THE ROYAL SAINTS OF
ANGLO-SAXON ENGLAND

Cambridge studies in medieval life and thought
Fourth series

General Editor:

J. C. HOLT
Professor of Medieval History and
Master of Fitzwilliam College, University of Cambridge

Advisory Editors:

C. N. L. BROOKE
Dixie Professor of Ecclesiastical History and
Fellow of Gonville and Caius College,
University of Cambridge

D. E. LUSCOMBE
Professor of Medieval History, University of Sheffield

The series Cambridge Studies in Medieval Life and Thought was inaugurated by G. G. Coulton in 1920. Professor J. C. Holt now acts as General Editor of a Fourth Series, with Professor C. N. L. Brooke and Professor D. E. Luscombe as Advisory Editors. The series aims to bring together outstanding work by medieval scholars over a wide range of human endeavour extending from political economy to the history of ideas.

Titles in the series

THE ROYAL SAINTS OF ANGLO-SAXON ENGLAND

A study of West Saxon and East Anglian cults

SUSAN J. RIDYARD

Fellow of Lucy Cavendish College, Cambridge

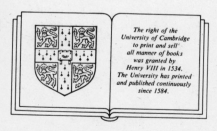

The right of the
University of Cambridge
to print and sell
all manner of books
was granted by
Henry VIII in 1534.
The University has printed
and published continuously
since 1584.

CAMBRIDGE UNIVERSITY PRESS

CAMBRIDGE

NEW YORK   NEW ROCHELLE   MELBOURNE   SYDNEY

Published by the Press Syndicate of the University of Cambridge
The Pitt Building, Trumpington Street, Cambridge CB2 IRP
32 East 57th Street, New York, NY 10022, USA
10 Stamford Road, Oakleigh, Melbourne 3166, Australia

First published 1988

Printed in Great Britain at the University Press, Cambridge

British Library cataloguing in publication data
Ridyard, Susan J.
The royal saints of Anglo-Saxon England:
a study of West Saxon and East Anglian
cults.
1. England. Royal families. Saints, *ca*
450–1066.
I. Title
274.2′02′0922

Library of Congress cataloguing in publication data
Ridyard, Susan J. (Susan Janet), 1957–
The royal saints of Anglo-Saxon England: a study of West Saxon
and East Anglian cults / Susan J. Ridyard.
p. cm. – (Cambridge studies in medieval life and thought:
4th ser., 9)
Bibliography.
Includes index.
ISBN 0-521-30772-4
1. Christian saints – Cult – England – History. 2. Anglo-Saxons –
Kings and rulers. 3. Great Britain – Kings and rulers. 4. England –
Church history – Anglo-Saxon period, 449–1066. 5. Anglo-Saxons –
Princes and princesses. 6. Great Britain – Princes and princesses.
I. Title. II. Series.
BR754.A1R53 1988
274.2′03—dc 19   88-3659 CIP

ISBN 0 521 30772 4

SE

CONTENTS

For my mother

ACKNOWLEDGEMENTS

I should like to express my gratitude to the many individuals and institutions without whose support this book could not have been written.

My first and greatest debt is to Professor Christopher Brooke, who has guided this project with unfailing patience, unflagging interest and stimulating advice drawn from his own wide-ranging and sensitive knowledge of the *legenda sanctorum*.

For access to and permission to cite manuscripts in their possession I am grateful to the Librarian of Trinity College, Cambridge, to the Master and Fellows of Corpus Christi College, Cambridge, to the Keeper of Manuscripts and Printed Books at the Fitzwilliam Museum, Cambridge, to the Keeper of Western Manuscripts at the Bodleian Library, Oxford, and to the British Library, Department of Manuscripts. The University Library in Cambridge and the Henry E. Huntington Library, San Marino, California, have each in their turn provided for me a pleasant and stimulating academic home.

For invaluable comments and advice I should like to thank my doctoral examiners, Dr Marjorie Chibnall and Dr Henry Mayr-Harting, and the general editor of Cambridge Studies in Medieval Life and Thought, Professor J. C. Holt, together with his colleague (with Christopher Brooke), Professor David Luscombe. I am grateful to Michael Lapidge for advice on the cults of the Winchester saints, to Martin Brett for palaeographical advice, to Diana Greenway for information on the work of Henry of Huntingdon, to Mark Blackburn for numismatic advice and to Stanley West and Glenys Putnam for introducing me to the fascinating and difficult world where history and archaeology meet. With Antonia Gransden and Cynthia Hahn I have enjoyed lively and interesting discussions of the cult of St Edmund: each has been generous in

Acknowledgements

permitting me to cite her as yet unpublished contribution to the 1986 Conference of the Charles Homer Haskins Society. Meryl Foster, Michael Franklin, Simon Keynes and Katharin Mack have likewise been generous with support and advice. To Eleanor Searle, my colleague and mentor at the California Institute of Technology in 1986–7, I owe a special debt: I have benefited greatly from her friendship and her knowledge. It is never easy finally to part with a book with which one has lived for years: I was helped to do so by the warm support and astute criticism of Professor Searle, Professor Warren Hollister and Mrs Phyllis Hetzel. For help in the preparation and checking of the typescript I am grateful to Catherine Heising, Joy Hansen and Flora Lewis. For both their patience and their expertise I am deeply indebted to William Davies and his colleagues at Cambridge University Press.

Some material from chapters six and seven of this book has been published in *Anglo-Norman Studies* (1987): it is here reproduced by kind permission of Boydell and Brewer.

Finally, I offer my special gratitude to my colleagues, the President and Fellows of Lucy Cavendish College: without their support and their friendship the story of the Anglo-Saxon royal saints would have remained untold.

My mother has lived long with this book: it is dedicated to her in love and in gratitude.

ABBREVIATIONS

AASS	*Acta sanctorum Bollandiana* (Brussels and elsewhere, 1643–)
AB	*Analecta Bollandiana*
ASC	*The Anglo-Saxon Chronicle*, tr. D. Whitelock, D. C. Douglas and S. I. Tucker (London, 1961); also *Two of the Saxon Chronicles parallel*, ed. C. Plummer, 2 vols. (Oxford, 1892–9)
ASE	*Anglo-Saxon England*
B	*Cartularium Saxonicum*, ed. W. de Gray Birch, 3 vols. and index (London, 1885–99)
BHL	*Bibliotheca hagiographica latina antiquae et mediae aetatis*, 2 vols. and supplement (Brussels, 1891–1901; supplement, 1911)
BL	British Library
BSS	*Bibliotheca sanctorum*, 12 vols. and index (Rome, 1961–70)
CCC	Corpus Christi College, Cambridge
CS	*Councils and synods, with other documents relating to the English church, I, A.D. 871–1204*, ed. D. Whitelock, M. Brett and C. N. L. Brooke, 2 vols. (Oxford, 1981)
DB	*Domesday book, seu liber censualis Willelmi primi regis Anglie*, ed. A. Farley, 2 vols., Record Commission (1783)
EETS	Early English Text Society
EHR	*English Historical Review*
GP	William of Malmesbury, *De gestis pontificum Anglorum*, ed. N. E. S. A. Hamilton, RS 52 (London, 1870)
GR	William of Malmesbury, *De gestis regum*

	Anglorum, ed. W. Stubbs, 2 vols., RS 90 (London, 1887–9)
HBC	F. M. Powicke and E. B. Fryde, *Handbook of British chronology*, Royal Historical Society Guides and Handbooks 2, 3rd edn, ed. E. B. Fryde, D. E. Greenway, S. Porter and I. Roy (London, 1986)
HBS	Henry Bradshaw Society
HE	Bede, *Historia ecclesiastica gentis Anglorum*, ed. B. Colgrave and R. A. B. Mynors, Oxford Medieval Texts (1969)
Heads	D. Knowles, C. N. L. Brooke and V. C. M. London, *The heads of religious houses: England and Wales, 940–1216* (Cambridge, 1972)
K	*Codex diplomaticus aevi Saxonici*, ed. J. M. Kemble, 6 vols. (London, 1839–48)
KH	D. Knowles and R. N. Hadcock, *Medieval religious houses: England and Wales*, 2nd edn (London, 1971)
LE	*Liber Eliensis*, ed. E. O. Blake, Royal Historical Society, Camden Third Series 92 (London, 1962)
Letters	*The letters of Osbert of Clare, prior of Westminster*, ed. E. W. Williamson (Oxford, 1929)
LVH	*Liber vitae: register and martyrology of New Minster and Hyde abbey, Winchester*, ed. W. de Gray Birch, Hampshire Record Society (London and Winchester, 1892)
MBHA	*The monastic breviary of Hyde abbey, Winchester*, ed. J. B. L. Tolhurst, 6 vols., HBS 69, 70, 71, 76, 78, 80 (London, 1932–42)
MO	D. Knowles, *The monastic order in England 940–1216*, 2nd edn (Cambridge, 1963)
Monasticon	W. Dugdale, *Monasticon Anglicanum*, revised edn, J. Caley, H. Ellis and B. Bandinel, 6 vols. in 8 (London, 1817–30; repr. 1846)
NLA	*Nova legenda Angliae*, ed. K. Horstmann, 2 vols. (Oxford, 1901)
ODS	D. H. Farmer, *The Oxford dictionary of saints* (Oxford, 1978)
PL	*Patrologiae cursus completus, series latina*, ed.

	J. P. Migne, 221 vols. (Paris, 1844–64)
RS	Rolls Series
S	P. H. Sawyer, *Anglo-Saxon charters: an annotated list and bibliography*, Royal Historical Society Guides and Handbooks 8 (London, 1968)
SC	*A summary catalogue of Western manuscripts in the Bodleian Library at Oxford*, 7 vols. (Oxford, 1895–1953)
TCC	Trinity College, Cambridge
TCD	Trinity College, Dublin
VCH	*Victoria history of the counties of England*
WS1	F. Barlow, M. Biddle, O. von Feilitzen, and D. J. Keene, *Winchester in the early Middle Ages: an edition and discussion of the Winton Domesday*, Winchester Studies 1 (Oxford, 1976)
WS2	D. J. Keene, with a contribution by A. Rumble, *Survey of medieval Winchester*, 2 vols., Winchester Studies 2 (Oxford, 1985)
WS4.i	M. Biddle and B. Kjølbye-Biddle, *The Anglo-Saxon minsters in Winchester*, Winchester Studies 4.i (Oxford, forthcoming)
WS4.ii	M. Lapidge, *The cult of St Swithun*, Winchester Studies 4.ii (Oxford, forthcoming)

For abbreviated titles of hagiographical works see the appropriate entry in the section headed Vitae etc. in the Bibliography (below, pp. 314–15)

Chapter 1

THE ROYAL SAINTS OF ANGLO-SAXON ENGLAND: SOME PROBLEMS OF INTERPRETATION

In the early days of January, in the momentous year 1066, 'King Edward, the beloved of God, languishing from the sickness of soul he had contracted, died indeed to the world, but was joyfully taken up to live with God.'[1] Thus wrote Edward's earliest biographer, probably within two years of his death. And almost a century later, on 7 February 1161, the apotheosis which he describes received universal recognition when Pope Alexander III announced the canonisation of Edward and decreed that his name should be enrolled among the confessors of the Christian church.[2]

Edward the Confessor was the last and most famous of the Anglo-Saxon royal saints: but he was far from unique. It is clear from Bede's *Historia ecclesiastica gentis Anglorum*, completed in the year 731, that already by that date Anglo-Saxon England was remarkable for the very considerable number of its kings, princes and royal ladies who, in an age before the development of papal canonisation, had come to be venerated as saints by the regional church.[3] A vernacular tract on the resting-places of the saints in England not only includes many royal saints but also is associated in its extant manuscripts with the so-called Kentish royal legend – an account of Kent's earliest Christian kings and their saintly families.[4]

---

[1] *The Life of King Edward the Confessor*, ed. F. Barlow, Nelson's Medieval Texts (1962), p. 55. It is unclear whether Edward died on 4 or 5 January: see *ibid.*, p. 80, n. 2. For the nature, date and authorship of the Life see *ibid.*, pp. xiv–xxx, xli–lix.

[2] For Edward's canonisation see *ibid.*, pp. xiii–xiv and App. D; F. Barlow, *Edward the Confessor* (London, 1970; repr. 1979); for the Bull of canonisation see *PL*, CC, cols. 106–7.

[3] *HE*; on the development of papal canonisation see E. W. Kemp, *Canonisation and authority in the Western church* (London, 1948).

[4] The tract, entitled *Secgan be þam Godes sanctum þe on Engla lande ærost reston*, together with the 'Kentish royal legend' (headed *Her cyð ymbe þa halgan þe on Angelcynne restað*) (hereafter *þa halgan*, is edited by F. Liebermann, *Die Heiligen Englands* (Hanover, 1889). On the *Secgan* see D. W. Rollason, 'Lists of saints' resting-places in Anglo-Saxon England', *ASE* 7 (1978), 61–93. The tract is preserved in Cambridge, Corpus Christi

Towards the end of the eleventh century the professional hagiographer Goscelin of Canterbury produced an impressive series of Lives of the English royal saints.[5] And William of Malmesbury, writing his history of the English kings almost forty years before the events of 1161, was able to preface his account of the Confessor with a special section devoted to that king's saintly predecessors and to write of the English saints that 'It is not necessary to name any of the common people but only the male and female members of the royal stock, most of them innocently murdered, who have been consecrated martyrs not by human conjecture but by divine acknowledgement.'[6]

Royal sanctity was not exclusively an Anglo-Saxon phenomenon. Continental parallels are found, for instance, in the royal saints of Merovingian Frankia and in the reputed sanctity of Henry II, king of Germany, and his consort, Kunigund.[7] The Celtic Christianity of Ireland and Wales was not unfamiliar with the concept of a saintly ruling family.[8] The Scandinavian world, in the persons of Olaf, king of Norway, and Cnut, king of Denmark, possessed its own royal martyrs.[9] In Eastern Europe, the death in

College, MS 201 (pp. 149–151) and in London, BL, MS Stowe 944 (fols. 34v–39). Rollason notes that the list was completed in its present form *c.* 1031, at which date it was entered in the Stowe MS. The second half 'in its present form was completed in or after 1013'; the first half seems 'to consist of more ancient material . . . as well as dealing with earlier saints and resting-places' ('Lists', p. 68). For discussion of the 'Kentish royal legend' see *Heiligen*, ed. Liebermann, p. xiii; Rollason, 'Lists', p. 73; and Rollason *The Mildrith legend: a study in early medieval hagiography in England* (Leicester, 1982), p. 28.

[5] For the life and works of Goscelin of Canterbury (also known as Goscelin of Saint-Bertin) see below, p. 37, n. 103.   [6] *GR*, i, 260–71, at 260.

[7] See especially F. X. Graus, *Volk, Herrscher und Heiliger im Reich der Merowinger* (Prague, 1965); R. Klauser, *Der Heinrichs- und Kunigundenkult im mittelalterlichen Bistum Bamberg* (Bamberg, 1957). Somewhat different but none the less interesting is the tradition of thaumaturgic rulership in Capetian France: see M. Bloch, *Les Rois thaumaturges* (Strasburg, 1924).

[8] Columba, who founded the Irish monasteries of Derry, Durrow and possibly Kells before travelling to Iona as an 'exile for Christ', was said to be a member of the royal clan of the Ui Neill (see *Adomnan's Life of Columba*, ed. A. O. and M. O. Anderson (London, 1961)). In Wales St Clydog, allegedly 'martyred' by a rival lover, was said to be one of the many saintly descendants of the legendary King Brychan (*ODS*, p. 85). On the Welsh royal saints see also M. Miller, *The saints of Gwynedd*, Studies in Celtic History 1 (Woodbridge, 1979), especially ch. 5; G. H. Doble, *Lives of the Welsh saints*, ed. D. S. Evans, 2nd edn (Cardiff, 1984), especially the introduction by D. S. Evans.

[9] Olaf was in large measure responsible for the conversion of Norway to Christianity. He was exiled following a rebellion in 1029; his death in the attempt to regain his kingdom was regarded as a martyrdom and his cult spread rapidly throughout the Scandinavian world and to England (B. Dickins, 'The cult of St Olave in the British Isles', *Saga-Book of the Viking Society* 12 (1937–45), 53–80). Cnut, king of Denmark, was murdered in 1086 by his brother and rebellious subjects; his cult was approved by Paschal II early in the

1038 of Stephen, king of Hungary, was followed by the performance of miracles at his tomb, and as late as the fifteenth century Poland acquired a royal saint in the person of Prince Casimir, who abandoned his secular and military role for a life of devotion and austerity.[10] And in Byzantine tradition the Emperor Leo appears as a worker of miracles and Constantine V as the object of a cult in Constantinople.[11]

What was characteristically Anglo–Saxon, however, was the ubiquity and the persistence of the royal cult. What was remarkable was the frequency with which new royal cults emerged and the consistency with which those cults, once established, continued to attract the attention of churchmen and hagiographers. For these reasons the tradition of Anglo–Saxon royal sanctity is of sufficient interest and importance to merit a specialised study. It has as yet received little attention from historians. A few detailed studies of individual cults, such as that of Professor Barlow on Edward the Confessor and that of David Rollason on St Mildrith of Thanet, have awakened interest in the subject. And Rollason's study of the cults of murdered royal saints has demonstrated the value of a comparative study of several cults of the same general type.[12] There has however been no comparative study of a number of royal cults of different dates and types. In particular there has been no study which seeks to arrive at an understanding of English royal sanctity by treating simultaneously and equally the cults of both men and women of royal birth. This book is a contribution towards filling that gap. It is focussed upon saints of the West Saxon and East Anglian royal dynasties and upon saints whose major Lives were written between the mid tenth and the mid twelfth centuries. It takes the form of a series of detailed case-studies – of Edmund, the *rex Christianissimus* martyred by the heathen, of Edward, a child

---

twelfth century (*Vitae sanctorum Danorum*, ed. M. Cl. Gertz (Copenhagen, 1910–12), I, 69–129; *ODS*, p. 68).

[10] *ODS*, pp. 363, 68–9. On the royal cults of Russia see I. Kologrivof, *Essai sur la sainteté en Russie* (Bruges, 1953), pp. 73–85; G. Fedotov, *Sviatyje drevnej Rusi* (Paris, 1931).

[11] G. Huxley, 'The Byzantine saint in iconoclasm', Discussion Paper presented at the University of Birmingham Fourteenth Spring Symposium of Byzantine Studies, March 1980.

[12] *Life of King Edward*, ed. Barlow; Rollason, *Mildrith legend*; Rollason, 'The cults of murdered royal saints in Anglo-Saxon England', *ASE* 11 (1983), 1–22. See also R. Folz, 'Saint Oswald roi de Northumbrie: étude d'hagiographie royale', *AB* 98 (1980), 49–74; Folz, 'Naissance et manifestations d'un culte royale: Saint Edmond roi d'Est Anglie', in K. Hauck and H. Mordek (eds.), *Geschichtsschreibung und geistiges Leben im Mittelalter: Festschrift für Heinz Löwe zum 65. Geburtstag* (Cologne and Vienna, 1978), pp. 226–46.

king allegedly murdered by his wicked step-mother and treacher-
ous subjects, of Æthelthryth, a royal lady who preserved her
virginity through two marriages and attained sanctity as the bride
of Christ, and of the other princesses and royal widows of Ely,
Winchester and Wilton, whose lives were dedicated *ad illum qui
speciosus est forma prae filiis hominum.*

These case-studies are not intended to provide comprehensive
histories of the growth and dissemination of the cults. My concern
is rather to approach an understanding of those cults by outlining,
and proposing tentative solutions to, three specific problems. Of
these the first concerns the theoretical relationship between royal
birth and the attainment of sanctity. A large issue is at stake here.
William Chaney almost twenty years ago portrayed the Anglo-
Saxon saint king as the lineal descendant of the sacral ruler of the age
of the migrations: his sanctity, being likened to sacrality, was an
almost inevitable adjunct of his kingship.[13] And the mystique of
the *stirps regia* extended beyond the king himself: for the princes
and royal ladies likewise sanctity might readily be expected or
assumed. A first step towards the understanding of England's royal
cults must be to determine whether this analysis accurately reflects
contemporary views on the relationship of royal birth and sanctity
– or whether the attainment of sanctity was perceived as being
dependent upon something more than membership in a numinous
group. Accordingly I seek briefly to outline the general context of
early medieval thought on the relationship of royal birth and
sanctity. More important, I analyse in some detail the interpretation – or interpretations – of that relationship offered by the
hagiographers of the royal saints. And I make some tentative
suggestions concerning the possible attitudes of contemporary
secular society. Analysis of these three views, of their relationship to
one another, and of their relative importance in the formation of
the royal cults suggests for those cults an origin and an interpretation both more Christian and more complex than Chaney allows.

The second problem is that of historical explanation. My pri-
mary objective is to establish the reasons for the growth and
continuing importance throughout the Anglo-Saxon period of the
individual cults. To the hagiographers the matter was quite
straightforward. The development of cult was dependent in the
first instance upon the expression of divine approbation by the

[13] W. A. Chaney, *The cult of kingship in Anglo-Saxon England: the transition from paganism to
Christianity* (Manchester, 1970), pp. 77–84.

bestowal upon the saint of miraculous powers: popular veneration traditionally followed hard on the heels of miraculous intervention. Historically, however, a saint did not perform miracles unless a substantial body of opinion was predisposed to believe in those miracles. Cults did not simply develop: they were developed. And their development owed less to divine acknowledgement than to successful advertising. At the centre of this study therefore lies the identification of the advertisers and the analysis of their aims: for what purpose was each cult conceived and in what sense, if any, was the royal status of its subject essential to the fulfilment of that purpose?

From the particular I shall attempt briefly to confront a very much more difficult problem – that of proceeding to the general. It is possible first to suggest, on the basis of the present case-studies, some general conclusions concerning the place of the royal saint within Anglo-Saxon society. And, taking the process one stage further, it is possible to derive from the history of the royal cults some general conclusions concerning the place of the monarchy – and of the royal dynasties – within that society. The issue of the relationship of royal sanctity to royal power has been highlighted by the work of the Polish scholar Karol Górski. In a paper entitled 'La Naissance des états et le "roi-saint": problème de l'idéologie féodale', Górski seeks to establish the incidence of saint kings in certain countries of Scandinavia and Eastern Europe as an index of progress towards state-formation. The incidence of saint kings, he argues, 'refléterait le potentiel de la puissance de l'organisation étatique du haut Moyen Age que l'Eglise a voulu, ou non, renforcer'.[14] Where the political power of the Crown was weak, the church sought to bolster royal authority by the creation of the saint king; where the monarchy was strong, the saintly ruler was conspicuously – and deliberately – absent. The theory is important; so too is the testing of its applicability to the royal cults of other countries. The present study, not least because it does not limit its inquiry to the male of the species, suggests that the English royal cults were produced by a society quite different from that of the Górski model.

A third and final problem remains – that of continuity. The year 1066 witnessed the death of the last of the Anglo-Saxon saintly

[14] K. Górski, 'La Naissance des états et le "roi-saint": problème de l'idéologie féodale', in T. Manteuffel and A. Gieysztor (eds.), *L'Europe aux IXe – XIe siècles: aux origines des états nationaux* (Warsaw, 1968), pp. 425–32, at p. 426.

kings and the establishment of a new ruling dynasty of Norman–
French origin. What, if anything, was the effect of the Norman
Conquest upon the veneration of the Anglo-Saxon royal saints?
The Norman antagonist to the Anglo-Saxon saint is a familiar
figure. His portrait is most strikingly drawn by David Knowles in
his masterly 1940 study of *The monastic order in England*.[15] Here
Knowles observes that the Norman treatment of the English
monasteries gave rise to complaints on three counts. First, they
claimed to have been robbed by the invaders of land and wealth.
Second, there were complaints about the imposition of knight
service on monastic lands. Finally, 'A third grievance, quite as
widespread, is more curious. The Norman abbots, it seems, frequently outraged the feelings of their monks by their disrespectful
attitude towards the old English saints.'[16] A number of examples is
cited. At St Albans, we are told, the Norman Abbot Paul slighted
the tombs of his predecessors, whom he condemned as *rudes et
idiotas*. At Abingdon the feasts of saints Æthelwold and Edmund
were allegedly banned on the grounds that the English were boors.
Abbot Warin of Malmesbury is said simply to have turned out
many relics of English saints. And Archbishop Lanfranc himself
allegedly set an example to the Norman sceptic by questioning the
sanctity of the English saint Ælfheah. To other writers on the
English church Norman scepticism – or worse – is simply an
assumed condition of the time. Thus Barlow writes generally of the
scepticism of the Norman abbots; Southern boldly of 'the contempt in which these saints were held by the Norman conquerors';
and Rollason with greater caution of 'the scepticism of certain late
eleventh-century churchmen towards the genuineness of the
Anglo-Saxon saints'.[17]

The Norman confrontation with the unfamiliar Anglo-Saxon
saints raises problems which cannot be resolved either by the
anecdotal approach of Knowles or by the generalising approach of
the other writers. The interaction of Norman monk or abbot with
the long-dead heroes of the English church can be understood only

[15] *MO*, pp. 118–20. For a more general study of the Norman reception of the English saints,
in which Knowles's argument is reviewed in detail, see S. J. Ridyard, '*Condigna veneratio*:
post-Conquest attitudes to the saints of the Anglo-Saxons', *Anglo-Norman Studies* 9
(1987), 179–206.   [16] *MO*, p. 118.

[17] F. Barlow, *The English church 1066–1154* (London, 1979), p. 191; R. W. Southern, *Saint
Anselm and his biographer: a study of monastic life and thought 1059–c.1130* (Cambridge,
1963), p. 249; Rollason, *Mildrith legend*, p. 59 (where it is however conceded that attitudes
towards the English saints were not always determined by racial considerations).

by detailed analysis of the individual cults within the context of the post-Conquest history of the religious houses in which those cults were centred. Such analysis, where the evidence permits, shows the Normans to have possessed a shrewd awareness that in accepting or rejecting the cults of the English saints, both royal and non-royal, they did something far more than pass judgement on a few rather suspect collections of bones. It shows them also to have proceeded shrewdly in the utilisation of that awareness for the furtherance of their aims. It calls for a radical reassessment of the relationship between Norman churchman and English saint.

Chapter 2

THE SOURCES

In the making of a cult the preservation or acquisition of relics and the establishment of a shrine was but a first step. The success of the shrine was dependent upon continuing effective publicity; and that dependence generated a specialised literature whose function was to document the earthly career of the individual and to demonstrate the authenticity and efficacy of the relics there venerated. Among sources for the history and interpretation of the cults of the saints that literature occupies a place of prime importance. For the great majority of cults hagiography provides the earliest and by far the most complete evidence; for some it provides the only evidence. More than this, because it was generally written in association with the promotion of a cult, hagiography was itself a product of the phenomenon which it describes: it opens a unique window on the meaning which the cult held for its promoters and for its clients. The problems inherent in the genre, however, have caused it to be viewed with deep suspicion by generations of historians: it is the purpose of the following pages to review some of those problems and to propose a working model for the constructive use of the legends of the saints.[1]

At the root of the traditional distaste for the Lives of the saints lies a major conceptual gulf between the task of the hagiographer and

[1] For general discussion of the nature and purpose of hagiography see especially H. Delehaye, *Les Légendes hagiographiques*, revised 3rd edn, Subsidia Hagiographica 18 (Brussels, 1927); Delehaye, *Cinq leçons sur la méthode hagiographique*, Subsidia Hagiographica 21 (Brussels, 1934); Delehaye, 'La Méthode historique et l'hagiographie', *Bulletin de la Classe des Lettres et des Sciences Morales et Politiques, Académie Royale de Belgique*, Fifth Series 16 (1930), 218–31; R. Aigrain, *L'Hagiographie: ses sources, ses méthodes, son histoire* (Paris, 1953); B. de Gaiffier, *Recherches d'hagiographie latine*, Subsidia Hagiographica 52 (Brussels, 1971); also Rollason, *Mildrith legend*, pp. 3–8.

that of the historian as it has generally been defined in the later nineteenth and twentieth centuries. The historian seeks the object-ive reconstruction and interpretation of the past; the hagiographer writes with a moral and often propagandist purpose. This purpose varies in accordance with the earthly career and the posthumous role of the individual saint: it may, however, be reduced to two essential elements. Hagiography aims to educate and to edify: accordingly its subject must present an example of Christian virtue in such a way as to encourage emulation.[2] More important, it seeks to increase the reverence felt for the individual saint;[3] closely related to this, it may seek also to enhance the prestige of the church or religious community which claimed to possess that saint's relics. Hence the hagiographer attempts not the detailed and critical reconstruction of past events but rather the creation of a literary vehicle for the fulfilment of a didactic or propagandist aim: the reliability of his account suffers accordingly.

It suffers, most obviously, because it is subject to a severe problem of bias. This bias may take many forms. It may consist simply of remembering the 'good' and omitting the 'bad' in an individual saint's career,[4] or, if the saint's earthly role was politi-cally controversial, of adopting a highly partisan stance in the portrayal of that role.[5] In other cases it may be possible to trace elements of bias to the personal interests of the hagiographer himself.[6] Most important, however, is the fact that a high propor-tion of the Lives were written by or for the communities which

---

[2] See Delehaye, *Les Légendes hagiographiques*, p. 2: 'pour être strictement hagiographique, le document doit avoir un caractère religieux et se proposer un but d'édification'.

[3] *Ibid.*: the title of hagiography must be given only to a work 'inspiré par le culte des saints, et destiné a le promouvoir'.

[4] See *Felix's Life of St Guthlac*, ed. B. Colgrave (Cambridge, 1956; repr. 1985), p. 80. After a lengthy account of Guthlac's pious youth the author devotes a mere two paragraphs to the nine years in which the saint 'cum adolescentiae vires increvissent, et iuvenili in pectore egregius dominandi amor fervesceret, tunc valida pristinorum heroum facta reminiscens, veluti ex sopore evigilatus, mutata mente, adgregatis satellitum turmis, sese in arma convertit'.

[5] For a good early example of this see *The Life of Bishop Wilfrid by Eddius Stephanus*, ed. B. Colgrave (Cambridge, 1927; repr. 1985). See also *The Life of St Anselm archbishop of Canterbury by Eadmer*, ed. R. W. Southern, Nelson's Medieval Texts (1962; repr. Oxford Medieval Texts, 1979) and the Lives of Thomas Becket contained in *Materials for the history of Thomas Becket, archbishop of Canterbury*, ed. J. C. Robertson and J. B. Sheppard, 7 vols., RS 67 (London, 1875–85).

[6] See for instance T. J. Hamilton 'Goscelin of Canterbury: a critical study of his life, works and accomplishments', 2 vols., unpublished Ph.D. thesis (University of Virginia, 1973), pp. 255–73, where it is suggested that Goscelin of Canterbury wrote in order to convince the Normans that the Anglo-Saxon saints were worthy of veneration.

claimed to possess the relics of the saint in question. They are accordingly heavily biased in favour of those communities, not only against rival claims to the relics but also as regards their wider political dealings.[7]

The reliability of hagiographical sources suffers also from the standardisation of their form and content. The much-decried adherence of later writers to the models provided by the earliest Lives – in particular by Athanasius's Life of St Anthony, Jerome's Life of Paul the Hermit and Sulpicius Severus's Life of St Martin – was not merely the result of slavish copying: it was the product rather of a shared moral aim.[8] Every saint who was to be a model of virtue must be cast in a clearly recognisable mould which could be traced back through the early Lives to the figure of Christ himself; and likewise the posthumous role of the 'patron saint' was from an early date a predetermined one. Hence, in the *Vita*, *Passio*, *Translatio* and *Miracula*, there evolved a series of literary forms of set type, whose purpose was to express and to illustrate certain standardised themes by means of standardised structure, standardised discursive passages and a standardised repertoire of miracle stories. Clearly the form and content of these texts were not invariable; clearly also they varied only within certain long-established and easily recognisable limits: hagiography depended for its intelligibility upon its conformity to convention.

For the historian, however, this conformity presents a serious problem – that of distinguishing the 'germ of truth' from what may appear to be an undifferentiated mass of hagiographical *topoi*. The problem is exacerbated by the fact that many of these *topoi* take the form of miracle stories which are not only unoriginal but also far from plausible. Such stories were central to the religious belief of the Middle Ages: 'not to have believed in miracles performed by the saints might well seem to the ordinary man to be equivalent to having no faith at all'.[9] The early church, threatened by an excess of popular piety, had treated this belief with some suspicion. It emphasised that only those miracles performed in Christ's name

[7] For the use of hagiography to lay claim to and defend ecclesiastical property see especially B. de Gaiffier, 'Les Revendications de biens dans quelques documents hagiographiques du XI^c siècle', *AB* 50 (1932), 123–38.

[8] For this dependence upon earlier models see P. Hunter Blair, *The world of Bede* (London, 1970), ch. 25; B. Colgrave, 'Bede's miracle stories', in A. Hamilton Thompson (ed.), *Bede, his life, times and writings* (Oxford, 1935), pp. 201–29, at p. 204; H. Mayr-Harting, *The coming of Christianity to Anglo-Saxon England* (London, 1972), pp. 229–39.

[9] See Colgrave's discussion of Bede's miracle stories in his introduction to the *HE*, pp. xxxiv–xxxvi, at p. xxxv.

were true miracles and it maintained that belief in the miraculous was not necessarily a sign of true faith; nor was the power to perform miracles the only sign of sanctity. But such subtleties were beyond the reach of the ordinary man, and so, 'although the theologians . . . knew well the difference between true faith and mere faith in the marvellous, yet they seem to have felt that the latter might be a stepping-stone to the former'.[10] Hence, for instance, both Gregory the Great and Bede were able to accept the importance of miracles in the process of conversion.[11] Hence also miracles came to constitute one of the principal instruments for the fulfilment of the hagiographer's didactic or propagandist aim: moral lessons were taught, individual saints extolled and an infinite variety of political interests advanced by means of those stories which in the nineteenth century were condemned as 'the most ridiculous and disgusting portions of the religious belief of the Middle Ages'.[12]

Finally, the reliability of hagiographical sources is further preju- diced by their generally retrospective nature. Only rarely do we encounter a contemporary Life composed by a disciple of its subject. More usually the extant sources represent either the belated growth of a retrospective tradition or an advanced stage in the development of a hagiographical tradition whose earlier stages are now lost. Often, moreover, it is difficult or impossible to distin- guish between these two types of retrospective source: the author of a work of the former type was unlikely to admit or to reveal by silence his ignorance concerning events before his own time. Again the problem arises in part from the moral purpose of hagiography and from the resultant belief that all saints must conform to an established model. It is a short step from the theory that a man must

[10] *Ibid.* See also R. C. Finucane, *Miracles and pilgrims: popular beliefs in medieval England* (London, 1977), ch. 1. For further comment on the importance of the miracles associated with holy relics and on the divergent views of secular piety and the ecclesiastical hierarchy on this subject in the early Christian period see H. Delehaye, *Les Origines du culte des martyrs*, 2nd edn, Subsidia Hagiographica 20 (Brussels, 1933) and P. Brown, *The cult of the saints: its rise and function in Latin Christianity* (Chicago, 1981).

[11] Colgrave, introduction to *HE*, pp. xxxv–xxxvi. Gregory's anonymous biographer, writing probably early in the eighth century, pointed out that miracles were important partly for the destruction of pagan idols, partly to strengthen the weak faith of the believers and partly to demonstrate the superior power of the Christian teachers in relation to that of the pagan priests (*The earliest Life of Gregory the Great*, ed. B. Colgrave (Kansas, 1968; repr. Cambridge, 1985), p. 78). On some of Gregory's qualms concern- ing the use of miracles see *HE*, I, 31.

[12] T. Wright, 'On saints' Lives and miracles', in *Essays on archaeological subjects*, 2 vols. (London, 1861), I, 227–67, at 227.

possess certain characteristics in order to be venerated as a saint to the belief that, because he was thus venerated, he must have possessed the requisite characteristics. Once this short step had been taken it became perfectly valid to invent the detail of an individual Life or to appropriate that detail from another source: for the production of a standardised Life of any saint there were endless blueprints to hand, and the hagiographers had not the slightest qualms about using them.[13]

Nor is differentiation between the two types of retrospective tradition necessarily facilitated in those cases where the writer purports to establish his own place within the hagiographical tradition by stressing that his work is founded upon earlier, reliable, written sources. The purpose of this literary device was the establishment of authority by appeal to witness: it was among the most common hagiographical *topoi* and it can be trusted only when the alleged written source still exists or can be shown to have existed and when the reliability of that source is capable of demonstration. Reliable oral tradition, likewise frequently cited by the hagiographers, must also be handled with care: in particular the closeness in time of the witness or chain of witnesses to the actual events described must be carefully weighed and the alleged reliability evaluated accordingly. A final and crucial point is that works of hagiography are rarely drawn from a single source, written or oral, reliable or unreliable: rather the individual work combines information and interpretation drawn from a number of distinct sources, both written and oral and of varying quality, in such a way as to fulfil its own immediate purpose. Few works therefore can readily be characterised as 'all good' or as 'pure fiction': much labour must be expended upon an assessment of their component parts.

Such are some of the problems inherent in the written legends of the saints. The nature of the genre is such that the objective reliability of a *Vita*, *Translatio* or collection of *Miracula* is often exceptionally difficult to assess. Indeed, if the value of a hagiographical text is to be measured solely in terms of such reliability, the temptation to dismiss that text as nothing more than a pious fiction is frequently almost too great. But how valid is this traditional equation between reliability and value? For the history and interpretation of the cults of the saints hagiography possesses a unique value which cannot be measured exclusively in terms of its

---

[13] See Delehaye, *Les Légendes hagiographiques*, ch. 3.

objective reliability and which is not necessarily forfeited even when such reliability is shown to be wanting.

The concern of the hagiographer was to outline, in whole or in part, the story of his subject's life, death and posthumous reputation in so far as this could be gleaned from his sources or elaborated by his imagination and in so far as it could be related without proving too much for his audience to digest. He might describe not only the virtues of his subject in this life but also the posthumous revelation of sanctity, the translation or translations of relics, the liturgical observance of festivals, the growth of pilgrimage to the shrine or shrines of the saint, and the associated geographical and social diffusion of the cult. The constructive use of this material is dependent upon the establishment both of date and of bias. The closer to a saint's own time that a hagiographical source can be placed, the greater is the likelihood that it may embody reliable traditions concerning the saint and the early history of his or her cult. But a retrospective tradition cannot be dismissed as worthless. A twelfth-century saint's Life may tell us little or nothing about its seventh- or tenth-century subject; but it may none the less be an invaluable source for the history of that subject's cult up to and during the author's own time. Indeed the emergence of a retrospective tradition itself raises an interesting and important question: for what reason was a hagiographical tradition introduced or augmented at a particular time? The answer may lie simply in a fashion-conscious dissatisfaction with the literary products of an earlier generation. Conversely, the emergence of that tradition may have been coincident with, and its nature may have been determined by, important developments or crises in the history of the religious community with which the saint was associated. At this point the question of bias becomes crucial. By whom and for what purpose was each hagiographical work written? How far does that orientation affect its reliability? And how informative is that orientation about the nature and function of the cult? These points are of particular importance when hagiography was produced by or for the community which owned or claimed to own the relics of the saint. Naturally that hagiography reflects the interests of the community in question; often it becomes indistinguishable from, or is incorporated into, monastic history. The resultant bias, far from robbing the work of its historical value, is of central importance to an understanding of the growth and continuing importance of the cult. It relates the development of that cult to the history of the house in which it was centred and it permits some analysis of the function of the cult within the framework of monastic history. A special interest attaches to those cults for which a substantial series of hagiographical sources survives. By detailed study of these sources it is possible to trace not simply the gradual bringing up to date of the hagiographical tradition but also the process by which the nature and function of a cult might vary in accordance with the changing requirements of its promoters.[14]

A biased and retrospective hagiographical tradition, therefore, can be of much value for the reconstruction of the cults of the saints; so too can a standardised tradition. Too much emphasis has traditionally been placed upon the separation of 'elements of truth' from supposedly valueless hagiographical *topoi*; too little importance has been accorded to analysis of the *topoi* themselves. Medieval hagiographers did not simply string together conventional stories and conventional discursive passages in order that their works might reach some notional minimum word limit. Each *topos* was selected – albeit from a relatively limited range of alternatives – specifically to clarify a major hagiographical theme. The hagiographer, by skilful selection and combination of *topoi*, was able to highlight the distinguishing characteristics of the cult which he wished to portray. The historicity of the *topos*, therefore, is less important than its nature. A saint who specialised in doing battle with serpents and sorceresses was clearly a very different creature from a saint whose principal function was to strike fear into the hearts of the invaders of monastic property. And, just as much can be learnt about the nature of a cult from the *topoi* of a single Life, so subsequent variations in *topoi* reflect not only changing literary fashions but also fundamental shifts in the nature and function of the cult.

The hagiographers, moreover, were not concerned only with the historical role of their subjects and with the posthumous development of cult; they were concerned also with the interpretation of sanctity. Among the most common hagiographical *topoi* are those discursive passages which define and extol the virtues of the saint in question. These passages were not introduced simply to provide a link between otherwise unconnected wonder tales. Like all other *topoi* they were carefully selected in order to fulfil a specific and important literary function. Their purpose was to provide a detailed theoretical statement both of the nature of sanctity in

---

[14] For a particularly interesting exploration of the relationship between the development of legend and the history of cult see Rollason, *Mildrith legend*.

general and of the rationale which led to the veneration as a saint of a particular individual. The definition of individual sanctity ranges from the relatively simple reiteration of themes such as that of the saint as *miles Christi* or as exile or pilgrim for Christ to the more detailed exposition of the nature of martyrdom or of the role of the female saint as *sponsa Christi*. Such themes may appear singly or, more usually, in complex combinations; they are supported by quotations from Scripture and from the Fathers and they are illustrated by the incorporation of miracle stories. The hagiographers, again by careful selection and combination, provided for their works a coherent thematic structure and presented a consistent and clearly enunciated interpretation of individual sanctity. In the present study therefore their works are of central importance not only for the reconstruction of the history of the English royal cults but also for an understanding of the theoretical relationship between royal birth and the attainment of sanctity.

The effect of this 'rehabilitation' of hagiographical source material is not, of course, to reduce the whole question of reliability to irrelevance. The assessment of reliability must remain the prerequisite for the constructive use of any hagiographical source, and for this reason, as well as to supplement the hagiographical material, reference must be made where possible to four major categories of source material. Of these the first comprises narrative sources in the form of general and monastic chronicles. The information afforded by these varies considerably in both quantity and quality. Like hagiography, they generally represent a retrospective or biased tradition – the latter especially in the case of monastic chronicles. More than this, there is often a danger that, far from providing independent corroboration of an extant hagiographical tradition, the account contained in such a narrative source may in fact be derived from that tradition, albeit sometimes in a slightly different recension. Hence the correct use of chronicle sources depends upon the establishment of their relationship to the extant hagiographical material.

A second category of written source, sometimes incorporated into narrative accounts and sometimes existing independently, comprises such documentary material as charters, wills and records of legal disputes. Such records usually tell us nothing about the life of the saint but, because the history of each cult was closely related to the fortunes of the religious community upon which it was centred, they afford a further insight into the circumstances in which that cult was able to flourish, into the importance of the cult as an instrument of ecclesiastical propaganda, into the role of the saint in attracting lay patronage and into the history of church dedications.

The importance of a cult at its principal centre may to some extent be established, and both the geography and the chronology of its diffusion from that centre traced, by reference to liturgical sources – in particular to calendars, litanies and *lectiones* for the festivals of the saints. Generally produced in order to fulfil the liturgical requirements of a specific religious community, these sources might be expected to provide sound contemporary evidence for the emergence and spread of the cults of the saints. They are however subject to a number of problems, of which the most important are those of dating, of provenance and of dependence upon the hagiographical tradition. A thorough investigation of the extant liturgical sources for the cults of the Anglo-Saxon royal saints, although much to be desired, would be a major and highly specialised undertaking far beyond the scope of this book. In the following chapters, therefore, I make only selective use of some of the most readily available and best-documented liturgical material.

A final type of supplementary source material is that which concerns the relics of the saints. The vernacular tract on the resting-places of the saints in England (the *Secgan*) provides a cumulative list of resting-places committed to writing towards the end of the Anglo-Saxon period; it can be supplemented by the more detailed, although generally later, relic lists of individual religious houses.[15] Taken together these sources may corroborate and even supplement the hagiographical and documentary tradition concerning both original resting-places and the subsequent diffusion of cult. Occasionally, too, where donors are named, relic lists provide an important insight into the mechanism of transmission of cult and allow some conclusions about the motivation of those involved.

ST EDBURGA OF WINCHESTER

St Edburga of Winchester was the daughter of Edward the Elder, king of Wessex from 899 to 924, and of his third wife, Edgiva.[16]

---

[15] For the *Secgan* see above, p. 1, n. 4; for a valuable guide to and discussion of medieval English relic lists see I. G. Thomas, 'The cult of saints' relics in medieval England', unpublished Ph.D. thesis (University of London, 1974).

[16] *AASS*, Iun. II (1698), 1070–1; *BSS*, IV (1964), cols. 902–3; *ODS*, p. 118. St Edburga of Winchester is to be distinguished from several other saints of the same name: (a) St

According to her legend, Edburga made a choice of the religious life when only three years old and as a result of that choice was sent by her father to St Mary's abbey, or Nunnaminster, at Winchester, where she remained until her death. Her withdrawal from the world is reflected in the silence of the sources. Only once does Edburga appear in contemporary records: in a charter of the year 939, preserved in the twelfth-century *Liber Wintoniensis*, King Athelstan grants an estate in Hampshire to his sister Edburga, who is described as a nun.[17] This apart, the earliest historical information concerning Edburga dates from the twelfth century and is generally limited to a naming of the saint among Edward's offspring, with a note recording her commitment to the religious life. Entries to this effect are found in the Worcester *Chronicon ex chronicis*, in the *Historia regum* attributed to Symeon of Durham and in Ailred of Rievaulx's *Genealogia regum Anglorum*.[18]

By the early twelfth century, however, Edburga had been endowed also with a well-developed hagiographical legend. The earliest extant full-length version of this legend, and the principal source for the early history of Edburga's cult, is a Life composed by Osbert of Clare, prior of Westminster.[19] The work is contained in

Edburga of Minster (d. *c.* 751), a disciple of St Mildrith and abbess of Minster-in-Thanet (*BSS*, IV, col. 902; *ODS*, p. 118). (b) St Edburga of Repton or Southwell (*c.* 700). She is described in the *Secgan* as lying at Southwell-on-Trent (*Heiligen*, ed. Liebermann, p. 11; see also *BSS*, IV, col. 901; *ODS*, p. 118). The traditional identification of this saint with the abbess of Repton who appears in Felix's Life of St Guthlac is rejected by Colgrave (*Felix's Life of St Guthlac*, p. 191). (c) St Edburga of Lyminge, allegedly a seventh-century nun of Lyminge whose relics were taken to Canterbury in the late tenth century (*BSS*, IV, col. 901). (d) a Mercian St Edburga, associated with Adderbury and Bicester (*BSS*, IV, col. 903; *ODS*, pp. 117–18). On this saint, and on the possible confusion of her legend with that of St Edburga of Winchester, see below, pp. 134–8. (e) St Edburga of Castor, said to have been a daughter of Penda of Mercia and a nun at Castor, near Peterborough (*BSS*, IV, col. 901).

[17] S446. The charter occupies fols. 101–102 of the *Liber Wintoniensis* (London, BL, Add. MS 15350) and is printed as B742. It is accepted as authentic by H. P. R. Finberg, *The early charters of Wessex* (Leicester, 1964), no. 57. The estate (at Droxford, Hants.) seems either never to have passed to Nunnaminster or rather quickly to have been lost by the community. It is not listed among the Domesday possessions of Nunnaminster, and part of it was regranted by Edwy in 956 (S600; B953; see also G. B. Grundy, 'The Saxon land charters of Hampshire with notes on place and field names', *Archaeological Journal*, Second Series 31 (1924), 31–126, at 74–9).

[18] 'Florence of Worcester', *Chronicon ex chronicis*, ed. B. Thorpe, 2 vols., English Historical Society (London, 1848–9), I (1848), 117; *Symeonis monachi opera omnia*, ed. T. Arnold, 2 vols., RS 75 (London, 1882–5), II (1885), 121; Ailred of Rievaulx, *Genealogia regum Anglorum*, ed. R. Twysden, *Historiæ Anglicanæ scriptores decem*, 2 vols. (London, 1652), I, col. 356. More detailed discussion of Edburga's career is found in the historical works of William of Malmesbury: see below, pp. 27–8.

[19] On the life and works of Osbert of Clare see H. Bradley, article entitled 'Clare, Osbert

Oxford, Bodleian Library, MS Laud Misc. 114 (fols. 85–120), of the second half of the twelfth century. It has not yet been edited in full, though extracts from it were printed by Leland and its introductory *epistola* is included in E. W. Williamson's collection of Osbert's letters.[20] An edition of the whole text, with a description of the manuscript, follows as Appendix 1 below.

The contents of the Life can be briefly summarised. After the introductory letter, in which the author is identified as Osbert, a native of Clare in Suffolk,[21] and a prologue on the theme of virginity, the *Vita* proper commences with a short genealogical introduction to the saint and a picturesque account of her vocation. Edward, wishing to know whether his daughter was destined for a career in the world or in the church, placed before her objects symbolic of both the secular and the religious life – the riches appropriate to her royal status and the chalice, paten and gospel-book of religion. Edburga showed no interest in the former but moved at once to the ecclesiastical objects; her movement was interpreted as a choice of the religious life, and she was accordingly committed for her upbringing to Æthelthryth, abbess of Nunnaminster.

Osbert goes on to outline the saint's subsequent growth in virtue, emphasising in particular her extreme humility, which is illustrated

de', in *Dictionary of national biography*, x, 386–7; 'La Vie de S. Edouard le Confesseur par Osbert de Clare', ed. M. Bloch, *AB* 41 (1923), 5–131; *Letters*, especially the introductory essay by J. Armitage Robinson; *Life of King Edward*, ed. Barlow, pp. xxx–xli and App. D; P. Chaplais, 'The original charters of Herbert and Gervase, abbots of Westminster (1121–1157)', in *A medieval miscellany for Doris Mary Stenton*, ed. P. M. Barnes and C. F. Slade, Pipe Roll Society, New Series 36 (London, 1962 for 1960), pp. 89–110; L. Braswell, 'St Edburga of Winchester: a study of her cult, a.d. 950–1500, with an edition of the fourteenth-century Middle English and Latin Lives', *Mediaeval Studies* 33 (1971), 292–333. Osbert's *Vita Edburge* is listed as *BHL*, no. 2385 and T. D. Hardy, *Descriptive catalogue of materials relating to the history of Great Britain and Ireland*, 3 vols. in 4, RS 26 (London, 1862–71), no. 1144. The work cannot be precisely dated. It is clear however that it was written after the removal of the Winchester New Minster to the suburban site of Hyde in 1110 (*Vita Edburge*, fol. 87v; KH, p. 81). Elsewhere Osbert notes that he was inspired to write the Life by a vision of the saint which he had experienced fifteen years earlier, at a time when he was 'eoquidem temporis spatio extra fines uirtutis in secularibus negotiis constituto'. The wording here is obscure, but it could imply that Osbert experienced the vision prior to his entry to the religious life. Osbert was sufficiently established in the religious life to be appointed prior of Westminster between *c*. 1117 and 1121 (*Letters*, p. 9). It is therefore possible that the *Vita Edburge* was written at a relatively early point in Osbert's career, perhaps in the 1120s. Conversely, however, the parallels with his *Vita Edwardi*, written in the 1130s (see below, pp. 20–1; the parallels are recorded in the notes to Appendix 1 below) may perhaps point to a later date.

20 J. Leland, *De rebus Britannicis collectanea*, ed. T. Hearne, 2nd edn, 6 vols. (London, 1770), I, 277–8; *Letters*, pp. 179–82 (no. 43).   21 *Vita Edburge*, fol. 85.

by reference to her custom, 'following the example of Our Lord's ministry', of secretly cleaning the shoes of the other nuns.[22] Edburga's growth in virtue was paralleled by the development of her miraculous powers. Osbert describes the cure of a blind woman by the application to her eyes of water in which the saint had washed her hands. And, more interesting, he outlines the fate of a group of nuns who, suspecting Edburga of some immoral liaison, followed her as she went to keep her nightly vigil in the nearby *monasterium* of St Peter: blinded in punishment for their suspicion, the nuns, after due repentance, received back their sight through the ministrations of the saint.[23]

An account of Edburga's confession and death is followed by a long and complicated history of the relics. Edburga's first translation, from an external grave to an honourable position within the church, was carried out by the community of Nunnaminster. A second translation, or elevation, was subsequently performed by St Æthelwold, bishop of Winchester from 963 to 984. And finally, late in the tenth century, a certain *comes Alwardus*, said to be the founder or refounder of Pershore abbey, was able by a singularly dubious transaction to procure relics of the saint for the endowment of that house. Thereafter the two religious communities were to become equal – though not always amicable – sharers in Edburga's patronage and Edburga's glory:

Although she has been divided into two shares in her relics, yet her virtue abounds in every particle: it offers a superiority to the nuns of Winchester, since the greater part of her body is there, while the oft-recited glory of her heavenly miracles gives lustre to the monks of Pershore.[24]

Osbert's *Vita Edburge* was composed almost two hundred years after the events which it purports to describe. It consists primarily of a conventional account of the saint's growth in conventional virtues; it is illustrated by conventional miracles and it culminates in a conventional death. Osbert's history of Edburga's relics raises at least as many questions as it answers. And, even though Osbert professed a special interest in the saint's shrine at Pershore, he was able to adduce only one unremarkable miracle to illustrate the nature of her cult at that house. How much, then, did Osbert of Clare really know about St Edburga of Winchester? And how, indeed, did he come to be writing about her at all?

[22] *Ibid.*, fols. 89–89v.
[23] On the identification of this *monasterium* see below, p. 277, n. 58.
[24] *Vita Edburge*, fol. 85v.

Osbert of Clare is a fascinating character. He is known to historians both as a dedicated but troublesome prior of Westminster and as a professional hagiographer of some standing. He first appears in the early 1120s, already a man of some importance, who seems to have been prior of Westminster for at least two years and who may even have been a serious candidate for the abbacy: if so, he had been disappointed by the appointment of Herbert in 1121.[25] He subsequently managed to incur the displeasure both of Herbert and of his successor Gervase; the result was two protracted periods of exile from his monastic home. Osbert seems to have accused Herbert of negligence in the government of Westminster: very probably a formal inquiry ensued, after which Herbert's decision to put his house in order may have been conditional upon the removal of his disruptive prior.[26] Osbert, probably with the assistance of Adelold, first bishop of Carlisle, was reinstated by the spring of 1134[27] and remained at Westminster throughout the 1130s. Once again, however, his zeal for the canonical government of the church proved fatal. News of the misgovernment of Abbot Gervase reached Innocent II; and Osbert again disappeared from the scene – 'banished to take charge of some small church or community which we cannot locate, miserably poor, and . . . writing constant begging letters to his friends of former days'.[28]

None the less, Osbert's achievement was considerable. As prior of Westminster he seems to have been closely involved in the foundation of a community of nuns at Kilburn. The foundation was doubtless undertaken for the greater glory of Westminster. The new community was to be in the custody of Westminster, and its members were to pray for the souls of all brothers and benefactors of that house, as well as for its royal founder, Edward the Confessor.[29] More important, Osbert stands out clearly as the man who masterminded Westminster's drive in the 1130s to secure the canonisation of that same royal patron. And central to Osbert's campaign was his skill as a hagiographer. Well aware of the need to provide a suitably impressive dossier on his subject, Osbert rewrote and brought up to date the earlier, only quasi-hagiographical Life upon which Edward's rather hesitant cult had hitherto been founded. Osbert dedicated his *Vita Edwardi* to Alberic of Ostia,

---

[25] *Letters*, pp. 1–4, 9.   [26] *Ibid.*, pp. 5–6.   [27] *Ibid.*, p. 11.
[28] *Ibid.*, pp. 18–19.
[29] *Ibid.*, pp. 16–17. On the nature of the community at Kilburn see KH, p. 259.

papal legate in England in 1138/9, and he used it as the basis of his case for Edward's canonisation when finally, probably in 1139, this was taken to Rome.[30]

Osbert's *Vita Edwardi* was the most outstanding product of a wide-ranging hagiological interest. He seems also to have played an important part in the deeply controversial revival of the festival of the Conception of the Blessed Virgin and in the promotion of the cult of St Anne.[31] He wrote a discourse for the edification of the faithful on the celebration of the former and composed a series of lections and hymns for the feast of the latter.[32] Closer to home, it was no doubt his loyalty to Westminster that, in part at least, occasioned his composition of a *Vita* or *Passio* of St Æthelbert, an East Anglian king 'martyred' by the Mercian Offa: Æthelbert's body was believed to rest at Hereford, but his head was claimed by Westminster.[33] During his first exile from Westminster, Osbert is known to have received hospitality at the abbeys of Ely and Bury St Edmunds.[34] His interest in the patron saint of the former is evident from a letter written to the monks of Ely, informing them of a miraculous appearance of St Æthelthryth in a humble wooden church on the Welsh border.[35] And his debt to the community of St Edmund received more elaborate acknowledgement – a series of *Miracula* of the ninth-century martyr king.[36]

Osbert's *Vita Edburge* fits rather neatly into this pattern of hagiographical works conceived to further the interests of, or to express gratitude towards, those religious communities with which Osbert had a significant personal connection. In his introductory *epistola*, Osbert writes at some length about the circumstances which led to the composition of the Life and about the sources upon which it was based. Foremost in his mind was the knowledge that he was writing at the request of the monks of Pershore – 'bound by the entreaties of the elders of the church of Pershore'.[37] And the familiarity with Pershore which this commission implies receives ample corroboration in one of Osbert's extant letters. Writing to

[30] On Osbert's role in the promotion of Edward's cult see especially *Letters*, pp. 17–19; *Life of King Edward*, ed. Barlow, App. D; Barlow, *Edward the Confessor*, ch. 12 and App. D. His *Vita Edwardi* is edited by Bloch, 'Vie de S. Edouard'. On the legation of Alberic of Ostia see *CS*, I, ii, 766–79. [31] *Letters*, pp. 11–15. [32] *Ibid.*, pp. 14–15.

[33] *Ibid.*, pp. 23–4. For the hagiography of Æthelbert see also Rollason, 'Cults of murdered royal saints', p. 9; 'Two Lives of St Ethelbert, King and Martyr', ed. M. R. James, *EHR* 32 (1917), 214–44. Osbert's *Passio* is preserved in Gotha, Landesbibliothek, MS I. 81; see P. Grosjean, 'De codice hagiographico Gothano', *AB* 58 (1940), 90–103, at 92–3.

[34] *Letters*, pp. 9–10, 11. [35] *Ibid.*, pp. 116–19 (no. 33). [36] See below, pp. 71–2.

[37] *Vita Edburge*, fol. 85.

Simon, bishop of Worcester, Osbert makes it clear that he has met Simon and Warin, his dean or prior, at the funeral of an abbot of Pershore.[38] The nature of Osbert's association with Pershore is not difficult to reconstruct. There is no evidence that Pershore was among the religious houses at which Osbert took refuge during his two periods of exile from Westminster. The funeral to which his letter alludes was almost certainly that of Abbot Wido, who died in 1136 or 1137:[39] hence his only attested visit to Pershore took place while he was enjoying a period of unparalleled security at Westminster. Very probably, therefore, Osbert's familiarity with Pershore is to be explained by a historical connection between that house and Westminster which dated back to the reign of the Confessor. Two of the three hundreds of Pershore had been granted by Edward for the endowment of Westminster; and the parish church of St Andrew had been built opposite Pershore abbey for the use of the Westminster tenants of Pershore.[40] Tenurial and administrative connections between the two houses were, therefore, close; and the cult of St Edburga may have been at least as important as that of St Edward to those Westminster tenants who worshipped within a few hundred yards of her shrine.

Edburga's cult, however, was not confined to Pershore; and nor, it seems, was Osbert's intended audience. He was prompted to write, he insists, not only by his love for the church of Pershore but also by his affection for the Winchester nuns.[41] I have been unable to find evidence of that direct connection with Nunnaminster which is implied by Osbert's words, but it is interesting to note that he did have access to at least one potential source of Winchester information – Henry of Blois, bishop of Winchester from 1129 to 1171 and papal legate from 1139 to 1143. When the community of Westminster decided to petition for the canonisation of its patron, Osbert turned for assistance to King Stephen; to the legate Alberic,

[38] *Letters*, pp. 77–9 (no. 12).

[39] *Ibid.* and p. 15. The deceased abbot is not named in Osbert's letter, but it is clear that his funeral took place when both Simon and Warin held office in Worcester. Simon was bishop from 1125 to 1150 and Warin held the office of dean or prior from *c.* 1124 until *c.* 1142 (*Heads*, p. 83). The only abbot known to have died in the period *c.* 1124–*c.* 1142 was Wido, who died in 1136/7 (*ibid.*, p. 59). His successor, William, was elected in 1138 and occurs only on the occasion of his election. The next recorded abbot, Thomas, first occurs 1143 × 5 (*ibid.*). It is therefore probable that Wido was the only abbot of Pershore to die during the relevant period and hence that it is to his death that Osbert's letter refers.

[40] *GP*, p. 298; S1040, 1043, 1143–6; *Letters*, p. 15; C. S. Taylor, 'Deerhurst, Pershore and Westminster', *Transactions of the Bristol and Gloucestershire Archaeological Society* 25 (1902), 230–50, at 240.   [41] *Vita Edburge*, fol. 85v.

22

cardinal bishop of Ostia, who in 1138 blessed as abbot of Westminster Gervase of Blois, probably an illegitimate son of the king; and to the king's brother, Henry of Winchester.[42] On his subsequent visit to the Curia, Osbert failed to secure Edward's canonisation: in the circumstances of 1139 his alliance with the house of Blois can have done his cause nothing but harm. He may, however, have been successful in other ways. It seems possible that he returned to England bearing relics of Pope Urban and his virgin disciple, Cecilia, and that he gave these not, as might be expected, to Westminster, but to Henry of Blois, who had sponsored his mission to Rome and who, probably as a result of Osbert's complaints, had been instructed by the pope to protect the estates of Westminster against the depredations of his own nephew, Abbot Gervase.[43]

Osbert, then, clearly had access to the traditions of Pershore; very probably too he was familiar, either through personal acquaintance or at second hand, with those of Nunnaminster. But the *Vita Edburge* was not, Osbert claimed, merely an amalgam of the oral traditions of the two communities upon which Edburga's cult was centred. Rather he was writing to provide for the Pershore monks a re-working of an earlier written source with which they had expressed dissatisfaction, apparently on stylistic grounds. Edburga's deeds had been set down in a style which lacked both clarity and elegance; Osbert's purpose, accordingly, was to produce a more polished literary work.[44]

The validity of this claim is not easy to assess. For the research of recent decades has highlighted a further intriguing aspect of Osbert's unconventional career. The eleventh and early twelfth centuries have been described as 'the golden age of medieval

---

[42] *Letters*, pp. 17–18, 80–7 (nos. 14–17, the former the dedicatory *epistola* to the *Vita Edwardi*); *Life of King Edward*, ed. Barlow, pp. 128–9; Barlow, *Edward the Confessor*, pp. 274–6. For a detailed study of the career of Henry of Blois see L. Voss, *Heinrich von Blois, Bischof von Winchester (1129–71)*, Historische Studien 210 (Berlin, 1932); for Henry's legation see *CS*, I, ii, 781–810.

[43] Thomas, 'Cult of relics', pp. 134–5, citing *Letters*, pp. 91, 96 (no. 22), 155–6 (no. 42), in each of which Osbert expresses his reverence for St Cecilia, and London, BL, MS Harley 3776, fol. 125r, a fourteenth-century martyrology listing Urban and Cecilia among the saints resting at Winchester. See also *Letters*, pp. 18–19, 88 (no. 20), Innocent II to Henry of Winchester bidding him protect the estates of Westminster.

[44] *Vita Edburge*, fol. 85: 'Quia uero illius gesta confusa uidebantur sermone contexta, nec in eis ordo uenustus radiabat insertus, precibus deuinctus seniorum Persorensis ecclesie, inculta studui diligentius elimare. Ut enim Seneca Cordubensis ait, "sepe bona materia cessat sine artifice", oratoris igitur color rethoricus hac maiestate debet excellere, ut in elegantia uerborum puritas sit aperta, et in compositione constructio respondeat equaliter perpolita, et in dignitate refloreat sententia pulchra uarietate distincta.'

forgery'[45] — an age in which forgery, while never ceasing to be regarded as a serious crime, came to be condoned and encouraged by even the most scrupulous churchmen as an almost 'respectable' way for religious houses to adapt their often inadequate muniments to the crises of the time.[46] In 1957, T. A. M. Bishop and Pierre Chaplais published their *Facsimiles of English royal writs*, in which it was suggested that a high proportion of the English forgeries of this period were the product of a single monastic scriptorium, and in which the scriptorium in question was tentatively identified as that of Westminster abbey.[47] The scale of the 'Westminster forgeries' was staggering: they included not only a large number of Westminster documents but also diplomas for Ramsey, Battle, Coventry, Gloucester and St Peter's, Ghent.[48] In 1962 Chaplais carried these researches a stage further: he identified the mind behind the 'Westminster forgeries'.[49] Chaplais took as his starting-point the fact that Osbert of Clare, seeking to bring together in his *Vita Edwardi* all the available evidence in support of his case for Edward's canonisation, incorporated into that work an account of Edward's benefactions to Westminster as these were allegedly contained in the king's diplomas. The diplomas to which Osbert alludes are three in number, of which two still survive in the original. The two extant originals are written in the same hand — a hand which recurs in a charter by which Abbot Herbert (1121–*c.* 1136) grants Powick

[45] A. Morey and C. N. L. Brooke, *Gilbert Foliot and his letters*, Cambridge Studies in Medieval Life and Thought, New Series 11 (Cambridge, 1965), p. 128. Chapter 8 of the same work provides a valuable general discussion of attitudes to forgery in this period. See also R. Vaughan, *Matthew Paris*, Cambridge Studies in Medieval Life and Thought, New Series 6 (Cambridge, 1958), chs. 8 and 10, and C. N. L. Brooke, 'Approaches to medieval forgery', in Brooke, *Medieval church and society: collected essays* (London, 1971), pp. 100–20.

[46] Morey and Brooke, *Foliot and his letters*, p. 128: 'In the eleventh and twelfth centuries social pressures were such that respectable men and respectable communities forged as they had not forged before and would never forge again.'

[47] *Facsimiles of English royal writs to A.D. 1100: presented to Vivian Hunter Galbraith*, ed. T. A. M. Bishop and P. Chaplais (Oxford, 1957), pp. xix–xxiv. The conclusions of Bishop and Chaplais had a long ancestry: see J. Tait, 'An alleged charter of William the Conqueror', in H. W. C. Davis (ed.), *Essays in history presented to Reginald Lane Poole* (Oxford, 1927), pp. 151–67, at p. 158, n. 2, where reference is made to a 'factory of forgeries' at Westminster.

[48] *Facsimiles*, ed. Bishop and Chaplais, pp. xx–xxii; see also Chaplais, 'Original charters', p. 92.

[49] Chaplais, 'Original charters', pp. 91–5. For an earlier suggestion that a single forger may have been responsible for a large proportion of the forgeries of this period see C. N. L. Brooke, 'The Canterbury forgeries and their author', *Downside Review* 68 (1950), 462–76, and 69 (1951), 210–31, at 230.

manor to the priory of Great Malvern.[50] There is, therefore, 'not the slightest doubt that all three documents were forged, and Osbert must have been aware of it'.[51] More than this, stylistic evidence shows that the same forger drafted all three charters, together with several other forged Westminster documents, a diploma of Edgar for Ramsey and diplomas of the Confessor for Coventry, Ramsey and St Peter's, Ghent. And analysis of the forged Westminster charters in relation to the *Vita Edwardi* reveals a number of incongruities which can be explained only by the supposition that, 'like the Life, the charters are the work of Osbert de Clare, who did not, as he claims, find the pretended charters of Edward among the muniments of Westminster abbey; he drafted them himself, at approximately the same time as he was writing his life of the Confessor'.[52] Osbert, therefore, was not only a controversial prior and a prolific hagiographer; he was also one of the most successful forgers of his time. Are we, then, to believe in the existence of Osbert's alleged written source for the *Vita Edburge*? Or did the work emanate rather from 'that world of fabricated history which Osbert of Clare was to make so much his own'?[53]

That Osbert did indeed have access to a written source is suggested, first, by a comparison of his work with the later accounts of St Edburga. These comprise a series of *lectiones* for the feasts of Edburga's deposition (15 June) and translation (18 July) contained in the late-thirteenth-century breviary of Hyde abbey,[54] an anonymous Latin Life contained in London, BL, MS Lansdowne 436[55]

---

[50] Chaplais, 'Original charters', pp. 91–2; *Vita Edwardi*, p. 91. The alleged charters of the Confessor are S1043, 1011 and 1041; K824, 779, 825 (respectively the so-called First, Second and Third charters of Edward to Westminster). Abbot Herbert's charter (Westminster Abbey Muniments XLIX) is printed in Chaplais, 'Original charters', p. 100 and a partial facsimile is provided at Plate VII(a).

[51] Chaplais, 'Original charters', p. 91. [52] *Ibid.*, pp. 92–3.

[53] *Life of King Edward*, ed. Barlow, p. 262.

[54] *MBHA*, III, fols. 264v–265 (15 June); IV, fols. 296–296v (18 July). The MSS upon which this edition is based – Oxford, Bodleian Library, MSS Rawl. liturg. e.1* and Gough liturg. 8 – were clearly together as two volumes of the same book prior to their incorporation into the Rawlinson and Gough collections. They are certainly of Hyde abbey provenance and were probably written during the abbacy of Simon de Kanings (1292–1304): see *ibid.*, I, vii–xi. On the provenance of these MSS see also N. R. Ker, *Medieval libraries of Great Britain: a list of surviving books*, Royal Historical Society Guides and Handbooks 3, 2nd edn (London, 1964), p. 104.

[55] This Life, entitled *De uita sanctae Edburgae uirginis*, is preserved on fols. 41v–43v of London, BL, MS Lansdowne 436, a Romsey MS of the early fourteenth century (see Ker, *Medieval libraries*, p. 164). The Life is listed as *BHL*, no. 2386 and Hardy, *Descriptive catalogue*, no. 1145 and is printed by Laurel Braswell ('St Edburga', pp. 329–33).

and a Middle English Life dating from the late thirteenth century.[56] These accounts, it is clear, were not derived exclusively from Osbert's work. For instance, the lections for Edburga's deposition contained in the Hyde abbey *sanctorale*, although providing a framework for Edburga's life which closely resembles that of Osbert's *Vita*, contain few verbal echoes of that work and on occasion provide information supplementary to that of Osbert's account.[57] The Hyde *sanctorale* history of Edburga's relics likewise preserves a tradition which differs in detail from that recorded by Osbert.[58] The Lansdowne Life, although resembling in outline Osbert's work and containing a number of verbal echoes, again gives some information unknown to or omitted by Osbert: in particular, its description of the saint's composition of seven hymns a day finds no parallel in any other extant source.[59] Its account of Edburga's Winchester translations resembles more closely that of Osbert than that of the Hyde *sanctorale*, but there are a number of verbal parallels with the latter source which are not shared by Osbert.[60] And the Middle English Life of the saint, as its editor notes, 'shows no conclusive relation to nor derivation from any of

---

[56] This Life is contained in London, BL, MS Egerton 1993, fols. 160–161, and in Oxford, Bodleian Library, MSS Eng. Poet. a. 1 ('Vernon'), fols. 32–32v and Bodley 779, fols. 282–293v. It is listed as Hardy, *Descriptive catalogue*, no. 1147 and is printed by Laurel Braswell, by whom it is tentatively dated to *c.* 1280 ('St Edburga', pp. 323, 325–9). Certainly it seems to belong to the reign of Edward I (1272–1307), for it incorporates a historical introduction unparalleled elsewhere in the Edburga literature which links the saint's father with subsequent ruling Edwards down to Edward I, who is said to have succeeded 'now late sine' (p. 325).

[57] For instance, the Abbess Æthelthryth, to whose care the infant Edburga was committed, is endowed with a royal ancestry which is absent from Osbert's account: *MBHA*, III, fol. 265; cited below, n. 96; cf. *Vita Edburge*, fol. 88.   [58] See below, p. 114.

[59] Braswell, 'St Edburga', p. 330: 'psalmos assidue canens nocte ac die, intendens animum ad psalmiste dictum: *Sepcies in die laudem dixi tibi* . . . Studebat per septenarium numerum ymnorum cotidie perficere. Quod haberetur in octaua beatitudine.' Both Osbert and the Hyde lections place considerable emphasis upon the saint's ability to sing, but neither provides this information (*Vita Edburge*, fols. 91v, 96–96v; *MBHA*, III, fol. 265). The Lansdowne Life closely resembles the Hyde *sanctorale* account in its endowment of the abbess Æthelthryth with a royal ancestry (see above, n. 57). But it omits several episodes which are central both to Osbert's account and to the Hyde lections — among them the saint's choice of the religious life at the age of three and the lengthy account of her acquisition for the nunnery of the estate known as *Canaga* (see below, p. 33).

[60] For example, *MBHA*, IV, fol. 296v: 'Tanta namque luce miraculorum radiabat, quatinus sancto swithuno Wintoniensi episcopo, concordia caritatis compararetur, ita quod infra mensem centum a diuersis infirmitatibus curarentur . . . Tanta eciam miraculorum gloria sanctus swithunus et beata edburga pollebant, et quasi miraculis uersificando deum laudarent: dum quando beatus swithunus unum sanabat, statim gloriosa uirgo edburga alium a quacumque infirmitate eripiebat.'

the extant lives, historical notices or liturgies'.[61] All this seems to indicate that there existed during the Middle Ages a rich and varied hagiographical tradition concerning Edburga which is represented by only a relatively small number of extant texts; and it is very probable that the origins of that tradition are to be traced to the period before Osbert wrote.

More concrete evidence for the early development of a hagiographical tradition is suggested by two twelfth-century sources. William of Malmesbury was able to incorporate into both his *Gesta regum* and his *Gesta pontificum*, each completed *c.* 1125, not only a conventional listing of the saint among Edward's offspring but also a longer, quasi-hagiographical account of her career.[62] William's account closely resembles that of Osbert's *Vita*. Like Osbert, he accords particular importance to the saint's early choice of the religious life, prompted by Edward's placing before her of both secular and ecclesiastical objects. He goes on to give an account of the saint's virtue in which *humilitas* receives special emphasis and is illustrated by reference to the shoe-cleaning incident. And, like Osbert, William portrays the cult as centred initially upon Winchester but as spreading also to a second centre at Pershore. This similarity does not imply that either work used the other as its source,[63] or even that they were derived from a

Cf. Braswell, 'St Edburga', p. 332: 'tanta enim in luce miraculorum radiebat, quatenus sancto Swithino Wyntoniensis episcopo concordia caritatis comparetur, ita quod infra mensem centum a diuersis infirmitatibus curarentur ad Christi honorem tantaque miraculorum gloria sanctus Swithinus et Edburga gloriosa uirgo pollebant dei misericordia ut quasi miraculis uerificando [*sic*] deum laudarent; dum quando gloriosus Swithinus unum sanabat, statim gloriosa uirgo Edburga alium a quacumque infirmitate detineretur eriperet'.

Cf. also *Vita Edburge*, fol. 102v, where Osbert writes on the same theme in markedly different words.

[61] Braswell, 'St Edburga', p. 311. On the unique historical introduction to this Life see above, n. 56.

[62] *GR*, I, 137: 'Suscepit etiam ex tertia uxore, Edgiua vocabulo, filios duos . . . filias duas, Edburgam et Edgiuam. Edburga, sacrata Christo uirgo, Wintoniae quiescit.' This sparse and unremarkable account is supplemented later in the same work (I, 268–9) by a quasi-hagiographical passage which Laurel Braswell, in her summary of the historical sources for the life of Edburga, fails to notice, attributing this lengthy account solely to the *Gesta pontificum* (*GP*, p. 174; Braswell, 'St Edburga', p. 305): in fact the Edburga passages in the two works are almost identical.

[63] Indeed, leaving aside the many cases where Osbert simply provides more detail than William, there are several significant differences between the texts which strongly suggest that this was not the case. First, Osbert describes the ecclesiastical objects placed before the saint as 'textum . . . euangelicum, et patenam et calicem' (*Vita Edburge*, fol. 88), whereas William mentions only the two latter (*GR*, I, 268; *GP*, p. 174). Conversely, William notes that the secular objects comprised 'armillas et monilia' (*GR*, I, 268; *GP*, p. 174), whereas Osbert speaks only in general terms of 'indumenta . . . regalia' and

common source. It does, however, strongly suggest that there was a hagiographical tradition in existence upon which both writers were able to draw.[64]

A single folio in the Bodleian Library may carry the story further. MS Bodley 451 contains an extract which Laurel Braswell has identified as part of a Life of St Edburga: it contains an account of the saint's healing of the blind woman and the beginning of the story of her secret vigils.[65] The main themes and the sequence of events closely resemble those of Osbert's Life, but the degree of verbal parallelism is not such as to suggest that the passage is taken from that work or from an abridgement of it. More important is the palaeographical evidence. The passage occupies the final folio of the last quire of a Nunnaminster manuscript written in the first half of the twelfth century.[66] The Edburga extract is in a different

'instrumenta . . . feminea' (*Vita Edburge*, fol. 88). Moreover, when describing the king's reaction to his daughter's choice, Osbert again speaks only in general terms of Edward's rejoicing, whereas William attributes to him a passage of direct speech (*GR*, I, 268; *GP*, p. 174). A further discrepancy arises in the context of the shoe-cleaning incident: Osbert uses the word *calciamenta*, while William employs *soccos* (*Vita Edburge*, fol: 89v; *GR*, I, 269; *GP*, p. 174).

[64] An account of Edburga almost identical to, and probably derived from, that of William of Malmesbury is found in London, BL, MS Harley 64 (fols. 84–85), where it is associated with an account of Edburga's translation to Pershore (briefly mentioned at fols. 47–47v) which is almost certainly derived from Osbert or from a later version of his work. The MS appears to be a compilation including extracts from Bede and Henry of Huntingdon together with miscellaneous Pershore material and a collection in a single hand of thirteenth-century documents: it is described in *A catalogue of the Harleian manuscripts in the British Museum*, 4 vols. (London, 1808–12), I, 16. I am grateful to Dr D. E. Greenway for advice on the contents of this MS, which also includes, on fols. 184–185v, a series of Edburga miracles. These comprise a prologue, with a vocation narrative and account of the saint's life almost identical to the William of Malmesbury account and to that on fol. 84v of the same MS, followed by an account of eight recent miracles performed through the saint's intercession at Pershore. The *Miracula* form part of the collection of thirteenth-century documents, where they appear in association with copies of papal correspondence addressed to Henry III (1216–72) and with accounts of the canonisations of Peter the Martyr (1253), St Francis (1228, with an account of his translation in 1230), and St Anthony (1232). Laurel Braswell notes ('St Edburga', p. 305, n. 56) that 'The miracles of St Edburga are considered by the writer contemporary and for one [f. 185] he gives the date 1260. On paleographical grounds the manuscript could not be much later than 1280.' The *Miracula* are listed as *BHL*, no. 2387 and Hardy, *Descriptive catalogue*, no. 1146.

[65] Braswell, 'St Edburga', p. 304. The extract is reproduced in Appendix 2 below.

[66] This is not a fly-leaf, as stated by Braswell ('St Edburga', p. 304). The MS is described in *A summary catalogue of Western manuscripts in the Bodleian Library at Oxford*, 7 vols. (Oxford, 1895–1953) (*SC*), no. 2401, where it is dated to *c.* 1100. N. R. Ker is more cautious in his attribution of the script to the first half of the twelfth century (*Medieval libraries*, pp. 201–2). Several factors point to the Nunnaminster origin of the MS. First, in addition to the major Edburga extract, the MS contains, on a fly-leaf (fol. ii), a note concerning the relationship of King Alfred to saints Edburga and Neot. The note takes as

hand, larger and less professional, but apparently of the same date. Hence the work from which this extract was taken seems either to have antedated Osbert's work or to have followed so closely upon it as to make it most unlikely that it represents a mere abridgement of that work. While it is not possible to identify the Bodleian fragment as taken from Osbert's actual source, that fragment provides further testimony to the prior existence of a literary tradition concerning St Edburga.

Analysis of Osbert's work, moreover, allows tentative conclusions to be reached concerning the date, the content and the provenance of his postulated written source. The latest events to be discussed in detail by Osbert are the saint's translation by Æthelwold and the acquisition of some of her relics by the abbey of Pershore: each of these is probably to be dated to *c.* 970.[67] But on three occasions Osbert makes reference to subsequent events. Twice he refers almost parenthetically to the Danish invasions of the late tenth and early eleventh centuries, and once he writes of assistance given to the Winchester nuns by Ælfwine, bishop of Winchester from 1032 until 1047.[68] It is not impossible that these references represent additions made by Osbert in order to bring up to date a Life of the late tenth century: but, in view of the fact that this updating would then end rather incongruously a century before Osbert's own time, it is most unlikely. Rather it seems probable that Osbert had before him a source which was itself produced in or following the mid eleventh century and which it was his aim not to update but, as advertised in his *epistola*, to re-write in a more acceptable style.[69]

its principal point of reference the year 1150 and was therefore probably written at about that date. The presence of these two items concerning Edburga in a MS which otherwise has no hagiographical content strongly suggests that the MS was a product of one of the houses in which the saint's cult was centred. Second, a note on fol. 119v informs us that the MS was written by a *scriptrix*. And, finally, the paste-downs of the medieval binding, taken from monastic accounts of 1334, include an item 'pro petris de Selborne': stone from the quarries of Selborne was frequently used for building in Winchester during the Middle Ages (see *VCH Hants.*, V, 312). On the provenance of the MS see also Ker, *Medieval libraries*, pp. 201–2 and the card index from which *Medieval libraries* was compiled and which is available for consultation in the Bodleian Library.

[67] See below, pp. 111, 132–3.   [68] *Vita Edburge*, fols. 88, 103v.

[69] See above, p. 23. One obvious candidate for the authorship of a later-eleventh-century Life would be Goscelin of Canterbury, who was composing Lives of the English saints in the relevant period, who included in his Life of St Edith a vocation narrative which closely resembles that of the *Vita Edburge*, and who may have had connections with the Winchester religious houses (see below, pp. 37–8, 83–4; *Life of King Edward*, ed. Barlow, pp. 99–100).

There is, however, at least a possibility that this postulated eleventh-century source was not without antecedents. This is suggested first by a single passage within Osbert's Life. Following his account of Edburga's translation by Æthelwold, Osbert writes of the Winchester saints Edburga and Swithun that 'The confessor and the virgin as it were alternately in disputation brought to conclusion novel miracles, while in alternate writings in prose and verse they strove among themselves, locked in mutual disputations.'[70] Osbert's meaning here is obscure, but the passage seems to suggest that, in the late tenth century, a certain rivalry between the two saints – and between the communities which those saints represented – came to be expressed in written form; and the natural vehicle for the expression of rivalry between saints was, of course, hagiography.[71] A further significant reference is found in a collection of Edburga's Pershore miracles compiled towards the end of the thirteenth century and contained in London, BL, MS Harley 64. Here the author explains his decision to include only the most recent of Edburga's miracles by stressing that the saint's life and early miracles had already received ample hagiographical coverage; and he makes it clear that this coverage had been not only in Latin but also in English.[72] Laurel Braswell provisionally identifies the English material to which the Harleian author alludes with the Middle English Life of Edburga, which seems to have been written almost contemporaneously with the Harleian *Miracula*;[73] but it is at least equally probable that the author had an Old English work in mind.

Some indication of the content and provenance of Osbert's postulated written source may be derived, first, from the fact that the Winchester traditions incorporated into his *Vita Edburge* seem in general to be both more detailed and more reliable than those

---

[70] *Vita Edburge*, fol. 102v: 'Certatim namque confessor et uirgo quasi quibusdam successibus noua determinabant miracula, dum tanquam in reciprocis apicibus in prosa et uersu inter se confligerent, et mutuis disputationibus altercarent.'

[71] On the development of a hagiographical tradition concerning St Swithun in the later tenth century see below, pp. 108, 109.

[72] London, BL, MS Harley 64, fol. 184v: 'Cuius uita celebs et cenobialis conuersatio quam ipsa sanctimonialis gesset in supradicto cenobio, quam inclita fuisset preclaris meritis, et quam preclara uirtutibus et signis, miracula in uita et post mortem antiquitus antiquioribus tam Anglice quam Latine de ipsa conscriptis literis commendant plurima, que templorum eius editui Persor' et Wynton' nescientibus uiua uoce pronuntiauit, unde nequaquam uetera iam amplius scribimus.'

For discussion of the Harleian *Miracula* see above, n. 64.

[73] Braswell, 'St Edburga', pp. 323–4, at p. 324.

concerning Pershore. For the latter house Osbert records only a single and unverifiable item of history –. the tenth-century refoundation of the house by *comes Alwardus*, with the associated translation of the relics of St Edburga.[74] This tradition concerning the foundation is preserved also by William of Malmesbury, who describes a foundation in the time of King Edgar by *Egelwardus dux Dorsatensis*:[75] the limited alternative sources speak of a foundation either by St Oswald or by King Edgar.[76] The *Alwardus/Egelwardus* in question is probably to be identified with Æthelweard, ealdorman of the Western provinces, patron of Ælfric and translator of the *Anglo-Saxon Chronicle*.[77] It is by no means impossible that he was a co-founder or an important patron of tenth-century Pershore; but it is most unlikely that he merits the elevated status of sole founder which he is accorded by Osbert of Clare.

With the monastic history of Winchester Osbert seems to have been more at ease. He provides, first, outline foundation histories of two of Winchester's religious houses, New Minster and Nunnaminster. Of these, the former is generally consistent with the other extant sources,[78] and the latter seems likewise to be founded

---

[74] *Vita Edburge*, fol. 107v: 'comes Alwardus . . . qui Persorense cenobium . . . construxit'. Cf. *ibid.*, fol. 108v, where Osbert writes of *Alwardus*'s return with the relics 'ad Persorense quod restauraueraat . . . cenobium'. On the historicity of *Alwardus*'s alleged acquisition of Edburga's relics see below, pp. 129–39.   [75] *GP*, p. 298.

[76] The Worcester annals attribute the foundation of Pershore to Oswald *s.a.* 883 (*Annales monastici*, IV, *Annales prioratus de Wigornia*, 369: this is probably an erroneously dated reference to the tenth-century reformer Oswald, on whose role in the refoundation of Pershore see *MO*, p. 51; Sir Ivor Atkins, 'The church of Worcester from the eighth to the twelfth century', *Antiquaries Journal* 17 (1937), 371–91, at 385; E. John, 'Some Latin charters of the tenth-century reformation', in John, *Orbis Britanniae and other studies* (Leicester, 1966), pp. 181–209, at pp. 199–204; D. H. Farmer, 'The progress of the monastic revival', in D. Parsons (ed.), *Tenth-century studies: essays in commemoration of the millenium of the Council of Winchester and 'Regularis concordia'* (London and Chichester, 1975), pp. 10–19, at p. 15. The alleged foundation charter of the abbey describes a foundation by King Edgar alone: S786; B1282. KH (p. 73) postulate a seventh-century foundation for secular canons, replaced consecutively by a community of monks and a community of seculars and nuns and with a refoundation *c.* 970 for Benedictine monks.

[77] On the career of Æthelweard see especially *The Chronicle of Æthelweard*, ed. A. Campbell, Nelson's Medieval Texts (1962), pp. xii–xvi; L. Whitbread, 'Æthelweard and the Anglo-Saxon Chronicle', *EHR* 74 (1959), 577–89; S. Keynes, *The diplomas of Æthelred 'the Unready', 978–1016: a study in their use as historical evidence*, Cambridge Studies in Medieval Life and Thought, Third Series 13 (Cambridge, 1978), pp. 187–8. Æthelweard's son, Æthelmaer, was responsible for the foundation of Cerne abbey in Dorset and of Eynsham abbey in Oxfordshire (see Keynes, *Diplomas*, p. 191; Whitbread, 'Æthelweard', p. 586).

[78] Osbert states that New Minster was founded by Alfred and brought to completion by Edward the Elder (*Vita Edburge* fol. 87v). For important discussion of this foundation see P. Grierson, 'Grimbald of St Bertin's', *EHR* 55 (1940), 529–61, at 551–7, where it is

on a local tradition with more than a grain of truth. Osbert attributes the foundation of Nunnaminster to Ealhswith, consort of Alfred, and records that the work was completed by Edward the Elder, or, elsewhere, by Edward in conjunction with an unnamed wife: Osbert's work is the earliest source to mention the role of Edward and the only source to mention that of his consort.[79] Ealhswith's central role in the foundation is attested by the *Liber uitae* of New Minster (*c.* 1030), where it is stated that Edward moved the remains of his father from the Old to the New Minster, in which Ealhswith, 'builder of the nuns' minster', was buried.[80] And further evidence concerning the establishment of Nunnaminster is found in a tenth-century addition to a much earlier book of prayers which seems to have passed into the nuns' possession. This comprises a vernacular account of the bounds of an estate belonging to Ealhswith; and these, Biddle notes, 'enclose the greater part of the area now occupied by St Mary's Abbey and suggest that Ealhswith provided the site for the foundation of the house'.[81] None of this, however, implies that Alfred's consort completed the foundation of Nunnaminster single-handed, and Osbert's statement that the work was completed by Edward seems to be corroborated by a passage in the late-tenth-century *Chronicle* of Æthelweard which describes the dedication by Archbishop Plegmund *c.* 908 of a tower in Winchester in honour of the Blessed Virgin.[82]

suggested that Alfred built for Grimbald a *monasteriolum* at Winchester and that the latter encouraged Edward to proceed with the foundation of a new monastery in accordance with Alfred's wishes. This interpretation is accepted by more recent scholars: KH, p. 81; M. Biddle, *'Felix urbs Winthonia*: Winchester in the age of monastic reform', in Parsons (ed.), *Tenth-century studies*, pp. 123–40, at p. 127; Biddle, 'Winchester: the development of an early capital', in H. Jankuhn, W. Schlesinger and H. Steuer (eds.), *Vor- und Frühformen der Europäischen Stadt im Mittelalter*, Abhandlungen der Akademie der Wissenschaften in Göttingen, 3 Folge, 83–4 (Göttingen, 1973–4), pp. 229–61, at p. 251; WS1, p. 313.

79 *Vita Edburge*, fols. 87v, 88v. The statement of WS1, p. 321, n. 9 that the earliest reference to Edward's role in the foundation is that of Leland (*Collectanea*, I, 413) is therefore mistaken: rather this is derived from Osbert's work. 80 *LVH*, p. 5.

81 WS1, p. 322; cf. Biddle, *'Felix urbs Winthonia'*, pp. 127–8. The bounds are printed in *An ancient manuscript of the eighth or ninth century: formerly belonging to St Mary's abbey, or Nunnaminster, Winchester*, ed. W. de Gray Birch, Hampshire Record Society (London and Winchester, 1889), p. 96, from London, BL, MS Harley 2965, fol. 40v.

82 *Chronicle of Æthelweard*, ed. Campbell, p. 52. P. Grierson suggests ('Grimbald', p. 557) that this passage refers to the dedication of New Minster, but it is pointed out in WS1 (p. 321, n. 10) that the original dedication of New Minster included not only the Blessed Virgin but also the Holy Trinity and St Peter: it therefore seems more likely that the dedication described by Æthelweard was that of Nunnaminster. Osbert attributes the dedication of Nunnaminster to 'Wintoniensis antistes Elphegus senior' (*Vita Edburge,*

Further evidence of Osbert's familiarity with Nunnaminster history is provided by an interesting story of royal patronage. King Edward, according to the hagiographer, visited his daughter at Nunnaminster and asked her to sing for his pleasure: in return, he granted to Nunnaminster the estate known as *Canaga*.[83] Among the estates of the nunnery recorded in the Domesday survey is that of All Cannings in Wiltshire.[84] The name appears in Domesday as *Caninge* or *Cainingha*, elsewhere as *Caneganmersc* or *Caningan maersc* and, in the mid twelfth century, as *Caninges, Canenghis, Canengis, Canninges* and *Caningas*.[85] Probably, therefore, Osbert's *Canaga* represents a version of this name. Certainly the estate of All Cannings is identified with that acquired as a result of Edburga's song in the series of lections for the saint's feast day contained in the Hyde abbey *sanctorale*. Here an account of Edburga's song is followed by the statement that the saint took advantage of her father's mellow mood to obtain from him for the use of the nuns 'the estate which is now called "allecaninga" on account of her song'.[86] We have no other evidence for the date and means of Nunnaminster's acquisition of All Cannings, and the length and detail of Osbert's account strongly suggests that he was dealing with an important local tradition whose core of truth lay in an act of patronage by Edward, stimulated at least in part by the presence of his daughter within the community.[87]

If Osbert was reliably informed about the foundation and endowment of Nunnaminster, he might be expected to speak with comparable authority of the history of its abbesses. His account of Edburga's own position within the monastic hierarchy is particularly important. A number of scholars, among them W. de Gray Birch, I. G. Thomas and Laurel Braswell, have attributed to Edburga the status of abbess of Nunnaminster.[88] The source of this

---

fol. 88v). This attribution is almost certainly erroneous, for Ælfheah did not succeed to the see of Winchester until 934/5 (*ASC*, A, *s.a*). On the foundation of Nunnaminster see also KH, p. 268, where a foundation by both Ealhswith and Alfred is suggested and the completion of that foundation by Edward the Elder is accepted.

[83] *Vita Edburge*, fols. 90–92v.   [84] *VCH Hants.*, II, 122; *VCH Wilts.*, II, 130.

[85] J. E. B. Gover, Allen Mawer and F. M. Stenton, *The place-names of Wiltshire*, English Place-Name Society 16 (Cambridge, 1939), pp. 249–50.   [86] *MBHA*, III, fol. 265.

[87] See also below, pp. 99–101; Osbert of Clare concludes his discussion of *Canaga* by noting that the estate remained in Nunnaminster's possession *adhuc hodie* (*Vita Edburge*, fol. 92v). If the identification of *Canaga* with All Cannings is correct, Osbert's statement is corroborated by evidence which demonstrates that the estate was still in the hands of the nunnery in the fifteenth century (*VCH Hants.*, II, 123).

[88] *Ancient MS*, ed. Birch, p. 6; Thomas, 'Cult of relics', p. 389; Braswell, 'St Edburga',

attribution appears to be the sixteenth-century antiquary, John Leland: it is corroborated neither by Osbert nor by the other extant medieval sources.[89] Of those who did attain abbatial status Osbert provides a tantalising account. The person appointed by Ealhswith, and still holding office when Edburga entered the nunnery, was an Abbess Æthelthryth.[90] Thereafter, Osbert names a certain Alfgheua or Alfghiua, abbess at the time of Edburga's translation by St Æthelwold and allegedly responsible for the sale of Edburga's relics to *comes Alwardus*.[91] A lady of the same name, described as *Alfgheua Coloniensis abbatissa*, is mentioned in association with Ælfwine, bishop of Winchester from 1032 until 1047.[92] And, finally, a certain Ælfleda is said to have been responsible for the restoration of the saint's shrine, which had been stripped of its gold and silver for the redemption of captives during the Danish invasions:[93] her abbacy is probably to be placed in the first half of the eleventh century. Osbert's account of these abbesses is not easy to disentangle[94] and on occasion seems to be contradicted by such other sources as are available.[95] It is, however, corroborated by

---

p. 292; also KH, p. 268. Those who have avoided this error include D. H. Farmer (*ODS*, p. 118) and the editors of *Heads* (p. 223).

89 Leland, *Collectanea*, I, 413. For Edburga's status within the nunnery see *Vita Edburge*, fols. 96–96v, an ambiguous passage which suggests that the saint may have held the office of precentrix; it may however mean simply that her love of singing was such that she seemed to be like a precentrix.

90 *Vita Edburge*, fols. 87v, 88.   91 *Ibid.*, fols. 103, 107v.

92 *Ibid.*, fol. 88. Elsewhere (fols. 104v–105) Osbert writes of Alfghiua 'uenerabilis abbatiss[a], que de Colonia ciuitate Germanie ex generoso sanguine natiuitatis traxit originem, et in nouo sanctimonialium uirginum monasterio quod Capitolium dicitur sancte religionis didicit honestatem'. The German house from which this abbess allegedly came is well-attested: see L. H. Cottineau, *Répertoire topo-bibliographique des abbayes et prieurés*, 3 vols. (Mâcon, 1935–70), I (1935), col. 838. I have, however, been unable to find further traces of Alfghiua herself.

93 *Vita Edburge*, fols. 103v–104. Presumably she is to be identified with the Alfletha who also appears at fol. 103v.

94 His account of Alfghiua/Alfgheua is particularly complicated, as he gives no indication of whether he is speaking of one abbess, whose abbacy must therefore have lasted from the time of Edburga's translation by Æthelwold until the time of Ælfwine, or of two, ruling in the second half of the tenth and the mid eleventh century respectively. The latter interpretation is chronologically the more plausible and seems to be supported by the fact that Osbert twice associates the lady with Cologne (*Vita Edburge*, fols. 88, 104v–105), whereas on one occasion (*ibid.*, fol. 107v) he endows her with a thoroughly English parentage, noting that 'Hec siquidem sanctimonialium magistra feminarum filia Aðeluuoldi comitis extitit, cui Ætheldrida que regi postmodum Eadgaro iuncta est conubio carnali genitura mater fuit.'

95 The most significant contradiction of alternative sources concerns the name of the abbess at the time of Edburga's translation by St Æthelwold. According to the Lives of St Æthelwold by Ælfric (1006) and Wulfstan (after 996) that saint appointed, at the time of

those later hagiographical works which it has been suggested were not exclusively dependent upon Osbert[96] and, especially as regards the eleventh century, Osbert's abbesses may very possibly fill some of the gaps left by the limited alternative sources. Osbert seems again to have had access to detailed and probably reliable local tradition; sadly, his information was rather clumsily used.

It seems clear, then, that Osbert knew more about the history of Nunnaminster than about that of Pershore, the house for which he claimed to be writing and with which he had a demonstrable personal connection. This seems to suggest that there was a considerable qualitative difference between Osbert's sources for the two houses – that his written source was concerned primarily if not exclusively to describe the saint's life and cult at Winchester. The point may be carried further. In one rather difficult passage Osbert summarised the changes which he planned to make when reworking his source: he intended, it seems, to divide a hitherto unitary work into two separate books, in order more clearly to distinguish the saint's life from her posthumous miracles.[97] But Osbert's work as it now stands is divided not into two sections but into three – a Life, an account of Edburga's posthumous career at

---

his refoundation of Nunnaminster, a certain Æthelthryth as abbess (*Three Lives of English saints*, ed. M. Winterbottom (Toronto, 1972), pp. 2, 3, 24, 47; also *Heads*, p. 223). Osbert, however, makes no reference to this Æthelthryth and names Alfghiua as abbess in the time of Æthelwold: unless we are to assume that Æthelthryth lived only for a very short time, his account stands in direct opposition to the earlier sources. The only other abbess of Nunnaminster recorded during the Anglo-Saxon period is Eadgyfu, who occurs *c.* 975 and again *c.* 990 × 2. Osbert's 'first' Alfghiua could just be inserted before Eadgyfu's abbacy, assuming Æthelthryth to have died soon after her appointment.

[96] The lections for the feast of Edburga's deposition contained in the Hyde abbey *sanctorale* give the abbess at the time of Edburga's entry to the nunnery as 'etheldrithe moribus et regali prosapia illustrissime' (though they do not state that she was the first abbess of the house; see *MBHA*, III, fol. 265). The lections for the saint's translation in the time of Æthelwold name Algiua as abbess (*ibid.*, IV, fol. 296v). The Lansdowne Life names the abbess at the time of Edburga's vocation as 'Edeldrida . . . femina gloriosa ex regali progenie orta' (Braswell, 'St Edburga', p. 330) and the abbess at the time of her translation to Pershore as Ælgina (*ibid.*, p. 332), a name which may well be derived from an Alfghiua/Alghiua tradition. The Middle English Life gives Aildred as abbess at the time of Edburga's vocation and Alkine as abbess at the time of her translation to Pershore (*ibid.*, pp. 327, 329). On the relationship of each of these sources to Osbert's work see above, pp. 25–7.

[97] *Vita Edburge*, fols. 85–85v: 'Artifex siquidem nouus in hac suscepi constitutione cum beniuolentia persuadere, ut opus recens legentes non fastidient, nec facta diuisione erga insolita animosius insolescant. Quod namque prius ueteres protulerunt sub uno, modernis a me temporibus sectum est in duo, ut uite uirginalis opera que gessit in corpore luculenter resplendeant insigni nouitate; sicque sequatur secundo iocunda translatio, ut ad scribendi concitum recurrant articulum, que per illam miracula Deus operatus est post triumphum.'

Winchester, and a description of her translation to and cult at Pershore.[98] It seems therefore that Osbert's written source provided the material for only two of the three sections of his finished work – that it dealt, in fact, only with the saint's life and cult at Winchester: Osbert's written source seems to have been exclusively a Winchester document.

If this interpretation of Osbert's written source is correct, it strongly suggests that the dissatisfaction of the Pershore monks with that source was based less upon stylistic than upon political considerations; and it may go some way towards explaining Osbert's involvement in the composition of a new Life of Edburga. By the early twelfth century the monks of Pershore possessed a set of relics which were believed to be those of St Edburga of Winchester. But the early history of Pershore had been troubled, and its records were no doubt poorly maintained.[99] There may have been no real knowledge of how or when the relics of the Winchester saint had passed into the hands of Pershore: very probably there was only a Winchester Life of the saint, which quite understandably made no reference to the transaction.[100] It was at this point that Osbert of Clare stepped in. It was Osbert's function to provide the Pershore relics with a history: he was to explain and to justify the claims of the Pershore monks to be equal sharers in the patronage and in the glory of the principal saint of one of England's leading nunneries. And he was to do so without calling down the

[98] These three sections occupy respectively Bodl. MS Laud Misc. 114, fols. 87v–98, fols. 98–107, and fols. 107v–120.

[99] Pershore was among those religious houses which suffered at the hands of the Mercian ealdorman, Ælfhere, in the so-called anti-monastic reaction which followed the death of King Edgar. Leland notes that 'Elferus abstulit praedia monachis' and that the damage caused by the father was subsequently rectified by Ælfhere's son, *Odda*, who died in 1056. He states also that the foundation was destroyed by fire at some unspecified date and was reoccupied in 1020 (Leland, *Itinerarium*, ed. T. Hearne, 2nd edn, 9 vols. (Oxford, 1744), v, 2; cf. *Collectanea*, i, 242–4). Thereafter the foundation seems to have had a continuous history throughout the eleventh century, although even then it suffered by the grant of some of its estates to King Edward's foundation at Westminster (see above, p. 22). For the history of Pershore see also Atkins, 'Church of Worcester', pp. 387–8, and the same continued in *Antiquaries Journal* 20 (1940), 1–38, 203–29, at 17; Taylor, 'Deerhurst, Pershore and Westminster', pp. 237–50; *MO*, pp. 53, 72; *Heads*, pp. 58–9.

[100] It is not impossible that the Pershore monks had produced a brief translation narrative which was used by Osbert and which may in one version have provided the basis for that contained in London, BL, MS Harley 64 (see above, n. 64). It seems more likely, however, that Osbert's account was derived from oral tradition and that the Harleian account was founded upon his own work or a later version of it.

wrath of that nunnery. It was a delicate diplomatic exercise, and its result was a neat but unconvincing compromise – a Winchester Life, with a Pershore appendix and a happily-ever-after ending.[101]

ST EDITH OF WILTON

St Edburga of Winchester was outdone in precocity by St Edith, daughter of King Edgar by his wife or concubine Wulfthryth, and principal patron of the nunnery of Wilton.[102] According to her legend the saint, while still an infant, was taken to Wilton by her mother, who withdrew from the secular life to that house. At the age of two, in a manner closely resembling that attributed by Osbert of Clare to St Edburga, she made her own choice of the religious life; she was to remain at Wilton until her death in her twenty-third year.

For the legend and cult of St Edith our earliest and most important source is a *Vita*, with associated *Translatio cum sequentibus signis*, composed by Goscelin of Canterbury.[103] The complete text is preserved in two manuscripts – Oxford, Bodleian Library, MS Rawlinson C 938 (s. xiii) and Gotha, Landesbibliothek, MS I. 81 (s. xiv);[104] a version of chapters 2–24 of the work which appears to represent a major revision by Goscelin himself is found in Cardiff,

---

[101] Williamson draws attention to the possibility that the work was put out in two forms, one addressed generally and having, as in the extant MS, a short 'Pershore' book, the other intended for the Winchester nuns and treating only the saint's life and her Winchester miracles. This is suggested by a discrepancy in the *incipits* and *excipits* given by Bale and Boston. Bodl. Laud Misc. 114 commences 'Fidelibus sancte matris ecclesie filiis', whereas Boston gives only 'Fidelibus' and Bale provides 'Fidelibus in Christo sororibus'. Boston makes 'Fidelibus' the beginning of a prologue, whereas in the Bodleian MS it introduces an *epistola*. Boston's *incipit* to the Life proper, 'Imperante', agrees with the Bodleian MS, but even here his *finis*, 'Omnium populorum', does not agree. See *Letters*, p. 25.

[102] For discussion of Edith's parentage see below, pp. 42–3.

[103] The career and writings of Goscelin of Canterbury have been the subject of an extensive literature: see especially 'La Vie de sainte Vulfhilde par Goscelin de Cantorbéry', ed. M. Esposito, *AB* 32 (1913), 10–26; A. Wilmart, 'Eve et Goscelin', *Revue Bénédictine* 46 (1934), 414–38; 'The *Liber confortatorius* of Goscelin of St Bertin', ed. C. H. Talbot, *Studia Anselmiana* 37 (Rome, 1955), 1–117; *Life of King Edward*, ed. Barlow, pp. xli–lviii, App. C; 'Texts of Jocelyn of Canterbury which relate to the history of Barking abbey', ed. M. L. Colker, *Studia Monastica* 7 (1965), 383–460; and Hamilton, 'Goscelin', which includes a useful attempt to establish a canon of Goscelin's works. Goscelin's *Vita Edithe* is edited by A. Wilmart, 'La Légende de Ste Edithe en prose et vers par le moine Goscelin', *AB* 56 (1938), 5–101, 265–307. (References to Wilmart's introduction are cited as: Wilmart, 'Légende de Ste Edithe'; references to Goscelin's work as: *Vita Edithe*.)

[104] For discussion of these MSS see Wilmart, 'Légende de Ste Edithe', pp. 8, 302–7.

Public Library, MS I. 381 (s. xii in.).[105] The work can be dated to
c. 1080. It was evidently written during the archiepiscopate of
Lanfranc (1070–89), for it is to that archbishop that Goscelin's
prologue is addressed.[106] More precisely, it must have been written, or at least completed, between the death in 1078 of Goscelin's
patron, the Lotharingian Herman, bishop of Wiltshire, and that of
William I in 1087: Goscelin writes that he was encouraged to
undertake the work by 'father Herman of blessed memory whose
follower I was' and speaks of William I as the reigning monarch.[107]

Like the *Vita Edburge*, then, the principal source for the life and
cult of St Edith was composed several generations after the events
which it purports to describe. But its context and its reliability have
been more fully studied and are more readily established than is the
case with Osbert's work. There can be no doubt that Goscelin's
Vita Edithe was firmly grounded in the traditions current at Wilton
in the final quarter of the eleventh century. Goscelin claims to be
writing at the request not only of Bishop Herman but also of the
community of Wilton;[108] he cites as his principal authority the oral
testimony of the abbess and nuns.[109] Goscelin's claim to be familiar
with Wilton is amply corroborated by what is known of his career.
Goscelin, a Fleming by birth and a monk of Saint-Bertin, whose
status as a hagiographer of the English saints was described by
William of Malmesbury as 'second to none after Bede',[110] emi-
grated to England between c. 1058 and c. 1065 to join Bishop
Herman.[111] It can be inferred that he became a member of
Herman's household and of the monastic community at Sherborne
and that prior to Herman's death in 1078 he travelled extensively
throughout the diocese; after a period of wandering between
religious houses, he spent his last years at St Augustine's, Canterbury.[112] In the *Vita Edithe* and elsewhere Goscelin shows much

---

[105] This composite MS seems to have taken its present form while in the possession of Sir
Robert Cotton. Fols. 81–120, containing Lives of St Æthelburga (with lessons for the
feast of St Hildelitha) and Edith and the *Passio* of St Edward the Martyr (see below, n.
159), dates from the first half of the twelfth century (N. R. Ker, *Medieval manuscripts in
British libraries*, II, *Abbotsford–Keele* (Oxford, 1977), 348–9; Wilmart, 'Légende de Ste
Edithe', p. 24 and n. 4 (where the relevant sections of the MS are dated to the later twelfth
century)). I see no reason to dispute Wilmart's view that the Cardiff text represents a text
revised and completed by Goscelin himself. The nature of the revisions is fully discussed
ibid., pp. 25–8, and the relationship between the original and revised texts is clearly
demonstrated in Wilmart's edition.

[106] *Vita Edithe*, pp. 34–9.   [107] *Ibid.*, pp. 37–8, 36.

[108] *Ibid.*, pp. 37–8.   [109] *Ibid.*, pp. 36–7.   [110] *GR*, II, 389.

[111] For the date of Goscelin's arrival in England see Hamilton, 'Goscelin', I, 143.

[112] *Life of King Edward*, ed. Barlow, pp. 93–104; Hamilton, 'Goscelin', I, 145–93.

familiarity with, and a special affection for, the community of Wilton. He was able, for instance, to describe in some detail both the *oratorium* of St Denys, built through the efforts of St Edith, and the new monastic church built by a later Edith, queen of the Confessor, and dedicated in 1065.[113] He was *au fait* with other important aspects of Wilton's domestic history – for example with the succession of its abbesses.[114] He was clearly familiar with the Wilton relic collection and with the traditions which had grown up around it: he makes reference to St Edith's clothes' chest, which miraculously escaped destruction by fire, and to an embroidered linen frontal from her first tomb;[115] he provides detailed accounts of Wulfthryth's acquisition for the nunnery of relics of the Passion and of St Iwi;[116] and, particularly interesting, he describes with great reverence the secondary cult of Wulfthryth, the 'hidden treasure and light' of the nunnery of Wilton.[117] Nor did minor details of monastic history escape his attention: he was able to make detailed references to incidents in the lives of the abbesses.[118] And in the *Liber confortatorius* he provides a vivid and moving picture of his own spiritual relationship with Eve, a Wilton nun who subsequently became a recluse at Saint-Laurent-du-Tertre at Angers. Thomas Hamilton rightly draws attention to the similarity in content between Goscelin's *Vita Edithe* and his *Historia translationis sancti Augustini*.[119] This suggests that the nature and extent of his knowledge of Wilton paralleled that which he possessed concerning St Augustine's and hence that this knowledge was acquired by similar means. We know that Goscelin's detailed knowledge of the buildings, traditions and community of St Augustine's was derived from a lengthy sojourn in that monastery, and it can therefore be deduced that the hagiographer had also spent some time in residence at the convent of Wilton; very probably he had served as chaplain to the Wilton nuns.[120]

---

[113] *Vita Edithe*, pp. 86–7, 295–7, 300–1.

[114] See especially *ibid.*, pp. 36, 99–100, 292, 294–7; cf. J. E. Nightingale, *Memorials of Wilton and other papers*, ed. E. Kite (Devizes, 1906), pp. 14ff.; *VCH Wilts.*, III, 241; *Heads*, p. 222.

[115] *Vita Edithe*, pp. 71–3, 100–1.   [116] *Ibid.*, pp. 73–5, 273–4.

[117] For an account of Wulfthryth's life and miracles see *ibid.*, pp. 271–7; at p. 278 Goscelin continues: 'Hec de abscondito thesauro et lucerna commendantur sub modio clausa; cetera celeberrima prosequamur de lampade fulgida et in domo Domini super candelabrum posita Editha.'

[118] See, for instance, *ibid.*, pp. 99–100, 294–7.

[119] 'Goscelin', I, 157–61.

[120] See *ibid.*, pp. 163–5; *Life of King Edward*, ed. Barlow, p. 94. Elsewhere Barlow places Goscelin in the context of a series of foreign chaplains who are known to have held office

Goscelin apparently had access during this postulated period of residence at Wilton not only to the oral traditions of the community but also to its written records. He makes no explicit claim to be working from an earlier Life of St Edith, but he does state that his information has been gleaned both from the testimony of the faithful and from existing books.[121] And one indication of the type of written source which was available to him is found at the end of his lengthy account of the cure of one of the epileptic dancers of Colebek: this story is said to have been related, and committed to writing in the vernacular, in the presence of the Abbess Brihtgifu.[122] It seems then that in this case there existed an Old English written record of an individual miracle; very possibly there were others, to which Goscelin makes no reference and of which no trace survives.

Whatever the sources of the Wilton tradition which Goscelin's work represents, it would be a mistake unreservedly to accept that tradition as reliable in all respects. Goscelin's familiarity with the domestic history of Wilton has been established beyond reasonable doubt; so too has his general reliability in the transmission of his sources.[123] None the less, the *Vita Edithe* contains a number of curious anomalies, and these are particularly evident when Goscelin seeks to intrude, or to explain the intrusion of, figures and events of national importance into his framework of monastic history. He provides, for instance, a very puzzling account of St Edith's translation at Wilton. This he claims to have been carried out by Archbishop Dunstan thirteen years after Edith's death.[124] It seems, however, that Goscelin believed Edith's death to have taken place *c.* 984; and Dunstan died in 988.[125] Goscelin, therefore, must

at Wilton: 'Wilton seems usually to have maintained two chaplains, and several of these had been Germans. The first holders of the office were Radbod monk of St Remi at Rheims and Benno canon of Trèves, the latter an artist. Later Osmund and Adelman were there, and, just before 1065 Beorhtric. Goscelin would fit in nicely.' (*Ibid.*, p. 98, citing *Vita Edithe*, pp. 50, 73, 87, 271–2, 301.)

[121] *Vita Edithe*, p. 39.   [122] *Ibid.*, p. 292.

[123] See *Life of King Edward*, ed. Barlow, pp. 94–9, 105–7; Hamilton, 'Goscelin', especially ch. 4.

[124] *Vita Edithe*, pp. 265–9.

[125] Goscelin notes (*ibid.*, p. 99) that a future abbess who was born on the thirtieth day after Edith's death was baptised by Ælfheah, who succeeded Æthelwold as bishop of Winchester from 19 October 984 until 1005 (*ASC*, A, *s.a.* 984; E, *s.a.* 1006). Clearly therefore Goscelin believed that Edith's death took place either immediately prior to Ælfheah's appointment to Winchester (i.e. 16 September 984) or at some point between that appointment and the death of Dunstan in May 988 (*ASC*, C, E, *s.a.* 988). His wording does not necessarily imply, as suggested by Wilmart, that the saint's death took

have misdated the saint's death, mistaken the length of time which elapsed before her translation, or attributed that translation to the wrong prelate. The latter error would be readily understandable. Throughout his narrative Goscelin seeks to enhance the prestige of his subject by her association with Dunstan and with other prominent churchmen;[126] her translation by Dunstan marked the culmination of that established association. If Goscelin did not know which prelate was responsible for the translation, then the name of Dunstan would spring most readily to mind; if he did know, then the cause of his subject's prestige may perhaps have been sufficient excuse for a little distortion of the facts.

Equally puzzling is Goscelin's account of the political events following the death of Edith's half-brother, Edward the Martyr.[127] Edward, according to Goscelin, was murdered on the instructions of his step-mother Ælfthryth and in support of his half-brother Æthelred's claim to the throne. The magnates, however, hearing of the murder and very rapidly putting two and two together, pronounced Æthelred unfit to rule and offered the throne instead to Edith. They were led in this extraordinary enterprise by no less a person than Ælfhere, ealdorman of Mercia, who is otherwise known as one of Æthelred's principal supporters, and in fulfilment of Edith's monastic vow they were prepared to place their own daughters in the nunnery of Wilton. This anecdote, unique to the *Vita Edithe*, is highly improbable. If true, its implications for the political history of Æthelred's reign would be of the highest importance; almost certainly, however, it must be regarded as the creation of an eleventh-century hagiographical imagination which found in the story of Edith's rejection of an earthly kingdom a poignant illustration of her devotion to the heavenly. Likewise Goscelin's story of the appointment of a reluctant Edith to rule three religious houses, although accepted by Wilmart, may be nothing more than an anecdote designed to emphasise the saint's

place in the actual year of Ælfheah's appointment. Edgar had married Ælfthryth by 964 (see below, note 142): Edith, then, must have been born before that date; and if Goscelin is correct in stating that she died in her twenty-third year, her death should be placed at the latest in 987.

[126] For instance Goscelin emphasises the role of Dunstan and Æthelwold in Edith's education, makes Dunstan responsible for the dedication of her *oratorium* of St Denys and records Dunstan's prophecy concerning her imminent death and ultimate incorruption (*Vita Edithe*, pp. 57–8, 87–8).

[127] *Ibid.*, pp. 82–3, 84–6; for discussion of Edward's reign and its aftermath see below, pp. 44–5, 154–68. For the relationship of Edith and Edward see below, p. 44, n. 142.

extreme reluctance to accept a position of authority and influence.[128]

Two final anomalies become apparent when Goscelin's account of St Edith is compared with that preserved by William of Malmesbury. The first concerns the parentage of the saint. William, in both the *Gesta pontificum* and the *Gesta regum*, displays some embarrassment on this point. In the former he notes that Edith was a daughter of Wulfthryth, who at the time of her liaison with Edgar was not a nun, as was commonly believed, but rather a lay girl who had taken the veil in an unsuccessful attempt to escape seduction by the king; he adds that St Dunstan's disapproval of the relationship resulted in his imposition of a seven-year penance on the king.[129] The *Gesta regum* presents a more confused account.[130] Here William relates Edgar's seduction of an unnamed 'virgin dedicated to God' and Dunstan's imposition of the seven-year penance. There follows a further 'seduction story' and then an account of Edgar's children, in which Edith's mother is again described as a lay girl who had taken the veil to escape seduction and whose liaison with the king called forth the archiepiscopal wrath: Wulfthryth is not explicitly identified with the unnamed virgin of the first 'seduction story', although such identification may well be implied. Nor does William explicitly state that Wulfthryth never became Edgar's wife: but his comments concerning the archbishop's disapproval are perhaps sufficient indication that he believed this to be the case.

Goscelin, in contrast, gives no hint that there was anything irregular about Edgar's relationship with Wulfthryth. Instead he likens the king's love for her to that of Jacob for Rachel and

---

[128] *Vita Edithe*, pp. 76–7: 'Vix ergo quindecennis processerat palmula in Christo dotalis Editha; iam paternus affectus Edgari, magis ecclesie quam regni propaginem pensans in filia, hanc super tria sanctimonialium, Deo dispensante, dispensat monasteria . . . Consecrat eam celesti aquila Adeluuoldus Uuintonie in monasterio quod Nonnarum nominatur. In monasterio quoque Berkinga dictum, in tercium etiam promota est patrocinium.'

Wilmart suggests (*ibid.*, p. 76, n. 6) that the incident may represent an attempt by Edgar, just prior to his death, to increase his daughter's landed endowment. He further suggests that the third foundation, whose name Goscelin did not provide, might be Amesbury. Edith is accepted by the editors of *Heads* (pp. 208, 223) as abbess of Barking but not as abbess of Nunnaminster. William of Malmesbury, in his Life of St Dunstan (*Memorials of Saint Dunstan*, ed. W. Stubbs, RS 63 (London, 1874), p. 310) claims that Edith was abbess of Wilton itself. Goscelin however clearly implies that this was not the case: Edith was reluctant to accept the abbacy of the three houses discussed above, 'malens matri subesse quam aliis praeesse, matrem timere quam aliis imperare' (*Vita Edithe*, p. 77) – she remained under the abbacy of her mother and was outlived by her.

[129] *GP*, pp. 190–1.   [130] *GR*, I, 179–80.

describes the 'indissoluble vows' which bound them together and which could be broken only by Wulfthryth's entry to the religious life.[131] Elsewhere the relationship of the Abbess Wulfthryth to the king is described as that of 'a sister who once was a wife'.[132] Goscelin's statement that Wulfthryth had been taken by Edgar from *ipsis scolis* perhaps suggests that she had been placed in a nunnery for her education: but there is no indication either that she was a professed nun or that she had taken the veil in order to escape from the king.[133]

It is of course possible that Goscelin either was ignorant of the facts or chose to conceal them; it would after all be difficult even for a medieval hagiographer to make saints of the daughter and concubine of a king who was a seducer of nuns, and still more so to reconcile this reputation with the alleged incorruption of Edgar's body and its possession of miraculous powers.[134] But it is equally possible that the error was William's. In particular he may have wrongly identified Wulfthryth as the 'victim' of a seduction story which makes its first appearance in the Lives of St Dunstan by Osbern and Eadmer: in Osbern's account that lady is an unnamed veiled virgin; in that of Eadmer she is an unnamed lay girl who is being educated at Wilton and who in a dramatic incident seizes a veil from one of the nuns as protection against the king.[135] Alternatively, he may have confused the story of Wulfthryth with that of Wulfhilda, another Wilton nun and future abbess of Barking, whose attempted seduction by Edgar was recounted in another context by Goscelin himself.[136] Whatever the case, it is clear that Goscelin (and Wilton) did not hold a monopoly on traditions concerning St Edith. By the twelfth century at the latest there were current two divergent traditions concerning the saint's parentage.[137]

[131] *Vita Edithe*, p. 41.   [132] *Ibid.*, p. 46.
[133] *Ibid.*, p. 41. In his *Vita Wulfhilde* Goscelin explicitly states that Wulfthryth was placed for her education in the nunnery of Wilton (see below, n. 136).
[134] For Edgar's posthumous reputation see *Vita Edithe*, p. 81.
[135] *Memorials of Saint Dunstan*, ed. Stubbs, pp. 111–12 (Osbern); 209–10 (Eadmer).
[136] *Vita Wulfhilde* (ed. Esposito), p. 17. Here it is noted that Edgar, unable to win Wulfhilda, took instead her kinswoman Wulfthryth 'eodem monasterio Vuiltonie in seculari habitu secum educatam, pari gloria forme, nobilitatis, et generosorum morum regno et regi condignam, que sidereo regi genuit celestem margaritam Eadgytham, ac post unicam prolem mutato honore regali in diuinum, mater diuturna prefulsit Vuintonie choro uirginum'.
[137] For important modern discussion of the marriage customs of the Anglo-Saxon kings see P. Stafford, *Queens, concubines and dowagers: the king's wife in the early Middle Ages* (Athens, Ga, 1983); Stafford, 'The king's wife in Wessex 800–1066', *Past and Present* 91

The existence of divergent traditions concerning St Edith is further attested by the contrasting accounts given by Goscelin and William of King Cnut's attitude towards her cult. Goscelin is full of praise for Cnut, describing at some length his devotion to the saint and his enrichment of her shrine.[138] William, in contrast, describes with some relish a fracas in which Cnut ridiculed the saint and received a fitting punishment at her hands.[139] Here again the development of the 'Edgar legend' may have had a part to play, for Cnut's is not the only reputation to suffer at William's hands. William puts into Cnut's mouth a succinct and striking explanation of his derision of St Edith: 'surely you can't expect me to believe that any daughter of Edgar can be a saint'.[140] If St Edith's hagiographer had access to this tradition, it is hardly surprising that he chose not to use it.[141]

ST EDWARD, KING AND MARTYR

King Edgar died in 975, leaving two young sons – Edward, son probably of his first wife Æthelflaed, and Æthelred, second and only surviving son of Ælfthryth.[142] There followed a succession crisis of a type not uncommon in tenth-century England, in which

(1981), 3–27; Stafford, 'Sons and mothers: family politics in the early Middle Ages', in D. Baker (ed.), *Medieval women, Studies in Church History*, Subsidia 1 (Oxford, 1978), pp. 79–100. King Edgar's marital history is discussed, and Wulfthryth accepted as Edgar's second legitimate wife, in *Queens, concubines and dowagers*, pp. 32, 74, 179, 180; 'King's wife', p. 14; 'Sons and mothers', pp. 79–81.

138   *Vita Edithe*, pp. 278–9.   139   *GP*, p. 190.   140   *Ibid.*

141   The later sources for the life and early cult of St Edith are based primarily on Goscelin's Life. They comprise a Latin abridgement of the work, contained in London, BL, MS Cotton Tiberius E. i and in Oxford, Bodleian Library, MS Tanner 15 (*BHL*, no. 2391; Hardy, *Descriptive catalogue*, no. 1184; pr. *NLA*, I, 311–15) and a Middle English history of the foundation of Wilton, with an account of the life, translation and miracles of the saint, contained in London, BL, MS Cotton Faustina B. iii (Hardy, *Descriptive catalogue*, no. 1186; *S. Editha sive Chronicon Vilodunense im Wiltshire Dialekt*, ed. K. Horstmann (Heilbronn, 1883)).

142   About Edward's parentage a number of traditions arose. Osbern, writing his Life of St Dunstan in the 1080s, made Edward an illegitimate son of Edgar by a nun of Wilton (*Memorials of Saint Dunstan*, ed. Stubbs, pp. xcix–c, 111–12). Eadmer, writing early in the twelfth century, made him a legitimate son by Edgar's wife, Æthelflaed (*ibid.*, p. 120). Edgar had married Ælfthryth by 964 (*Anglo-Saxon Wills*, ed. D. Whitelock (Cambridge, 1930), p. 121) and we can therefore probably assume that Edward was born before that date and was at least eleven years old at the time of his father's death. Æthelred was the second son of Edgar and Ælfthryth (the first, Edmund, dying in 971): probably therefore he was born no earlier than 966 and was no more than nine at the time of his father's death; William of Malmesbury gives his age in 975 as only seven (*GR*, I, 181). For further discussion of Edward's parentage see Keynes, *Diplomas*, pp. 163–5; P. Stafford, 'The reign of Æthelred II: a study in the limitations on royal policy and

tensions within the ruling family 'proved a major focus for many issues and resentments' and in which the allegiance of the leading magnates was accordingly determined less by loyalty to an individual claimant to the throne than by mutual rivalries whose roots lay elsewhere.[143] In this case the precise disposition of forces cannot be reconstructed, but it seems that Edward had the support of Archbishop Dunstan, possibly of St Oswald, and of the ealdormen Æthelwine of East Anglia and Brihtnoth of Essex. Æthelred's most prominent supporters appear to have been his mother, Ælfthryth, and Ælfhere, ealdorman of Mercia; he may also have had the support of the third of the great monastic reformers, St Æthelwold.[144] After some initial conflict, Edward's cause won the day. Æthelred's supporters, however, were far from acquiescent, and on 18 March, probably in 978, 'King Edward was killed. And in this same year the atheling Ethelred his brother succeeded to the kingdom.'[145]

The 'Chronicle' account

For Edward's death and the subsequent rapid development of his cult we are fortunate in possessing a number of early sources. Prominent among these is the account preserved in the Northern recension manuscripts of the *Anglo-Saxon Chronicle*.[146] Here it is recorded *sub anno* 979 that Edward was killed in the evening of 18 March at *Corfes geate* and was buried at Wareham without any royal honour. There follows a brief lament for the dead king which probably dates from the tenth century[147] and which therefore

action', in D. Hill (ed.), *Ethelred the Unready: papers from the millenary conference*, British Archaeological Reports, British Series 59 (Oxford, 1978), pp. 15–46, at p. 21, where it is suggested that Edward may have been a son of Edgar by Wulfthryth; see also the works of Stafford cited above, n. 137.

[143] On disputed successions in tenth-century England, and on that of 975 in particular, see Stafford, 'Reign of Æthelred II', pp. 17–24.

[144] For the disposition of forces in 975 see D. J. V. Fisher, 'The anti-monastic reaction in the reign of Edward the Martyr', *Cambridge Historical Journal* 10 (1950–2), 254–70; Stafford, 'Reign of Æthelred II', p. 21; Keynes, *Diplomas*, p. 166.

[145] *ASC*, A, *s.a.* 978. For a summary of the evidence for the dates of Edward's murder, Æthelred's accession and Æthelred's coronation see Keynes, *Diplomas*, pp. 232–4 and n. 7. Keynes notes that where Æthelred's diplomas supply a regnal year, that year is calculated variously from a point in 978 and a point in 979: 'the only conceivable explanation is that the earlier point represents the king's accession (therefore 18 March 978) and the latter one his coronation (therefore 4 May 979)' (*ibid.*, p. 233).

[146] *ASC*, D, E, *s.a.* 979; for the date of these MSS see *ASC*, pp. xiv, xvii.

[147] Keynes, *Diplomas*, p. 167.

testifies to the speed with which Edward came to be regarded as a saint and martyr. It stresses the magnitude of the sin involved in the murder of a king – 'And no worse deed than this for the English people was committed since first they came to Britain.' – and it emphasises the divine vindication of the fallen lord:

Men murdered him, but God honoured him. In life he was an earthly king; he is now after death a heavenly saint. His earthly kinsmen would not avenge him, but his heavenly father has greatly avenged him. The earthly slayers wished to blot out his memory on earth, but the heavenly avenger has spread abroad his memory in heaven and in earth. Those who would not bow to his living body, now bend humbly on their knees to his dead bones. Now we can perceive that the wisdom and contrivance of men and their plans are worthless against God's purpose.

Finally, after describing Æthelred's accession, these manuscripts supply, *sub anno* 980, a note recording the solemn removal of Edward's remains from Wareham to Shaftesbury: 'In this year ealdorman Ælfhere fetched the holy king's body from Wareham and bore it with great honour to Shaftesbury.'[148]

Archbishop Wulfstan's view

A further early source much preoccupied with sin is the *Sermo lupi ad Anglos*, composed by Wulfstan II, archbishop of York, and first preached in 1014.[149] The *Sermo* was a product of the military defeat and political disaffection which characterised the final decade of Æthelred's reign. The Danish scourge, its author argued, was a product of moral degeneracy; the alleviation of the country's suffering could accordingly be achieved only by moral reform: hence Wulfstan's bitter indictment of the manifold sins allegedly prevalent in English society. Prominent among these was the sin of disloyalty, and Wulfstan's work moves to a forceful climax as he demonstrates that the evil of disloyalty not only pervaded the lower ranks of society and its less important transactions but also eroded its most fundamental relationships and threatened even the institution of kingship itself: 'Edward was betrayed and then killed, and afterwards burnt, and Æthelred was driven out of his country.'[150] The structure of the *Sermo* is such that considerable emphasis falls upon Wulfstan's indictment of disloyalty to the king:

---

[148] *ASC*, D, E, *s.a.* 980.
[149] *Sermo lupi ad Anglos*, ed. D. Whitelock, 3rd edn (London, 1963); for the date of the *Sermo* see *ibid.*, p. 6.   [150] *Ibid.*, pp. 56–7.

the regicide of 978 was the greatest sin that the archbishop could conceive. But there is no suggestion that Wulfstan regarded Edward as a saint. Particularly puzzling is his statement that Edward's murder was followed by the burning of the body. This finds no support in the earlier sources or in the later hagiographical tradition; but, as Keynes points out, 'the authority of Wulfstan is considerable, and the discrepancy only emphasises the existence of more than one tradition about Edward's death'.[151] It is worth bearing in mind that those concerned to promote Edward's cult had a vested interest in the existence of relics: that cult was centred upon a royal corpse which, far from having returned to dust and ashes, remained 'untouched by any corruption'.[152]

The Life of St Oswald

The earliest extant detailed account of Edward's murder and its aftermath is found in a passage inserted somewhat parenthetically into the *Vita Oswaldi archiepiscopi Eboracensis* composed, probably by Byrhtferth of Ramsey, between 995 and 1005.[153] The passage commences with reference to the political disorders which followed Edgar's death and which centred on the problem of the succession. It goes on to note that Edward's initial success was followed by his murder, while on a goodwill visit to Æthelred, by 'the thegns who supported his brother'.[154] As in all good murder stories, there follows the concealment of the body, this time in the house of an unimportant man. Edward's remains, however, were eventually raised from the earth, found to be whole and uncorrupt, and solemnly taken by Ealdorman Ælfhere to be buried with due honour at an unnamed location. Thereafter the divine vindication of the saint is contrasted with the chastisement of his unrepentant murderers. The whole seems to testify to the existence of a developed hagiographical tradition not more than twenty-eight and possibly only eighteen years after Edward's death – well before the end of the reign of the man whose succession could be procured

---

[151] *Diplomas*, p. 167.
[152] *Passio Edwardi*, ed. C. E. Fell, *Edward King and Martyr*, Leeds Texts and Monographs, New Series 3 (Leeds, 1971), p. 9. See also below for the account of the *Vita Oswaldi*.
[153] *Vita Oswaldi archiepiscopi Eboracensis*, in *Historians of the church of York and its archbishops*, ed. J. Raine, 3 vols., RS 71 (London, 1879–94), I (1879), 399–475, at 448–52. For the authorship and date of the *Vita Oswaldi* see ibid., p. lxv; M. Lapidge, 'The hermeneutic style in tenth-century Anglo-Latin literature', *ASE* 4 (1975), 67–111, at 91–5.
[154] *Vita Oswaldi*, p. 449.

only by Edward's murder. And the author concludes with a note which, though conventional in form, seems to imply the existence of a flourishing cult and to suggest that a serious attempt was being made to record the miracles performed at Edward's tomb. Within a few years, we are told, 'so many miracles took place at his tomb that it was impossible to write them down as quickly as they happened'.[155]

The 'Passio Edwardi'

The earliest extant full-length account of Edward's murder and cult is an anonymous *Passio et miracula sancti Eadwardi Regis et Martyris* produced late in the eleventh century or in the first years of the twelfth: the work has been tentatively attributed by Christine Fell to Goscelin of Canterbury.[156] Certainly Goscelin was composing Lives of the English saints in approximately the right period, and the anonymous author's familiarity with that part of Dorset which was the scene of Edward's murder and subsequent veneration accords well both with Goscelin's custom of collecting information about a saint at the centre of that saint's cult and with what is known of his movements in England.[157] The author of the *Passio*, more-over, speaks with respect of, and allows a prominent role in one of

[155] *Ibid.*, p. 452.

[156] The *Passio* is listed as *BHL*, no. 2418 and Hardy, *Descriptive catalogue*, no. 1164. It is edited by Fell, *Edward King and Martyr*, pp. 1–16. (References to Fell's introduction are cited as: Fell, *Edward*; references to the *Passio* itself as *Passio Edwardi*.) Fell's edition is based on Oxford, St John's College, MS 96, of the twelfth century. This is collated with eight other MS versions of the *Passio*: the several MSS are described, and their relationship discussed, by Fell, *Edward*, pp. v–xi.

   For the date of the *Passio* there is good internal evidence. The author, concluding an account of a miracle which took place during the Confessor's reign, notes that its subject remained at Shaftesbury for the rest of his life, 'de quo omnes paene ibi manentes qui eum uiderunt usque hodie testimonium perhibent' (*Passio Edwardi*, p. 14). Clearly, then, the work was composed within the lifetime of those who knew the subject of the miracle. A further miracle is said to have taken place some time after this and to have reached the author by 'relatione spectabilium personarum quae hoc uiderunt' (*Passio Edwardi*, p. 14). Here again the author was writing within living memory of the events which he describes, and in this case those events are said to have taken place during the episcopate of Herman, bishop of Wiltshire from 1058 until 1078. Furthermore, the fact that the work ends almost immediately after this miracle seems to suggest that it was committed to writing late in the eleventh or early in the twelfth century. For the tentative attribution of the work to Goscelin, with a suggested date of *c.* 1070–80, see Fell, *Edward*, p. xx.

[157] For the local topographical knowledge of the anonymous author see *Passio Edwardi*, p. 4; for his familiarity with the abbeys of Shaftesbury and Wilton and with the identity of local prelates see pp. 8–15, *passim*. For Goscelin's custom of collecting information at the

Edward's miracles to, Goscelin's patron, Bishop Herman.[158] It may also be significant that the *Passio* is associated in two of its extant manuscripts with other, well-authenticated works by Goscelin.[159] Finally, and perhaps most importantly, references to Edward are found in a number of Goscelin's well-authenticated works.[160] In particular, the *Vita Edithe* includes a chapter on the nature of Edward's rule and the manner of his death; Goscelin's interpretation of the latter accords well with that of the *Passio*; and his account is followed by a hymn in honour of St Edward.[161] The *Passio*, in turn, shows a marked interest in the history of Wilton and in the activities of St Edith.[162]

To the accounts preserved in the earlier sources the *Passio* adds an attribution to Ælfthryth of the initiative in Edward's murder, a more complex account of the disposal of the body, a description of Edward's translation at Shaftesbury in 1001 and an account of three miracles which took place after that event. It is founded, its author stresses, exclusively upon written sources or reliable oral testimony;[163] and on three occasions material is explicitly rejected because it is inadequately recorded.[164] Christine Fell notes that oral testimony is adduced for two of the three post-1001 miracles: this suggests that the written sources to which the author refers were the sources for the *Passio* itself (that is, for the entire pre-1001 portion of the work).[165] Such sources can be traced, however, only for those passages which deal with events of national importance or with the historical traditions of Shaftesbury abbey. Thus the account of King Edgar's promotion of the monastic reform is derived from the *Regularis concordia*, and the author seems to have been familiar with Shaftesbury traditions as these are recorded in the abbey's cartulary.[166] If the author's claims are to be believed, however, he

principal centre of a cult see 'Liber confortatorius', ed. Talbot, p. 13 and Hamilton, 'Goscelin', I, 146–69; for his movements in England see above, pp. 38–9.

[158] *Passio Edwardi*, pp. 14–15. Goscelin's association with Herman is discussed above, p. 38.

[159] Oxford, St John's College, MS 96, where the *Passio* precedes Goscelin's work on St Augustine, and Cardiff, Public Library, MS 1. 381, where it comes between Goscelin's *Vita Edithe* and his work on the Barking saints. See Fell, *Edward*, p. xx.

[160] See Hamilton, 'Goscelin', I, 69ff. Edward is introduced into Goscelin's Life of Wulfsige, bishop of Sherborne ('The Life of Saint Wulfsin of Sherborne by Goscelin', ed. C. H. Talbot, *Revue Bénédictine* 69 (1959), 68–85, at 76) and into his account of the translation of St Yvo (*Vita sancti Yuonis*, in PL, CLV, cols. 79–90, at col. 88).

[161] *Vita Edithe*, pp. 82–4.

[162] *Passio Edwardi*, pp. 8–9, where the author provides a vivid description of Edith's presence on the occasion of Edward's translation to Shaftesbury.

[163] *Ibid.*, p. 11.   [164] *Ibid.*, pp. 11, 13, 15.   [165] Fell, *Edward*, p. xviii.

[166] *Ibid.*, pp. xviii–xix. The Shaftesbury cartulary is London, BL, MS Harley 61; the

must have been using a written source for the whole of the *Passio*. It is therefore tempting to conclude that behind the *Passio* as we now have it there lies an earlier hagiographical source, probably of Shaftesbury origin. This suggestion is corroborated by the curious time-gap between the translation of 1001 and the final three miracles, which commence in the time of the Confessor. 'It is to be expected', writes Fell, 'that Shaftesbury abbey would have provided itself with a life of Edward fairly early; the lack of information on miracles immediately after 1001 suggests that such a life was composed shortly after the events of that year.'[167]

THE ROYAL LADIES OF ELY

The 'dynasty' of royal ladies, descendants of the East Anglian king Anna (c. 635–54), who came to be venerated at the abbey of Ely form a natural group. Of these, by far the most important was Æthelthryth, or Etheldreda, foundress and first abbess of Ely. She was succeeded as abbess by her sister Sexburga, widow of Eorcenbert, king of Kent, and foundress of a religious community on the island of Sheppey. A third sister, Withburga, allegedly entered the religious life at East Dereham in Norfolk and was translated to Ely late in the tenth century. Sexburga's daughter, Eormenilda, widow of Wulfhere of Mercia, apparently succeeded her mother as abbess, first of Sheppey and subsequently of Ely. Werburga, daughter of Eormenilda, was principally remembered for her work in the Mercian monasteries and had her final resting-place at Chester: she did, however, spend some time as a nun and possibly abbess of Ely. To these may be added two saints whose connection with Ely was very much more tenuous. Æthelburga, a further daughter of Anna, became abbess of the Frankish monas-

---

relevant charters are S357 and 899, grants respectively of Alfred and of Æthelred II to Shaftesbury.

167 Fell, *Edward*, p. xix. It is not impossible that the account of Edward preserved in the *Vita Oswaldi* was derived from such an early hagiographical source. The variations between that account and the *Passio*, however, make it unlikely either that the author of the *Passio* made use of the *Vita Oswaldi* (Fell, *Edward*, p. xviii) or that the two works shared a common source.
   A detailed description of the later Latin and vernacular accounts of St Edward is provided by Fell (*Edward*, pp. iii–v, xiv–xv); on the chronicle sources for the saint see *ibid.*, pp. xvi–xvii; and on the printed versions of the *Passio* see *ibid.*, pp. xi–xiv. Fell rightly emphasises the central importance of the *Passio* in the evolution of the Edward legend; for an alternative view, which stresses the importance of saga-telling and which disregards the *Passio* entirely, see C. E. Wright, *The cultivation of saga in Anglo-Saxon*

tery of Faremoûtier-en-Brie; and Eorcengota, daughter of Sexburga, became a nun at the same house.

The 'Liber Eliensis'

For the history of Ely and of its royal cults the single most important source is the *Liber Eliensis*, a compilation made at Ely between 1131 and 1174 and providing a detailed history of St Æthelthryth's church from its foundation until the compiler's own time.[168] The nature, sources and value of the *Liber Eliensis* have been extensively discussed by E. O. Blake in his masterly edition of the work;[169] only a few introductory remarks are needed here. The *Liber Eliensis* is essentially a derivative work and as such is of considerable value as a repository of domestic historical tradition and documentary material. Particular importance attaches, for example, to those chapters of Book II which derive from the *Libellus quorundam insignium operum beati Æthelwoldi episcopi*, itself translated from a vernacular account of Æthelwold's re-endowment of the house and of the legal disputes arising from his transactions.[170] It must be emphasised, however, that the decision to gather together in a single work the historical traditions and documentary resources of the abbey of Ely was the product of a series of crises in the history of that house: the contents of the *Liber*

England (London and Edinburgh, 1939), pp. 161–71; see also R. M. Wilson, *The lost literature of medieval England*, 2nd edn (London, 1970), pp. 101–3.

[168] *LE*, pp. xxiii–lviii. The principal MSS of the *LE* are Cambridge, Trinity College, MS O.2.1 and a MS in the possession of the Dean and Chapter of Ely. These and a number of related MSS are described, with full references, by Blake (*LE*, pp. xxiii–xxvii). Blake notes (pp. xlvi–xlix) that the work was certainly composed by a monk of Ely and that the strongest candidate for its authorship is Richard, who is known to have produced two works in defence of the community's rights and who is probably to be identified with the later sub-prior and prior of that name: 'His name would lend considerable authority to the *Liber Eliensis*, at least for its twelfth-century portions' (p. xlvii). On the date of the *LE* Blake writes: 'Book I must have been written later than 1131, when *Florence*, the latest source used in it, could have become available. The compiler then allowed enough time to pass before beginning Book II to warrant an apology for the delay, and this book cannot have been completed before 1154. Book III was finished after 1169, when Bishop Nigel died, – and the first reference to his death comes as early as ch. 57 – and, as no mention is made of his successor, before 1174' (p. xlviii).

[169] *Ibid.*, especially pp. xxviii–xlii, xlix–lviii. A valuable discussion of the pre-Conquest documents used by the compiler of the *LE* is provided by Dorothy Whitelock in her foreword to Blake's edition.

[170] See *LE*, pp. ix–x, xxxiv, li–liii. The *Libellus*, from which cc. 1–49 of *LE*, Book II are derived (except cc. 5, 6, 9, 16, 28, 29, part of 39, 40), survives in London, BL, MS Cotton Vespasian A. xix (fols. 2–27v) and Cambridge, Trinity College, MS O.2.41 (pp. 1–64v),

Eliensis were accordingly determined less by the desire to record objective history than by the exigencies of twelfth-century ecclesiastical politics. In other ways too the compiler's treatment of his sources poses severe problems. He shows, for instance, a disappointing tendency to adhere to mainstream sources at points where an interesting local tradition might have been expected;[171] and elsewhere he hopelessly confuses local tradition by misunderstanding his narrative sources,[172] by uncritically incorporating two conflicting accounts of the same event,[173] or by inserting documentary material at inappropriate points in his narrative.[174]

The *Liber Eliensis*, then, is far from providing an objective or definitive history of Ely; and there is some truth in Blake's statement that the work is most valuable where the compiler's contribution 'can be altogether undone and the compilation be dissolved into its component parts'.[175] This is true not only of its historical and documentary but also of its hagiographical sections. The compiler made extensive use, particularly in Book I, of local hagiographical sources; and in so doing he produced a work of exceptional value for the analysis of the function and importance of the monastic cult within the framework of monastic history. Nevertheless, it is clear that the hagiographical content of the *Liber*

both of the twelfth century. This record of Æthelwold's transactions and of the legal disputes arising from them had been written originally in Old English and had been translated at the instigation of Bishop Hervey (1109–31); it seems to have been known as the *Liber de terris sancti Æðelwoldi* (see *LE*, II, proem; App. A, p. 395). Blake notes (*LE*, pp. li–liii) that: 'Whether the translator was the first to arrange documents, separately preserved, consecutively in a book, or whether he was working from an existing collection, we are not expressly told. But there are indications that he is translating a register compiled soon after the time of the events described . . . Taken as a whole, the *Libellus* provides no firm evidence of the date when the postulated Old English original could have been compiled. It could fit equally well before or after the death of Æthelwold, but the probable limits are after the accession of Æthelred and before the death of Abbot Brihtnoth [996 × 9].'

[171] For instance in his account (*LE*, II, 90) of the death at Ely of the atheling Alfred, which is derived mainly from 'Florence', *Chronicon*, ed. Thorpe, I, 191–2 and from William of Poitiers, *Gesta Guillelmi ducis Normannorum et regis Anglorum*, ed. R. Foreville, Les Classiques de l'Histoire de France au Moyen Age 23 (Paris, 1952), pp. 8–10.

[172] Especially evident in the account (*LE*, II, 102–11) of Hereward's rebellion of 1071/2; see especially below, pp. 196–7.

[173] As at *LE*, I, 15, where he notes first that St Æthelthryth received the island of Ely *iure dotis* from her first husband and then goes on to repeat Bede's statement that Ely was part of the territory of the East Angles and that the saint wished to have her monastery there because she sprang from the race of the East Angles; see below, pp. 177–8.

[174] As in the account of the political activities of Bishop Nigel preserved in *LE*, III, 62–78. For an attempt to reconstruct the events of Nigel's episcopate see *LE*, App. E, pp. 433–6.

[175] *LE*, p. lviii.

Eliensis represents an advanced stage in the development of a relatively well-documented tradition. It is clear too that the nature of the *Liber Eliensis* as a monastic history vindicating both the spiritual and the material status of the twelfth-century community has led variously to abridgement, development and distortion of the pre-existing hagiographical tradition. The history of the veneration of the saints at Ely is accordingly intelligible only by analysis of the entire corpus of early sources; it cannot be written with reference to the *Liber Eliensis* alone.

The legend of St Æthelthryth

For the legend of Ely's royal founder a number of hagiographical and quasi-hagiographical sources survive. The account upon which all later works are based is that of Bede's *Historia ecclesiastica*, written only half a century after the saint's death and founded at least in part upon the testimony of her friend and adviser Bishop Wilfrid.[176] Bede explains that the saint was a daughter of Anna and that she was twice married, first to Tonbert, *princeps* of the South Gyrwe, and subsequently to Ecgfrith, king of Northumbria; she was distinguished by her preservation of virginity throughout these marriages. Finally she obtained Ecgfrith's permission to withdraw from the secular life. She became a nun under Ecgfrith's aunt, Æbbe, at Coldingham and one year later was constituted abbess of a community of her own foundation at Ely. Bede goes on to describe the saint's special virtues, her death and humble burial at Ely, and her translation after sixteen years by her sister Sexburga, who had succeeded her as abbess. Bede's personal devotion to St Æthelthryth is shown by his incorporation into the *Historia ecclesiastica* of a hymn in praise of virginity which he had previously composed in her honour.[177]

---

[176] *HE*, IV, 19. Bede's account is listed as *BHL*, no. 2632. Earlier but incidental references to the career of Æthelthryth are found in *Life of Bishop Wilfrid*, ed. Colgrave, pp. 40, 44–6, x–xi. For recent discussion of this work see D. P. Kirby, 'Bede, Eddius Stephanus and the "Life of Wilfrid"', *EHR* 98 (1983), 101–14. This source describes the successful rule of Ecgfrith, king of the Northumbrians and second husband of Æthelthryth, as long as he and the queen were obedient to Wilfrid, and notes the decline in the king's fortunes following his disagreement with Wilfrid and his separation from Æthelthryth. It explains also that Æthelthryth provided Wilfrid with an estate for the foundation of his church of St Andrew at Hexham. Colgrave points out (*Life of Bishop Wilfrid*, p. xii) that Bede made use of Eddius without acknowledgement in his account of Wilfrid. It is clear, however, that Bede's information concerning Æthelthryth was not derived solely, if at all, from this source; and Bede names Wilfrid himself as the source for his information concerning the incorruption of the saint's body.   [177] *HE*, IV, 20; *BHL*, no. 2633.

An English version of Bede's account of Æthelthryth was produced between 992 and 1002 by Ælfric, later abbot of Eynsham, as
part of his collection of saints' Lives.[178] Ælfric adds nothing to
Bede's narrative, although the sequence of events is slightly modi-
fied; like Bede, he concludes with a passage in praise of virginity.
A further vernacular account of the saint, likewise based on Bede,
and possibly antedating Ælfric, is found in the *Old English martyrology*.[179] And the saint's parentage, her marriage to Ecgfrith and
her burial at Ely are briefly recorded in *Þa halgan*.[180]

Among the post-Bedan sources for the saint's life and cult
particular importance has traditionally been attached to the first
book of the *Liber Eliensis*, which 'has the form, obscured in part by
additional material and an emphasis on chronological order, of a
saint's Life and Miracles'.[181] This form strongly suggests that the
book was derived from an earlier hagiographical source, and the
existence of such a source is further attested by analysis of two
extant Lives, contained in Cambridge, Corpus Christi College, MS
393 (fols. 3–33v) and in Trinity College Dublin, MS 172 (pp. 259–
75). The Corpus manuscript, written in a single hand of the twelfth
century, contains a Life in rhyming prose, followed by a book of
miracles in a different style; of these the last four form a separate
group which can be dated to the time of Bishop Hervey (1109–
31).[182] There follows (fols. 33v–55) a metrical version of this Life
by Gregorius, a monk of Ely, who was writing in the time of
Henry I;[183] hence the prose Life from which he worked must have

---

[178] *Ælfric's Lives of saints*, ed. W. W. Skeat, 4 vols., EETS, Original Series 76, 82, 94, 114
(Oxford, 1881–1900; repr. in 2 vols., 1966), I, 314–35. The Lives are dated by Skeat to *c.*
996–7 (II, xxvii) and by Clemoes to the decade 992–1002 (P. A. M. Clemoes, 'The
chronology of Ælfric's works', in Clemoes (ed.), *The Anglo-Saxons: studies presented to
Bruce Dickins* (London, 1959), pp. 212–47, at p. 244). Ælfric's Life of Æthelthryth is listed
as Hardy, *Descriptive catalogue*, nos. 721 and 722.

[179] *An Old English martyrology*, ed. G. Herzfeld, EETS, Original Series 116 (London, 1900;
repr. 1973), pp. 102–3. The MSS of the martyrology are discussed by Herzfeld (pp. xi–
xiii). The work is listed as Hardy, *Descriptive catalogue*, nos. 723–4.

[180] *Heiligen*, ed. Liebermann, pp. 5–7.

[181] *LE*, p. xxx. This account is listed as *BHL*, nos. 2634, 2638 and as Hardy, *Descriptive
catalogue*, nos. 714–15. For accounts of the saint which rely heavily upon this source see
J. Bentham, *The history and antiquities of the conventual and cathedral church of Ely*, 2nd edn
(Norwich, 1812), pp. 45–57; D. J. Stewart, *On the architectural history of Ely cathedral*
(London, 1868), pp. 1–12.

[182] These four miracles, of which the first is dated 1116, are incorporated into the *LE* as
Book III, cc. 33–6. The other miracles of the Corpus Life can all be dated to the period *c.*
870 – *c.* 970 and are related to *LE*, I, 43–9; see *LE*, p. xxxii.

[183] The metrical Life commences 'Incipit prologus in libello de Vita et gestis Beate

---

been completed some time before Henry's death in 1135. The Dublin Life is one of a collection of *Vitae* compiled in the thirteenth or fourteenth century.[184] It is followed by a book of miracles which, except for the omission of the later group, shares the contents of Corpus. There are many striking resemblances between the Lives, but they are not identical. Nor are they derived from the *Liber Eliensis* or it from either or both of them. Rather it seems that the *Liber Eliensis* account must be derived from a lost version of the Life, closely related to both Corpus and Dublin but identical with neither of them.[185] Discussion of the legend and cult of St Æthelthryth, therefore, must be based not only upon the better-

Æðelðreðe uirginis quem uersifice composuit Gregorius Eliensis monachus' (CCC 393, fol. 33v). It is discussed by Blake (*LE*, p. xxx and n. 12). The miracles of Bishop Hervey's time are described as *nostro tempore* (CCC 393, fol. 50v) and are prefaced by a eulogy on Henry I (CCC 393, fols. 51–51v). The metrical Life ends incomplete after the first of these miracles and the scribe left a space in his list of chapter headings for the three remaining miracles: 'This suggests that this copy was made while Gregorius was still at work and therefore belongs to the reign of Henry I. Also one of the miracles of Bishop Nigel's time (Book 3, c. 60) is dated 1134–35 and this was presumably not yet available for copying into the Corpus book. The handwriting and the decorated initial at the beginning of the MS would suit a date in the second quarter of the twelfth century' (*LE*, p. xxx, n. 12). On the Corpus MS see also *BHL*, no. 2639 and Hardy, *Descriptive catalogue*, no. 716, each of which makes reference only to the verse Life. The MS is described by M. R. James, *A descriptive catalogue of the manuscripts in the library of Corpus Christi College, Cambridge*, 2 vols. (Cambridge, 1912), II, 251–3. Ker dates the MS to the twelfth century and notes that it is of Ely provenance (*Medieval libraries*, p. 78). It contains, in addition to the Lives of Æthelthryth, a Life of Withburga (see below, p. 59), *lectiones* for the feasts of Sexburga (see below, p. 58) and Eormenilda (see below, p. 60), a Life of Werburga (see below, p. 60) and an extract on saints Æthelburga and Eorcengota (see below, p. 61).

[184] *LE*, p. xxx. The MS is described by T. K. Abbott, *Catalogue of the manuscripts in the library of Trinity College, Dublin* (Dublin and London, 1900), no. 172, where it is dated to the thirteenth and fourteenth centuries. A more detailed description is found in the new catalogue under preparation by M. L. Colker and available in typescript in the library of Trinity College, Dublin (vol. IV, no. 172); here the MS is dated to the second half of the fifteenth century. Grosjean dates the MS to the thirteenth century (P. Grosjean, 'Catalogus codicum hagiographicorum Latinorum bibliothecarum Dublinensium', *AB* 46 (1928), 81–148, at 86–8).

[185] The relationship of the Corpus, Dublin and *LE* Lives is discussed in detail by Blake, *LE*, p. xxxi. Of the relationship of the lost version to Dublin and Corpus Blake writes: 'It is possible that Dublin, which is closest to Bede, was the first to be produced and that from it a revised version, now lost, was made which in turn was the source of Corpus and the *Liber Eliensis*. But there may have been another link in the chain . . . a lost version, based on Bede, divided into two parts, the first of which ended with Etheldreda's death. From this Dublin would derive, merging the two parts into one and moving the concluding phrase of the first part to the end of the second. From this same lost version there would also derive a second lost version, which retained the division into two parts, but made other alterations in phrasing and order, and which was used by Corpus and the *Liber Eliensis*.'

known work but also upon the surviving representatives of the tradition upon which that work was founded.[186]

The legend of St Sexburga

For the life and cult of Ely's second abbess the sources are more limited. Sexburga makes her first appearance in the pages of Bede, where she is treated with markedly less enthusiasm than her virgin sister: only her marriage to Eorcenbert, her succession to Ely and her translation of Æthelthryth are recorded, and in each case her appearance seems to be little more than incidental.[187] *Þa halgan* highlights, albeit briefly, a different aspect of the saint's activities – her role as queen of the Kentish people and as founder of St Mary's *mynster* on the island of Sheppey.[188] And the two perspectives on Sexburga's career are combined in the earliest extant full-length account of the saint, a Life contained in two important Ely manuscripts of the twelfth century – Cambridge, Trinity College, MS O.2.1 (fols. 215–228)[189] and, with some variations, in London, BL,

[186] Further sources for the legend and cult of St Æthelthryth include an account preserved in London, Gray's Inn, MS 3 (fols. 143v–145), of the twelfth century; this is merely an extract from Bede (Hardy, *Descriptive catalogue*, no. 720). A separate booklet on the translation of Æthelthryth in 1106 is contained in London, BL, MS Cotton Domitian xv, of the late thirteenth or early fourteenth century. Blake notes that this was probably compiled from the *LE* (*LE*, pp. xxxvi–xxxvii; see also *BHL*, no. 2637). A short Life is contained in London, BL, MS Cotton Tiberius D. iii (fols. 232v–233v), of the thirteenth century (Hardy, *Descriptive catalogue*, no. 718). A metrical Life is preserved in Oxford, Trinity College, MS vii. 2, of the fifteenth century (Hardy, *Descriptive catalogue*, no. 719). A short Life is preserved in London, BL, MS Cotton Tiberius E. i and in Oxford, Bodleian Library, MS Tanner 15 (*BHL*, no. 2640; Hardy, *Descriptive catalogue*, no. 717; pr. *NLA*, I, 424–9). Middle English Lives are found in London, BL, MS Cotton Faustina B. iii and in Oxford, Bodleian Library, MS Bodley 779, both of the fifteenth century (Hardy, *Descriptive catalogue*, nos. 725–6). Each of the Lives listed above closely follows Bede, only that in Tiberius D. iii departing appreciably from his language and introducing some rhyming prose (see *LE*, p. xxxi, n. 6).

[187] *HE*, III, 8, where Bede is primarily concerned with Sexburga's daughter Eorcengota, and IV, 19, which forms part of his account of Æthelthryth.

[188] *Heiligen*, ed. Liebermann, p. 5.

[189] The MS is of great importance for the history of Ely: it contains an Ely calendar (ed. F. Wormald, *English Benedictine kalendars after A.D. 1100*, 2 vols., HBS 77 and 81 (London, 1939–46), II (1946), 1–19) (hereafter: Wormald (ed.), *After 1100*), a list of the abbots and bishops of Ely, the *Liber Eliensis*, the *Inquisitio Eliensis*, a record of the plea of 1071 × 5 (for the two latter see *Inquisitio comitatus Cantabrigiensis subjicitur Inquisitio Eliensis*, ed. N. E. S. A. Hamilton, Royal Society of Literature (London, 1876), pp. 97–195), the Life of Sexburga and material relating to Eormenilda, Eorcengota, Æthelburga, Werburga and Withburga. It is described by Blake, *LE*, pp. xxiii–xxiv and by M. R. James, *The Western manuscripts in the library of Trinity College, Cambridge: a descriptive catalogue*, 4 vols. (Cambridge, 1900–4), III (1902), 79–82. On its date and Ely provenance see also Ker, *Medieval libraries*, p. 78.

MS Cotton Caligula A. viii (fols. 108–120v).[190] The Life focusses first on the saint's upbringing and reluctant but fruitful marriage to Eorcenbert; it provides a lengthy account of her withdrawal after Eorcenbert's death to a religious community at *Middeltona* and of her subsequent foundation of and rule over Minster-in-Sheppey; it moves on to her 'third career' and death at Ely; and it closes with an account of two posthumous miracles.

The date and sources of the Life are not easily established. Blake notes that the Trinity Life is a copy appended to the manuscript of which the *Liber Eliensis* forms part; hence the compiler of the *Liber Eliensis*, when incorporating material from the Life, must have had access to an earlier manuscript version.[191] It is unlikely that this earlier version is to be identified with the Life in the Cotton manuscript, for the passages which the *Liber Eliensis* shares with the Life of Sexburga are more closely related to the Trinity than to the Cotton Life. It is accordingly necessary again to postulate one or more lost versions from which all the extant sources derive. In the form in which we now have it the *Vita Sexburge* was put together after 1106, for its opening passages refer briefly to the translation of Withburga in that year.[192] The *Vita* proper, however, makes no

---

[190] *BHL*, no. 7693; Hardy, *Descriptive catalogue*, no. 845: neither of these works refers to the Life in TCC O.2.1. Blake mistakenly claims that the Life of Sexburga is found only in the Trinity MS, noting that Caligula A. viii contains only a series of *lectiones* on Sexburga (*LE*, p. xxxiv, n. 1). In fact a text of the Life varying only slightly from that in the Trinity MS is found in Caligula A. viii. The MS is described in the *Catalogue of the manuscripts in the Cottonian library deposited in the British Museum* (London, 1802), p. 44. Ker notes that this is a composite MS, of which the first portion (fols. 4–47), of the thirteenth to fifteenth centuries, was the property of the Premonstratensian abbey of Beauchief in Derbyshire (*Medieval libraries*, p. 8). Its second part (fols. 59–191) is a hagiographical compilation of the twelfth century ascribed to Ely on the grounds of an inscription of ownership by an individual member of the community (p. 78). Its Ely material comprises a Life of Werburga, with *lectiones* for her feast, *lectiones* for the feasts of Sexburga and Eormenilda, a collection of miracles of Withburga and the Life of Sexburga.

[191] *LE*, p. xxxiv; material from the *Vita Sexburge* is incorporated at Book I, cc. 18, 32, 35.

[192] TCC O.2.1, fols. 216v–217; Caligula A. viii, fol. 110: reference is made to Withburga who 'post trescentos quinquaginta annos tota integra est reperta'. The chronology of this passage is confused. The F MS of the *ASC* states *s.a.* 798 that Withburga's uncorrupt body was found at Dereham, this being fifty-five years after her death. On this reckoning Withburga's death must be placed in 743 and the discovery of her uncorrupt body after 350 years in 1093. That the translation of 1106 is intended by the author of the *Vita Sexburge* is however clear from a similar passage which, following an account of that translation, concludes the Life of Withburga in CCC 393: 'De beate autem Wihtburge integritate, taliter in chronicis anglicis recitatur. Anno Domini septingentesimo nonagesimo octauo, corpus sancte Wihtburge sine corruptione inuentum est post annos fere quinquaginta quinque in Dyrham. His septingentis nonaginta octo additis duobus et ducentis completi sunt mille anni. Quos alii centum et

reference to the events of 1106, when Sexburga herself was translated with her 'sisters' to a new church at Ely;[193] instead the last dateable incident in the *Vita* concerns the Viking invasions of the ninth century.[194] Hence it seems possible that the parenthetical reference to the events of 1106 was merely an addition by a twelfth-century writer who, far from composing a new work, was simply refurbishing a much older account. This suggestion seems to be corroborated by that writer's statements that he has amended earlier documents, and that his information is gathered partly from the testimony of faithful men and partly from 'ancient writings of the English'.[195] His account of Sexburga's career at Sheppey is closely related to a brief Old English fragment written between the Danish invasions of the ninth century and the second half of the eleventh century and preserved in London, Lambeth Palace, MS 427 (fol. 211): this is identified by Rollason as a version of the Mildrith legend which may have been in origin a product of Minster-in-Sheppey.[196] The author of the *Vita Sexburge* may have derived his information concerning Sheppey from this version of the Mildrith legend.[197] It is also possible that both the *Vita Sexburge* and the Sheppey information in the Lambeth fragment were derived from a vernacular Life of Sexburga.

In the Cotton manuscript the *Vita Sexburge* is associated with a series of eight lessons for the saint's festival (fols. 93v–95v). These occur also in Corpus 393 and appear to be an abridgement of the Latin Life, omitting in particular all reference to the saint's connection with Sheppey.[198]

sex subsecuti faciunt insimul trecentos et quinquaginta quattuor annos a dormitione ipsius beate Wihtburge usque ad hunc nostri temporis diem quo incorrupto ostensa est corpore' (CCC 393, fol. 69).

The same faulty chronology was preserved when the account of the translation provided by the *Vita Withburge* was incorporated into *LE*, II, 147.   [193] *LE*, II, 145.

[194] TCC O.2.1, fols. 226v–227; Caligula A. viii, fol. 119v. There follows one further miracle for which no date can be established.

[195] TCC O.2.1, fol. 215; Caligula A. viii, fol. 108v: 'Huius ergo gesta, caritate fratrum instigante compulsus, emendatioribus scedulis donare disposui . . . Quedam ipsius opera ex antiquis Anglorum scriptis sunt comperta, quedam nobis fidelium uirorum relatione cognita, que ad Dei laudem et gloriam pro nostra eruditione simplici stilo sunt exaranda.'

[196] Rollason, *Mildrith legend*, pp. 29–31. For a summary of the content of the Lambeth fragment see *ibid.*, pp. 86–7. The fragment is printed in 'A fragmentary Life of St Mildred and other Kentish royal saints', ed. M. J. Swanton, *Archaeologia Cantiana* 91 (1975), 15–27, at 26–7.

[197] See Rollason, *Mildrith legend*, p. 30.

[198] CCC 393, fols. 69–71v; Caligula A. viii, fols. 93v–95v. The *lectiones* are listed as *BHL*, no. 7694; Hardy, *Descriptive catalogue*, no. 846. A later Life of Sexburga exists in London,

The legend of St Withburga

For the legend of St Withburga the earliest hagiographical sources are Lives contained in Trinity O.2.1 (fols. 236v–240v) and in Corpus 393 (fols. 59–69).[199] It is possible that these Lives, similar but not identical, may derive from a common source: the extracts concerning St Withburga incorporated into the *Liber Eliensis* seem to derive from a Life of the Corpus type.[200] Both accounts describe the saint's royal birth and virtuous youth, her withdrawal to Dereham, her death and humble burial, and her translation after approximately fifty-five years from the common graveyard to the church at Dereham.[201] Thereafter the Trinity Life ends abruptly with a single miracle story, while the Corpus Life supplies an account of Withburga's translations to Ely in the tenth century and at Ely in 1106. The Trinity author is disarmingly honest about his ignorance concerning the saint. His account of how that ignorance came about, however, is perhaps rather suspect: he explains that an early written work was destroyed by the people of Dereham following the loss of their saint and that his own narrative was therefore pieced together from scanty references in 'chronicles and ancient writings'.[202]

These Lives are supplemented by a collection of miracles, preserved in Caligula A. viii (fols. 102–107v).[203] The miracles have a separate prologue and contain no material in common with the Lives. They were certainly put together after 1106 and the first of them must have been written during or after the time of Everard, bishop of Norwich (1131–45).[204]

BL, MS Cotton Tiberius E. i and in Oxford, Bodleian Library, MS Tanner 15 (*BHL*, no. 7695; Hardy, *Descriptive catalogue*, no. 847; pr. *NLA*, ii, 355–7).

[199] *BHL*, no. 8979; Hardy, *Descriptive catalogue*, nos. 1017–18. On the unproven attribution of this work to Goscelin of Canterbury see Hamilton, 'Goscelin', pp. 51, 54–63, 68–76, 123–4. The saint's burial at Ely is briefly recorded in *Þa halgan* (*Heiligen*, ed. Liebermann, p. 7). An abridgement of the Corpus/Trinity Life is found in London, BL, MS Cotton Tiberius E. i and in Oxford, Bodleian Library, MS Tanner 15 (*BHL*, no. 8981; Hardy, *Descriptive catalogue*, no. 1019; pr. *NLA*, ii, 468–70).

[200] See *LE*, p. xxxvii and n. 3.

[201] Cf. *ASC*, F, *s.a.* 798.   [202] TCC O.2.1, fol. 237.

[203] *BHL*, no. 8980; Hardy, *Descriptive catalogue*, no. 1020.

[204] Of the saint's translation in 1106 the author writes: 'Cuius post trecentos quinquaginta annos moderno tempore tota integra caro est reperta, ita ut in nostra etate plures uiderimus in carne superstites, qui sacratissimum illius corpus uidere et propriis attrectare meruerint manibus' (Caligula A. viii, fol. 102). The *Miracula*, therefore, must have been committed to writing within living memory of the translation, though not perhaps in its immediate aftermath. The first of the miracles concerns the miraculous punishment of Bishop Everard.

Saints Eormenilda and Werburga

For both Eormenilda and Werburga the earliest extant source is *Þa halgan*, which records that Eormenilda married Wulfhere, son of Penda of Mercia, and that the union produced a saintly daughter, Werburga, who was buried at the minster of *Heanburh* and subsequently translated to Chester; Eormenilda was buried at Ely with her mother and aunt, Sexburga and Æthelthryth.[205] A short account of Eormenilda's life and of two posthumous miracles, in the form of *lectiones* for her feast, is included in each of the three Ely hagiographical collections.[206] The earliest extant Life of Werburga is likewise contained in each of these manuscripts;[207] it was composed after the translation of Werburga's relics to Chester between 907 and 958, and after the translation of Cyneburga, Cyneswitha and Tibba to Peterborough in 963.[208] The Life seems to be based upon a work written at Hanbury in the late ninth or early tenth century and to have taken its present form at Chester in connection with the promotion of Werburga's cult there.[209] It tells us little about its subject's role at Ely and makes no reference to her cult at that house.

Saints Æthelburga and Eorcengota

For each of these saints the sources are exceptionally limited. Æthelburga, like Sexburga, is introduced somewhat parenthetically

[205] *Heiligen*, ed. Liebermann, p. 7.

[206] TCC O.2.1, fols. 228–230v; CCC 393, fols. 71v–75; Caligula A. viii, fols. 95v–98. In TCC O.2.1 the work is headed 'Incipit vita beate Ermenilde'; in the two other MSS it is presented as a series of lessons for the saint's feast. The content of the three MSS is identical except for a few scribal variations. The piece seems to have been composed in association with the *lectiones* for the feast of Sexburga which immediately precede it in the Corpus and Cotton MSS: it commences 'De beata et Deo digna Eormenhilda eadem fere recensemus, que de matre eius sanctissima retulimus.' The work is listed as *BHL*, no. 2611; Hardy, *Descriptive catalogue*, no. 864. A further short account of Eormenilda is found in London, BL, MS Cotton Tiberius E. i and in Oxford, Bodleian Library, MS Tanner 15 (*BHL*, no. 2612; Hardy, *Descriptive catalogue*, no. 865; pr. *NLA*, II, 405–6).

[207] TCC O.2.1, fols. 231v–236; CCC 393, fols. 75–81v; Caligula A. viii, fols. 86–91v. The *Vita* is also found in Trinity College, Dublin, MS 172 (pp. 253–9). It is listed as *BHL*, no. 8855; Hardy, *Descriptive catalogue*, nos. 949–51 and is printed by Migne, *PL*, CLV (1854), cols. 93–110. It is followed in the Cotton MS by an abridgement in the form of eight lessons for the saint's feast (fols. 91v–93v). These are listed as *BHL*, no. 8856; Hardy, *Descriptive catalogue*, no. 951. A further abridgement is found in London, BL, MS Cotton Tiberius E. i and in Oxford, Bodleian Library, MS Tanner 15, with other MSS (*BHL*, no. 8857; Hardy, *Descriptive catalogue*, no. 953; pr. *NLA*, II, 422–5).

[208] See Rollason, *Mildrith legend*, p. 26. The work's traditional attribution to Goscelin of Canterbury cannot be verified: see Hamilton, 'Goscelin', pp. 51, 54–63, 68–76, 123–4.

[209] Rollason, *Mildrith legend*, pp. 26–7.

into Bede's account of Eorcengota.[210] Bede notes that the scarcity of
religious houses in seventh-century England led many to enter the
religious life in continental communities. Among those to do so
were Saethryth, step-daughter of Anna, and Anna's own daughter
Æthelburga, each of whom became abbess of Faremoûtier-en-
Brie. Æthelburga's sanctity was demonstrated by the incorruption
of her body on its translation seven years after her death, and her
feast was accordingly celebrated at Brie on 17 July. Eorcengota
likewise became a nun, though never abbess, of Brie. Her sanctity,
Bede notes, was revealed by many wonders, prominent among
them her prophecy concerning her own death. Each of the saints
receives a brief notice in *Þa halgan*.[211] This apart, the only other
early material for Æthelburga and Eorcengota is a short account of
each saint preserved in Trinity O.2.1 and in Corpus 393: in each case
this is taken directly from Bede and has no independent historical
value.[212]

ST EDMUND, KING AND MARTYR

The historical Edmund, king of the East Angles, is an elusive
figure.[213] In our earliest source, the 'Parker' manuscript of the
Anglo-Saxon Chronicle, compiled *c.* 890, he appears memorable
only for the manner of his death, and even this is recorded with no
greater comment than are those of the many ealdormen slain in the
Viking wars; the annal for 870 reads thus: 'In this year the raiding
army rode across Mercia into East Anglia, and took up winter
quarters at Thetford. And that winter King Edmund fought against
them, and the Danes had the victory, and killed the king and
conquered all the land.'[214] Asser, writing his Life of King Alfred in
893 and making use of the *Chronicle*, is similarly laconic:

---

[210] *HE*, III, 8.   [211] *Heiligen*, ed. Liebermann, p. 7.
[212] TCC O.2.1, fols. 230v–231, 236–236v; CCC 393, fols. 1–2v. See Hardy, *Descriptive
catalogue*, nos. 892 (Æthelburga), 866 (Eorcengota).
[213] Edmund was born *c.* 841/2, succeeded *c.* 855 and died in the winter of 869/70. Written
sources record no king of the East Angles between Æthelbert (d. 794) and Edmund, but
numismatic evidence supplies the names of at least two rulers for this period – Æthelstan
(*c.* 825) and Æthelweard (*c.* 850); it seems likely that Edmund succeeded the latter. For
Edmund's earthly career and for the development of his legend see especially D.
Whitelock, 'Fact and fiction in the legend of St Edmund', *Proceedings of the Suffolk
Institute of Archaeology* 31 (1967–9), 217–33; G. Loomis, 'The growth of the Saint
Edmund legend', *Harvard Studies and Notes in Philology and Literature* 14 (1932), 83–113;
A. P. Smyth, *Scandinavian kings in the British Isles 850–880* (Oxford, 1977), especially ch.
16; Folz, 'Saint Edmond'.
[214] *ASC*, A (Cambridge, Corpus Christi College, MS 173), *s.a.* 870; for the date of this MS
see *ASC*, p. xi; Whitelock, 'Fact and fiction', p. 217 and n. 2. The compiler of the *ASC*

In the year of the Lord's Incarnation 870 . . . the Viking army mentioned above passed through Mercia to East Anglia, and spent the winter there at a place called Thetford.

In the same year, Edmund, king of the East Angles, fought fiercely against that army. But alas, he was killed there with a large number of his men, and the Vikings rejoiced triumphantly; the enemy were masters of the battlefield, and they subjected that entire province to their authority.[215]

Such was Edmund as he appeared before his story was subjected to the accretion of legend. In these nearly contemporary sources there is no reference to his parentage or childhood, to the date or means of his rise to power or even to the nature of his rule. Nor is there any indication that his death was regarded as a martyrdom: the *rex sanctissimus* of later hagiographical tradition appears here simply as one among the many leaders and rulers of the Anglo-Saxons who lost both their kingdoms and their lives in the years preceding the 'Alfredian revival' of the late ninth century.[216]

The tenth-century tradition

The earliest hagiographical account of St Edmund was produced over three generations after the events of 869/70 and by a writer of continental origin. Towards the end of the tenth century Oswald, bishop of Worcester and archbishop of York, seeking a scholar capable of instructing his English monks, sent a delegation to the Frankish house of Fleury, which had provided much of his own

---

for the Alfredian period began his year on 24 September; thus Edmund's death, which in the 'Parker' MS appears *s.a.* 870, in reality took place in the autumn of 869 (see especially M. L. R. Beaven, 'The beginning of the year in the Alfredian Chronicle, 866–87', *EHR* 33 (1918), 328–42, at 336 and n. 36).

215 *Asser's Life of King Alfred*, ed. W. H. Stevenson (Oxford, 1904), pp. 25–6 (tr. S. Keynes and M. Lapidge, *Alfred the Great* (Harmondsworth, 1983), pp. 77–8). For the date of the work see *Asser's Life of King Alfred*, pp. lxxi–lxxiv; Keynes and Lapidge, *Alfred the Great*, p. 53.

216 Loomis points out that two MSS of the *ASC* style Edmund 'Sce Eadmund' and regards this as evidence for his early veneration as a saint ('Growth of the Saint Edmund legend', pp. 83–4). Of these, however, MS E (Oxford, Bodleian Library, MS Laud 636) seems to be written in a single hand as far as *c.* 1121 and MS F (London, BL, MS Cotton Domitian A. viii) was produced late in the eleventh or early in the twelfth century (*ASC*, p. xvi). Both are therefore late versions of the *ASC* and, though both are based on earlier sources, their testimony is not to be preferred to that of the 'Parker' MS: their references to 'Sce Eadmund' may well be textual additions and do not in themselves constitute proof that Edmund's cult had emerged within a few years of his death. The substantial alternative evidence for the early development of the cult is discussed below, pp. 211–23.

monastic training.[217] The man chosen to travel to England was
Abbo, a renowned author and teacher and a future abbot of
Fleury.[218] Abbo, having miraculously survived a hazardous jour-
ney, arrived at the Fenland abbey of Ramsey, where he taught the
monks for two years.[219] He also produced a major hagiographical
work – his *Passio sancti Eadmundi Regis et Martyris*.[220]

Abbo's visit to England, and his composition of the *Passio*, can be
dated with some precision to the period 985–7.[221] As so late an
authority the *Passio* might reasonably be regarded with much
suspicion; but the credentials adduced in Abbo's introductory
epistola are far from implausible. Abbo claims to have heard
Edmund's story from Archbishop Dunstan, who in turn had been
present when the story was related to King Athelstan by a very old
man who claimed to have been Edmund's armour-bearer on the
day of his martyrdom.[222] There is no reason to reject the role here
attributed to the armour-bearer. Edmund was killed in the winter
of 869/70; Athelstan succeeded in 924; Dunstan was born *c.* 909.[223]
If, therefore, the story was related to Athelstan soon after his
accession, Dunstan would have been between fifteen and twenty
years old and the armour-bearer, assuming him to have been young
at the time of Edmund's martyrdom, would have been in his
seventies – the *senex decrepitus* described by Abbo: the *Passio*,
accordingly, 'must be treated with respect'.[224]

It would be a mistake, however, to regard the *Passio* as simply a

217 P. Cousin, *Abbon de Fleury-sur-Loire* (Paris, 1954), p. 65.
218 For detailed discussion of Abbo's career, together with complete lists of his literary
works and correspondence, see *ibid*. Abbo's Life was written by his disciple Aimon (*Vita
sancti Abbonis auctore Aimoino monacho*), in *PL*, cxxxix, cols. 375–414.
219 *Vita Abbonis*, col. 392.
220 The most recent edition of the *Passio*, and that cited throughout this work, is in *Three
Lives*, ed. Winterbottom, pp. 67–87, from London, BL, MS Cotton Tiberius B. ii (fols.
2–19v), of the eleventh century. For an earlier edition see *Memorials of St Edmund's abbey*,
ed. T. Arnold, 3 vols., RS 96 (London, 1890–6), I (1890), 3–25. The *Passio* is listed as
BHL, no. 2392; Hardy, *Descriptive catalogue*, no. 1098.
221 The *Passio* commences with a dedicatory *epistola* addressed to Archbishop Dunstan: the
work must therefore have been completed before Dunstan's death in 988. Abbo's work
was translated into English by Ælfric, whose prologue describes in more detail the
circumstances in which the *Passio* had been written. He notes (*Ælfric's Lives of saints*, ed.
Skeat, II, 314) that Abbo came to Dunstan three years before the latter's death and that
within two years he returned to the continent and was almost immediately made abbot
of Fleury. As Dunstan died in May 988, Abbo's arrival should be placed early in 985 and
his departure early in 987; he became abbot of Fleury in the following year (*Vita Abbonis*,
cols. 393–4; Cousin, *Abbon*, p. 92): hence it is to the period 985–7 that the composition of
the *Passio* must be dated.   222 *Passio Edmundi*, p. 68.
223 J. Armitage Robinson, *The times of St Dunstan* (Oxford, 1923), pp. 92ff.; Whitelock,
'Fact and fiction', pp. 218–19.   224 Whitelock, 'Fact and fiction', p. 219.

direct and straightforward reproduction of the armour-bearer's story. Abbo stresses that, with the exception of its final miracle, his narrative is derived from Archbishop Dunstan.[225] That narrative concerns not only Edmund's martyrdom at the hands of the pagan *Hinguar* but also the subsequent discovery and burial of the body with its severed head, the translation of the whole and uncorrupt body to *Bedricesgueord* (later Bury St Edmunds) and the development of Edmund's reputation as a wonder-working saint. It is at no point made clear precisely what proportion of this narrative derived originally from the armour-bearer. His testimony may have concerned the martyrdom alone; more likely it included also the recovery of the body; perhaps it covered the translation to *Bedricesgueord*.[226] Almost certainly it did not cover anything which took place after the very early years of Athelstan's reign. By the mid tenth century at the latest there was a religious community, probably a small group of priests, established around St Edmund's shrine at *Bedricesgueord*,[227] and it seems clear that the latter part of Abbo's narrative – an account of the saint's incorruption, for which Abbo adduces the testimony of a certain Oswen, and a miracle which is dated to the time of Theodred, bishop of London in the first half of the tenth century – derived not from the armour-bearer but from the traditions of that community as mediated through St Dunstan. Abbo, moreover, had plainly made his own investigations into the history of the cult. His final miracle, concerning the chastisement of an arrogant young man who demanded that the uncorrupt body of the saint be shown to him, must have been derived from the traditions of *Bedricesgueord* itself, either directly or through the community of Ramsey.[228] More than this, both Dunstan and Abbo had almost certainly embellished the armour-bearer's story by constructing their own relatively sophisticated interpretation of

---

225 *Passio Edmundi*, p. 68.

226 Abbo states that the initial disposal of Edmund's body by his killers was witnessed by 'quidam nostrae religionis' (*Passio Edmundi*, p. 80). It is unclear whether this is intended as a reference to the armour-bearer himself, to the source of this part of the armour-bearer's information or to an independent source. No statement is made concerning the authority for the translation to *Bedricesgueord*.

227 For the history of this community see below, pp. 219–20, 222–3, 224–5, 227.

228 It seems that Abbo wrote rather for the community of Ramsey, where according to Aimon he was based during his stay in England (*Vita Abbonis*, col. 392), than for that of *Bedricesgueord*: this seems to be the natural interpretation of the statement in his introductory *epistola* that: 'Postquam a te, uenerabilis pater [Dunstan], digressus sum cum multa alacritate cordis et ad monasterium quod nosti festinus redii, coeperunt me obnixe hi cum quibus, fraterna karitate detentus, hospitando hactenus degui pulsare

the events of 869/70. One further point deserves mention. Antonia Gransden has pointed out that the three earliest extant manuscripts of the *Passio* all date from the late eleventh century and all contain a number of variations from the text of Abbo as this is preserved in Ælfric's English translation.[229] These variations bear a direct relationship to the propaganda current at Bury in the time of Abbot Baldwin (1065–97): taken together they seem to suggest that the text of Abbo as we now have it represents an interpolated version circulated by that abbot in the aftermath of the Norman Conquest.[230] In the absence of any earlier manuscript version of the *Passio*, the post-Conquest interpolation of Abbo must remain a hypothesis. Nevertheless, Dr Gransden's work provides a further warning that the *Passio Edmundi* may be far removed from the simple story of an ageing armour-bearer. Embellished by the addition of later information, and coloured by the didactic and perhaps even propagandist aim of those responsible for its transmission, it might be expected to obscure or to distort the events which it purports to describe.

Nowhere has this possibility of distortion proved more controversial than in Abbo's account of the crucial events of 869/70. Abbo describes the whole course of the Viking invasions in a manner rather different from that of the earlier sources. In the *Chronicle* and in Asser the descent on East Anglia in 869 appears merely as one in a long series of heathen incursions: in particular it was preceded by an attack on the same area in 865, when the raiding army was bought off by the provision of horses.[231] Abbo makes no reference to this initial invasion of East Anglia, though he does show some familiarity with the scale of the Viking military operations and he was aware that the 869 attack was preceded by an expedition to

manu sancti desiderii ut mirabilium patratoris Eadmundi regis et martyris passionem litteris digererem, asserentes id posteris profuturum.'

This should not, however, obscure the possibility that Abbo may have paid a visit to *Bedricesgueord*. The fact that the Ramsey monks were interested in commissioning a Life of the *Bedricesgueord* saint in itself suggests that relations between the two communities were close and it is possible that the Ramsey monks in or shortly after this period were actively involved in the introduction of regular Benedictine monasticism to *Bedricesgueord* (see A. Gransden, 'The legends and traditions concerning the origins of the abbey of Bury St Edmunds', *EHR* 100 (1985), 1–24, at 24).

[229] A. Gransden, 'Baldwin, abbot of Bury St Edmunds, 1065–1097', in R. Allen Brown (ed.), *Proceedings of the Battle Conference on Anglo-Norman Studies* 4 (1982), 65–76, at 72–3.
[230] For further discussion of this point see below, p. 231 and n. 80.
[231] *ASC*, A, E, s.a. 866; *Asser's Life of King Alfred*, p. 19 (tr. Keynes and Lapidge, *Alfred the Great*, p. 74).

Northumbria.[232] And, in his account of the 869 invasion itself, he makes the Vikings arrive in East Anglia by sea, whereas the historical sources state that they rode over Mercia to Thetford.[233] Most important, however, is the striking discrepancy between the historical and hagiographical accounts of the circumstances of Edmund's martyrdom. According to the historical sources, Edmund fought against the Vikings and was defeated and killed by them. Abbo's Edmund died rather by deliberate moral choice: his martyrdom followed not upon his defeat by, but upon his refusal to accept the overlordship of, a great pagan leader.[234]

The conflicting nature of these sources poses a major problem which cannot be satisfactorily resolved. Several possibilities suggest themselves. Most straightforwardly the sources can be reconciled by the assumption that Abbo merely telescoped the events of 865 and 869. On the former occasion the heathen had indeed come to East Anglia by sea and had indeed carried out negotiations with the king, perhaps in circumstances in which he was unable to raise an army.[235] Alternatively, it has been noted that the *Chronicle* does not explicitly state that Edmund was killed *in battle*; rather its wording leaves room for the possibility that the king was slain *in the aftermath of* a military defeat.[236] Antonia Gransden, conversely, suggests that the *Chronicle*'s phrase *þone cining ofslogan* 'does not exclude the possibility that Edmund was killed in battle and not martyred at all'[237] – thus consigning the whole of Abbo's martyrdom narrative to the realm of hagiographical fantasy. Each of these explanations is plausible; but none is wholly convincing. For each involves the assumption that Abbo, as a result either of ignorance or of his hagiographical purpose, simply omitted all reference to a well-attested battle. It is hard to believe in Abbo's ignorance of such a battle – for it is hard to believe that Edmund's armour-bearer would have passed over it in silence. Nor is it easy to find a hagiographical purpose behind its omission from Abbo's account: there was little reason to invent a 'peace king' when 'To die fighting

232 *Passio Edmundi*, p. 72. For the Viking activities in the north see especially Smyth, *Scandinavian kings*, chs. 12–14.

233 *Passio Edmundi*, p. 72; cf. *ASC*, A, E, s.a. 870; *Asser's Life of King Alfred*, p. 26 (tr. Keynes and Lapidge, *Alfred the Great*, p. 77).   234 *Passio Edmundi*, pp. 74–9.

235 For the possibility that Abbo telescoped the events of the two years see Whitelock, 'Fact and fiction', p. 221.

236 *Ibid.*, pp. 217–18 and p. 221, where it is noted that both Gaimar and Roger of Wendover reconciled their conflicting sources 'by assuming a passage of time between Edmund's defeat in battle and his capture by the Danes'.

237 Gransden, 'Legends and traditions', p. 2.

the heathen was an adequate claim to sanctity.'[238] Moreover, if Abbo did intend to present Edmund as a peace king, or as an unresisting victim, he was both singularly unspecific and singularly inconsistent about so doing. Rather he makes quite clear his belief that Edmund had a considerable reputation as a warrior.[239] And, having done so, he had little reason to cheat his audience of its anticipated battle scene – unless, as was the whole point of his narrative, there was no battle.

It is, I believe, at least possible that Abbo's narrative is a more reliable source for the death of St Edmund than either the *Chronicle* or Asser. 'When dealing with events outside Wessex', writes Smyth, 'the Chronicle is concerned not with details but with basic issues – the laconic noting of the deaths of kings and the outcomes of major battles.'[240] Perhaps in the case of St Edmund a combination of ignorance and lack of interest led the compiler of the *Chronicle*, and Asser likewise, to place too great a reliance upon an assumed connection between the deaths of kings and the outcomes of battles. Perhaps, as Abbo claims, the martyrdom of St Edmund followed upon his defeat not in battle but in diplomacy. An initial point in Abbo's favour is the fact that he alone of the early sources was able to name Edmund's killer: his *Hinguar* is probably to be identified with Ivarr inn beinlausi, son of Ragnar loðbrok, who seems to have been prominent among the leaders of the Vikings in England from the mid 860s until *c.* 871.[241] The *Chronicle*, in

---

[238] Whitelock, 'Fact and fiction', pp. 217–18.

[239] Whitelock notes (*ibid.*, p. 221) that 'hagiographical writers would not be averse to depicting Edmund as all along an unresisting victim'. But this is precisely what Abbo did not do. He emphasised, first, that Edmund's story had been recounted by the man who had been his armour-bearer on the day of his martyrdom: a king who had no interest in fighting the invaders would have had little need to be accompanied in his final hours by an armour-bearer. Nor would the reputation of such a man prompt the Viking leader to put his followers to death in order to prevent him from raising an army (*Passio Edmundi*, p. 73). Nor again is it likely that such a man would be captured *proiectis armis* – having seized his arms but been powerless to use them (*Passio Edmundi*, p. 78). And nor, finally, would such a man have used the following argument when urged by his bishop to submit to the heathen demands: 'Et quid suggeris? Ut in extremis uitae, desolatus meo satellite, fugiendo inferam crimen nostrae gloriae? Semper delatoriae accusationis calumniam euitaui, numquam relictae militiae probra sustinui, eo quod honestum michi esset pro patria mori: et nunc ero mei uoluntarius proditor, cui pro amissione carorum ipsa lux est fastidio?' (*Passio Edmundi*, p. 75).
Abbo's Edmund was a warrior king cast in a traditional Christian-heroic mould. He adopted the role of sacrificial victim, 'ut aries de toto grege electus', only following his capture – when it became apparent that he had little alternative (*Passio Edmundi*, pp. 78–9).   [240] Smyth, *Scandinavian kings*, p. 205.

[241] For this identification, and for the career of Ivarr, see especially Smyth, *Scandinavian kings*, chs. 12–18. On the later medieval incorporation of the Edmund story into the

contrast, shows not the slightest interest in the names of the Scandinavian leaders until the latter year, when Wessex itself was for the first time directly threatened by the invaders.[242]

More important is analysis of Abbo's version of the events leading up to the martyrdom. *Hinguar*, he notes, came to East Anglia from Northumbria, leaving his associate *Hubba* in the north.[243] His omission of any reference to the expedition of 865 may be explained either by ignorance or by the fact that it was extraneous to his principal theme; his statement that the invaders arrived by sea is less readily intelligible. Arriving at an unnamed East Anglian town, *Hinguar* began immediately to slaughter its inhabitants, together with those of the surrounding countryside, in order that Edmund, who was known to be a skilled warrior, would be unable to raise an army.[244] The strategy worked: the king, isolated some distance from the town at *Haegilisdun* (or *Haeglesdun*), was cut off from all means of resistance. Abbo's account is not implausible. We know that the Danes had made peace with the East Angles in 865 and that they had spent the following years in Northumbria and Mercia. Their return in 869, therefore, must have been unexpected and might easily have crippled Edmund's powers of resistance. And the incident accords well with what is known of Ivarr's cunning and political opportunism. Just as, in 866, he had taken advantage of the weakness of the divided Northumbrian kingdom to prepare the way for a large-scale onslaught,[245] so in 869 he was able to make good use of the simple device of surprise. Quite possibly Edmund made some preparations for war, and quite possibly there was some sporadic fighting, but equally possibly there was never a battle worthy of the name: there is no inherent improbability in Abbo's statement that the king was finally captured not on a battlefield but *in palatio*,[246] bearing arms but hopelessly unprepared for war.

After slaughtering Edmund's supporters, Abbo explains, *Hinguar* was able to open negotiations with the king – to demand that the Christian monarch share with him his lands and his riches

'Loðbrok legend' see *ibid.*, ch. 4; Whitelock, 'Fact and fiction', pp. 228–31; Loomis, 'Growth of the Saint Edmund legend', pp. 90–113; Loomis, 'St Edmund and the Lodbrok (Lothbroc) legend', *Harvard Studies and Notes in Philology and Literature* 15 (1933), 1–23.   [242] *ASC*, A, E, *s.a.* 871; Smyth, *Scandinavian kings*, p. 224.
[243] *Passio Edmundi*, p. 72.   [244] *Ibid.*, p. 73.
[245] *ASC*, A, *s.a.* 867; for detailed discussion of the Scandinavian conquest of Northumbria see Smyth, *Scandinavian kings*, chs. 12–14.   [246] *Passio Edmundi*, p. 78.

and rule as a Danish underking over his own realm.[247] The
situation which Abbo here describes was not unparalleled in the
history of Scandinavian England. In 867, for example, it seems that
the Vikings had established an Englishman, Egbert, as just such a
'puppet' ruler over part of Northumbria.[248] And in 874, after
driving Burgred of Mercia out of his kingdom, 'they gave the
kingdom of the Mercians to be held by Ceolwulf, a foolish king's
thegn; and he swore oaths to them and gave hostages, that it should
be ready for them on whatever day they wished to have it, and he
would be ready, himself and all who would follow him, at the
enemy's service'.[249] It is by no means impossible that in the case of
East Anglia the negotiations elsewhere carried out with a 'collabo-
rating elite' were entered into with the king himself. Abbo's
account of these negotiations, I would suggest, was not merely a
hagiographical invention designed to exonerate a failed warrior by
his transmutation into a peace king. It is perhaps best understood as
an indication that the Vikings proceeded with the conquest of East
Anglia in a manner which was wholly characteristic of their *modus
operandi* elsewhere. The only obstacle to the perfect conquest was
that the Christian king refused to play; his capture and execution
was the inevitable consequence of that refusal.[250]

The post-Conquest tradition

In 1095 the body of St Edmund was solemnly translated into the
presbytery of a new Norman church: 'Symbolically, and to some
extent in reality, this event can be seen as inaugurating Bury's

[247] *Ibid.*, p. 74.
[248] *Historia Dunelmensis ecclesiae*, in *Symeonis monachi opera omnia*, ed. Arnold, 1 (1882), 55;
cf. Smyth, *Scandinavian kings*, pp. 207–8.
[249] ASC, A, s.a. 874; cf. *Asser's Life of King Alfred*, p. 35 (tr. Keynes and Lapidge, *Alfred the
Great*, p. 82).
[250] Cf. Smyth, *Scandinavian kings*, p. 206: 'When we study Abbo's elaborate account in
detail, we find that many aspects of his story are not only plausible but conform to a
pattern of Danish activities observable elsewhere in the British Isles and Scandinavia.'
Smyth has put forward the suggestion that the manner of Edmund's death was itself
paralleled in the history of other rulers who unsuccessfully resisted the Vikings:
Edmund, he claims, was subjected to a form of ritual slaying, the 'blood-eagle' sacrifice,
thereby becoming a victim of the cult of Oðinn (*Scandinavian kings*, ch. 14, especially
189–92, 210–13). Smyth's arguments are persuasive: but recent analysis of the skaldic
and saga sources for the 'blood-eagle' sacrifice has cast serious doubt not only upon the
suggestion that St Edmund met his death by this means but also upon the existence of the
rite among the Scandinavians of the ninth and tenth centuries (R. Frank, 'Viking
atrocity and skaldic verse: the rite of the blood-eagle', *EHR* 99 (1984), 332–43, especially
341–3).

greatest era as a focus of pilgrimage in England.'[251] The rise of this pilgrimage centre is reflected in the rapid development during the Norman period of a local hagiographical tradition. Abbo's work, mediated through the West Saxon court, put together with partial reference at most to the community which possessed St Edmund's body, and over a century out of date, was a hopelessly inadequate basis for the principal cult of one of England's most prestigious religious houses. It was accordingly supplemented, first, by a collection of miracles composed by Hermann the archdeacon.[252] This work was produced at the request of Abbot Baldwin and was probably completed within a few years of his death in 1097.[253] It includes an account of Edmund's initial burial and translation to *Bedricesgueord* which differs in detail from that of Abbo, followed by a series of posthumous miracles and culminating in the translation of 1095; the whole becomes inextricably intermingled with a history of the religious community at Bury St Edmunds.

[251] 'Geoffrey of Wells, *De infantia sancti Edmundi (BHL 2393)*' ed. R. M. Thomson, *AB* 95 (1977), 25–42, at 26.

[252] *Hermanni archidiaconi liber de miraculis sancti Eadmundi*, in *Memorials of St Edmund's abbey*, ed. Arnold, I, 26–92. Arnold's edition is based upon the text in London, BL, MS Cotton Tiberius B. ii. Further texts of the *De miraculis* are preserved in Oxford, Bodleian Library, MSS Digby 39 and Bodley 240 and in Oxford, St John's College, MS 75. The work is listed as *BHL*, nos. 2395–6 and Hardy, *Descriptive catalogue*, no. 1109. Arnold suggests (*Memorials of St Edmund's abbey*, I, xxviii–xxix) that Hermann was in the confidence of Herfast, bishop of Thetford, at the time of the latter's attempt to establish his see at Bury and that he may subsequently have become a monk at Bury; cf. Gransden, 'Baldwin', p. 65. Hermann is named by Landon as the first archdeacon of Norwich (L. Landon, 'The early archdeacons of Norwich diocese', *Proceedings of the Suffolk Institute of Archaeology and Natural History* 20 (1930), 11–35). It seems probable, however, that Hermann was not a diocesan archdeacon but an official of the abbey of Bury (see *Ungedruckte Anglo-Normannische Geschichtsquellen*, ed. F. Liebermann (Strassburg, 1879), pp. 226–7; J. le Neve, *Fasti ecclesiae Anglicanae 1066–1300, II, Monastic cathedrals (northern and southern provinces)*, compiled by D. E. Greenway (London, 1971), p. 62; J. Sayers, 'Monastic archdeacons', in C. N. L. Brooke *et al.* (eds.), *Church and government in the Middle Ages: essays presented to Christopher Cheney* (Cambridge, 1976), pp. 177–203, at pp. 179–80; C. N. L. Brooke, 'The archdeacon and the Norman Conquest', in *Tradition and change: essays in honour of Marjorie Chibnall*, ed. D. Greenway *et al.* (Cambridge, 1985), pp. 1–19, at pp. 7–8.

[253] *De miraculis*, p. 27. Hermann notes that he is writing at the request of 'felicis memoriae patris Baldewini' and of 'fratrum . . . sibi subjectorum'. His description of Baldwin makes it clear that the abbot was already dead at the time of writing, and the work ends abruptly shortly after describing the 1095 translation. In the collection of miracles preserved in Oxford, Bodleian Library, MS Bodley 240 six additional miracle stories are ascribed to Hermann. R. M. Thomson has accordingly suggested that 'Hermann must have made more than one redaction of his work, adding to the later one(s) more miracles which had come to his attention' ('Two versions of a saint's Life from St Edmund's abbey: changing currents in XIIth century monastic style', *Revue Bénédictine* 84 (1974), 383–408).

Thereafter the local hagiographical tradition continued to flourish. Before *c.* 1125 the Office of St Edmund was rewritten to include a series of *lectiones* based upon Hermann's work.[254] And the same period saw the production of a new series of *Miracula* which 'brought Hermann up to date, repeated his stories in a more literary and fashionable style, and filled in the uncomfortably long period of silence between Edmund's martyrdom and the earliest of Hermann's miracles with a series of appropriate wonders'.[255] Each of these is included in New York, Pierpont Morgan Library, MS Morgan 736, which contains also a fine series of thirty-two full-page miniatures illustrating the life and miracles of the saint: the manuscript is dated by R. M. Thomson to 1124–5.[256] Particularly problematical is the relationship between the Morgan *Miracula*, the miracles known to have been collected by Osbert of Clare, and a further collection made in the late twelfth century and contained in London, BL, MS Cotton Titus A. viii (s. xiii).[257] Both Bale and Boston of Bury provide *incipits* for Osbert's work, and traces of that work survive in the miracle collections of Titus A. viii and Oxford, Bodleian Library, MS Bodley 240 (s. xiv).[258] The Titus A. viii collection is divided into two books, and the prologue to Book I contains no indication of its author's identity; that to Book II, however, is ascribed in a marginal note of the fourteenth century to Osbert of Clare, and traces of a similar attribution are found opposite the *epistola* which follows and opposite miracles 8–20 of Book II.[259] The same miracles occur in the Bodleian manuscript, where they are ascribed to Osbert in a marginal note by the

---

[254] See '*De infantia*', ed. Thomson, p. 26.

[255] *Ibid.*, pp. 26–7. For detailed discussion of this work see Thomson, 'Two versions'.

[256] R. M. Thomson, 'Early Romanesque book-illustration in England: the dates of the Pierpont Morgan "Vitae sancti Edmundi" and the Bury Bible', *Viator* 2 (1971), 211–25; E. Parker McLachlan, 'The scriptorium of Bury St Edmunds in the third and fourth decades of the twelfth century: books in three related hands and their decoration', *Mediaeval Studies* 40 (1978), 328–48; O. Pächt, C. R. Dodwell and F. Wormald, *The Saint Albans Psalter* (London, 1960), especially pp. 141–2; C. M. Kauffmann, 'The Bury Bible', *Journal of the Warburg and Courtauld Institutes* 29 (1966), 60–81. The miniature-cycle occupies fols. 7–22v, the *Miracula* fols. 23–76, a text of Abbo's *Passio* fols. 77–86 and the Office of St Edmund fols. 87–100v, ending imperfectly due to loss of leaves.

[257] The Titus A. viii collection is printed under the title *Samsonis abbatis opus de miraculis sancti Ædmundi* in *Memorials of St Edmund's abbey*, ed. Arnold, I, 107–208.

[258] See *Letters*, pp. 26–7. On these MSS see also *Memorials of St Edmund's abbey*, ed. Arnold, I, xlv–xlvii; Thomson, 'Two versions', p. 385.

[259] See *Memorials of St Edmund's abbey*, ed. Arnold, I, xxxix; Thomson, 'Two versions', p. 388. Thomson identifies the hand which made the marginal notes as that of Henry de Kirkestede, prior and armarius at Bury *c.* 1360–80.

scribe.[260] The remaining miracles of Titus A. viii are likewise incorporated into Bodley 240, where they are attributed to Abbot Samson of Bury (1182–1211): it was on the basis of this attribution that Arnold named Samson as the author or compiler of the whole collection.[261] A different interpretation was put forward by E. W. Williamson, who suggested that the Morgan and Titus *Miracula* represented respectively an early and a late recension of the work by Osbert of Clare.[262] The two collections are closely related,[263] but there are strong reasons for rejecting Williamson's proposed identification and for assigning the Morgan *Miracula* to an anonymous Bury writer of the first quarter of the twelfth century.[264] The most plausible reconstruction of the subsequent sequence of Bury hagiographical works is that of Thomson, who has suggested that Osbert's work was composed after his visit to Rome in 1139 and comprised only miracles not included in the Morgan collection; thereafter Abbot Samson revised the Morgan collection and added an appendix to one of its miracles; and finally, late in the twelfth or early in the thirteenth century, a further Bury compiler conflated Osbert's miracles with those of Abbot Samson to produce the collection now extant in Titus A. viii.[265]

Abbo's *Passio* and the twelfth-century miracle collections are concerned exclusively with Edmund's death and posthumous reputation; with his birth, youth and reign they deal only in the

---

[260] See *Memorials of St Edmund's abbey*, ed. Arnold, I, xxxix; Thomson, 'Two versions', p. 389.

[261] *Memorials of St Edmund's abbey*, ed. Arnold, I, xxxix–xl, liii–lvi; cf. Thomson, 'Two versions', p. 389.   [262] *Letters*, pp. 29–31.

[263] The preface and cc. 1–15 of Titus A. viii agree with the preface and cc. 1–15 of the Morgan MS, with some variations in length and word order. At c. 16 the Morgan MS adds a miracle which appears as Book II, c. 11 of Titus A. viii. Thereafter the first book of the Morgan collection concludes with a lengthy *Excusatio historiologi* and Book II begins with a new prologue: neither of these is included in Titus A. viii. Book II, cc. 1–5 of the Morgan MS agree with Book II, cc. 1, 3, 4–7 of Titus A. viii, and at this point the Morgan MS breaks off.

[264] First, the thirteen miracles attributed in Titus A. viii to Osbert of Clare are omitted entirely from the Morgan MS. Second, Osbert's highly distinctive style can be more readily detected in the miracles attributed to him in Titus A. viii than in the miracles common to the Titus and Morgan collections. Third, Boston's *incipits* for Osbert's work at no point appear in the Morgan *Miracula* but do find parallels in the sections of Titus A. viii ascribed to Osbert. Fourth, the Morgan *Miracula* as incorporated into Titus A. viii have been quite ruthlessly abridged: it seems most unlikely that Osbert of Clare, in order to create a second recension of his *Miracula*, would have willingly indulged in such wholesale pruning of his own work. For further detailed criticism of Williamson's suggestion that Osbert was the author of both the Titus and the Morgan *Miracula* see Thomson, 'Two versions', pp. 391–3.   [265] *Ibid.*, pp. 389–93.

most cursory fashion. In the mid twelfth century, however, a further development of the St Edmund legend took place: in a work entitled *De infantia sancti Edmundi* the martyred king was provided with a past.[266] The *De infantia* was composed *c.* 1155 by Geoffrey of Wells, probably a member of one of the religious houses of Thetford, at the request of Sihtric, prior of Bury.[267] It solves the mystery surrounding Edmund's early years by endowing him with a continental origin. Offa, Edmund's alleged predecessor in East Anglia, was said to have set out on pilgrimage to the Holy Land in the hope that his prayers for an heir might be granted. On the way, while passing through Saxony, he encountered the king's son, Edmund, to whom he was in some unspecified way related.[268] On his return to England, Offa fell ill and, having failed to produce the desired heir, instructed his subjects to adopt Edmund as their king. Edmund was duly brought from Saxony, landed on the Norfolk coast and spent a year being educated at Attleborough before being accepted as king of the East Angles and taking up residence at Bures on the Suffolk–Essex border. Geoffrey's work was clearly founded upon such traditions concerning the saint as were current in Norfolk in the mid twelfth century; the bulk of his material is either 'fictional, folkloric or legendary'.[269] The author's achievement, as Thomson has pointed out, was to incorporate that material into a work characterised by 'the presence and employment of a historical sense' and by a marked interest in the delineation of Christian kingship.[270]

---

[266] The work is edited by Thomson, '*De infantia*', pp. 34–42; an earlier edition is that of Arnold in *Memorials of St Edmund's abbey*, I, 93–103. The work is listed as *BHL*, no. 2393 and Hardy, *Descriptive catalogue*, no. 1117.

[267] '*De infantia*', ed. Thomson, pp. 27, 34.

[268] The starting-point for Edmund's assumed 'continental connection' seems to have been Abbo's statement that the saint was 'ex antiquorum Saxonum nobili prosapia oriundus' (*Passio Edmundi*, p. 70).   [269] '*De infantia*', ed. Thomson, p. 28.

[270] *Ibid.*, pp. 29–31. The later versions of the St Edmund legend are numerous. For detailed discussion of the evolution of the legend see especially Whitelock, 'Fact and fiction'; Loomis, 'Growth of the Saint Edmund legend'; Loomis, 'St Edmund and the Lothbrok legend'; 'A new *Passio beati Edmundi Regis (et) Martyris*', ed. J. Grant, *Mediaeval Studies* 40 (1978), 81–95. See also *BHL*, nos. 2392–2403; Hardy, *Descriptive catalogue*, nos. 1098–1117.

Chapter 3

ROYAL BIRTH AND THE FOUNDATIONS OF SANCTITY: THEORETICAL INTERPRETATIONS

J. M. Wallace-Hadrill, in his masterly study of early Germanic kingship, concluded a brief examination of the Merovingian royal cults with the statement that 'Frankish respect for the Merovingians never reached the point where it was possible to expect or assume royal sanctity.'[1] A random glance at Bede's *Historia ecclesiastica* might suggest that, in contrast, such a point was reached, and reached at a relatively early date, in Anglo-Saxon England. Indeed, William Chaney has noted of the Anglo-Saxon period that 'the sacral nature of kingship, pagan and Christian, would lead the folk to expect God to honour the *stirps regia*. The recognised form of this in the new religion was sainthood.'[2] For Chaney the Christian saint king was the lineal descendant of the sacral ruler of the age of the migrations: sanctity simply was carried in the blood or went with the job of the Anglo-Saxon kings and, by extension, of their consorts and their offspring.[3] It is the purpose of this chapter, first, to demonstrate that the reality was nothing like so simple and, second, to review the statements made about the relationship between royal birth and sanctity by the hagiographers of the royal saints.

---

[1] J. M. Wallace-Hadrill, *Early Germanic kingship in England and on the continent: the Ford Lectures delivered in the University of Oxford in the Hilary Term 1970* (Oxford, 1971), p. 53.

[2] Chaney, *Cult of kingship*, p. 81.

[3] *Ibid.*, pp. 77–84; at p. 77 Chaney notes that 'The royal role in mediatorship with the divine continues in the special role assigned many kings in the new religion – the bestowal on them of sainthood.' For an important response to Chaney's view see J. Nelson, 'Royal saints and early medieval kingship', in D. Baker (ed.), *Sanctity and secularity, Studies in Church History* 10 (Oxford, 1973), 39–44.

ASCRIBED OR ACHIEVED? SANCTITY AND THE ROYAL
STATE IN THE EARLY MIDDLE AGES[4]

Kingship, as every medieval churchman knew and as every medieval ruler was informed, was instituted by divine concession: it was exercised *Dei gratia*. The kingdom, accordingly, had the status of a divine trust, in relation to which the ruler functioned not in or by his own right but rather as God's vice-gerent upon earth – as the holder of an office with more or less well-defined rights and duties and with a more or less well-defined scope and purpose. In general terms, that scope and purpose may be described as protection of the trust. And because the definition of kingship became, in the post-conversion centuries, exclusively a prerogative of the church, that protection was directed towards a very special group and was given a very special character: it was protection of the Christian church and of Christian society. Protection, at its most straightforward, meant the duty of the ruler to combat paganism and to guarantee the security of the church: hence Gregory the Great, in a letter to the newly converted Æthelbert of Kent, made it clear that Æthelbert had been designated by God as ruler over the English in order that through him his people might come to the Christian faith.[5] But conversion and the advancement of the church were the very least that was expected of the Christian ruler. That ruler's overriding concern was rather with the attainment of national *felicitas* – with *pax*, *prosperitas* and national salvation. The attainment of that goal was dependent in part upon the ruler's own right

---

[4] For the following discussion of general themes in the history of early medieval kingship I am indebted to the following: W. Ullmann, *The Carolingian Renaissance and the idea of kingship*, The Birkbeck Lectures in Ecclesiastical History, 1968–9 (London, 1969); J. L. Nelson, 'National synods, kingship as office, and royal anointing: an early medieval syndrome', in G. J. Cuming and L. G. D. Baker (eds.), *Councils and assemblies, Studies in Church History* 7 (Oxford, 1971), 41–59; Nelson, 'Ritual and reality in the early medieval *ordines*', in D. Baker (ed.), *The materials, sources and methods of ecclesiastical history, Studies in Church History* 11 (Oxford, 1975), 41–51; Nelson, 'Symbols in context: rulers' inauguration rituals in Byzantium and the West in the early Middle Ages', in D. Baker (ed.), *The orthodox churches and the West, Studies in Church History* 13 (Oxford, 1977), 97–119; Nelson, 'Inauguration rituals', in P. H. Sawyer and I. N. Wood (eds.), *Early medieval kingship* (Leeds, 1977), pp. 50–71; P. E. Schramm, *A history of the English coronation*, tr. L. G. Wickham-Legg (Oxford, 1937); Wallace-Hadrill, *Early Germanic kingship*; Wallace-Hadrill, 'The *via regia* of the Carolingian age', in *Trends in medieval political thought*, ed. B. Smalley (Oxford, 1965), pp. 22–41; Wallace-Hadrill, 'Gregory of Tours and Bede: their views on the personal qualities of kings', *Frühmittelalterliche Studien* 2 (1968), 31–44.
[5] *HE*, I, 32.

relationship with God: by providing an example of personal virtue he was to act as moral *rector* to his people. It was dependent also upon the public *utilitas* of the ruler. That *utilitas* comprised, first, leadership in war; internal peace was to be the product of external security. And, second, it comprised the special and all-enveloping royal virtue – that of *iusticia*, with its associated power of *correctio*.

Medieval government was, with very rare exceptions, government by kings, and it was with the status and duties of kings that contemporary writers were primarily concerned: we possess no detailed analysis of the status and function of royal women. On the few occasions when a woman was called upon to perform regal functions, her role was in no way distinguished from that of the male of the species. More usually, the status of the royal lady was that of consort and her function was dynastic and supportive. The Christian queen was expected to encourage her husband in the paths of virtue and, more important, to provide him with heirs: the church 'lacked any definition of the role of queens beyond what was required of all Christian wives'.[6]

The Christian church in its early centuries created and promulgated a theory of useful rulership. But what did the rulers themselves stand to gain from acceptance of this theory? What, from the point of view of the early medieval king, was the purpose and product of the correct execution of the royal *ministerium*? On this point there was little controversy: the church had an answer which it knew would appeal to even the most reluctant of Christian kings. The ruler who conformed to the standards laid down by the church could expect a two-fold reward. He would receive success in this world – victory in battle, peace at home and lasting fame among men. And he would obtain salvation after death – a place in an eternal kingdom presided over by a ruler who was *rex regum*.[7]

One thing, however, did not feature either among the conventional attributes of Christian rulership or among the rewards promised by the churchmen as their part of the 'bargain' between the secular and ecclesiastical powers – an automatic ticket to sanctity. Sanctity, unlike the sacrality of pagan rulership, was not an assumed attribute of the Christian king: in neither a continental

---

[6] Wallace-Hadrill, *Early Germanic kingship*, pp. 92–3. For an interesting illustration of the importance accorded to queens in exhorting their husbands to virtue see *HE*, II, 11, a letter in which Pope Boniface urges Queen Æthelburga to secure the conversion of her husband, the Northumbrian king Edwin, 'ut profecto sacrae scripturae testimonium per te expletum indubitanter perclareat: "Saluabitur uir infidelis per mulierem fidelem."'

[7] See, for instance, *HE*, I, 32, Gregory's letter to Æthelbert of Kent.

nor an insular context was it considered a part of the normal paraphernalia of rulership. Indeed it seems clear that the saint king, far from being a lineal descendant of the sacral ruler, was a fundamentally different creature. Sacrality involves the transmission of other-worldly powers into the world of men; sacral rulership, accordingly, transcends the division between clerical and secular. It constitutes, moreover, 'an ascribed not an achieved status, for its bearer possesses magical powers by definition. Nothing has to be proved or approved: sacrality goes with the job, is carried in the blood.'[8] A presupposition of Christian thought, in contrast, is the monopoly of sacral power by the Christian priesthood. The consecrated king was created by that priesthood, and was made 'not replete with magical powers but capable, through grace, of fulfilling his this-worldly royal function'.[9] That king was, Janet Nelson has convincingly argued, 'the church's model of desacralised rulership'.[10] And sacrality was not simply replaced by sanctity. Sanctity, in direct opposition to sacrality, could not be an ascribed status granted to certain classes by definition. It could only be an achieved status, awarded posthumously and in recognition of particular qualities; there could accordingly 'be no sanctification of royalty *per se*'.[11] The status and function of the Christian king was carefully defined by generations of ecclesiastical writers whose theme was that the ruler must work hard in order to attain salvation; they were in no doubt that he must work very much harder in order to attain sanctity.

The transition from paganism to Christianity in early medieval Europe in general and in Anglo-Saxon England in particular was of course a process of great complexity. The Christian church did not grow up in a cultural and political vacuum: its beliefs and practices were framed with continuous reference to those of the pre-Christian world within which it was to make its way and which it was eventually to supersede. The traditions which the church thus inherited included not only the northern and pagan, upon which the Chaney thesis is centred, but also the Mediterranean and the Hebraeo-Christian: the scale and complexity of the problem of cultural transmission cannot be overestimated. Chaney's book, in emphasising the continuity between pagan and Christian England, 'heavily and repeatedly underlines what is clearly true'.[12] The book

[8] Nelson, 'Royal saints', p. 42.   [9] *Ibid.*, pp. 42–3, at p. 43.
[10] *Ibid.*, p. 43.   [11] *Ibid.*
[12] R. Brentano, review of Chaney's *Cult of kingship*, in *Speculum* 47 (1972), 754–5, at 755.

fails however adequately to acknowledge that, in the matter of kingship, the church did far more than simply adopt the traditions of pre-Christian society. Its concern was rather to mould the rulership which it inherited in accordance with its own societal needs – to create a new model of useful rulership. In so doing it produced a radical reinterpretation of the traditions to which it was heir. Kings might be expected to do much the same things; but the principles underlying that expectation were new and challenging. Form might remain; meaning was changed. The problem of the transition from old to new religion has a further dimension. The Christian leaders created a kingship which was not sacral, and a sanctity which differed fundamentally from sacrality. We cannot know, though we can perhaps guess, how fully their theoretical subtleties were appreciated by a contemporary secular audience – by the rulers themselves and by the *folc* who might indeed expect God to honour the *stirps regia*. Allowance must be made for a measure of ambiguity, confusion or syncretism in the belief of that audience, even indeed in the beliefs or actions of some of the churchmen who were drawn from and obliged to operate within the secular world. Ambiguity of practice must be acknowledged; so too, however, must clarity of principle. Sanctity did not flow in the veins of the early medieval English kings: it found no place among the expected or assumed attributes of the Anglo-Saxon rulers or among those of their daughters and consorts.

THE HAGIOGRAPHERS AND THE ROYAL STATE

The hagiographers of the royal saints did not of course write primarily as political theorists seeking to analyse the nature and function of kingship. Nor, however, did they limit their discussion of rulership and of the royal state to direct interpretative comment on the relationship between the royal birth of their subjects and their attainment of sanctity. As educated churchmen, they generally had more than a passing interest in the theory of rulership, and for two more specific reasons kings, and to a lesser extent their consorts, played a prominent part in their narratives. It was necessary, first, for each hagiographer to place his subject within a recognisable historical context. Accordingly he was at some pains to discuss those rulers with whom his subject was connected by birth or marriage and, where possible, to glorify that subject by reference to the deeds of his or her ancestors and associates. Second, hagiography tended to shade into monastic history; and monastic history was determined in large measure by the activities, benevolent and otherwise, of kings and of royal ladies. The hagiographers, therefore, had ample opportunity – and very good reason – to make known their views on the private virtues and public duties of kings and their consorts.

The hagiographers created a number of memorable kings. Osbert of Clare produced interesting *vignettes* of both Alfred and Edward the Elder, the grandfather and father of his subject; Goscelin provided a clearly delineated picture of Edgar, which was paralleled in outline by several other writers; the Ely hagiographers produced a finely drawn Eorcenbert of Kent. Each of the rulers thus created was characterised by personal virtue: his own right relationship with God was assured. In Osbert's Alfred this virtue received its expression in the king's love of learning and devotion to the Scriptures;[13] Eorcenbert, we are told, was educated by his saintly consort in the Christian virtues;[14] Edgar was likened by Goscelin to the Old Testament model of Solomon.[15] In each case also private virtue was translated into public *utilitas*. Special emphasis was placed upon the advancement of Christianity and the patronage of the church. Osbert's Alfred was *cultor Dei*; with his consort and his heir he was renowned for his foundation and patronage of the religious houses of Winchester.[16] Edgar was remembered for his patronage of Wilton and for his part in the refoundation of Ely.[17] More generally, he was the *rex philosophicus* whose reign provided that golden age of concord between *regnum* and *sacerdotium* in which the monastic revival of the tenth century was able to take root.[18] Eorcenbert, according to Bede, ruled for twenty-four years *nobilissime*, the first English king to order the destruction of idols and the observance of the Lenten fast.[19] But these rulers were not memorable only as patrons of the church. That patronage was one part of a wider scheme; it was one of several means to the attainment of both national and personal salvation. Thus, for instance, the author of the Life of Sexburga characterised the age of Eorcenbert and his consort as one of harmony between *regnum* and *sacerdotium* in which

[13] *Vita Edburge*, fol. 87v.
[14] TCC O.2.1, fol. 217v; Calig. A. viii, fol. 110v (*Vita Sexburge*, cited below, n. 71).
[15] *Vita Edithe*, p. 39.   [16] *Vita Edburge*, fol. 87v.
[17] *Vita Edithe*, p. 46; *LE*, II, 1–3.   [18] See especially *Vita Edburge*, fols. 101v–102.
[19] *HE*, III, 8.

the church of God flourished and bore fruit . . . Good faith throve, and the guile of dishonesty grew weak. Piety grew to maturity, and wickedness was destroyed. Invincible steadfastness endured, and the madness of fury grew feeble. Virtue reigned, and dishonour was cast down. Continence found favour, and passion stood condemned. Iniquity yielded to justice; sobriety restrained dissolute luxury . . . Thus both at home and abroad all things were calmed and made peaceful, so that Christian peace reigned supreme throughout their dominion.[20]

The point was made even more explicitly in Goscelin's description of the end of Edgar's reign:

Edgar, the prince of peace, after filling Britain with monasteries, after magnifying the glory of the churches, after pacifying the people with the best of laws, after all his work of piety and justice, was translated from earthly empire to a heavenly crown placed upon him by the judge of kings.[21]

Such are some of the rulers who figure prominently in the Lives of the royal saints. They are among the best-documented examples, but they are by no means isolated. Other kings were very clearly created in the same mould. Among the East Angles, for instance, Sigebert, responsible for the reconversion of the kingdom after a three-year lapse into paganism, was 'a devout Christian and a very learned man in all respects';[22] Anna was characterised by 'Wondrous devotion to the worship of God, wondrous concern for the building of churches';[23] Offa, alleged predecessor of Edmund, was *iusticie cultor, pacis amator* and *rex peregrinus*.[24] Among the Northumbrians, Ecgfrith was 'pleasant of speech, courteous of manner, a man vigorous in arms, and a close friend of the blessed Wilfrid'.[25] Wulfhere was the first native ruler of the Mercians to embrace and enforce the Christian religion: his virtues received their expression in his work as 'builder of many churches' and their reward in the kingdom of heaven.[26] The hagiographers' interpretation of Christian rulership, moreover, is made clear not only by

---

[20] TCC O.2.1, fols. 217v–218; Calig. A. viii, fols. 110v–111: 'Conueniunt inter se regnum et sacerdotium, quorum mundus splendide concordia regitur, et ecclesia Dei florere solet et fructificare . . . Fides uiget, fraudis dolositas eneruatur. Pietas maturescit, destruitur scelus. Constantia inuincibilis perseuerat, uesania furoris effeminatur. Honestas regnat, turpitudo deicitur. Continentia approbatur, dampnatur libido. Equitati cedit iniquitas, temperantia luxurie fluxa restringit . . . Ita domi forisque omnia sedata sunt et pacata, ut pax Christiana in toto corum optinuerit principatum imperio.'
[21] *Vita Edithe*, p. 80.
[22] *HE*, II, 15 (tr. Colgrave and Mynors, p. 191). [23] *LE*, I, 7.
[24] *De infantia*, ed. Thomson, p. 35. [25] *LE*, I, 8. [26] *Vita Werburge*, col. 102.

the distribution of praise but also by the application of censure. That censure was directed against those rulers who rejected the Christian faith, who refused to co-operate with the church or who were known despoilers of it. Thus the Ely writer's initial praise of Ecgfrith was paralleled by his condemnation following that king's reluctant acceptance of his wife's withdrawal and his quarrel with Bishop Wilfrid.[27] And, just as it was repeatedly emphasised that the righteous would receive their reward in heaven, so it was made abundantly clear that the wages of sin would be misfortune, death and disgrace.[28]

The Lives of the royal saints, it is clear, are wholly representative of early medieval thought on the nature of kingship: they are indeed one of the most important sources upon which analysis of that thought can and should be based. The rulership which they portray is a rulership conferred by God, justified by virtue and consummated by an ultimate translation to the kingdom of heaven. The qualities of their rulers are the conventional ones of private virtue and public *utilitas*, and these are expressed through the conventional channels of protection of the faith, patronage of the church, the exercise of *iustitia*, and the attainment of *pax* through military and political domination. Royal ladies, where they appear at all, do so as rather useful appendages to their husbands: they encourage those husbands in Christian virtue, they join with them in the patronage of the church, and they provide them with heirs.[29] The end product is a deliberately and highly idealised view of the royal state, and the hagiographers leave us in no doubt that their subjects, born into this royal tradition, were the beneficiaries from the outset of its reflected glory: they might even be expected to attain a degree of piety. But it is made clear also that birth into the ruling dynasties of Anglo-Saxon England did no more than create an expectation of piety. The rulers and the consorts of whom the hagiographers wrote in general terms were not saints, and they were sharply differentiated from those royal persons who formed the subjects of the Lives and who *had* attained sanctity. The hagiographers, moreover, far from assuming a sanctification of

[27] *LE*, I, 8–11; see below, n. 49.
[28] *HE*, II, 5 (the sons of Saebert of Essex); III, I (the Northumbrians Osric and Eanfrid), 7 (Cenwalh of Wessex), 22 (Sigebert of Essex); IV, 26 (Ecgfrith of Northumbria).
[29] See *Vita Edburge*, fol. 87v, concerning Ealhswith's patronage of the church, and below, pp. 89–90, concerning the activities of Sexburga and Eormenilda prior to their entry to the religious life.

royalty *per se*, perceived that for each individual the relationship between royal birth and the attainment of sanctity was both crucial and complex. The definition of that relationship was of central importance in their writings.

THE ROYAL LADIES

The earliest and most concise interpretation of the sanctity of the royal ladies is found in Bede's account of St Æthelthryth. Bede's initial concern was with the saint's royal origin and connections: his opening sentences read like the beginning of some glorious dynastic history.[30] But that beginning was not sustained. Bede's interest in Æthelthryth was hagiographical rather than dynastic or political; and it was not in a dynastic or political role that the foundations of sanctity lay. For the daughter of Anna sanctity derived not from worldly duty but from religious vocation. The theme is developed with skill. Bede's brief genealogical introduction centres on the saint's second marriage, to the Northumbrian Ecgfrith; it is immediately juxtaposed with the statement that 'Though she lived with him for twelve years she still preserved the glory of perfect virginity.'[31] Bede goes on to outline the testimony of Bishop Wilfrid concerning Æthelthryth's refusal to consummate her marriage and to describe the 'divine miracle' of her incorruption after death – the most certain sign 'that she had remained uncorrupted by contact with any man'.[32] The centrality of *uirginitas* is underlined by the hymn which follows. Bede's hymn in honour of St Æthelthryth is also a hymn in honour of *uirginitas*: the royal lady takes her place alongside Agatha and Eulalia, Thecla and Euphemia, Agnes and Cecily, all virgin martyrs of the early church:

> Nor lacks our age its AETHELTHRYTH as well
> Its virgin wonderful nor lacks our age.[33]

It was, then, as a virgin saint that the royal lady Æthelthryth won fame and inspired devotion. And about the relationship of this role to the royal state Bede is unambiguous. The preservation of *uirginitas* was not simply an optional extra, to be added to the conventional catalogue of royal virtues: for a royal lady to be twice married and still to remain a virgin was rather an explicit denial and

---

[30] *HE*, IV, 19.   [31] *Ibid.* (tr. p. 391).
[32] *Ibid.* (tr. p. 393).   [33] *Ibid.*, c. 20 (tr. p. 399).

contravention of her royal duty. It culminated in a choice between two distinct and incompatible worlds: after twelve years of marriage and entreaty Æthelthryth finally was permitted 'to relinquish the affairs of this world and to serve Christ, the only true King, in a monastery'.[34] Æthelthryth's sanctity, far from being a product of her royal status, was conditional upon the renunciation of that status and upon commitment to the alternative goal of the monastic life:

> Of royal blood she sprang, but nobler far
> God's service found than pride of royal blood.[35]

Bede's Æthelthryth was wholly typical of the royal ladies created by the hagiographers. In each case hagiography began with genealogy. A genealogical introduction served to locate the saint within a recognisable historical context and to enhance her prestige by reference to the deeds of her ancestors.[36] It also had, as in Bede's account of St Æthelthryth, a further and less obvious function. It provided the starting-point for the elaboration of the theme that sanctity could not derive simply from membership in a royal dynasty: the royal ladies, exalted by birth, were even further exalted by their deeds. Those deeds, moreover, and their relationship to the royal state, were clearly defined. Sanctity was founded upon the preservation of *uirginitas*[37] and upon commitment to the monastic ideal; as such it represented the negation of royal status. In both the *Vita Edburge* and the *Vita Edithe* the point is underlined by a vocation narrative which is skilfully juxtaposed with the genealogical introduction. Edburga, summoned before her father when only three years old, was presented with two groups of objects, symbolising the secular and ecclesiastical lives; her instinctive movement towards the ecclesiastical objects represented her aban-

---

[34] *Ibid.*, c. 19 (tr. p. 393).   [35] *Ibid.*, c. 20 (tr. p. 399).

[36] St Edburga, for instance, was placed in context by a brief introduction to the reigns of her grandfather and father, Alfred and Edward the Elder; her prestige was enhanced by the hagiographer's decision to highlight the patronage of the church as the most noteworthy feature of those reigns (*Vita Edburge*, fol. 87v). Goscelin achieved the same effect by identifying St Edith as the daughter of Edgar and by characterising that king as a man of piety and his reign as one of peace (*Vita Edithe*, pp. 39–40). The genealogies of the descendants of Anna are generally more elaborate. Most notable is that of the *Vita Werburge* (cols. 97–101), in which the saint's descent is traced from the royal lines of Kent, Frankia, Mercia and East Anglia and full notice is given of the role of her ancestors in the propagation of the faith and of those among them who had come to be venerated as saints. For the derivation of this genealogy see Rollason, *Mildrith legend*, pp. 26–7.

[37] An exception must be made here of the royal widows Sexburga and Eormenilda and of Wulfthryth, mother of St Edith: for discussion of these ladies see below, pp. 89–92.

donment of the world and her commitment to the church.[38] Goscelin's account is more evocative. The infant Edith, he notes, had been taken by her mother to the nunnery of Wilton. There, at the age of two, she was visited by her father, who placed before her 'regal dignity and ladies' finery, golden coronets, cloaks woven with gold, jewelled robes, bracelets, rings and necklaces'. Her mother, in contrast, laid out 'the black veil of purity, the chalice and paten, vessel of Our Lord's Passion, and the Psalter of Holy Scripture'. The infant moved at once to the latter objects: 'without hesitation, from the middle of the spendid colours, she picked out the veil alone and set it in place of a crown upon her head'.[39]

The hagiographers, however, having made it clear that the foundation of sanctity lay in the renunciation of royal status, did not thereafter lose interest in that status. Rather it retains considerable thematic importance throughout the *Vitae*: its function becomes that of an inherited status with which to contrast the saint's actual role. The principal themes of the monastic life – those of *castitas*, *obedientia* and *paupertas* – are delineated with continuous reference to the antithetical assumptions of the royal state.

Most crucial and most poignant is the interpretation of *castitas*. The saint, in choosing the religious life, had renounced the most fundamental duty and privilege of the royal lady and had committed herself to an alternative which could be realised only by the fulfilment of a role – that of *sponsa Christi* – antithetical to that into which she was born. St Edith, for instance, is said to have abandoned *spes filiorum regum* and to have perceived her life as a pilgrimage to the heavenly bridal chamber.[40] For Withburga, commitment to the religious life was paralleled by the rejection of earthly suitors: ' "Farewell", she said, "kingly suitors and sons of kings; attend to your weddings, princes and nobles. I have found a bridegroom whom my soul loves; I am already firmly wedded to him." '[41] The theme receives particularly interesting elaboration in

[38] *Vita Edburge*, fol. 88.
[39] *Vita Edithe*, pp. 44–5. The Trinity version of the *Vita Withburge* preserves an interesting anecdote in which the saint's subsequent choice of the religious life is foreshadowed when, as a child playing on the beach with her friends, she constructed a church of pebbles on the edge of the water (TCC O.2.1, fols. 237v–238).
[40] *Vita Edithe*, pp. 51, 45.
[41] TCC O.2.1, fol. 239; CCC 393, fol. 59v: ' "Valete", ait, "amatores reges et regum nati; agite uestras nuptias principes et proci. Ego sponsum quem diligit anima mea inueni, iam illi inseparabiliter nupsi." ' For similar portrayals of the rejection of earthly marriage and of the saint's role as bride of Christ see *Vita Werburge*, col. 101; *HE*, III, 8, on Æthelburga and Eorcengota.

the legend of St Æthelthryth. Bede's narrative is centred upon
Æthelthryth's second marriage and upon her subsequent entry to
the religious life: her virtuous life up to that point is assumed but not
explored. Later writers, however, found it necessary to labour the
point. Thus the Corpus/Dublin Life stresses that each of
Æthelthryth's marriages was contracted with the greatest reluctance and solely in order to comply with the dynastic policies of her
family;[42] on each occasion the reluctant bride jealously guarded her
chastity.[43] The verse rendering of the Life goes further. Gregorius
writes of Æthelthryth's first marriage in such a way that one
wonders whether the unfortunate Tonbert, in dying soon after the
marriage, simply took the line of least resistance:

Uncorrupted by the bridal bed, she was a wife in name alone. A virgin, she
fled from, she hated, she knew not man's touch and the marriage act. The
deeds of the marriage bed she knew not, since she, the chaste one, was
devoted to virtue. Worthy of the heavenly marriage chambers, bride of
the groom immortal, she fled the desires of the flesh, she triumphed as a
second Judith.[44]

The saint's marriage to Ecgfrith becomes a struggle from which she
emerges uncompromisingly victorious;[45] her departure for
Coldingham is a flight from evil.[46] The Life contained in the *Liber
Eliensis* completes the process. The saint's opposition to her first
marriage is even more vehement;[47] that marriage is followed by a

---

[42] CCC 393, fol. 3v: 'seculari more Australium Gyruiorum principi Tonberto nomine
iungitur copulatione maritali uoto parentum unanimi, ipsa uero inuita si posset reniti
contra'; cf. TCD 172, p. 260. CCC 393, fol. 4: 'datur iterum in coniugium uoluntate
parentum Northymbre Ægfrido regi desponsanda in matrimonium'; cf. TCD 172,
p. 260.

[43] CCC 393, fol. 3v: 'Ecce quod insolitum mundo nouum miratur omnis homo, ut queuis
desponsata maneat inmaculata'; cf. TCD 172, p. 260. CCC 393, fol. 4: 'Cuius consortio
duodenis annis usa, perpetue uirginitatis integritate manens gloriosa, compos uoti prioris
animi nil affectat dultius quam que sunt Dei, habens odibile quod esse Deo nouit
abhominabile, non aliquid seculi captans suadibile'; cf. TCD 172, p. 260.

[44] CCC 393, fol. 35: 'Incorrupta thoro, fit coniunx nomine solo. / Virgo, uiri tactus fugit,
odit, nescit et actus. / Nescit facta thori, dum seruit, casta, pudori. / Digna Dei thalamis et
sponsi sponsa perennis, / Carnis uota fugit, sic uincit, ut altera Iudith.'

[45] *Ibid.*, fol. 35v: 'Virginitatis honor, quem nullus decoquit ardor, / Perpetuus mansit, nec in
hac sua gloria transit, / Exulta gemino uictrix bellona triumpho. / Iam tibi uirgo tuus
geminatur in hoste triumphus. / Ut prius, exulta, uicisti, plaude, resulta. / Laurea debetur
uictrici, pugna meretur.'

[46] *Ibid.*, fol. 36: 'Fugit ab Egypto, fugit, Pharaone relicto. / Dumque fugit Sodomam; non
respicit ipsa Gomorram. / Vicinam Sodome Segor; fugit, atque Gomorre. / Ignes dum
metuit; montes secura petiuit; / Deseruit thalamos humilis regina superbos.'

[47] *LE*, I, 4. Æthelthryth 'solius Dei suspirabat ad thalamum, cui uirgineum sollempniter
epitalamium concinebat'. Her father, however, agrees that she should be given in

preliminary withdrawal to the religious life;[48] and the downfall of Ecgfrith is complete. The frustrated but ultimately flexible Christian king of the Bedan narrative becomes the agent of the *hostis antiquus* who even attempts forcibly to remove his erstwhile wife from the monastery at Coldingham.[49]

Castitas was associated in the monastic ideal with the virtue of *obedientia*, and in the Lives of the royal ladies the closely related attributes of *obedientia* and *humilitas* figure prominently. Goscelin, in his description of the community of Wilton, notes that 'just as the most precious jewel Edith outshone the others in rank, so too she surpassed them all in humility'.[50] Osbert of Clare writes of Edburga in similar vein: 'though by birth she was exalted above the rest, in the dignity of service she rendered herself most lowly of all'.[51] And he goes on to provide striking illustrations of Edburga's humility and commitment to the service of others. He describes first an incident in which the prioress came upon a member of the community reading alone and, in punishment, administered a sound beating. Thereafter, on discovering that the errant nun was none other than Edburga, she rapidly had second thoughts and apologised profusely to the *filia principis*. Edburga, in contrast, set little store by her royal status. Moved by the humility of her monastic superior, she too prostrated herself, begged forgiveness

marriage to Tonbert: 'Quod illa audiens multum perhorret, diu recusat, diu denegat, utpote que omni desiderio vitam in virginitate optabat implere. Sed vincit parentum auctoritas, immo animi eius sententiam divina immutat providentia que eam presciebat ex matrimonii sarcina gloriosiore coronandam castitatis laurea.'   [48] *Ibid.*, c. 8.

[49] *HE*, IV, 19. Ecgfrith, according to Bede, needed much persuasion but eventually sanctioned his wife's withdrawal and allowed her to depart peacefully to Coldingham. The Corpus/Dublin Life likewise is far from hostile towards Ecgfrith: see especially CCC 393, fols. 5–5v: 'O laudabilis uiri uita, annis duodenis constans et firma, qua non impetitur sibi maritata ulla quod hominum est carnali lasciuia. Inter eos quidem frigescit carnis lasciuies, calescit autem amoris Domini temperies.' The compiler of the *LE* notes that Ecgfrith's reign, so long as he was sympathetic to his wife, was one of peace and prosperity. Thereafter, however, Ecgfrith becomes the tempter who urges the saint 'ad carnales illecebras' and from whom she receives special divine protection (*LE*, I, 8). We are told, for instance, that on one occasion the king followed Æthelthryth as she went to prayer: 'Nec mora, rex concitus advenit ad hostium, introspexit et ecce domus illa, quasi inflammata, intrinsecus tota reluxit. Unde nimio terrore correptus, pedem pro stupore retraxit atque ad eam clamando recessit, dicens: "Noli, bona mulier, noli estimare me tibi ulterius velle illudere. Dominus Deus protector tuus est et adiutor fortis"' (*ibid.*, c. 9). With great reluctance Ecgfrith finally allowed Æthelthryth to enter the religious life at Coldingham (*ibid.*, c. 10). Thereafter, however, he had second thoughts and on the advice of his followers attempted 'cum furore et fremitu' to seize her from the monastery (*ibid.*, c. 11). The saint took flight, was saved by being miraculously marooned on a headland for seven days, and finally arrived safely at Ely.

[50] *Vita Edithe*, p. 62.   [51] *Vita Edburge*, fol. 88v.

for her error and swore that in future she would in no way transgress the precepts of the Rule: the royal child was to claim no privilege.[52]

There follows an account of the saint's custom, 'following the pattern of Our Lord's ministry', of secretly cleaning the shoes of the other nuns.[53] Just as Christ himself, by washing the feet of the disciples, had proclaimed the glory of humility, so too Edburga became to the sisters an example of that same virtue: every night she would secretly steal away their shoes, wash them and soften them with grease. This custom met with an interesting, and at first sight rather curious, response. When Edburga was finally identified as the author of the secret good deed she was brought before the assembled community and, far from receiving gratitude or praise, was publicly rebuked for an act of service which was perceived as a betrayal of her royal status:[54] the *humilitas* of the *uirgo regia* had far exceeded the expectations of the church.

Goscelin likewise places much emphasis on the virtue of *humilitas*. St Edith, rejecting the preoccupations of the world, 'by the ladder of humility strove towards heaven'.[55] Like Edburga, she was committed to the service of others;[56] in particular she was concerned for the outcasts and marginal of society. Turning aside from the praises of those of her own rank, she devoted herself instead to the care of the sick and the destitute:[57] even the criminal benefited from her care, her concern for thieves being likened to that which she felt for her brothers Edward and Æthelred.[58] Edith's *humilitas* was expressed in her refusal to exercise in person abbatial authority over three religious houses, 'preferring to be subject to

[52] *Ibid.*, fol. 89.

[53] *Ibid.*, fols. 89–89v. For a similar demonstration of royal humility see Bede's statement that Æthelthryth would only take a hot bath before the greater feasts 'et tunc nouissima omnium, lotis prius suo suarumque ministrarum obsequio ceteris quae ibi essent famulis Christi' (*HE*, IV, 19; followed in the later Æthelthryth hagiography).

[54] *Vita Edburge*, fol. 89v, cited below, p. 99.

[55] *Vita Edithe*, p. 60 (cf. Rule of St Benedict, c. 7).

[56] *Vita Edithe*, p. 61: 'Iam non se meminit regno natam, ut ancillarum Christi exhiberet ancillam. Non arrogat longam regum genealogiam, sed neque matris dignam imperio prosapiam, malens a domino humilium gratiam et gloriam. Exerta lacertos ad obedientiam, ad seruitutem omnium primam, ad dignitatem reddidit postremam.' For this theme see also *Vita Werburge*, col. 102.

[57] *Vita Edithe*, pp. 62–3, at p. 63: 'Virgo sullimior in Christo mundi imperio, terrenis celsitudinibus ac fauoribus iam ualedicit; languidis ac destitutis se impendit, lazaros Christi regum natis preponit, elefantiosis seruire regno pretendit, ulcerosis uestigiis quasi scabello Domini adiacere, eaque lauacris, capillis, osculis fouere mauult quam imperare. Quanto quisque apparuerat morbis deformior, tanto hec offertur benignitate compacientior et famulatu suffusior.' [58] *Ibid.*, p. 64.

her mother than to rule over others';[59] it culminated in the rejection of an earthly throne.[60] This latter incident is immediately
juxtaposed with an account of the devotion with which Edith
constructed at Wilton an *oratorium* dedicated to St Denys. There
could be no clearer illustration of the hagiographer's fundamental
theme: '"My kingdom is not of this world."'[61]

Renunciation of dynastic aspirations and of this-worldly honour
went hand in hand with rejection of the trappings of secular
womanhood. Æthelthryth in her later years accepted with good
grace the growth of a tumour on her neck: '"I know well enough
that I deserve to bear the weight of this affliction in my neck, for I
remember that when I was a young girl I used to wear an unnecessary weight of necklaces; I believe that God in his goodness would
have me endure this pain in my neck in order that I may thus be
absolved from the guilt of my needless vanity."'[62] Wulfthryth
planned for her daughter a harsh childhood in which the pleasure
conventionally taken in fine clothes and cosmetics was replaced by
a commitment to virtue and learning:

Her mother sought not to bind her shining tresses with gold, to obscure
the citadel of the cross with gems hanging over her brow . . . or to add
anything to her natural beauty; rather she strove only for those things
befitting the marriage chamber of Our Lord. She taught not the use of
rouge, of ceruse, of antimony, but only modesty; she prepared her
daughter not with varied adornments but rather with the grace of letters
and of virtue, by which she might shine forth more eminently to give light
to the church.[63]

The pleasure conventionally derived from riches and personal
adornment was replaced in Edith by a commitment to the poor and
to the aims of the church: Goscelin tells us that she valued wealth
only in so far as it could be used for the good of others.[64] Osbert of
Clare similarly writes at length of his subject's personal charity.[65]
And by far the most striking renunciation of personal riches comes
in a speech attributed by Osbert to St Edburga. King Edward,
coming with his companions to Winchester, asked his daughter to

---

[59] *Ibid.*, p. 77.   [60] *Ibid.*, pp. 84–6.
[61] *Ibid.*, p. 86, citing John 18:36.   [62] *HE*, IV, 19 (tr. p. 397).
[63] *Vita Edithe*, p. 49. One might doubt whether Wulfthryth was entirely successful.
Elsewhere (*ibid.*, pp. 70–1) Goscelin recounts a confrontation between Edith and
St Æthelwold, who rebukes the young royal lady for the unseemly fineness of her dress.
Edith, evidently a lady of some spirit, is not slow to reply: 'Crede, o pater reuerende,
nequaquam deterior mens Deo aspirante sub hoc habitabit tegmine quam sub caprina
melote.'   [64] *Ibid.*, p. 65.   [65] *Vita Edburge*, fols. 92v–93.

sing for their entertainment. Edburga was reluctant, fearing that she might be led into the sin of pride. Edward, however, was finally able to prevail by the promise of a just reward. He may have found his daughter's aspirations a little surprising:

'Listen, o king, to a virgin who speaks for the virgins, to a nun who speaks for the nuns; attend, o father, to the words of your daughter; give heed, o parent, to your own flesh. I do not seek from you a weight of diverse metals; I do not ask for silver flowers decorated by the craftsman's hand or for splendid garments woven with gold and jewels. It is not this that my purpose demands.'[66]

The unfortunate ruler, having no doubt expected to provide for his daughter a relatively small gift of a personal nature, was persuaded instead to part with the estate of *Canaga* for the benefit of the nunnery.

To the hagiographers of the royal virgins, therefore, sanctity and secularity were mutually exclusive. Sanctity was located exclusively within the monastic context and as such was founded upon a life both divorced from and antithetical to that conventionally expected of a young royal lady. The themes of the royal *Vitae* differ less in kind than in degree from those more generally applied to women entering the religious life.[67] The renunciation of the royal lady was perhaps greater because she had more to lose; and one suspects that the hagiographers derived some pleasure from pointing out that, for the royal lady, the rewards of the religious life were particularly appropriate: dominion over the earthly kingdom would be replaced by glory in the heavenly. Thus Edburga, having renounced her this-worldly role, is *sponsa summi regis*;[68] and Æthelthryth is designated 'this queen and bride of Christ, and therefore truly a queen because the bride of Christ'.[69]

There remains a further group of royal ladies – those whose saintly daughters furnished living proof that they could lay no claim to the preservation of *uirginitas*. The Lives of Sexburga and Eormenilda each begin with genealogy and go on to outline their subject's fulfilment of her political and dynastic function within the world.[70] In each case the saint receives high praise for her conduct

---

[66] *Ibid.*, fol. 92.
[67] There are, for instance, close thematic parallels between Goscelin's *Vita Edithe* and his *Liber confortatorius*, addressed to the former Wilton nun Eve.
[68] *Vita Edburge*, fol. 96v.   [69] *HE*, IV, 20 (tr. p. 397).
[70] The importance of the political and dynastic function is made particularly clear in the *lectiones* for the feast of Eormenilda, where it is noted that following the saint's marriage

as Christian consort: she leads her husband in the ways of virtue and she provides him with worthy heirs;[71] Sexburga is even said to have governed the kingdom in the interval between her husband's death and the accession of her young son.[72] But the hagiographers provide no model for the attainment of sanctity within the world and through the fulfilment of royal duty. Instead the translation of virtue into sanctity is seen to have derived from a single and crucial turning-point within the career of the royal lady – from a timely widowhood and a hasty withdrawal to the religious life. It is made clear that the saint's earthly duty had been fulfilled with the utmost diligence, but that it had been endured rather than enjoyed. Both Sexburga and Eormenilda, although they submitted to marriage with better grace, are said like Æthelthryth to have entered it with reluctance;[73] each is said to have maintained as far as possible the monastic virtues within the royal court;[74] and for each the religious life represented a refuge from a dynastic and political role which, although tolerated, was barely tolerable.[75]

to Wulfhere of Mercia 'hac . . . mediatrice Cantuarii et Mercii facta sunt uti unum regnum' (TCC O.2.1, fol. 28v; CCC 393, fol. 72; Calig. A. viii, fol. 96).

71 The *Vita Sexburge* notes that 'Collateralem suum regem in dies cotidie ad studium beate imortalitatis accendere, ad sacrarum edium domicilia statuenda, ad terenda sancte ecclesie limina, ad uigilias sanctorum deuotis excubiis exercendas, ad monasteria in quibus non erant locis construenda, ad ruinas morum reficiendas, insignis matrona animum induxit' (TCC O.2.1, fol. 217v; Calig. A. viii, fol. 110v; cf. CCC 393, fols. 70–70v; Caligula A. viii, fol. 94v (*lectiones* for Sexburga's festival). For Sexburga's children see TCC O.2.1, fol. 217; Caligula A. viii, fol. 110 (*Vita*): 'Reges duo Egbertus et Lotharius, tanquam duo planete in celo lucentes oriuntur. In altero sexu Ærmenilda et Erkengoda, tanquam duo sidera preclara apparent.' Cf. CCC 393, fols. 69v–70; Calig. A. viii, fol. 94 (*lectiones*).
    For similar themes in the Life of Eormenilda see TCC O.2.1, fols. 228v–229; CCC 393, fols. 72–73v; Calig. A. viii, fols. 96–96v.

72 See Swanton, 'Fragmentary Life of St Mildred', pp. 26–7; TCC O.2.1, fols. 218–218v; Calig. A. viii, fol. 111v.

73 For Sexburga's reluctant marriage see TCC O.2.1, fol. 216; Calig. A. viii, fols. 109–109v (*Vita*); CCC 393, fol. 69v; Calig. A. viii, fol. 94 (*lectiones*). Cf. the account of Eormenilda in TCC O.2.1, fols. 228–228v; CCC 393, fol. 72; Calig. A. viii, fols. 95v–96.

74 See, for instance, the *Vita Sexburge*: 'Regina uero beata diuersorum calamitatibus sulleuandis intenta, palatium instituit receptaculum miserorum, quos languore et inedia consumptos et egrotantes de plateis colligere et refouere faciebat. Non inuenit in illam auaritia quod quateret, superbia quod inflaret, ambitio quod delectaret' (TCC O.2.1, fols. 217–217v; Calig. A. viii, fol. 110v; cf. CCC 393, fol. 70; Calig. A. viii, fols. 94–94v (*lectiones*)). Cf. *Vita Werburge*, col. 101, on Eormenilda.

75 The hagiographers effectively employ the theme of marriage and the secular life as a prison or tempest from which refuge is finally sought in religion. The author of the *Vita Sexburge* notes that his subject came, on her husband's death, to the monastery at *Middeltona*, 'ad cuius ecclesie portum de mundi huius naufragio nuda euasit' (TCC O.2.1, fol. 218v; Caligula A. viii, fols. 111v–112; cf. CCC 393, fol. 71; Caligula A. viii, fol. 95 (*lectiones*)). Of Eormenilda it is written that on the death of Wulfhere 'almiflua regina Ermenhilda quamquam pie defleret excidium sociale tota iam anima cum uulnerata

Following their withdrawal from the world, the sanctity of the royal widows is defined in terms directly analogous to those applied to the virgins. The hagiographer of Werburga, for instance, drew close parallels between the virtues of the virgin daughter and those of the widowed mother, Eormenilda: 'Mother and daughter competed in piety, testing who was the more humble, who could be the more lowly: the mother exalted above herself the virginity of the child she had borne; the daughter held her mother's authority in greater esteem.'[76] And the *Vita Sexburge* provides an interesting comparison between that saint and her virgin sister Æthelthryth. It is fitting, we are told, that just as both were sisters in the flesh, both were queens on earth and both became the brides of Christ, so both should receive worthy veneration. They were not, however, of equal merit, for their virtues were different in kind. Æthelthryth was famed for *uirginitas*, Sexburga for *continentia*. Æthelthryth remained inviolate amid the temptations of the flesh; Sexburga 'dwelt in holy devotion among the embraces of the flesh'. Æthelthryth preserved her virginity in two marriage chambers; Sexburga 'in married union abounded in the fruits of good works'.[77] Both here and in what follows there is perhaps a slightly uncomfortable awareness that Sexburga, as the exponent rather of *continentia* than of *uirginitas*, represented, within the hierarchy of monastic values, something of a 'second best'. But this slight discomfort was not such as to persuade the hagiographer to bring his subject 'down to earth' and to seek out a more positive relationship between her fulfilment of royal duty and her attainment of sanctity. The hagiographical solution to the problem of the

---

caritate exultabat in Christi libertate . . . Tunc inquam in luce apparuit, qualis sub coniugali nexu in oculis Domini uixerit, quibus estibus, crucibus, gemitibus, suspiriis, uitam beatissime germane sue Erkengode uirginis Christi in se zelata sit, et hunc diem non maritalis funeris sed diuine obsequutionis desiderauerit. Extimplo ad precellentissimum Elig monasterium confugit' (TCC O.2.1, fols. 229–229v; CCC 393, fol. 73v; Caligula A. viii, fols. 96v–97).

76 *Vita Werburge*, col. 102. Cf. the role accorded to Wulfthryth as teacher of and moral example to her virgin daughter throughout the *Vita Edithe*.

77 TCC O.2.1, fols. 224v–225; Caligula A. viii, fols. 117v–118: 'Condecens igitur est ut quemadmodum ambe sorores germane, ambe regine in seculo, ambe unius professionis titulo decorate, ambe regis eterni insignite sponsalibus extiterunt, ambas condigna ueneratione condignis prosequamur laudibus. Non ut in illis paribus paria conferamus, quippe cum equalis eas dicamus non fuisse meriti, quas diuina gratia dispari uirtutum flore perornauit. Illam uirginitate, istam continentia. Illam inter carnis incendia inuiolatam, istam inter carnales complexus in sancta deuotione seruauit. Illam inter duorum coniugum thalamos perpetua uirginitate dotauit; istam in maritali copula bonorum operum fecundauit incrementis.'

royal widow was, in the last resort, little more than a compromise: Sexburga and her daughter, reluctant victims of the political institution of marriage, are somewhat crudely portrayed as frustrated virgins redeemed only by the accident of their widowhood and their consequent belated entry into the religious life. For the royal widows as for their virgin daughters the only path to sanctity lay through the cloister.

'REX ET MARTYR'

It was not only among the royal ladies of Anglo-Saxon England that the religious life exercised a strong appeal. In Bede's *Historia ecclesiastica*, for instance, both the crowned monk and the pilgrim king found a place. Sebbi, king of the East Saxons, ended his days as a monk; the West Saxon Caedwalla abdicated in order to receive baptism at Rome; Cenred of Mercia and Offa of Essex each ended their lives as monks in Rome.[78] But Bede's reaction to rulers of this type was ambivalent. In one particularly poignant story he provides some insight into the tensions created by kingly withdrawal from the world. Sigebert, seventh-century king of the East Angles, abdicated and retired to a monastery which he had founded. Thereafter the kingdom was invaded by the heathen Penda of Mercia, and the uncomprehending East Angles begged their erstwhile ruler to go with them into battle. When he refused, they dragged him from the monastery to the battlefield, where, refusing to carry more than a stick, he was killed by the heathen 'and the whole army was either slain or scattered'. Bede's praise of Sigebert is muted. He is not described as a saint, and there is at least a hint that the withdrawal so praised in the royal ladies was perhaps deemed inappropriate in a king – that Sigebert, although a good and religious man, was ultimately rather misguided.[79]

In the figure of Oswald, king of Northumbria, Bede found a model of kingly sanctity which was more to his liking. Oswald, like Sigebert, was killed by Penda; but the circumstances of his death were very different. For the almost accidental death of Sigebert was substituted a death in battle *pro patria* and *contra*

[78] *HE*, IV, 11; V, 7, 19.
[79] *Ibid.*, III, 18 (tr. p. 269). Bede seems to have regarded with similar ambivalence the monastic aspirations of the East Saxon Sebbi. Such actions, he seems to suggest, although laudable, were not quite kingly: 'multis uisum et saepe dictum est, quia talis animi uirum episcopum magis quam regem ordinari deceret' (*ibid.*, IV, 11).

paganos. Bede seems to have had little hesitation in recognising as a saint a ruler who, far from renouncing his royal duty, met his death by its fulfilment.[80]

Abbo's Edmund was a variation on the theme of *rex et martyr*. Like Oswald, and in striking contrast to the royal ladies, Edmund attained sanctity not by the manner of his life but rather by the nature of his death, by his suffering martyrdom at the hands of the pagan. To Abbo as to Bede, the single and crucial act upon which sanctity was founded represented not the renunciation of royal status but the fulfilment of royal duty. The background which Abbo sketches in his opening passages is of central importance to his interpretation of Edmund's sanctity. Here the hagiographer carefully draws out the tragic contrast between Edmund, a highly idealised Christian king, and the tyranny of the Danes. Edmund, we are told, was from his earliest childhood 'a devotee most true of the Christian faith'; he was elevated to the throne not so much by due course of election as by the ardent will of the people; he bore himself with courtesy and modesty; he was pleasing in appearance, his physical beauty reflecting his inner peace. Personal virtue was translated into righteous government. Abbo's Edmund was *rex iustus*, dispensing benefits to the meek and censure to the wicked; he was helper of the helpless, protector of the widow and the orphan; his guiding principle was the Biblical 'Have they made you a prince? Be not exalted, but be among them as one of them.'[81] The Danes, in stark contrast, were agents of 'the enemy of the human race',[82] whose aim it became to test the patience of the Christian king. Their leader was 'minister of evil',[83] and the nature of their rule is shockingly revealed in Abbo's account of their arrival in Edmund's kingdom. The pagan leader *Hinguar*

landed by stealth at a city in that region, entered it and before the citizens knew what was happening set it on fire. Boys, and men old and young, whom he met in the city streets were killed; and he paid no respect to the

[80] For Oswald's death see *ibid.*, III, 9: the king 'pro patria dimicans a paganis interfectus est'. Bede does not call Oswald a martyr, but his special reverence for the king is suggested by his statement that 'Cuius quanta fides in Deum, quae deuotio mentis fuerit, etiam post mortem uirtutum miraculis claruit.' The following cc. 10–13 are devoted to the history of Oswald's relics and the miracles performed through his intercession.

[81] *Passio Edmundi*, pp. 70–1 (citing Ecclus. 32:1). Abbo's Edmund corresponds closely to the author's concept of the ideal Christian king as this is revealed in his other writings: see Abbo, *Collectio canonum*, in *PL*, CXXXIX, cols. 473–508. The theme of Edmund as ideal Christian king was later adopted and elaborated by Geoffrey of Wells in his *De infantia, sancti Edmundi*. [82] *Passio Edmundi*, p. 71. [83] *Ibid.*, p. 72.

chastity of wife or virgin. Husband and wife lay dead or dying on their threshold; the infant, snatched from its mother's breast, was killed before her eyes. The wicked soldiers scoured the town in fury, thirsting after every crime which might satisfy the tyrant who from sheer love of cruelty had ordered the massacre of the innocent.[84]

In the sequel it becomes apparent that Edmund is to be denied the opportunity to meet the tyrant in battle; his men have been massacred in order to prevent such an encounter. Instead his trial is that of the Christian king forced to enter into negotiations with the heathen. *Hinguar*, Abbo notes, sent to Edmund a messenger bearing an ultimatum:

'My master, the invincible king *Hinguar*, a terror by land and sea . . . has come with a great fleet to the shores of this province to winter here; and on that account he commands that you share with him your ancient treasures and your hereditary wealth and reign in future under him. But if you despise his power . . . you will be judged unworthy both of your kingdom and of your life.'[85]

Edmund's dilemma is clear. He must rule as sub-king under a pagan leader whose beliefs and actions were directly antithetical to those of the Christian ruler; or he must be prepared to meet his death at the hands of that pagan leader. In a series of carefully constructed speeches, addressed in part to one of Edmund's bishops and in part to the heathen messenger, Abbo works out the response of the Christian king. Rejecting the bishop's advice that he either submit or take flight, Edmund expresses his distaste for the self-betrayal which such action would represent[86] and stresses, in Christian-heroic terms, his reluctance to outlive his slaughtered companions. At the heart of his argument, however, lay the question of faith. His decision centres on what is in effect a confession of faith: 'The almighty disposer of events is present as my witness that, whether I live or die, nothing shall separate me from the love of Christ, the ring of whose faith I took upon me in the sacrament of baptism.'[87] Submission to the heathen would be a betrayal not only of his pride and of his people but also, and more importantly, of his God:

'And thus . . . I have determined to be the benefactor of the English people, in scorning to bow my neck to any yoke but that of the service of God . . . He allows me life, for which I no longer care; he promises me a kingdom, which I already have; he would give me riches, for which I have

---

84 *Ibid.*, pp. 72–3.   85 *Ibid.*, p. 74.
86 *Ibid.*, p. 75, cited above, p. 67, n. 239.   87 *Ibid.*

no need. For these things should I now begin to serve two masters – I, who have dedicated myself in the presence of my court to live and to rule under Christ alone?'[88]

The sequence culminates in Edmund's own ultimatum to *Hinguar*: 'Know therefore that for the love of this earthly life the Christian king Edmund will not submit to a heathen chief unless first you come fully to share in our religion; he would rather be a standard-bearer in the camp of the eternal king.'[89] The action of the pagan leader was swift: Edmund's martyrdom was a direct and immediate product of that moral choice which represented the ultimate fulfilment of his duty as a Christian king.

A very different approach to the sanctity of a 'martyred' ruler is found in the *Passio Edwardi*. Edward was murdered by fellow-countrymen and fellow-Christians for reasons of political expediency. His death, moreover, involved no moral choice: it took place quite simply because he had the misfortune to be in the wrong place at the wrong time and with the wrong people. It was accordingly difficult for even the most thoughtful hagiographer to formulate any direct relationship, positive or negative, between Edward's status as a Christian king and his attainment of sanctity by 'martyr-dom'. The author of the *Passio* did not even try. He did portray Edward as a good Christian king,[90] and he did present his murder as the devil's work:[91] but he drew no significant conclusions either concerning Edward's moral state or even concerning the general evil of regicide. In so far as his work has any central theme at all, it belongs to a quite distinct hagiographical tradition – that of the martyred innocent. Edward the king is absorbed into, and dominated by, Edward the meekest of lambs going forth unsuspecting to the slaughter.[92]

---

[88] *Ibid.*, p. 76.   [89] *Ibid.*, p. 78.

[90] *Passio Edwardi*, p. 3. The earlier account of the *Vita Oswaldi* in contrast mentions only the harshness of Edward's temperament, citing this as a reason for the opposition of some magnates to his succession (p. 449).   [91] *Passio Edwardi*, pp. 3–4.

[92] Edward, going alone to visit his brother at Corfe, 'tanquam agnus mitissimus tendit, neminem uerens aut pertimescens, qui nec in minimis quidem aliquem se offendisse recognoscebat'; he is *rex innocens*; and one of the conspirators, who offered the kiss of peace to the victim, is likened to Judas, betrayer of Christ (*Passio Edwardi*, pp. 4, 5, 8). The author of the *Vita Oswaldi* writes in similar vein (p. 449): 'Insidiantes et maligni quærebant animam innocentis, cui Christus prædestinavit et præscivit consortem fieri martyrii dignitatis.' This narrative, like the *Anglo-Saxon Chronicle*, shows a greater awareness than does the *Passio* of the special horror of the crime of regicide.

Chapter 4

THE CULT OF ST EDBURGA AT WINCHESTER AND PERSHORE

THE HISTORICAL EDBURGA

Ita generosa uirgo et sponsa summi regis Eadburga uite subtracta presentis ergastulo, in confessione uere fidei et unius Dei cognitione migrauit ad celum, cum sacris coronanda uirginibus sanctorum subuecta presidiis angelorum . . . Et quia uestibus auro textis que regio generi congruunt nullatenus gloriabatur, nec suorum splendore natalium insolescere uoluit, circumdata uarietate uirtutum, agnum sponsum meruit uirgineo uellere candidatum.[1]

The Edburga created by Osbert of Clare was a royal lady whose sanctity was a product exclusively of her role within the church. As such, it was founded upon the renunciation of royal status and duty, upon commitment to the ideal of chastity and upon the fulfilment of a role antithetical to that commonly expected of a young lady of royal birth. But how real was this theoretical – and highly conventional – antithesis between the *uirgo regia* and the *sponsa summi regis*? Did the hagiographer, in selecting this as his principal theme, perhaps obscure the real role of the historical Edburga?

For an understanding of Edburga's historical role the scene is set by Osbert's introductory genealogical passages. It has been suggested above that these passages serve a two-fold purpose within the *Vita*.[2] First, they enhance the prestige of the saint by her association with a highly praised tradition of Christian rulership; second, and by no means incongruously, they provide a starting-point for the working out of the theme that sanctity might be attained only by renunciation of that same royal association. But Osbert's genealogical passages have a third function, of at least equal importance, within his narrative. They establish a historical connection between the West Saxon royal house and the religious

---

[1] *Vita Edburge*, fol. 96v.   [2] See above, pp. 83–4.

community within which Edburga's life was to be spent. In so doing, they place the saint within a political context; and they strongly suggest that the ecclesiastical role upon which Edburga's sanctity was founded could not be separable from, but was rather a direct product of, her birth into the West Saxon royal dynasty.

Osbert's account of Edburga's ancestry is centred upon the importance of her family in the foundation and endowment of the religious houses of Winchester.[3] Thus a general introduction to Alfred's piety and love of learning culminates in the statement that, among his other good works, 'inspired by divine grace, he began the New Minster at Winchester'. And of his consort's activities only one was considered relevant to Osbert's narrative – her initiative in the foundation of Nunnaminster. Osbert goes on to draw out the full implications of these acts of royal piety, making clear both the central importance of royal involvement in every stage of foundation and the continuity of that involvement. Thus Ealhswith is said to have been responsible at Nunnaminster for each of the four major processes of foundation – for the construction of monastic buildings, for the collection of a group of nuns, for the appointment of Æthelthryth as abbess and for the provision of the community's endowment. And it is emphasised that, following the death of both king and consort, their son, Edward the Elder, brought to completion their plans: the establishment of the church in Winchester became part of the inherited tradition of West Saxon royal obligation. Osbert here describes a relationship of a very specific kind between the West Saxon royal house and the religious communities of Winchester. Alfred and Ealhswith had each created a royal *Eigenkloster* on a traditional model, within which the founder remained in a real sense the proprietor of the new community, within which proprietary rights over land and buildings were translated into supervisory rights over the community, and within which those rights were vested not only in the original founder but also in his or her successors in the royal line.[4] To the members of the

---

[3] *Vita Edburge*, fol. 87v.

[4] For the history of the *Eigenkloster*, and in particular of the royal *Eigenkloster*, in England see especially H. Boehmer, 'Das Eigenkirchentum in England', in Boehmer *et al.* (eds.), *Texte und Forschungen zur Englischen Kulturgeschichte: Festgabe für Felix Liebermann* (Halle, 1921), pp. 301–53; W. Levison, *England and the continent in the eighth century: the Ford Lectures delivered in the University of Oxford in the Hilary Term, 1943* (Oxford, 1946; repr. 1973), pp. 27–33; *MO*, pp. 569–70, 589–90; Barlow, *English church, 1000–1066*, pp. 315–17. For the royal nunneries of Wessex see especially M. A. Meyer, 'Patronage of the West Saxon royal nunneries in late Anglo-Saxon England', *Revue Bénédictine* 91 (1981), 332–58.

house of Cerdic that relationship was significant as an expression of piety and as a path to prestige; to New Minster and Nunnaminster it represented the whole means of origin and survival: the religious houses of the late ninth and early tenth centuries were no less dependent upon royal support than were those of the 960s and 970s whose debt received elaborate acknowledgement in the *Regularis concordia*.

The religious community to which the infant Edburga was sent was, therefore, bound by the closest ties of dependence to the family of the saint. And to the members of that community the presence of the *uirgo regia* had a profound symbolic and political significance. It constituted, first, a potent symbol of the strength and continuity of the bond which existed between royal dynasty and royal foundation. The point was clearly appreciated by Osbert, who chose to conclude his account of Edburga's vocation by reminding his audience of Nunnaminster's royal origin: 'The church of the Blessed Virgin Mary, Mother of God, which St Edburga's grandmother, Queen Ealhswith, began and was prevented by death from completing, having been finished by King Edward and his pious consort, was dedicated by Ælfheah the Elder, bishop of Winchester.'[5] The political significance of Edburga's entry to the nunnery can be more fully documented. Osbert's exposition of the saint's spiritual excellence is centred upon five major episodes – upon Edburga's *contretemps* with the prioress, demonstrating her *patientia* and *humilitas* (c. 3), upon her secret shoe-cleaning ministry and its sequel (cc. 4 and 5), upon the *Canaga* episode (cc. 6 and 7), upon her charity to the poor (c. 8) and upon her pious death (cc. 11–12). Each of these episodes is intended to illustrate that devotion to the monastic ideal, and to the needs of others, which the hagiographer presented as a product of the saint's renunciation of her secular status. Taken together, they demonstrate that devotion to the church depended for its effectiveness upon precisely that secular status which the saint had in theory renounced.

Of these episodes the two first provide a fascinating insight into the attitude of the Winchester nuns towards their royal charge. On one occasion, we are told, the prioress, finding a member of the community reading alone and disturbed by this breach of monastic discipline, beat the errant nun without realising her identity.

---

[5] *Vita Edburge*, fol. 88v.

Thereafter, on recognising that the culprit was none other than Edburga, she immediately prostrated herself before her and begged forgiveness.[6] Her apologies, it seems, were the product not of any recognition of Edburga's special virtue but rather of the respect due to her royal status. The prioress apologised because she had struck, not a saint, but *principis filiam*: it was taken for granted that the royal child should stand outside the rules which bound the rest of the community; she should be handled, even when plainly disregarding monastic discipline, with kid gloves. A similar attitude underlies the story of the saint's secret shoe-cleaning ministry. The hagiographer's enthusiasm for his subject's *humilitas* was clearly not shared by the beneficiaries of her good deed. Instead she received a public rebuke for an act of service which was seen as a betrayal of her royal status: '"It is unseemly", they said, "for a royal child to bow her neck to such humble service and to set about the work of a common slave; it is harmful to the dignity of her illustrious birth."'[7] That virtue most praised by the hagiographer was regarded with the greatest trepidation by a religious community which sought nothing more than that Edburga should act in accordance with the conventions of her royal status.

The reason for this monastic trepidation is made explicit in the sequel to the shoe-cleaning incident. King Edward, the hagiographer notes, came to Winchester and, with suitable paternal concern, made discreet enquiries about the conduct of his daughter. He received from the nuns a generally favourable report, but it was nevertheless clear that they were holding something back: 'Still they wavered and trembled . . . afraid to relate that deed which was detestable to all, lest they be struck down by the king's anger.'[8] Edward, however, was not easily put off; the nuns were eventually compelled to 'come clean' – and one can almost hear the corporate sigh of relief when the king reacted favourably to the news of his daughter's somewhat unorthodox behaviour.

Good relations, then, were maintained between Edward and the nuns, and the value of those good relations to the religious community is made clear in the following chapters 6 and 7 of Osbert's work. Together these recount the manner in which Edburga persuaded her father to endow Nunnaminster with the estate of *Canaga*, which had passed into his hands through the exercise of royal justice. The story may not be accurate in all its details; but

[6] *Ibid.*, fol. 89.   [7] *Ibid.*, fol. 89v.   [8] *Ibid.*, fol. 90.

there is no reason to doubt that such an incident took place, and the amount of space which Osbert devotes to it suggests that it was of considerable importance within Edburga's career.[9] The occasion of the gift of *Canaga* to Nunnaminster was a further visit of Edward to Winchester 'to see again his beloved child in the holy community'.[10] The king, wishing Edburga to sing for his entertainment, overcame her very proper reluctance by the promise of a just reward. This promise provided the cue for Edburga to disavow all worldly interests and to outline instead the needs of the church. Her emphasis fell upon Nunnaminster's origin in an act of royal patronage and upon Edward's continuing royal obligation: '"Let your royal will bring to fruition that which your mother's bounteous love began, and let the maidenly throng receive for their subsistence that which has fallen to you through the misdeed of your followers."'[11] The child's plea was successful, and *Canaga* passed to the nunnery, in whose possession it remained until Osbert's day.

Nunnaminster's acquisition of *Canaga* was not a more or less accidental by-product of Edburga's characteristic *humilitas* and self-denial. Rather it seems to have been the result of a carefully conceived plan, initiated not by the saint herself but by the nuns among whom she had been placed. During Edward's reign, Osbert informs us, the sole endowment of Nunnaminster was an estate within Winchester itself, presumably that granted by Ealhswith at the time of the original foundation.[12] This was less than adequate to meet the needs of the community, and so the nuns came to rely for assistance upon Edburga.[13] Their reliance, it seems, was not founded upon recognition of Edburga's special virtue and consequent access to divine protection. Rather the protection which the nuns sought lay very firmly in this world, and it was in her this-worldly connections that Edburga's usefulness lay: she was begged to appeal to her father for a gift which might solve the community's problem.[14] There follows in Osbert's narrative a detailed account of the forfeiture to the king of *Canaga* following a brawl in the royal court between two soldiers, Alla and Muluca. The nuns seized the opportunity. Having ascertained that the estate was suitable for their purposes, they 'whispered in the saint's ear' that this would be an appropriate moment to approach her father. Edburga, left in no doubt as to the urgency of the matter, accord-

[9] For discussion of this incident see above, p. 33 and n. 87. The story occupies fols. 90–92v of the *Vita Edburge*.   [10] *Vita Edburge*, fol. 91.   [11] *Ibid.*, fol. 92.
[12] *Ibid.*; see above, p. 32.   [13] *Vita Edburge*, fol. 90v.   [14] *Ibid.*

ingly strove to carry through the wishes of her fellows, 'so that through her efforts the wealth of the nunnery might be greatly increased'.[15] It was, therefore, at the bidding of the community that Edburga approached the king for the grant of *Canaga*; and it was surely with the this-worldly needs of the nuns in mind that she spoke to her father thus:

There are some, established in the wilderness, who on account of the grief of their pilgrimage and their ardent desire to contemplate the face of God are prevented neither by the pains of hunger nor by thirst from divine contemplation. These, because they have risen above the sufferings of the flesh, abhor the pleasures of the flesh. And while they seek to provide for the spirit, they easily deny themselves the delights of corporal food. But the weaker multitude and the inferior sex are not endowed with that fortitude; for them it is impossible to live without bodily sustenance.[16]

The saint, it appears, was manipulated from the outset by those of the nuns who had made a careful assessment of her potential usefulness. And, within the *sancta congregatio*, the usefulness of the *uirgo regia* was, first and foremost, that of *mediatrix ad regem*.[17]

Edburga's presence at Nunnaminster, then, provided for that community an important means of access to the king: the saint became a crucial focus for the working out in practice of the relationship between the religious community and the royal dynasty to which it was bound. More than this, the commitment of the royal child to that house in itself constituted an act of patronage. Not only did it substantially enhance the prestige of the house; it also meant the immediate acquisition of wealth. Edburga's entry to the religious life must have been accompanied by a gift to the community either in land or in moveable wealth.[18] Osbert makes no explicit reference to such a gift or dowry, but he does give some indication of the type of moveable wealth which was believed to have entered the nunnery with the king's daughter and to have remained there after her death. He describes the subsequent fate of the gospel-book which was placed before Edburga on the occasion of her vocation, and in so doing he gives some indication of the

---

[15] *Ibid.*, fol. 91.   [16] *Ibid.*, fol. 92.
[17] *Ibid.*, fol. 90v: introducing the story of Alla and Muluca, Osbert notes 'Hec est occasio que se ultro intulit qua ad regem uirgo regia mediatrix accessit.'
[18] The early history of the gift at entry or 'dowry' of those entering the religious life is difficult to reconstruct in detail. For an interesting examination of the subject see J. H. Lynch, *Simoniacal entry into religious life from 1000 to 1260: a social, economic and legal study* (Ohio State University Press, 1976), with an introduction on the Rule of St Benedict and the history of the gift at entry prior to 1000.

wealth which the richly adorned codex represented: 'That gospel-book of which I have already spoken was stripped of its gold and silver by the Danes who raged madly through England, but many years later . . . it was skilfully restored to its former splendour.'[19]

On two further occasions Edburga is seen to have used wealth of a personal nature for the benefit of the community and for the furtherance of its aims. Osbert notes, first, that the saint was renowned for her charity to the poor.[20] Here he quite explicitly alludes to, and justifies, that retention of personal wealth within the community which to the monasticism of a later age was wholly uncanonical: 'At that time the nuns of that house were allowed to have an abundance of personal riches, since all that they possessed was used for the maintenance of religion . . . The law of the stricter Rule by which God is now served in the monasteries was still at that time completely unknown and the teachings of the holy father Benedict were not yet observed.'[21] Second, Osbert describes thus the mourning which followed Edburga's death: 'The daughters of Syon wept for the daughter of Juda, who in affection had divided among them those things which were hers, so that by benefits of this kind she might be more assiduously commended to them.'[22] It was by their endowment with what remained of her earthly property that Edburga ensured that her soul would be speeded on its way to heaven by the prayers of the nuns. The saint's death was significant not simply as the culmination of a virtuous life: it brought also a final act of patronage.

It seems, then, that Osbert of Clare, in presenting Edburga's sanctity as the product of an ecclesiastical role both divorced from and antithetical to her royal status, told only a part of the story: and, in so doing, he seriously obscured the historical Edburga. Edburga's sanctity, according to the hagiographer, was founded upon her withdrawal from the world: relinquishing *et populum suum et paternam domum*,[23] she devoted herself instead *ad illum qui speciosus est forma prae filiis hominum*.[24] But to look below the surface of the hagiographical theory is to reveal a reality in which the saint's withdrawal had rather limited practical consequences. In physical terms it meant no more than a short stroll from her father's palace in Winchester to her monastic home;[25] certainly it did not lead to complete severance from her royal father. More than this, the

---

[19] *Vita Edburge*, fol. 88.   [20] *Ibid.*, fol. 93.   [21] *Ibid.*   [22] *Ibid.*, fol. 96v.
[23] *Ibid.*, fol. 99, citing Ps. 44:11.   [24] Cf. *ibid.*, fols. 104, 110, citing Ps. 44:3.
[25] On the presence of a royal residence in Winchester see below, p. 115.

monastic environment into which Edburga moved was a highly politicised one. Her withdrawal was not to those religious who, 'established in the wilderness', were in no circumstances distracted from the service of God; it was to a royal foundation within an important *ciuitas regia*.[26] The community was, no doubt, predominantly aristocratic in composition: so much is suggested by Osbert's statement that the initial community was assembled by Alfred's consort and by his endowment of the abbess Alfghiua with a thoroughly aristocratic genealogy.[27] And the nuns retained a close interest in the political affairs of the royal and aristocratic world. The *Canaga* episode shows them to have been thoroughly conversant with the workings of the royal court and to have proceeded with sound political sense in the utilisation of their knowledge for the furtherance of their corporate aims.

In these circumstances the saint, in theory 'far removed from worldly cares',[28] was neither expected nor allowed actually to forget her royal status. Rather that status became both a symbol and a tool in the hands of a religious community which realised with some trepidation that the presence of the *uirgo regia* was potentially either its greatest asset or a tremendous liability. At best, it represented to the Winchester nuns a symbol of royal approval, a source of considerable immediate wealth and a means of continued access to the ear of the king; at worst, it made ever-present the fear of the royal wrath. In the delicate task of bringing up the royal child, the Winchester nuns took a gamble and won. Edburga lived up to their expectations; and that she did so was a result not of the renunciation of her royal status and connections but rather of the readiness with which she allowed that status and those connections to subserve the needs of the religious community. In practice, there could be no antithesis between the *uirgo regia* and the *sponsa summi regis*. Edburga's story was not only one of piety but also one of patronage: her ecclesiastical function is intelligible only in terms of the services rendered by the *filia principis* to the *filie Syon*.

THE INCEPTION OF CULT

Quieuit itaque aliquanto tempore in eodem quo condita est loculo Eadburga incorruptibilis et splendida uirgo, donec choruscantibus miraculis sepultura ipsius celebris habita est et insignis, et signorum

[26] *Vita Edburge*, fol. 107; cf. below, pp. 114–15.   [27] *Vita Edburge*, fol. 107v.
[28] *Vita Edburge*, fol. 97.

celestium ex undanti plenitudine per mundum sparsit radios immortalis
uite.[29]

Edburga died, according to Osbert, in her thirtieth year,[30] and was
buried in a humble tomb outside the monastic church. Here she
remained until a specific miraculous occurrence reminded the nuns
that their royal sister perhaps merited a more honourable resting-
place.[31] Adjacent to the saint's tomb was a window which it was
the duty of one of the sisters to close every evening. On one
occasion, however, she was prevented from doing so by a mysterious pressure from outside. At first she assumed that this was a quite
ordinary human prank, but when she failed to trace the culprit, and
when the mysterious event was repeated on three successive
evenings, she became convinced of its divine origin and accordingly drew the matter to the attention of her fellows. The event was

---

[29] *Ibid.*, fols. 97v–98.

[30] The date of Edburga's death cannot be accurately established. It is placed by Laurel
Braswell, I. G. Thomas and D. H. Farmer, none of whom name their sources, at the year
960 (Braswell, 'St Edburga', p. 292; Thomas, 'Cult of relics', p. 106; *ODS*, p. 118). *VCH*
and KH, in contrast, each cite the year 925 (*VCH Hants.*, II, 122; KH, p. 268). Osbert of
Clare unfortunately gives his reader no dates, but he does provide a chronology which
seems to cast doubt on each of these proposed death dates. He states that Edburga was
placed in the nunnery at the age of three and that she died in her thirtieth year (*Vita
Edburge*, fols. 88, 97v). This chronology – if we are to take it seriously – suggests that, if
Edburga's death is to be placed in 925, her birth must be dated to *c.* 895 and her entry to
Nunnaminster to *c.* 898: but the foundation of Nunnaminster seems not to have been
completed until after the accession of Edward in 899 (see above, p. 32). Osbert also
stresses that the commitment of the three-year-old child to Nunnaminster took place on
the initiative of her father. Edward died in 924: hence, if Osbert's narrative is to be
accorded any credence, his daughter's birth must be dated, at the latest, to *c.* 921 and her
death, at the latest, to *c.* 951. Three further pieces of evidence combine to suggest a date in
the early 950s for the saint's death. First, Edburga was Edward's daughter by his third
wife: I have been unable to trace a date for the marriage of Edward and Edgiva, but it is
interesting to note that the future King Edmund, one of the sons of the marriage, was
probably born in 921 (*HBC*, p. 26). Second, the charter of Athelstan to his sister
Edburga, if genuine, clearly indicates that the saint was still alive in 939 (see above, p. 17).
And, third, the Worcester annals include a prayer to St Edburga *s.a.* 953 (*Annales de
Wigornia*, p. 370), thus indicating that by the fourteenth century this was believed to be
the date of her death: it is not impossible that for once these notoriously untrustworthy
annals preserve a reliable tradition.

Yet another tradition places the saint's death in the early 930s. The Harleian account
notes that Edburga died in 932, in her thirtieth year (MS Harley 64, fol. 84v). And the
flyleaf note in MS Bodley 451 (see below, Appendix 2) states that 219 years elapsed
between Edburga's death and the year 1150. This death date of 931/2 does not conflict
with Osbert's account of Edburga's commitment to Nunnaminster by her father at the
age of three and of her death in her thirtieth year. It is, however, incompatible with the
Athelstan charter of 939 and – unless we are to assume that the saint actually died in her
early teens – with the fact that she was Edward's daughter by his third wife. More likely,
therefore, it is to the early 950s that the saint's death is to be dated.

[31] *Vita Edburge*, fols. 100–101v.

immediately hailed as a manifestation of the divine will: the window which could not be closed was perceived as a sign that Edburga should be raised from her humble tomb and translated to a more worthy resting-place. Great excitement ensued; the community's previous negligence was duly lamented; and Edburga was rather hastily raised from her unworthy tomb and given a second burial outside the choir of the monastic church.[32] This, however, was not the end of the matter. The saint appeared to the nuns and expressed her continuing dissatisfaction. The nuns tried again, this time with more success: the saint was moved, in accordance with her own command, to a still more prestigious resting-place beside the high altar of the church.[33]

The inception of St Edburga's cult is portrayed by Osbert of Clare as a product less of human devotion than of divine bullying. The virtues and the will of the saint were made manifest by her performance of miracles, and the unfortunate nuns were dragooned into behaving accordingly. But a faulty window becomes a sign of the divine will only to those who wish to perceive it as such, and saintly messages are relayed in visions only to those who have an interest in hearing those messages. The real initiative in the promotion of Edburga's cult came, it is clear, from the Winchester nuns. And in these circumstances the 'sanctification' of the *uirgo regia* is intelligible only in terms of her historical role within the community of Nunnaminster. That role was not only one of vigils, *uirginitas* and exaggerated humility. It was also, perhaps more importantly, one of patronage: Edburga had been both a much-loved and an extremely useful member of the community. It is not therefore surprising that the nuns were predisposed to look for miracles in the vicinity of her tomb. Nor is it surprising that, having found those miracles, they were predisposed to take the all-important step of arranging a translation. The history of the inception of St Edburga's cult at Nunnaminster is that of the transition of royal patron into patron saint.

ST EDBURGA AND THE TENTH-CENTURY REFORM

The establishment of Edburga's cult at Nunnaminster was a direct product and an appropriate culmination of her historical role as sister and patron within that community. But to explain the

---

[32] *Ibid.*, fol. 101v.   [33] *Ibid.*

inception of cult is to tell only a part of the story. A cult, once established, did not simply develop under its own momentum: it had to be actively fostered and advertised, and it had to be adapted to serve needs which would from time to time slacken or intensify and which might on occasion undergo a complete reorientation. Under what circumstances, then, was Edburga's cult sustained? And what were the factors which stimulated its further development?

Osbert of Clare placed that development firmly within the context of the tenth-century monastic reform.[34] He speaks first of the concord of *regnum* and *sacerdotium* which characterised the reign of Edgar and which made possible the establishment of regular Benedictine monasticism. Thereafter we are given a brief guided tour of the monastic foundations of St Æthelwold and an introduction to his work as promoter of the cults of the saints. Finally Osbert notes that the bishop, witnessing Edburga's miracles, recognising her glory and encouraged by visions, determined that her relics should be translated to a silver shrine. The abbess and community of Nunnaminster were duly consulted and with their support, in the presence of the conventional crowd of clergy and people, the saint was raised from her tomb and laid to rest in a richly decorated shrine.

Osbert's account of this translation is wholly consistent with what is known of the nature and history of the tenth-century reform both within Winchester and elsewhere. Æthelwold, formerly abbot of Abingdon, was appointed by King Edgar to the see of Winchester in 963.[35] Within a year of his consecration, and after a dramatic confrontation, he had expelled from his cathedral church the 'evil-living clerics' and had replaced these with monks from Abingdon; the clerks of New Minster had likewise been replaced by monks; and in Winchester's third religious house a community of nuns had been established under the leadership of an

---

[34] *Ibid.*, fols. 101v–103v.
[35] *ASC*, A, E, *s.a.* 963. Two early Lives of Æthelwold survive – a *Vita* by Ælfric, dateable to the year 1006, and a *Vita* by Wulfstan, written after Æthelwold's translation in 996. The most recent edition of each of these Lives is that of Michael Winterbottom (*Three Lives*, pp. 17–29 (Ælfric), 33–63 (Wulfstan); see also pp. 1–4, 6–7.). For Æthelwold's role in the tenth-century reform the secondary literature is extensive: see especially *MO*, pp. 36–57; Robinson, *Times*, ch. 5; Farmer, 'Progress of the monastic revival'; E. John, 'The king and the monks in the tenth-century reformation', in John, *Orbis Britanniae*, pp. 154–80; John, 'The beginning of the Benedictine reform in England', in *Orbis Britanniae*, pp. 249–64.

Abbess Æthelthryth.[36] Osbert of Clare makes no explicit reference to Æthelwold's refoundation of Nunnaminster but notes generally that the churches of Winchester were the first to benefit from Æthelwold's work of refoundation.[37] Thereafter, having set his own house in order, Æthelwold turned his attentions elsewhere – to the establishment of the new monasticism at Ely, Peterborough and Thorney.[38]

The monastic revival thus instituted by Æthelwold, together with his contemporaries Dunstan and Oswald, is best known as a spiritual movement having as its purpose the introduction and enforcement of regular Benedictine monasticism.[39] It was also, of necessity, a material and political reform, involving both the reconstruction and the re-endowment (or, at the very least, reorganisation of the endowment) of the religious houses.[40] And equally importantly – and this aspect of the revival has been too little emphasised by historians – it was a movement closely associated with the promotion of the cults of the saints. In the overwhelming majority of cases the cults thus promoted were those of men or women who had been associated with a religious community in an earlier, generally pre-Viking, incarnation. As such they provided for that community a link with its historical or legendary past; and they provided also a wonder-working patron in the present – a source not only of corporate prestige but also of considerable revenue.[41] Hence, for instance, Æthelwold's

---

[36] *Three Lives*, ed. Winterbottom, pp. 22–4 (Ælfric), 44–7 (Wulfstan); cf. *ASC*, A, *s.a.* 964; *GP*, p. 174.   [37] *Vita Edburge*, fol. 102.

[38] Ibid.; cf. *Three Lives*, ed. Winterbottom, pp. 24–5 (Ælfric), 47–8 (Wulfstan).

[39] See especially *MO*, pp. 42–8; *Regularis concordia anglicae nationis monachorum sanctimonialiumque*, ed. T. Symons, Nelson's Medieval Texts (1953); Symons, 'Regularis concordia: history and derivation', in Parsons (ed.), *Tenth-century studies*, pp. 37–59.

[40] For the implications of the reform for the endowments of religious houses see especially John, 'King and monks', where it is argued that the demise of English monasticism in the late ninth and early tenth centuries had been the result less of the depredations of the Danes than of *secularium prioratus* (*Regularis concordia*, ed. Symons, p. 7) – the dissipation of endowments by grants to local landowners, together with a tendency for individual members of religious communities to hold prebends *quasi propria*. In these circumstances, refoundation in the late tenth century may in many cases have involved not the creation of a new endowment but rather the reorganisation of an existing one – by the resumption of estates which had been granted either to local landowners or to individual members of the community and by the subsequent communalisation of this endowment. It is likely that reorganisation of this kind took place at both Winchester and Worcester (see John, 'King and monks', pp. 162–5); and for a suggestion that something of the sort was also happening at Ely see below, pp. 181–5.

[41] The importance of the cults of the saints within the refounded communities of the tenth century was highlighted by Thomas, 'Cult of relics', pp. 325–6. The spiritual and

refoundation of Ely was followed by the promotion of the cults of saints Æthelthryth, Sexburga and Eormenilda and by the thinly disguised theft from Dereham of the relics of St Withburga.[42] The relics of St Botulf and of his alleged brother Athulf were translated to the refounded Thorney, along with those of a mysterious trio, Tancred, Torhtred and Tova, said to have been hermits martyred by the Danes.[43] And in Northumbria Oswald was said to have been responsible for the translation at Ripon not only of that church's most famous saint, the royal martyr Oswald, but also of four early abbots of the house.[44]

Among the cults promoted during this period one in particular attained a sudden and staggering success – the cult at Winchester cathedral of Swithun, bishop of Winchester from *c.* 852 to *c.* 862. For the existence of Swithun's cult prior to Æthelwold's refoundation of Old Minster there is not a shred of evidence. By *c.* 975, however, Lantfred, a Winchester monk of continental origin, had produced a detailed and contemporary account of the emergence of that cult.[45] Its story began about the year 968, when Swithun began to work miracles and, in particular, to express dissatisfaction with his humble resting-place outside the west door of the church; it culminated on 15 July three years later, when Swithun's relics were solemnly translated into the church.

Swithun's translation seems to have coincided with the start of building work on the Old Minster church.[46] Certainly reconstruc-

political role of the local saint in this period has not, however, received the detailed attention which it undoubtedly deserves. I hope that this study of St Edburga, together with that of St Æthelthryth which follows in ch. 6, will do something to redress the balance; for more detailed examination of this subject see Ridyard, 'The cults of the saints in the tenth-century monastic revival', in M. J. Franklin and S. J. Ridyard (eds.), *Church and society in England, 500–1215* (forthcoming).

42 See below, pp. 185–6.

43 These saints are located at Thorney by the *Secgan* (*Heiligen*, ed. Liebermann, p. 15), and by a twelfth-century list in London, BL, MS Add. 40,000, fol. 11v. For full discussion of the Thorney cults see Thomas, 'Cult of relics', pp. 231–8.

44 *Vita Oswaldi*, p. 462.

45 The date of *c.* 975 for Lantfred's work is suggested by Michael Lapidge, to whom I am much indebted for my understanding of Swithun's cult. For Lapidge's detailed analysis of the legend and cult of St Swithun see WS4.ii. Lantfred's work is partially printed in *AASS*, Iul. 1 (1719), 321–37, and the remainder of the work is edited by E. P. Sauvage, 'Sancti Swithuni Wintoniensis episcopi translatio et miracula, auctore Lantfredo monacho Wintoniensi', *AB* 4 (1885), 367–410: my references are to this edition.

46 For the architectural history of Old Minster see WS4.i; also Biddle, '*Felix urbs Winthonia*', pp. 136–9; WS1, pp. 306–13. For a preliminary study based on written sources see R. N. Quirk, 'Winchester cathedral in the tenth century', *Archaeological Journal* 114 (1957), 28–68; for the excavations of 1961–71 see M. Biddle and R. N. Quirk, 'Excavations near Winchester cathedral, 1961', *Archaeological Journal* 119 (1962),

tion can hardly have begun before that event, for Swithun's grave
was in the open at the time of the translation, and the new building
dedicated in 980 was centred on the site of his original grave.[47] That
new building seems to have been intended as a shrine-church or
martyrium.[48] This design, however, was apparently never carried
out, and the completed building took the form of a west-work of
continental type, centred on the site of the saint's initial tomb, over
which a monument had been raised.[49] Biddle notes that 'The
connection between west-works, the tombs of saints, and the cult
of relics, well known on the Continent, seems clearly reflected
here, not least in the circumstance that this west-work had emerged
from an adaptation of an earlier and apparently unfinished
martyrium.'[50]

The cult of Swithun seems, therefore, to have been of central
importance in determining the form of the reconstructed Old
Minster church. Its importance is also reflected in the rapid development of a hagiographical tradition,[51] in the wide dissemination
of Swithun's relics[52] and in the entry of his two major feasts (the

150–94, and thereafter M. Biddle, 'Excavations at Winchester, 1962–   ', interim reports
published annually in *Antiquaries Journal* as follows: *2nd interim*, 44 (1964), 188–219; *3rd
interim*, 45 (1965), 230–64; *4th interim*, 46 (1966), 308–32; *5th interim*, 47 (1967), 251–79;
6th interim, 48 (1968), 250–84; *7th interim*, 49 (1969), 295–329; *8th interim*, 50 (1970),
277–326; *9th interim*, 52 (1972), 93–131; *10th interim*, 55 (1975), 96–126, 295–337. For
Swithun's translation and the commencement of reconstruction see Biddle, '*Felix urbs
Winthonia*', p. 136; WS1, p. 307.

47 'Lantfred, *Translatio*', ed. Sauvage, pp. 394–5; Biddle, *7th interim*, pp. 320–1; Biddle,
'*Felix urbs Winthonia*', pp. 136–8; WS1, p. 307. Rebuilding continued after 980 with the
reconstruction and extension of the east end, which was dedicated in 993/4.

48 Biddle, '*Felix urbs Winthonia*', p. 136.

49 That the reconstructed Old Minster church took the form of a west-work of continental
type was first suggested by Quirk, 'Winchester cathedral', pp. 43–56. This conclusion,
based on the evidence of the Swithun hagiography, was corroborated by the excavations of 1966–9: see Biddle, *8th interim*, pp. 315–17, 320–1; Biddle, '*Felix urbs Winthonia*',
p. 138; WS1, pp. 307–8. For the general architectural background see H. M. Taylor,
'Tenth-century church building in England and on the continent', in Parsons (ed.),
Tenth-century studies, pp. 141–68. See also, for a possible parallel to the Winchester west-
work, F. Kreusch, *Beobachtungen an der Westanlage der Klosterkirche zu Corvey*, Beihefte
der Bonner Jahrbucher 9 (Cologne–Graz, 1963).

50 Biddle, '*Felix urbs Winthonia*', p. 138; cf. Quirk, 'Winchester cathedral', p. 53.

51 For the early hagiography of Swithun see WS4.ii; the currently available editions are:
'Lantfred, *Translatio*', ed. Sauvage; *Frithegodi monachi breviloquium vitae beati Wilfredi et
Wulfstani cantoris narratio metrica de sancto Swithuno*, ed. A. Campbell (Zurich, 1950),
pp. 65–177; *Ælfric's Lives of saints*, ed. Skeat, I, 441–73; 'Vita sancti Swithuni
Wintoniensis episcopi auctore Goscelino, monacho Sithiensi', ed. E. P. Sauvage, *AB* 7
(1888), 373–80.

52 Swithun's name appears in relic lists of the following: Abingdon; Bath, cathedral priory;
Christ Church cathedral priory, Canterbury; Glastonbury; Meaux; Peterborough;

deposition of 7 July and the translation of 15 July) into the English calendars, where they remained ubiquitous throughout the Middle Ages.[53] Thus, as Osbert points out, in the time of Æthelwold, 'Swithun, the illustrious confessor of God, made known his glory by a new revelation, whom also the glory of new miracles daily extolled to the heavens.'[54] Within a few years a ninth-century bishop so obscure that his earliest hagiographers confessed to their total ignorance concerning his earthly career had been transformed into the principal heavenly patron of the leading church of Wessex and one of the most enduringly famous of the Anglo-Saxon saints.

The creation or rehabilitation of the cult of the saint was, it is clear, an integral and important part of the process of monastic revival. If the establishment of regular Benedictine monasticism provided a community with spiritual credibility, and if the establishment of a landed endowment and the building of a great church provided wealth, prestige and power, then the promotion of a local cult ensured both spiritual and political stability by providing for the community a historical identity and a powerful protector in heaven. Against this background the translation of Edburga's relics by Æthelwold becomes immediately intelligible. The history of Nunnaminster, even in the period of the tenth-century reform, is notoriously obscure. But we do know that the house, following its refoundation by Æthelwold, shared in the general reorganisation, adjustment and enclosure of monastic lands by which that bishop sought to provide for the religious houses of Winchester an ordered and secure monastic life *a ciuium tumultu remoti*.[55] It is likely too that reform was followed by reconstruction – certainly if we are to believe William of Malmesbury's statement that Edburga's

Reading; St Albans; Salisbury, secular cathedral; St Paul's, London, secular cathedral; Waltham; Warwick, secular college of St Mary (Thomas, 'Cult of relics', p. 463).

[53] For the feast of Swithun's deposition see *English kalendars before A.D. 1100*, ed. F. Wormald, HBS 32 (London, 1934) (hereafter referred to as Wormald (ed.), *Before 1100*), nos. 1 (to which the feast was added in the eleventh century), 2 (where the feast is wrongly described as that of the saint's translation), 5–20; Wormald (ed.), *After 1100*, 1, 8, 25, 40, 57, 74, 90, 106, 123; 11, 14, 33, 69, 85, 98. For the feast of Swithun's translation see *Before 1100*, nos. 1 (to which the feast was added in the eleventh century), 5–20; *After 1100*, 1, 8, 25, 174; 11, 14, 69, 85, 98. [54] *Vita Edburge*, fol. 102.

[55] S807 (B1302), charter of King Edgar to Old Minster, New Minster and Nunnaminster, 963 × 970. For Æthelwold's reorganisation of the monastic precinct at Winchester see also S1449 (B1163); 1376 (K1347); WS4.i; Biddle, 'Felix urbs Winthonia', pp. 132–6; WS1, p. 308. Old Minster seems to have gained some land from New Minster and to have obtained an extension eastwards from private lands; its domestic buildings were rebuilt and provided with a water system, and the three religious houses were enclosed by a new boundary wall.

monasteriolum was by Æthelwold's time 'almost in ruins'.[56] And a natural concomitant of refoundation and reconstruction was the promotion of cult and the translation of relics. Translation may indeed simply have been necessitated by rebuilding; or, as in the case of Old Minster, reconstruction and the promotion of cult may have been more closely associated as two essential elements in a many-sided process of reform. One further point is worthy of note: analogy with Old Minster strongly suggests that reconstruction and the translation of relics may have represented the culmination of a long and complex process of refoundation and might therefore be dated rather to the 970s than to the previous decade.

But the events of Æthelwold's episcopate do more than provide a general context into which Edburga's translation by that bishop can neatly be fitted: they suggest also a very specific motive for that measure. Winchester was unique among the centres of the monastic revival in the multiplicity of its religious houses. And the rivalry between those houses forms an important *leitmotiv* of their history. It is reflected, for instance, in the tenurial arrangements carefully negotiated by Æthelwold in the hope of minimising conflict between them.[57] Likewise, it has been suggested that the six-storey tower somewhat hastily erected at New Minster during the 980s was undertaken 'in a spirit of ostentatious competition' with the Old Minster west-work, which had risen only twenty metres away.[58] And it is clear that the ultimate removal in 1110 of New Minster to the suburban estate of Hyde was occasioned at least in part by the uncomfortable proximity of the Old and New Minsters: according to William of Malmesbury 'the two churches stood so close together, their walls adjacent to one another, that the voices of the monks chanting in the one clashed with the voices in the other'.[59] In these circumstances, the relative status of the three Winchester houses must have been determined at least in part by their ability to attract the pilgrimage, the prayers and the patronage of the faithful. And nothing attracted the faithful so much as a wonder-working saint. Hence it might be expected that each of the houses should have attempted to enhance its own prestige by promoting the cults of its principal saints – and that the rivalry between the houses should have coalesced around, and should have

---

[56] *GP*, p. 174.   [57] See above, n. 55.
[58] Biddle, '*Felix urbs Winthonia*', p. 136; cf. R. N. Quirk, 'Winchester New Minster and its tenth-century tower', *Journal of the British Archaeological Association*, Third Series 24 (1961), 16–54, at 21.   [59] *GP*, p. 173.

been expressed in terms of, the rivalry between those saints. Certainly it seems that something of the sort was taking place between the Old and New Minsters. Lantfred describes at great length the case of a man who fell victim to a kind of witchcraft exercised by two fearsome women, 'like two of the three Furies'.[60] Coming to Winchester, he was met by friends and relatives, who persuaded him to seek a cure at the New Minster shrine of St Judoc, a Breton prince whose relics had been brought to Winchester from Saint-Josse-sur-Mer.[61] The sick man, however, deferred the pilgrimage until the following day; and in the meantime he experienced a vision of a splendid figure in episcopal regalia, from whom he received unambiguous instructions:

'If you wish to obtain the most speedy aid in your sickness, you should be carried not to the New Minster but instead to the stone cross which stands before the most ancient church, behind the tomb of one of the bishops; and, spending the night there, while you keep your wakeful vigil, through Christ's aid you shall receive back the health which you have recently lost.'[62]

The visit to St Judoc was duly abandoned, and a cure was obtained, as promised, at the tomb of the bishop saint. The point which Lantfred wished to make is clear. The obscure Old Minster bishop was a patron more effective than the foreign prince of New Minster: and the prestige of Old Minster was increased accordingly.

Against this background, one passage of Osbert's *Vita Edburge* is particularly interesting. Osbert stresses that Æthelwold was prompted to undertake Edburga's translation by witnessing her miracles. And those miracles are described not in isolation but with explicit reference to those of Swithun:

the blessed confessor of God Swithun shone forth throughout the city of Winchester with his miracles, and the glorious and blessed virgin Edburga gleamed with countless famous wonders ... The splendour of the holiness of each banished the ill health of the sick, and all those who came as faithful suppliants obtained without difficulty that which they sought.[63]

[60] 'Lantfred, *Translatio*', ed. Sauvage, p. 388.
[61] *Ibid.*, pp. 390–1. The presence of Judoc's relics at New Minster is recorded in the *Secgan* (*Heiligen*, ed. Liebermann, p. 15). For the legend of Judoc, and for his arrival in Winchester, see *MBHA*, III, fols. 189–191; IV, fols. 403v–406; *Liber monasterii de Hyda*, ed. E. Edwards, RS 45 (London, 1866), p. 82; Thomas, 'Cult of relics', p. 188.
[62] 'Lantfred, *Translatio*', ed. Sauvage, pp. 391–2.   [63] *Vita Edburge*, fols. 102–102v.

Swithun and Edburga, then, exercised a dual patronage within Winchester. They were, Osbert stresses, equally prominent in the performance of miracles: the 'glorious confessor' shone forth 'like the heavenly sun'; the 'royal child' gleamed 'as the moon among the stars'.[64] Dual patronage, however, was not always amicable, and Osbert goes on to demonstrate the ease with which it could, and apparently did, degenerate into mutual rivalry:

The confessor and the virgin as it were alternately in disputation brought to conclusion novel miracles, while in alternate writings in prose and verse they strove among themselves, locked in mutual disputations. To those whom the holy bishop Swithun seemed to deny a remedy the blessed virgin Edburga held out her hand of compassion. And those to whom she did not grant freedom from sickness the glorious man of God deemed worthy of intercession.[65]

In all this we cannot exclude the possibility that Osbert was simply employing the common hagiographical device of enhancing the prestige of his subject by comparison with a better-known figure. Conversely, this passage serves to highlight the very strong probability that, by perhaps the early 970s, Edburga's cult had been given fresh impetus by the sudden and unexpected competition of Swithun – that in the Winchester of the tenth-century reform the cult of the royal patron had attained unprecedented importance as an instrument of monastic rivalry. The one major objection to this interpretation of Edburga's translation – that it was allegedly carried out on the initiative not of the nuns but of Æthelwold – is easily countered; for behind Æthelwold's familiarity with the deeds of St Edburga is surely to be detected the hand of the Nunnaminster propagandists.

The foregoing provides, I believe, the most plausible reconstruction of the origin and early history of St Edburga's cult in Winchester. But a further possibility remains. Osbert's account of the saint's translation by Æthelwold is followed by a further enigmatic passage concerning the relationship between the Old Minster and Nunnaminster cults. He writes of a period of desolation in Winchester before Edburga began to work miracles there. In particular, he notes, the emergence of Swithun's cult had caused the community of Nunnaminster great distress; it was not until a later date that, following the commencement of Edburga's miracles, the nuns found their own patron:

[64] *Ibid.*   [65] *Ibid.*, fol. 102v.

The fame of God's bishop Swithun drew everybody to the festive celebration of his miracles, and on that account the neglected virgins were tormented by their decline and desperation. But after the sun of justice shone upon them in the splendour of the glorious virgin's miracles there grew in that church the rites of heaven, and the joy of the saints was multiplied.[66]

Osbert's chronology, here as elsewhere, leaves much to be desired, and it is very probable that this passage, intended as an introduction to Edburga's miracles, alludes simply to that revitalisation of an existing cult which I have already proposed. Conversely, however, the passage may invite some reinterpretation of the early history of Edburga's cult. For it seems to imply that the cult in no way antedated that of Swithun but rather was promoted in the aftermath of, and specifically in reaction to, that of the ninth-century bishop saint. This in turn suggests that the transition of the royal patron into the patron saint, far from being a natural or immediate sequel to Edburga's this-worldly role, was exclusively a product of the tenth-century reform and of the monastic rivalries engendered or fuelled by it. The 'sanctification' of the royal patron, in short, may have taken place only when the Winchester nuns were forced to search their corporate memory for a worthy antagonist to Swithun. This interpretation of Edburga's cult is just compatible with Osbert's chronologically vague account, in which Edburga's translation by the nuns and her translation by Æthelwold are linked by the unspecific phrase *Ea tempestate*.[67] It perhaps receives some support from the later Hyde *sanctorale* and Middle English Lives of the saint, each of which describes not a two-stage process of cult-development but only a translation of relics carried out by Æthelwold in conjunction with the Winchester nuns.[68] It must remain, however, no more than a hypothesis.

ROYAL WINCHESTER AND THE ROYAL CULT

St Edburga's life was spent, and her posthumous reputation formed, in a city with rather a special nature and history. The term

[66] *Ibid.*, fol. 104.   [67] *Ibid.*, fol. 101v.
[68] *MBHA*, IV, fol. 296v: Edburga remained in her original grave for some time, until a heavenly sign demonstrated her dissatisfaction: 'Nam in visione quibusdam sororibus apparuit, et ut, se inde deberent levare admonuit. Quibus negligentibus manifeste revelationem eius translacionis, aliis atque aliis iterumque apparuit, ne dubitarent eam transferre quam misericors deus collocaverat in sanctorum ordine et sanctus denique adelwoldus Wyntoniensis episcopus crebris admonitionibus revelationum admonitus

'capital city', when applied to a society in which government remains essentially personal and itinerant, is dangerously anachronistic. None the less, it is clear that, within the Wessex and the England of the tenth and eleventh centuries, political pre-eminence belonged to the *felix urbs Winthonia*. That pre-eminence was founded upon a traditionally close relationship between Winchester and the West Saxon royal house. Martin Biddle has argued convincingly that Winchester was, from the mid seventh century if not before, the site of an important royal residence.[69] By the eleventh century the city had attained central importance in both the business and the ceremonial of the royal court. It seems, for instance, to have served as the principal repository for the royal treasure; certainly it was from Winchester that all Cnut's best valuables were seized by Harold in 1035.[70] And the last of the Anglo-Saxon kings is known to have paid at least seven visits to Winchester, of which two may have been associated with full gatherings of the witan.[71]

A corollary of Winchester's royal status was its ecclesiastical prosperity and pre-eminence. The close connections between the royal house and the religious communities of New Minster and Nunnaminster have already been outlined, and Old Minster was likewise a royal foundation, probably established by King Cenwalh in the 640s and apparently intended not for immediate

---

est. Algivam tunc temporis abbatissam, congregationemque sanctimonialium ammonuit, quatinus sanctissima virgo christi edburga a tumulo transferretur ad scrinium.'

For the similar, but much briefer, account of the Middle English Life see Braswell, 'St Edburga', p. 329. It is unfortunately unclear whether these sources represent an independent tradition or whether they merely give a confused rendering of the two-stage process recounted by Osbert of Clare.

[69] Biddle, '*Felix urbs Winthonia*', pp. 123–6; Biddle, 'Winchester: development', pp. 237–41; WS1, pp. 289–90. There follows in each of these works an account of the development of royal Winchester throughout the Anglo-Saxon period. It is interesting to note that the royal and ceremonial role of Winchester seems to have been complemented by that of *Hamwih*, Saxon Southampton, as an industrial and commercial centre: see P. V. Addyman and D. H. Hill, 'Saxon Southampton: a review of the evidence', *Proceedings of the Hampshire Field Club* 25 (1968), 61–93, and 26 (1969), 61–96; P. V. Addyman, 'Saxon Southampton: a town and international port of the 8th to the 10th century', in Jankuhn *et al.* (eds.), *Vor- und Frühformen*, pp. 218–28.

[70] *ASC*, C, D, *s.a.* 1035; and cf. *ibid.*, E, *s.a.* 1086. For Winchester's role as a repository for the royal treasure see especially WS1, pp. 290–2; V. H. Galbraith, *Studies in the public records* (London, 1948), pp. 41–6; F. M. Stenton, *Anglo-Saxon England*, 3rd edn (Oxford, 1971), pp. 643–4; Barlow, *English church, 1000–1066*, pp. 120–4; J. le Patourel, *The Norman empire* (Oxford, 1976; repr. 1978), pp. 147–50.

[71] WS1, p. 290; T. J. Oleson, *The witenagemot in the reign of Edward the Confessor: a study in the constitutional history of eleventh-century England* (Oxford, 1955), Apps. T and O.

use as the seat of the bishopric but rather to serve an adjacent royal palace.[72] The royal associations of the Winchester churches are reflected in the traditional use of both Old and New Minsters as places of royal burial. Among the rulers of Wessex or England buried in or translated to Winchester were Cynegils, Cenwalh, Cynewulf, Æthelwulf, Alfred, Edward the Elder, Edred, Edwy, Edmund Ironside, Cnut and Harthacnut.[73] Very probably too those royal associations, along with the developing cult of Swithun, were among the factors determining the form of the reconstructed Old Minster church of the 970s. The most striking feature of that church was the west-work which rose probably to a height of between forty and fifty metres directly opposite the royal palace. West-works of this kind 'were sometimes arranged to accommodate the throne of the local ruler at first- or second-floor level, in a position from which he could observe the whole or greater part of the interior of the church. This may well have been one of the functions of the Winchester west-work.'[74] Certainly the tenth-century reform saw the continuity and strengthening of the traditional bonds between the churches of Winchester and the West Saxon royal house. It was no accident that the king bestowed upon the three principal reformers the sees of Canterbury, York and Winchester. Nor is it surprising that it was from Winchester that the *Regularis concordia*, the royally approved manifesto of the reform movement, was issued in the early 970s. The concord of *regnum* and *sacerdotium* to which Osbert of Clare so nostalgically alludes reached its apogee in the Winchester of Edgar and Æthelwold.

In the tenth and eleventh centuries, therefore, the city of Winchester was made great by the strengthening of its traditional royal associations: it became the principal *ciuitas regia* of Anglo-Saxon England. And the royal character of the city carries interesting implications for the history of the Anglo-Saxon royal cults: in Winchester, if anywhere, the cults of the royal saints might be expected to attain a particular ubiquity and a particular importance.

This, however, they signally failed to do. The point may be illustrated by reference to the *Secgan*, the earliest complete text of

---

[72] For New Minster and Nunnaminster see above, pp. 95–6. For Old Minster see *ASC*, F, *s.a.* 648; KH, pp. 80–1, where the foundation is dated 642–3; Biddle, 'Felix urbs Winthonia', p. 125; Biddle, 'Winchester: development', pp. 237–9; WS1, pp. 306–7.
[73] See WS1, p. 290, n. 3 and references therein cited.   [74] *Ibid.*, pp. 307–8.

which is found in a Winchester manuscript of *c.* 1031.[75] This provides a list of the saints resting in each of the Winchester houses. Old Minster is represented by Birinus, the seventh-century apostle of the West Saxons, whose seat was at Dorchester-on-Thames; Haedde, bishop in the late seventh century; Swithun; and the tenth-century bishops Frithestan, Byrnstan, Ælfheah and Æthelwold. To this list of bishop saints was added Justus, a boy martyr of Beauvais whose relics had been translated to Winchester.[76] The New Minster list includes Grimbald, who seems to have headed a small secular community at Winchester immediately prior to the foundation of New Minster, and Judoc, whose relics were said to have been brought from Saint-Josse-sur-Mer.[77] Nunnaminster is represented by St Edburga alone.[78]

The evidence of the *Secgan* is corroborated by that of the liturgical sources. There is unfortunately no extant calendar which can safely be attributed to Nunnaminster, but Francis Wormald, in his *English kalendars before A.D. 1100*, prints four eleventh-century calendars of the other Winchester houses.[79] Of these the two earliest (nos. 9 and 10), contained in London, BL, MS Cotton Titus D. xxvii and in Cambridge, Trinity College, MS R.15.32, are

---

[75] London, BL, MS Stowe 944, the *Liber vitae* of New Minster; see *Heiligen*, ed. Liebermann, p. xiii; above, p. 1, n. 4.

[76] For the Old Minster list see *Heiligen*, ed. Liebermann, p. 15. For a general history of the Old Minster relic cults see Thomas, 'Cult of relics', pp. 132–7. For the career of Birinus see especially *HE*, III, 7; *MBHA*, IV, fols. 396–397; for Haedde see *HE*, IV, 12; *MBHA*, IV, fols. 285–286v; for Swithun see above, pp. 108–10; for the tenth-century bishops see *MBHA*, IV, fols. 371–372 (Byrnstan), 309–310, 341v–342 (Æthelwold; see also above, n. 35). For the Winchester traditions concerning St Justus see *MBHA*, IV, fols. 362–362v.

[77] For the New Minster list see *Heiligen*, ed. Liebermann, p. 15. For a general history of the New Minster relic cults see Thomas, 'Cult of relics', pp. 187–95. For Grimbald see also Grierson, 'Grimbald'; for Judoc see above, p. 112.

[78] *Heiligen*, ed. Liebermann, p. 15; see also Thomas, 'Cult of relics', p. 196.

[79] A particularly enigmatic calendar is that preserved on fols. 3–8v of London, BL, MS Cotton Nero A. ii (Wormald (ed.), *Before 1100*, no. 3). This calendar was assigned by Wormald to Wessex and dated to the eleventh century. N. R. Ker has suggested (*Catalogue of manuscripts containing Anglo-Saxon* (Oxford, 1957), pp. 198–201) that fols. 3–13 of the MS have been detached from BL, MS Cotton Galba xiv and that the original MS was a Winchester document, probably associated from the early eleventh century with Nunnaminster. This attribution seems, however, to be improbable, for the calendar contains no feast of St Edburga and few of the other major feasts local to Winchester; instead it shows a marked interest in those saints who were venerated primarily in the extreme west of England. For the most recent discussion of the calendar see M. Lapidge, 'Some Latin poems as evidence for the reign of Athelstan', *ASE* 9 (1980), 61–98, at 84–6. Here it is suggested that the calendar originates from furthermost Wessex, possibly from St Germans in Cornwall; its date, calculated from the associated Easter tables, is placed in the second quarter of the eleventh century.

attributed to New Minster and are dated to *c.* 1023–35 and *c.* 1025 respectively.[80] Nos. 11 and 12, in London, BL, MS Arundel 60 and in London, BL, MS Cotton Vitellius E. xviii, are each dated to *c.* 1060;[81] the latter is tentatively assigned to New Minster.[82] With the single exception of Frithestan, who receives no liturgical veneration, the local saints commemorated in these calendars are identical with those whose relics receive mention in the *Secgan*; the calendars allow no individual to be added to the list of Winchester saints.[83]

The churches of Winchester, it is clear, produced only one royal cult – that of St Edburga. The saint, it is true, received consistent and considerable veneration, the feasts of both her deposition and

---

[80] For the date and provenance of the calendar in the Cotton MS see Wormald (ed.), *Before 1100*, pp. vi, 113; Ker, *Catalogue*, p. 265. For the calendar in the Cambridge MS see Wormald (ed.), *Before 1100*, pp. vi, 127; Ker, *Catalogue*, p. 135.

[81] Wormald (ed.), *Before 1100*, pp. 141, 155; Ker, *Catalogue*, pp. 166, 298; see also below, p. 126.

[82] Wormald (ed.), *Before 1100*, p. vi, where it is stated that the calendar probably came from New Minster, 'though early in its history it crossed the road to the cathedral'. This calendar is discussed in detail by N. J. Morgan, 'Notes on the post-Conquest calendar, litany and martyrology of the cathedral priory of Winchester with a consideration of Winchester diocese calendars of the pre-Sarum period', in A. Borg and A. Martindale (eds.), *The vanishing past: studies of medieval art, liturgy and metrology presented to Christopher Hohler*, British Archaeological Reports, International Series 111 (1981), pp. 133–71, at p. 134 and notes 10 and 11. In note 11 Morgan suggests that 'the Calendar represents the pre-Conquest text of the Cathedral (the date of the manuscript may in fact be shortly after the Conquest)'. For further discussion of the calendar see K. Wildhagen, 'Das Kalendarium der Handschrift Vitellius E. XVIII', in Boehmer *et al.* (eds.), *Festgabe für Felix Liebermann*, pp. 68–118; *The Bosworth Psalter*, ed. F. A. Gasquet and E. Bishop, (London, 1908), *passim*; J. B. L. Tolhurst, 'An examination of two Anglo-Saxon manuscripts of the Winchester school: the Missal of Robert of Jumièges and the Benedictional of St Æthelwold', *Archaeologia* 83 (1933), 27–44, at 30–4; J. L. Rosier, *The Vitellius Psalter* (Ithaca, 1962); *The missal of the New Minster*, ed. D. H. Turner, HBS 93 (Leighton Buzzard, 1960), pp. xi, xiii; Ker, *Catalogue*, pp. 298–301.

[83] The local feasts commemorated in the Winchester calendars are as follows:

9 Jan.	tr. Judoc	4 Sep.	tr. Birinus
12 Mar.	Ælfheah (10, 12 only)	10 Sep.	tr. Æthelwold
15 June	dep. Edburga	18 Oct.	Justus
2 July	dep. Swithun	30 Oct.	ordination Swithun (12 only)
7 July	Haedde	4 Nov.	Byrnstan
8 July	dep. Grimbald	3 Dec.	dep. Birinus
15 July	tr. Swithun	10 Dec.	octave Birinus (11, 12 only)
18 July	tr. Edburga	13 Dec.	dep. Judoc
1 Aug.	dep. Æthelwold		

The following feasts were added to no. 12 in the thirteenth century: octave of the deposition of Swithun (9 July), octave of the translation of Swithun (22 July), translation of Grimbald (3 September).

her translation being entered in each of the four Winchester calendars.[84] None the less, her isolation is striking. With the exception of the peripatetic saints Justus and Judoc, the churches of Winchester were concerned chiefly to promote the cults of those upon whose work the city's ecclesiastical status had been founded – the bishop saints of Old Minster, the alleged founder of New Minster and the royal patron of Nunnaminster. The concord of *regnum* and *sacerdotium* had not found its expression in the sanctification of kingship: Winchester, despite its profusion of potential royal relics, was not an important centre for the promotion of royal cults and in no way took upon itself the role of shrine to the West Saxon royal house.

The point may be carried further. For it seems that the West Saxon royal house was itself conspicuous only for its lack of interest in Winchester's single royal saint. The cult portrayed by Osbert of Clare owed its inception to the Winchester nuns and was sustained by those nuns with the support of St Æthelwold. This history stands in marked contrast to that of Swithun's cult as described by Lantfred, who was at pains to stress that his subject's translation took place not only in response to the demands of the saint and with the backing of Æthelwold but also in accordance with the command of King Edgar.[85] About the subsequent history of Edburga's cult in Winchester, and about its diffusion from thence, Osbert of Clare reveals disappointingly little. That history is condensed into a chronologically vague account of five conventional miracles – the first four curative in nature and concerning respectively a Winchester cripple, two poor women whose place of origin is not specified, a clerk of Saint-Quentin who had been seized by madness and a Wilton man similarly 'possessed by a demon', the fifth concerning the liberation of a man bound in chains at the king's command.[86] Two points, however, are immediately striking.

[84] St Edburga also occupies a place of some importance among the English virgins in the litany associated with calendar no. 11, in BL, MS Arundel 60: see F. Wormald, 'The English saints in the litany of Arundel MS 60', *AB* 64 (1946), 72–86, at 82.

[85] 'Lantfred, *Translatio*', ed. Sauvage, pp. 394–5.

[86] *Vita Edburge*, fols. 104–107. The first of these miracles is associated with Osbert's 'second' Abbess Alfghiua, until whose time its subject is said to have lived (fol. 104v). The third miracle is said to have taken place in the time of 'prefate de qua diximus abbatisse' (fol. 105v) and the fourth in that of the abbess 'de qua prelibauimus' (fol. 106v). As no other abbess is named in this part of the narrative, it is possible that Osbert intended to place at least three of the five miracles in the time of the 'second' Alfghiua. But the point cannot be established with certainty; and on the general problems inherent in Osbert's account of the Nunnaminster abbesses see above, pp. 33–5.

First, the recorded clientele of St Edburga's shrine was drawn primarily from Winchester itself or from its region; even the clerk of Saint-Quentin who sought a cure there did so rather because he happened to be receiving hospitality at Nunnaminster than because news of the saint's miracles had travelled overseas. Second, that clientele seems to have been drawn principally from the lower social strata: St Edburga neither extended favours to nor received favours from bishops, archbishops, secular magnates or members of the West Saxon royal house. On only one occasion does Osbert provide an oblique and uninformative reference to royal interest in and patronage of the cult. He notes that the saint's shrine was refurbished by the abbess Ælfleda/Alfletha 'with the assistance of the devout queens'.[87] This apart, the cult which he describes was exclusively local and popular in appeal: it was a cult which had failed entirely to become fashionable.

The argument from silence cannot of course be wholly satisfactory. It is clear that Nunnaminster survived and prospered throughout the late tenth and eleventh centuries. Its survival and prosperity were founded in large measure upon royal goodwill and patronage, and it would be rash to discount the possibility that such goodwill and patronage may have been determined in part by interest in Nunnaminster's royal saint.[88] Nevertheless, the absence from all the hagiographical sources of any reference to royal involvement in Edburga's translations, together with the parenthetical nature of Osbert's single reference to royal patronage of the shrine, strongly suggests that the cult of St Edburga was in no sense a royal creation. And this in turn implies that the cult of St Edburga carried no political implications which might profitably be utilised by the kings of the later Anglo-Saxon period. The point is underlined by the marked absence of aristocratic interest in the cult. St Edburga's shrine seems never to have become a fashionable place of pilgrimage for those magnates who surrounded the royal court in Winchester. That shrine, therefore, clearly had no political relevance for them: the magnates of Æthelred and Edward the Confessor could make no political statement and reap no political

---

[87] *Vita Edburge*, fol. 104.

[88] In 1086 Nunnaminster was in possession of estates in Winchester itself, at Lyss, Froyle, Leckford Abbess, Long Stoke, Timsbury and Ovington in Hampshire; Coleshill in Berkshire; and Urchfont and All Cannings in Wiltshire (*VCH Hants.*, II, 122). For royal grants in favour of Nunnaminster see S526, 807, 1503, 1515. See also Meyer, 'Patronage of the West Saxon royal nunneries', p. 348.

advantage by a display of reverence towards the saintly ancestor of those kings; and the magnates of Cnut likewise attached no special significance to this saint whose dynasty that king had usurped. The cult of St Edburga became neither a symbol nor a tool in the high politics of the late Old English state. Within the principal *ciuitas regia* of late Anglo-Saxon England, the cult of the *filia principis* was exclusively local and monastic in origin, inspiration and implication: it was significant only in the context of Nunnaminster politics and Nunnaminster spirituality.

THE NORMAN CONQUEST AND THE CONTINUITY OF CULT

The cult of St Edburga was that of an Anglo-Saxon *uirgo regia* transformed into an Anglo-Saxon patron saint in accordance with the dictates of Anglo-Saxon monastic policy and politics. How, then, did that cult fare under the rule of the Normans? Osbert of Clare composed his *Vita Edburge* probably in the third or fourth decade of the twelfth century.[89] That he did so in itself suggests that Edburga's cult did not suffer a total demise in the aftermath of conquest. But as a source for the more detailed history of that cult, and in particular for the crucial years immediately following 1066, Osbert's *Vita* fails us completely. It contains not a single reference to the coming of the Normans and not a single episode which can be dated to the post-Conquest years. Even the evidence to be derived from the structure of the work is ambiguous. That structure suggests that Osbert's major source, probably a Winchester Life of the saint, was written in or after the mid eleventh century:[90] perhaps, then, it was a product of a revival of interest in the cult after the Conquest. Conversely, Osbert's own work is remarkable for its total failure to bring up to date the history of the cult: this perhaps suggests that, from the mid eleventh century onwards, interest in that cult had been so slight that Osbert could unearth no record of its history under Norman rule.

Two lines of inquiry, the local historical and the liturgical, tend to support in outline that impression of general, long-term continuity which is implied by Osbert's composition in the twelfth century of a Life of St Edburga; but they do little to fill in the detail. It is clear, first, that the effect of the Norman Conquest upon royal Winchester was far from catastrophic. The city remained an im-

---

[89] See above, p. 17, n. 19.   [90] See above, p. 29.

portant royal residence and centre for court business and ceremonial. In the immediate aftermath of conquest the new Norman
ruler began the construction of a castle within the walled city,[91]
and by *c.* 1069/70 work had commenced on a new royal palace.[92]
Thereafter William seems to have made it his custom, whenever he
was in England, to spend Easter at Winchester; a similar practice
seems to have been followed by William Rufus and, until *c.* 1108,
by Henry I.[93] For the prosperity and pre-eminence of royal
Winchester the crucial turning-point came not in 1066 but in the
middle years of the reign of Henry I;[94] and the seal was perhaps set
on Winchester's decline in the year 1141, when the city, its
churches, St Edburga's nunnery and the royal palace were destroyed, allegedly by the forces of its own bishop, the enigmatic
Henry of Blois.[95]

The church of Winchester entered the Norman period in an
anomalous and embarrassing position. Its bishop was Stigand, who
from 1052 had held the see in plurality with that of Canterbury,
whose archiepiscopal status had been recognised only by the anti-
pope Benedict X, and who formed the principal target of the
Norman and papal reformers.[96] The unorthodox bishop was
quickly disposed of: deposed by the legates of Alexander II in 1070,
he was replaced, at the king's instance, by the Norman Walkelin;[97]
and – perhaps around the same time – the cathedral community
received a new prior in the person of Walkelin's brother Simeon,
formerly a monk of Saint-Ouen at Rouen.[98] Following this
takeover, the see of Winchester seems to have preserved and even
gradually enhanced its status. At the Council of Windsor in 1072
the bishop of Winchester seems to have been seated in order of
consecration; at the Council of London in 1075, where the prece-

---

[91] WS1, pp. 302–5; cf. F. Barlow, 'Guenta', *Antiquaries Journal* 44 (1964), 217–19.

[92] *LVH*, pp. 1–3. For the siting and history of the palace see WS1, pp. 292–302.

[93] See *ASC*, E, *s.a.* 1086, where it is stated that, as often as he was in England, William wore
his crown three times a year, at Easter at Winchester, at Whitsuntide at Westminster, at
Christmas at Gloucester; on each of these occasions all the great men of the kingdom
would be assembled about him. For a summary account of the visits of William and his
successors to Winchester see WS1, pp. 295–6.

[94] See especially WS1, pp. 296–302.

[95] *LVH*, p. 2 (where the destruction of the city is dated to 1140); see WS1, p. 297 and n. 4 for
evaluation of this account.

[96] For the career of Stigand see especially Barlow, *English church, 1000–1066*, pp. 77–81,
302–8; also H. E. J. Cowdrey, 'Pope Gregory VII and the Anglo-Norman church and
kingdom', *Studi Gregoriani* 9 (1972), 79–114, at 84.   [97] *CS*, I, ii, 565ff.

[98] *Annales de Wintonia*, p. 33 (*s.a.* 1082). Simeon left Winchester in 1081/2 to become abbot
of Ely (*Heads*, p. 80); the date of his arrival in Winchester cannot be recovered.

dence of the English bishops was established, he joined the small group whose sees were acknowledged to possess special dignity: 'it was amicably determined that the archbishop of York should be seated to the right of the archbishop of Canterbury, the bishop of London to his left and the bishop of Winchester next to York. And if York is absent, London should be seated to the right of Canterbury, Winchester to the left.'[99] Initially relations between Walkelin and the community of his cathedral priory may have been strained. William of Malmesbury wrote at some length about that community's hostility to its foreign bishop and about the conciliatory measures adopted by Walkelin.[100] He implies, moreover, that in one way at least the new bishop deserved some of the criticism meted out to him: he diverted three hundred pounds' worth of land from the endowment of the monks for the use of himself and his successors.[101] Smaller ripples in the pool of monastic tranquility may have been caused by the reforming activities of two foreign priors. Of these the second, Godfrey of Cambrai (1082–1107), seems to have instituted a reform of the divine office.[102] And about the revolutionary measures of the first, Simeon, the Winchester annals provide a more amusing anecdote. The new prior, we are told, was disturbed by the eagerness with which the monks consumed meat in the refectory. His approach to this dietary problem was subtle: he had prepared for them an exquisite meal of fish; and the monks, duly impressed, were quickly converted from their carnivorous habits.[103] Change, therefore, there undoubtedly was; but major conflict seems to have been avoided. Internal stability and public prestige were complemented by growth and reconstruction. By the late 1070s work had commenced on a new cathedral church: 'The immense size of the new church, 162 metres in length, was undoubtedly a response to the eminence of the city in royal and ecclesiastical affairs. No other church in England or Normandy even approached this scale until the second half of the twelfth century, and then only rarely.'[104] And if the splendour of Walkelin's church symbolised the inauguration of a new and self-consciously Norman era, it did not do so entirely at the expense of the past. The new church was dedicated in

---

[99] *CS*, I, ii, 612–13; cf. *GP*, p. 67; *Annales de Wintonia*, p. 30. For the proceedings and significance of this council see also C. N. L. Brooke, 'Archbishop Lanfranc, the English bishops and the Council of London of 1075', *Studia Gratiana* 12 (Bologna, 1967), 41–59, especially 47–50. [100] *GP*, p. 172. [101] *Ibid*. [102] *Ibid*.
[103] *Annales de Wintonia*, p. 33 (*s.a.* 1082). [104] WS1, p. 310.

1093 and 'On the feast of St Swithun, having processed from the new to the old church, they brought the shrine of St Swithun and placed it with honour in the new church.'[105]

New Minster, like the cathedral priory, was subject to fairly rapid Normanisation. Its abbot, Ælfwig, seems to have been among those killed at Hastings; and a further abbot, Wulfric, was deposed in 1072 and replaced by Riwallon. The latter died probably in 1088 and the abbey passed into the hands of Rufus's judge and tax-collector *par excellence*, Ranulf Flambard, until the appointment of Robert Losinga *c.* 1091.[106] The destruction by fire in 1065 of a number of the conventual buildings, together with the subsequent encroachment of William's new palace, must have caused severe problems and made even more apparent the disadvantages of New Minster's cramped city-centre site.[107] The year 1110 accordingly saw the removal of the community to Hyde: 'the king caused the monastery of St Grimbald to be moved from the precinct of the episcopal church to a northern suburb of the city'.[108] As in the case of Old Minster, however, change did not mean the abandonment of the past. Just as St Swithun had accompanied his monks to the new Norman cathedral, so New Minster moved to Hyde 'with its monks and its relics'.[109]

The two major religious houses of Winchester seem, therefore, to have survived the Norman Conquest with some anxious moments but without catastrophe. By the early twelfth century they were thriving institutions, with extensive estates and spectacular new buildings. And within those brash new buildings the relics of the Old and New Minsters had been reverently enshrined: the cults of the Anglo-Saxon saints were far from having outlived their usefulness. Sadly we have no such detailed evidence for the history of Nunnaminster in the years following 1066. The Winchester annals preserve some record of the abbatial succession and make it clear that by 1084 at the latest the abbey was under foreign,

---

[105] *Annales de Wintonia*, p. 37. See also Thomas, 'Cult of relics', p. 133, where it is noted that the relics of the other Old Minster saints seem to have been translated at the same time.

[106] *Heads*, pp. 81–2; *Annales de Wintonia*, pp. 30, 36. Ælfwig's name is recorded in *LVH*, p. 35, where a slightly later hand has added 'abbas . . . occisus in Bello'. The editors of *Heads* accept this information as 'well authenticated'; for criticism of the later traditions that Ælfwig was Harold's uncle and that he died at Hastings along with twenty of his monks see Round in *VCH Hants.*, I, 417–19.

[107] *LVH*, p. 2; WS I, pp. 292–5, 316–17.   [108] *Annales de Wintonia*, p. 43.

[109] *Ibid*. See also Thomas, 'Cult of relics', pp. 188–90, where it suggested that the relics thus translated included those of Grimbald but not those of Judoc.

probably Norman, control: they record the death in that year of an abbess Beatrice and her replacement by Alice.[110] The archaeological evidence suggests that some rebuilding took place late in the eleventh or early in the twelfth century,[111] and the abbey church was rededicated in 1108.[112] Very possibly reconstruction was accompanied, as at Old Minster, by the translation of relics; certainly the dedication of the church to St Edburga implies a continuing interest in her cult during the post-Conquest decades. This apart, Nunnaminster failed entirely to hit even the local headlines until it was burned during the siege of Winchester in 1141. There is no reason to assume that its experience of conquest was more traumatic than that of the other Winchester houses; and there is no reason to assume that the relics of its patron were less reverently treated than were those of saints Swithun and Grimbald.

Some evidence bearing directly upon the continuity of cult may be derived from a brief investigation of liturgical sources. These suggest a general pattern of continuity, both as regards the high veneration accorded to Edburga within Winchester itself and as regards the diffusion of her cult from thence. Again, however, the pattern can be traced only in outline. For Winchester itself, no post-Conquest calendar can with any certainty be attributed to Nunnaminster and none can be firmly dated to the crucial decades immediately following the Conquest. From New Minster there survives a missal (Le Havre, Bibliothèque Municipale, MS 330) which can be located within the second half of the eleventh century but which cannot be more precisely dated: here the feast of Edburga's deposition is commemorated, that of her translation omitted.[113] Whatever the reason for this omission, it seems not to have marked the beginning of a decline in Edburga's local impor-

---

[110] *Annales de Wintonia*, p. 34; *Heads*, p. 223.

[111] WS1, p. 322 and n. 10, where it is noted that in 1973 excavations by the Winchester City Rescue Archaeologist revealed the south-west corner of the late Saxon monastic block, to which a vaulted undercroft had been added in the early Norman period.

[112] *Annales de Wigornia*, p. 375 (*s.a.* 1108): 'Ecclesia Sanctæ Edburgæ Wyntoniæ dedicata est.' It has been noted (WS1, p. 322, n. 10; addendum at p. 556) that the Worcester annals here follow the thirteenth-century Winchester annals preserved in London, BL, MS Cotton Vespasian E. iv, fols. 153–201: 'the reference is clearly to St Mary's Abbey, for the same annals, also following the Winchester source, refer in the same terms to the burning of the nunnery in August 1141' (see *Annales de Wigornia*, p. 379 (*s.a.* 1140)).

[113] *Missal of New Minster*, ed. Turner, fol. 102. On the provenance and date of this MS see *ibid.*, pp. viii–xiii. Two further sources commemorate the saint's deposition in almost identical terms – an extract from a late-eleventh-century missal preserved in London, BL, MS Cotton Vitellius A. xviii, and a missal fragment of the twelfth century found in Oxford, Bodleian Library, MS Rawlinson D. 894. Of these the former is printed in *The*

tance. In the thirteenth century the saint was receiving high veneration at Hyde abbey: the breviary of that house includes twelve lessons for the feast of the saint's deposition and four for that of her translation; its calendar likewise includes both feasts of the saint, and Edburga's name ranks highly among the English virgins invoked in its litany.[114]

For Winchester cathedral priory no proper post-Conquest calendar or reliable litany survives; these have, however, been carefully reconstructed, from scattered and fragmentary sources, by Nigel Morgan.[115] Among those sources is the calendar in MS Cotton Vitellius E. xviii, which was written either just before or immediately after the Conquest and which was corrected and graded in the thirteenth century to conform to the then current usage of the cathedral priory.[116] This history is in itself significant. The calendar may have been written while the community which produced it was still under English rule: if so — unless we are to assume that the cathedral community of the thirteenth century suddenly decided to rescue a neglected document from dusty oblivion – the implication seems to be that the calendar remained in use in its original form, or with only gradual modification of that form, until the thirteenth-century revision. Alternatively, the calendar may have been produced by a community in the early days of its domination by the Normans: if so, the fact that its contents are wholly consistent with those of the pre-Conquest Winchester calendars[117] would tend towards the same conclusion – that the events of 1066 were not followed at Winchester by a radical change in liturgical practice. As regards the post-Conquest veneration of St Edburga in particular, her deposition is entered as a feast of twelve lessons in the Vitellius calendar and in two others of the manuscripts upon which Morgan's reconstruction is founded: Milan, Biblio-

Leofric Missal, ed. F. E. Warren (Oxford, 1883), p. 305; the latter, item no. 31 in a MS of liturgical fragments, is unprinted (see *SC*, no. 13660).

[114] *MBHA*, III, fols. 264v–265; IV, fols. 296v–297. The New Minster calendar and litany also survive in New York, Pierpont Morgan Library, MS Glazier 19 (s. xiv) and London, British Library, MS Harley 960 (s. xiv); the litany is also found in Rome, Bibliotheca Apostolica Vaticana, MS Ottob.Lat.514.   [115] Morgan, 'Notes'.

[116] For the date and provenance of the calendar see above, n. 82; for its thirteenth-century correction see Morgan, 'Notes', p. 134. The calendar in BL, MS Arundel 60 likewise cannot with certainty be located on either side of the Conquest.

[117] See above, n. 83. The Vitellius calendar, far from reducing the number of local feasts, includes one – the ordination of Swithun – which is unparalleled in the other Winchester calendars and two – the feast of Ælfheah and the octave of Birinus – which are each paralleled in only one other Winchester calendar.

theca Braidense, MS AF. XI. 9, a mid-twelfth-century psalter with an ungraded calendar of Ely cathedral priory which was rather carelessly corrected in the fourteenth century to conform to the usage of Winchester cathedral priory, and Madrid, Bibliotheca Nacional, MS Vit. 23–8, a manuscript of *c.* 1140–50 including a calendar with major feasts indicated by capitals.[118] The feast of Edburga's translation occurs in the Milan[119] and Madrid manuscripts and in Oxford, Bodleian Library, MS Rawlinson C. 489, a fragmentary breviary written in 1424 by Brother William Vincent;[120] the feast has been deleted from the Cotton manuscript.[121] In general the highest gradings are reserved, naturally enough, for the saints of universal importance and for the Old Minster saints:[122] but in the Madrid Psalter both feasts of Edburga are placed among those whose high rank is indicated by capitals.[123] Edburga is one of only two English virgins to be included in the post-Conquest litany of Winchester cathedral priory.[124]

Neither before nor after the Norman Conquest, however, was the liturgical cult of St Edburga restricted to Winchester. Indeed the earliest evidence for the saint's liturgical veneration is found not in a Winchester document but in a calendar which Wormald attributes to the West Country.[125] The calendar dates from *c.* 969–78 and includes the feast of Edburga's deposition; its date is wholly consistent with the suggested impetus given to Edburga's cult following the refoundation of Nunnaminster in the 960s. The feast of Edburga's deposition also appears in the calendar of the Bosworth Psalter,[126] and by the second half of the eleventh century

---

[118] For discussion of the calendars in the Milan and Madrid MSS see Morgan, 'Notes', p. 134. The relevant part of the text is missing from the remaining calendars used by Morgan – those preserved in Oxford, Bodleian Library, MS Rawlinson C. 489, in Westminster, Abbey Library, CC 24, and in Sotheby Sale, 24 June 1980, lot 71 (acquired by BL).

[119] In the fourteenth-century amendment of this MS the feast of Edburga's translation was added as a feast of twelve lessons: see Morgan, 'Notes', pp. 141, 148.

[120] See *ibid.*, p. 134.

[121] See *ibid.*, p. 141; Wormald (ed.), *Before 1100*, no. 12. The month of July is missing from the remaining calendars used by Morgan (see above, n. 118).

[122] Morgan, 'Notes', pp. 146–7.   [123] *Ibid.*, p. 149.

[124] *Ibid.* The other English virgin listed in this litany is Æthelthryth of Ely. Morgan's reconstruction of the litany is based upon the following MSS: (a) Oxford, Bodleian Library, MS Auct. D. 2. 6., of the mid twelfth century; (b) London, BL, MS Cotton Vitellius E. xviii, a litany added in the second half of the twelfth century and badly damaged by fire; (c) Sotheby Sale, 24 June 1980, lot 71 (BL).

[125] Salisbury, Cathedral Library, MS 150, fols. 3–8; Wormald (ed.), *Before 1100*, no. 2.

[126] London, BL, MS Add. 37517, fols. 2–3; Wormald (ed.), *Before 1100*, no. 5. The calendar was attributed by Wormald to St Augustine's, Canterbury, *c.* 988–1012, and by Bishop

it had spread throughout the West Country and to a number of centres in the East and West Midlands. It appears in the calendar of the early eleventh-century Missal of Robert of Jumièges, variously attributed to Ely or to Thorney,[127] in a Bury calendar of *c.* 1050[128] and in a Crowland calendar of about the same date.[129] Other documents recall the problems posed by the Vitellius calendar: they cannot with certainty be located on either side of the Conquest. These include a calendar attributed to Wells under Bishop Giso (1061–88),[130] a West Country calendar of the second half of the eleventh century,[131] a Sherborne calendar of *c.* 1061[132] and two calendars of probable Worcester provenance dating from the second half of the century.[133] Here, as in the case of the Vitellius calendar, the precise date of writing is perhaps less significant than the evidence of continued relevance: in no case has the feast of St Edburga fallen victim to the hand of a later corrector. Further evidence of the continued and widespread veneration of St Edburga is supplied by the later medieval calendars. Edburga's

to Christ Church, Canterbury, *c.* 988–1023 (*Bosworth Psalter*, pp. 34–7). More recently P. Korhammer has attributed the MS with its calendar (said to have been added between 988 and 1008) to Christ Church, Canterbury, or possibly to Westminster abbey ('The origin of the Bosworth Psalter', *ASE* 2 (1973), 173–87).

127 Rouen, Bibliothèque Publique, MS Y. 6, fols. 6–11v; Wormald (ed.), *Before 1100*, no. 15 (not printed); Sir Ivor Atkins, 'An investigation of two Anglo-Saxon kalendars (Missal of Robert of Jumièges and St Wulfstan's Homiliary)', *Archaeologia* 78 (1928), 219–54 (text printed; attributed to Thorney); Tolhurst, 'Examination of two Anglo-Saxon manuscripts' (attributed to Ely).

128 Rome, Vatican, Cod. Reginen. Lat. 12, fols. 7–12v; Wormald (ed.), *Before 1100*, no. 19.

129 Oxford, Bodleian Library, MS Douce 296, fols. 1–6v; Wormald (ed.), *Before 1100*, no. 20.

130 London, BL, MS Cotton Vitellius A. xviii, fols. 3–8v; Wormald (ed.), *Before 1100*, no. 8; cf. *Missal of New Minster*, ed. Turner, p. vii.

131 Cambridge, University Library, MS Kk. v. 32, fols. 50–55v; Wormald (ed.), *Before 1100*, no. 6. The calendar is attributed to Glastonbury by J. Armitage Robinson, in B. Schofield, *Muchelney memoranda*, Somerset Record Society 42 (1927), pp. 172–8. N. R. Ker points out (*Catalogue*, p. 39) that fol. 59 has a table of years from 1000 to 1061 and that the portion of the MS containing the calendar is written in an English Caroline minuscule of the first half of the eleventh century; together these facts suggest that the text of the calendar is probably of pre-Conquest date.

132 Cambridge, Corpus Christi College, MS 422 (the so-called Red Book of Darley); Wormald (ed.), *Before 1100*, no. 14. Cf. Ker, *Catalogue*, pp. 119–21, where it is noted that the hand of this part of the MS is dateable to soon after 1060. A table of years on fols. 44–45 runs from 1061 to 1098.

133 Cambridge, Corpus Christi College, MS 391, fols. 3–14; Wormald (ed.), *Before 1100*, no. 17, where it is attributed to St Mary's cathedral priory, Worcester. Cf. Ker, *Catalogue*, pp. 113–15, where the MS is dated to the time of Wulfstan II (1062–95). Oxford, Bodleian Library, MS Hatton 113, fols. iii–viii; Wormald (ed.), *Before 1100*, no. 16, where the calendar is tentatively attributed to Evesham; cf. Ker, *Catalogue*, pp. 391–9, where the MS is attributed to Worcester.

deposition is commemorated in the Benedictine calendars of Abbotsbury,[134] Barking,[135] Chertsey,[136] St Werburga's, Chester,[137] Glastonbury,[138] Shaftesbury,[139] Winchcombe,[140] Westminster[141] and York.[142] And although no calendar survives for Pershore itself[143] the cult of St Edburga certainly flourished in the West Midlands' houses within which Pershore influence might have been felt. Edburga's deposition occurs in calendars of Deerhurst,[144] Evesham,[145] St Peter's, Gloucester,[146] Worcester,[147] Tewkesbury[148] and, a little to the south, Malmesbury.[149] The liturgical evidence combines with the historical to demonstrate that the cult of St Edburga retained, in the decades and the centuries following 1066, both its local importance and its widespread popularity. We cannot reconstruct in detail the circumstances of Edburga's survival; but there can be little doubt that her cult was as at least as vital in the mid twelfth century as it had been in the late tenth.

ST EDBURGA AT PERSHORE: A CASE OF MISTAKEN IDENTITY?

The culmination of Osbert's otherwise unspectacular account of the diffusion of Edburga's cult comes in that final section of his

[134] London, BL, MS Cotton Cleop. B. ix, fols. 54–60 (*c.* 1300); Wormald (ed.), *After 1100*, I, 7.

[135] *The ordinale and customary of the Benedictine nuns of Barking abbey*, ed. J. B. L. Tolhurst, HBS 65 (London, 1927), pp. 1–12.

[136] Oxford, Bodleian Library, MS Lat. Lit. e. 6, fols. 4–8v (s. xiv in.); Wormald (ed.), *After 1100*, I, 89.

[137] Oxford, Bodleian Library, MS Tanner 169*, pp. 3–14 (s. xii ex.); Wormald (ed.), *After 1100*, I, 105. The feast is a fifteenth-century addition with the grading *in albis*.

[138] 'The liturgical calendar of Glastonbury abbey', ed. F. Wormald, in J. Autenrieth and F. Brunhölzl (eds.), *Festschrift Bernhard Bischoff* (Stuttgart, 1971), pp. 325–45.

[139] Cambridge, Fitzwilliam Museum, MS 2–1957; see Morgan, 'Notes', pp. 156, 167, n. 66.

[140] London, BL, MS Cotton Tiberius E. iv; Valenciennes, Bibliothèque Municipale, MS 116; see Morgan, 'Notes', pp. 157, 167, n. 66.

[141] Oxford, Bodleian Library, MS Rawlinson liturg. g. 10, fols. 1–6v (s. xv); Wormald (ed.), *After 1100*, II, 68.   [142] See Morgan, 'Notes', p. 167, n. 66.

[143] See below, p. 132.

[144] Yale, University Library, MS 578 (before 1467); see Morgan, 'Notes', pp. 156, 167, n. 66.

[145] Oxford, Bodleian Library, MS Barlow 41, fols. 158v–163v (s. xiv); Wormald (ed.), *After 1100*, II, 32.

[146] Oxford, Jesus College, MS 10, fols. 1–6v (s. xii); Wormald (ed.), *After 1100*, II, 49.

[147] *The Leofric Collectar*, ed. W. H. Frere, 2 vols., HBS 45, 56 (London, 1918), II, 587–600.

[148] London, BL, MS Royal 8. C. vii; Cambridge, University Library, MS Gg. 3. 21; see Morgan, 'Notes', pp. 156, 167, n. 66.

[149] Oxford, Bodleian Library, MS Rawlinson liturg. g. 12, fols. 95v–107 (1521); Wormald (ed.), *After 1100*, II, 84.

work which concerns the saint's translation to and her patronage of the abbey of Pershore. It is clear both from Osbert's account and from that of William of Malmesbury that by the twelfth century the monks of Pershore possessed a set of relics which were believed to be those of St Edburga of Winchester.[150] But I have suggested above that, because the early history of Pershore had been troubled, there may have been little corporate recollection of precisely when and how those relics had been acquired. Very probably the monks received little or no assistance from written records: in particular there seems to have been only a Winchester Life of the saint, which understandably made no reference to the cult of St Edburga at Pershore. In these circumstances, it was the function of Osbert of Clare not simply to re-write in a more literary style a pre-existing Life of the saint but also, perhaps more importantly, to provide the Pershore relics with a history.[151]

Osbert's approach to his task was quite straightforward. He explains that among those to be impressed by the Winchester miracles of St Edburga was the elusive *comes Alwardus*, alleged refounder of Pershore abbey.[152] *Alwardus* accordingly determined to acquire for his foundation some relics of the saint: 'So from Alfghiua, the abbess of that time, he eagerly sought, with the daring of a relative, that which because he was her nephew she, the mother of the community, did not deny. He obtained from the abbess the skull of the precious virgin, together with some ribs, some smaller bones and other relics, for which he secretly paid a hundred pounds.'[153] About the subsequent development of Edburga's cult at Pershore Osbert's account is enthusiastic but less than informative. *Alwardus*'s acquisition of the relics was vindicated by the saint's performance of miracles at Pershore. Within a year, Osbert claims, a hundred of the sick were restored to health;[154] and, to emphasise the point, 'those who on hearing of her miracles deserted other shrines came in throngs to seek the novel protection of St Edburga'.[155] It is unfortunate that the hagiographer was able to provide a detailed account of only one unremarkable miracle in support of his

150 *Vita Edburge*, fols. 85–86; *GP*, p. 298; cf. *GR*, i, 269.
151 See above, pp. 30–7, especially pp. 36–7.
152 *Vita Edburge*, fol. 107v; for *Alwardus* see above, p. 31.
153 *Vita Edburge*, fol. 107v. *Alwardus* is designated *nepos* of the abbess, a term which can mean either 'nephew' or 'cousin'; the former is the more common and seems the more likely here.   154 *Ibid.*, fol. 110.   155 *Ibid.*, fol. 109.

rather extravagant claims for the success of Edburga's cult at Pershore.[156]

The translation was followed, according to Osbert, by a period of recrimination and rivalry between the houses of Nunnaminster and Pershore. The role of the abbess in the sale of the relics seems to have been, and to have remained, unpopular in the extreme: 'there are many', the hagiographer notes, who, while praising *Alwardus* for his devotion to the saint, condemn the abbess for her avarice in parting with the relics for gain.[157] The saint too, it appears, was far from delighted with this somewhat cavalier treatment of her body; and her wrath fell not only upon the abbess but also upon the whole of the *sancta congregatio* – even, indeed, upon the city of Winchester: following the removal of a part of the holy body 'the miracles of the glorious virgin Edburga were rarely seen to adorn the city'.[158] Osbert's narrative, here as elsewhere, is chronologically imprecise. With no indication of the duration of Edburga's diplomatic dudgeon, he notes that eventually the nuns were forced to go barefoot to Pershore in order to plead with the saint for the resumption of her patronage.[159] This obtained, the cult which Osbert portrayed as existing in his own time was not simply one which had been appropriated from Nunnaminster to Pershore but rather one which was centred upon two houses with equal claims to the patronage of the saintly princess.[160]

Osbert's account of Edburga's translation to and cult at Pershore has the appearance of a brief and self-contained appendix, conceived as an instrument of monastic propaganda, and rather clumsily tacked on to the end of what remains, in essence, a Winchester Life of the saint: as such it is far from convincing. Moreover, because the early history of Pershore is notoriously obscure, its reliability is exceptionally difficult to assess. It has been shown that Osbert's attribution of the refoundation of Pershore to *comes Alwardus*, although corroborated by William of Malmesbury, is itself not above suspicion.[161] And on the subject of *Alwardus*'s acquisition for the house of Edburga's relics even William is silent: he clearly believed that Pershore possessed relics of Edburga, but he hazards no guess as to how they came to be there.[162] Among later sources, the Hyde breviary makes no reference to the Pershore relics of Edburga; the Harleian translation narrative and the

---

[156] *Ibid.*, fols. 110–110v. The miracle concerns the cure of a paralysed woman at Edburga's Pershore shrine. [157] *Ibid.*, fol. 107. [158] *Ibid.*, fol. 108v. [159] *Ibid.*, fol. 110. [160] See above, p. 19. [161] See above, p. 31. [162] *GP*, p. 298.

Lansdowne Life parallel in outline Osbert's account;[163] the Harleian *Miracula* offer no explanation of the presence of Edburga's relics at Pershore; and the Middle English Life states in a matter-of-fact way that:

> þe abbesse solde hir scolle to þe abbeiȝe of Pershore
> Vor þe erl þat began þat hous an hondred pound ȝaf þerfore.[164]

There is no extant Pershore calendar against which Osbert's October date for the feast of Edburga's translation to that house can be checked; but the position of the *Vita Edburge* within MS Laud Misc. 114 strongly suggests that his date was fully in accordance with the local practice of the twelfth century.[165] And it is possible that the considerable body of evidence for the early and consistent celebration in the Worcester area of the feast of the saint's deposition may be explained by the presence of some of her relics at Pershore.[166] Two further points may tend in Osbert's favour. The first abbot of the refounded Pershore, Foldbriht, was a disciple of St Æthelwold.[167] As such he may have been well informed about the inception of Edburga's cult at Winchester and about any possible opportunity for the acquisition of her relics. More than this, such an opportunity may well have arisen at precisely the time when the refounded Pershore was most in need of a saintly patron. The refoundation of Pershore is probably to be dated to *c.* 970. And Æthelwold's translation of Edburga may have taken place in the early 970s, at which time the refoundation of Nunnaminster may have been nearing completion.[168] Medieval translations were quite commonly regarded as opportunities for the dissemination of relics;[169] hence it is possible that Edburga's translation by

163 MS Harley 64, fols. 47–47v, 84–85; Braswell, 'St Edburga', p. 333.

164 Braswell, 'St Edburga', p. 329.

165 For the Pershore feast of St Edburga see *Vita Edburge*, fol. 110v. For a suggestion that MS Laud Misc. 114 may comprise portions of a martyrology intended for Pershore use, and for the significance of the position of the *Vita Edburge* within this MS, see below, pp. 256–7. On the absence of Pershore liturgical documents see Morgan, 'Notes', p. 133 and n. 2.

166 See above, p. 129. Because this feast was very widely commemorated in pre-Conquest England the significance of its celebration in the Worcester area is not easy to assess: it need not necessarily imply a relic cult in that area. Likewise the continued celebration of the feast after the Conquest, while it may have been stimulated in part by the relic cult which we know to have existed by Osbert's day, sheds no light upon the origin of that cult.

167 *MO*, p. 51; Atkins, 'The church of Worcester', p. 388; *Chronicon monasterii de Abingdon*, ed. J. Stevenson, 2 vols., RS 2 (London, 1858), I, 124; II, 257–8.

168 On the refoundation of Pershore see above, p. 31 and n. 76; on that of Nunnaminster and Edburga's translation by Æthelwold see above, pp. 106–14.

169 Two interesting English examples may be cited. In the early thirteenth century the

Æthelwold provided the occasion for the division of her relics and for the sale of some of them to *comes Alwardus*, or perhaps to Æthelwold's disciple, the first abbot of Pershore.

The events of the early 970s, then, provide a plausible context for the transaction described by Osbert – a sale of relics, perhaps not entirely above board, which the Winchester nuns came rapidly to regret. But three other explanations for the relic cult of St Edburga at Pershore deserve serious consideration. First, it is possible that the relics of the Winchester saint were indeed acquired in the tenth century but in a manner rather different from that described by Osbert. The dissemination of relics in the Middle Ages did not always take place by fair means; and a translation such as that of *c.* 970 would have provided a prime opportunity for a little holy theft:[170] the alleged purchase of relics may in reality have been a judiciously concealed theft by some representative of the Pershore community. Such an explanation would do much to explain the note of monastic discontent which rumbles ominously through the closing section of Osbert's work. And it might add a more sinister significance to the nuns' barefoot pilgrimage to Pershore: perhaps that pilgrimage belongs less to the history of medieval piety than to the lost history of monastic skulduggery. One point, however, is puzzling. If indeed we were dealing with a case of theft, we might expect to find some attempt in the Winchester sources to repudiate

cathedral of Worcester was rebuilt; in 1218 it was rededicated to saints Mary, Peter, Oswald and Wulfstan and the relics of St Wulfstan were translated into a new shrine (*Annales de Wigornia*, pp. 409–10). This translation seems to have provided the occasion for the division of the saint's relics. William, abbot of St Albans, is said to have returned home bearing a rib of St Wulfstan, and the bishops of Norwich and Salisbury, whose presence at the ceremony is recorded in the Worcester annals, may have fared equally well, for each of their cathedrals later claimed relics of the saint (Thomas, 'Cult of relics', p. 139). Likewise Faricius, abbot of Abingdon (1100–17), who seems to have been of central importance in promoting the relic cults of that house, was present at the Winchester translation of St Æthelwold in 1111 (*Chronicon monasterii de Abingdon*, II, 46; *Annales de Wintonia*, p. 44): here he acquired the arm and shoulder-blade of St Æthelwold which appear in an Abingdon relic list compiled after an investigation of the relic collection in 1116 (*Chronicon monasterii de Abingdon*, II, 155–8). Thomas suggests that Faricius may have acquired at the same time the relics of other Winchester saints, including Edburga, whose names appear in the Abingdon list ('Cult of relics', p. 154 and n. 5).

170 For a general study of relic thefts in the Middle Ages see P. Geary, *'Furta sacra': thefts of relics in the central Middle Ages* (Princeton, 1978). One interesting point highlighted by Geary is that hagiographical texts frequently explain and justify relic thefts by reference to the piety and special devotion to the saint of the thief (*ibid.*, pp. 139–40). In the *Vita Edburge* Osbert of Clare frequently uses this device to explain and to justify the purchase of Edburga's relics by *comes Alwardus*: see for instance fol. 107v: 'Unde zelo succensus flagrabat superno ut pretiose uirginis Eadburge reliquias adquireret'; cf. *ibid.*, fols. 108–109 *passim*.

Pershore's claim to the relics. It seems unlikely, though it is not impossible, that Osbert's postulated Winchester source included such a repudiation; and the Hyde breviary simply ignores the existence of Edburga's cult at Pershore. There survives only one enigmatic passage in the Winchester annals to indicate that all was not well with the relics of the Nunnaminster saint, and this speaks darkly of conflict not with Pershore but with the abbey of Great Malvern. The accession of Edward the Elder is noted, with the statement that 'His daughter was St Edburga, whose holy body in truth rests in Winchester at Nunnaminster; although the monks of Malvern falsely claim to have it.'[171] There is, so far as I can ascertain, no other evidence that the monks of Malvern laid claim to any part of St Edburga's body, and it is possible that the two Worcestershire houses of Pershore and Great Malvern had been confused by the compiler of the annals. In the case of St Edburga's relics, therefore, theft may, perhaps should, be suspected; it is unlikely ever to be proved. A second explanation for the Pershore cult of St Edburga involves ignorance rather than fraud: it is possible that the Winchester relics were acquired at a later stage in the history of Pershore and in a manner which was hopelessly confused even by Osbert's day – perhaps through that *Odda*, son of Ealdorman Ælfhere, who was said by Leland to have been an important patron of Pershore.[172] The third, and most interesting, possibility is that we may be dealing with a case of mistaken identity: were the relics whose presence at Pershore Osbert sought to explain really those of St Edburga of Winchester?

There existed during the Middle Ages an obscure and confused tradition of another, Mercian, Edburga. Christopher Hohler, in an important study of the legend of St Osyth, draws attention to the fact that the 'First Essex Life' of that saint, although written for the Essex community of Chich (later St Osyth), nevertheless endows its subject with a Mercian genealogy.[173] Osyth is said to have been a grandchild of Penda of Mercia by his daughter Wilburga and her

---

[171] *Annales de Wintonia*, p. 10.   [172] See above, p. 36, n. 99.
[173] C. Hohler, 'St Osyth and Aylesbury', *Records of Buckinghamshire* 18 (1966–70), 61–72, at 63. The possession of Osyth's relics was disputed between the Essex community and the church of Aylesbury, Buckinghamshire. Hohler notes that: 'The Essex church had, formally, the better of the argument, but the matter was not officially settled till 1502, in spite of the inequality of the contest between a rich and important Augustinian abbey near London and what throughout the later Middle Ages was the parish church of a singularly undistinguished town. Aylesbury's strong card was that its claim was almost certainly correct' (*ibid.*, pp. 61–3).

husband Fredeswald. The hagiographer goes on to explain that
Penda, although himself a pagan, had many Christian descendants,
and to name among his children King Peada and St Cyneburga,
both well attested, and a mysterious St Edburga.[174] Further information concerning this Edburga seems to have been embodied in
the Life of St Osyth composed by William de Vere, bishop of
Hereford (1186–98); the Life is lost, but extracts from it were
preserved by Leland.[175] William, an Essex man with Buckinghamshire connections, incorporated into his work a Buckinghamshire
tradition according to which St Osyth was brought up by her
maternal aunt, Edith, who lived at Aylesbury; this Edith is said to
have had a sister, Edburga, who lived at Adderbury in Oxfordshire.[176] Leland implies that Edith had been in charge of some kind
of religious community, and very probably the same was true of
the Edburga *uirgo* of Adderbury. The existence and local importance of this Edburga is further attested by the Mercian place-name
evidence. Adderbury clearly takes its name from a lady called
Edburga: it appears as *Ead(b)urggebyrig* and *Eadburgebyrig* in wills of
c. 950 and *c.* 1015 respectively, and as *Eadburgberie* in the Domesday
survey.[177] More than this, Hohler was able to put forward an
interesting and convincing argument in favour of the existence of
an early Life of the Adderbury saint.[178] Finally, a small group of

---

The so-called First Essex Life of the saint is preserved in London, BL, MS Lansdowne
436 and in Gotha, Landesbibliothek, MS 1.81. For a detailed analysis of the Osyth legend
see D. Bethell, 'The Lives of St Osyth of Essex and St Osyth of Aylesbury', *AB* 88 (1970),
75–127.

[174] On Peada and Cyneburga see the Mercian genealogy in 'Florence', *Chronicon*, I, 252.
The genealogy of the 'First Essex Life' includes also St Mildrith, St Werburga and two
mysterious ladies, St Elftreda and St Elgida. Hohler identifies the former as Ælfthryth,
the abbess of Repton who appears in Felix's Life of St Guthlac ('St Osyth', p. 63; *Felix's
Life of St Guthlac*, p. 84 and note) and the latter with a lady said by Hugh Candidus to be
buried at Bishop's Stortford ('St Osyth', p. 63; *The Chronicle of Hugh Candidus*, ed.
W. T. Mellows (London, 1949), p. 62).

[175] See Hohler, 'St Osyth', p. 64; Leland, *Itinerarium*, VIII, 41.

[176] Leland, *Itinerarium*, VIII, 41: 'Ositha filia Fredewaldi regis, et Wilburgæ Pendæ regis
filiæ. Ositha adhæsit doctrinæ Edithæ et Eadburgæ, quarum neptis erat. Fredewaldus
rex paganus. Editha domina de Ailesbirie, quam villam non ex patris dono, sed extortam
matris adepta gaudebat. Ositha famulabatur Edithæ in Ailesbury. Eadburga, soror
Edithæ, habitabat apud Edburbiry, quæ a nomine virginis, quæ vico prævidebat, nomen
hoc sortita est, ab Ailesbyri decem stadiis interfuluum habens amnem, qui sæpe turgidus
inundatione pluviarum et ventorum impulsione itinerantibus molestum facit
transitum.' For discussion of this passage see Hohler, 'St Osyth', pp. 64–5.

[177] M. Gelling, *The place-names of Oxfordshire*, 2 parts, English Place-Name Society 23
(Cambridge, 1953–4), II (1954), 391; *Wills*, ed. Whitelock, pp. 10, 108–14, 56, 167–74;
cf. above, n. 176.

[178] Hohler, 'St Osyth', pp. 64–6. Hohler suggests that an early Life of the Adderbury

calendars seem to attest to the liturgical veneration of this saint –
unfortunately on the same day as the Winchester translation of the
West Saxon Edburga.[179]

The existence of this second, Mercian, Edburga is problematical.
If we are to accept the existence of this distinct Mercian saint, we
must accept also the possibility that the relics claimed by the
Pershore monks were in fact relics of this saint – an obscure local
lady, probably foundress of some forgotten nunnery, of whom
nothing remained except a few bones and the vague memory of a
name. Perhaps Osbert of Clare, seeking to provide this local
Mercian saint with an identity and a more-than-local reputation,
simply appropriated the legend of the better-known West Saxon
saint, justifying that appropriation by the invention of a dubious
translation of relics. If this was the case, moreover, we cannot know
whether Osbert was the originator of the tradition of mistaken

Edburga may have been the source from which the author of the 'First Essex Life' of St
Osyth was working when he supplied his subject with a Mercian genealogy. He notes,
first, that in order to have hit upon saints of such obscurity as Edburga, Elftreda and
Elgida the author of the 'First Essex Life' must have been using a written source which
came from somewhere north west of London. Second, it is clear from the subsequent
history of the Osyth legend that the St Osyth to whom this source referred was made to
live, die and be buried in Aylesbury: this explains why the genealogy was the only
portion of the source to be incorporated into the Essex Life. Further, William de Vere
incorporated into his Life of St Osyth a number of Buckinghamshire traditions,
including a particularly grandiose description of the river Cherwell (cited above, n.
176). Hohler suggests that this description must have formed the setting for some
hagiographical anecdote which Leland did not copy out. The nature of this anecdote,
however, may be deduced from the work of an eleventh-century Irishman,
Conchubran, who came to England in search of materials to improve the Life of St
Monenna, abbess of Killeavy, who allegedly crossed the Irish Sea on a floating island.
Conchubran, on encountering the legend of St Modwenna, who was said to be buried at
Burton-on-Trent, decided that this lady must be identifiable with Monenna. In his
subsequent attempt to enhance the glory of Monenna/Modwenna he introduced into
his narrative a certain Ite and a maiden Osid, whose sole function was to be sent by
Ite to give a book to Monenna/Modwenna, to fall into the river Anker *en route*, and
to be resurrected three days later – still clutching the undamaged book – by
Monenna/Modwenna. Of this legend Hohler writes: 'It can be pretty well taken for
granted that St Modwenna was not a protagonist in this story before Conchubran got
hold of it. But "Ite" and "Osid", notably the latter, are primarily introduced into his
narrative as part of it and it must have been related about them before it reached
Conchubran's ears. This is obviously the story for which Leland, following de Vere,
gives us the setting; and I think it is clear that its source is the legend of St Edburga, whom
Conchubran has replaced by St Modwenna as nonchalantly as he has replaced the
Cherwell by the Anker' (*ibid.*, p. 66).

[179] For discussion of these calendars, see Hohler, 'St Osyth', p. 71, n. 13. The calendar in
London, St Paul's cathedral, MS 83c. 19 has for 18 July the mysterious entry 'Eadburge
virginis. Ositha', and that in Cambridge, Clare College, MS Kk. iii. 6 has 18 July as the
only feast of Edburga.

identity under which the Pershore monks were evidently
labouring, or whether, as seems more likely, he had for once been at
the receiving end of a confused and corrupt tradition which was
already established at Pershore and which he was merely required
to commit to writing.

The problem, however, does not end here. In the early 1180s the
Augustian priory of Bicester was founded by Gilbert Basset. The
house was dedicated to St Edburga, and the remains of her shrine
from Bicester can still be seen in the church of Stanton Harcourt.[180]
But which St Edburga was enshrined at Bicester? And to which St
Edburga did the dedication of the house refer? In the thirteenth
century it was assumed that the Winchester saint was intended. The
Middle English Life of that saint notes that

> Þe abbeiȝe of Perschore of Seint Eadborw is,
> And þe nonnerie of Winchestre ek, þer heo was nonne iwis,
> And Burcestre þer biside Oxneford þre canones beþ
> Of Seint Ædborw hii beþ all þreo, as men al day seþ.[181]

And the medieval seals of both Pershore and Bicester portrayed the
Blessed Virgin, together with St Edburga, crowned and bearing in
her right hand a cup and in her left a book:[182] the allusion is almost
certainly to the chalice and gospel-book of the Winchester legend.

The truth, however, may have been nothing like so simple. It has

---

[180] For the early history and dedication of the Augustinian priory of Bicester see KH, p. 147
(St Edburga); *Heads*, p. 151 (St Edburga and St Mary); J. C. Dickinson, *The origins of the
Austin canons and their introduction into England* (London, 1950), pp. 141, 148 (St Edburga);
VCH Oxon., II, 94 (St Edburga), *Monasticon*, VI, i, 432 (St Mary and St Edburga); White
Kennett, *Parochial antiquities attempted in the history of Ambrosden, Burcester and other
adjacent parts in the counties of Oxford and Buckinghamshire* (Oxford, 1695), pp. 134ff.
(St Edburga). Kennett printed a number of early Bicester charters, but these provide no
evidence for the dedication of the house. The Stanton Harcourt shrine of St Edburga is
discussed by E. A. G. Lambourn, 'The shrine of St Edburg', *Reports of the Oxfordshire
Archaeological Society* 80 (1934), 43–52.
[181] Braswell, 'St Edburga', p. 329. Later writers have held various opinions as to the identity
of the Bicester Edburga. Leland wrote simply that the priory church was dedicated to
'St Edburge the Virgine' (*Itinerarium*, VII, 4). White Kennett believed that the Mercian
saint was intended (*Parochial antiquities*, p. 137) and the same view is taken by Christopher Hohler ('St Osyth', pp. 63ff.) and D. H. Farmer (*ODS*, p. 118). Laurel Braswell,
though clearly aware of the danger of confusion between the West Saxon and Mercian
saints, nevertheless simply accepts the statement of the Middle English Life that the
Bicester and the Winchester saint were identical ('St Edburga', p. 297), and I. G. Thomas
tentatively identifies the Bicester saint with the West Saxon Edburga ('Cult of relics',
p. 196). Historians have also shown a tendency to confuse the Edith whom Leland's notes
locate at Aylesbury with the Edburga who is placed by those notes at Adderbury: the
result is a curious hybrid, St Edburga of Aylesbury (see, for instance, Kennett, *Parochial
antiquities*, p. 137; *ODS*, p. 118).   [182] *VCH Worcs.*, II, 136; *VCH Oxon.*, II, 95.

been shown that the story of St Edburga's translation from Winchester to Pershore must be treated with extreme caution. More than this, we have no evidence for a translation either from Winchester itself or from Pershore to the Augustinian foundation at Bicester. In these circumstances it is impossible to establish whether the three houses of Nunnaminster, Pershore and Bicester possessed the relics of one and the same Edburga or whether we are dealing with two distinct saints, a Mercian and a West Saxon, whose legends and cults had become the object of confusion. In these circumstances too there remains a final and intractable problem: were the relics enshrined at either Pershore or Bicester those of *either* the Mercian *or* the West Saxon saint of whom we have alternative information? The refounded Pershore of the tenth century was established on the site of, and may have been a direct successor to, an earlier religious community.[183] And the priory of Bicester shared its dedication to St Edburga with a parish church which seems to have been an important mother church even before the Conquest: the church was given by Gilbert Basset to the priory and it is quite possible that it was from here that the priory obtained its relics of Edburga.[184] In each case the new foundation may have succeeded to the relics of an earlier community;[185] and those relics may have been treated with all the respect due to their antiquity but with little understanding of their history and local significance. In each case it would have been the easiest thing in the world for the new community to assume that the local relics of Edburga *uirgo* were those of the relatively well-known West Saxon saint and to establish a dedication, a shrine and a seal on the basis of that assumption. Perhaps, to the Pershore monks of the tenth century and to the Bicester canons of the twelfth, a cult based on mistaken identity of St Edburga of Winchester was both more convenient and more prestigious than a cult of the obscure founder or patron of a small, transient and forgotten Anglo-Saxon community, whose relics had been jealously guarded but whose legend was irretrievably lost.

The history of the Pershore relics of St Edburga must remain, at

[183] See above, p. 31 and n. 76.
[184] *VCH Oxon.*, II, 94; VI, 40; Leland, *Itinerarium*, VII, 4; Kennett, *Parochial antiquities*, p. 136.
[185] Kennett (*Parochial antiquities*, p. 137) knew of a document of the reign of Edward I which referred to a spring at Bicester called 'Edburg's well' and to a path between the town and the priory known as *Edburghes grene way* or *Via sanctæ Edburgæ*. These names may testify to the existence of a tradition concerning a local St Edburga; alternatively they may have evolved simply from association with the church or priory.

least for the present, an unsolved puzzle. The story told by Osbert of Clare, probably in accordance with twelfth-century Pershore tradition, is neat but not wholly convincing. Analysis of that story does, however, open a window upon the wide range of human deeds and motives which may have determined the diffusion of Edburga's cult. It permits some exploration of the meaning which that cult may have held for men and women who can be variously understood as devout, mercenary, competitive, opportunist, fraudulent or simply confused. And it suggests something of the complex relationship of actuality and belief in the transmission of cult. It is only to be regretted that Osbert reveals so little of the use which the Pershore monks made of the belief, accurate or not, which they so successfully fostered.

Chapter 5

THE CHILDREN OF EDGAR

EDITH AT WILTON: THE ROYAL PATRON

Goscelin's *Vita Edithe* provides a finely drawn portrait of a royal child who, renouncing her secular status, became an exile from her earthly home and sought instead the heavenly and immortal land, 'showing in the preservation of chastity that she sought the virgin's son and seeking by a pilgrim's life on earth to win a heavenly spouse above'.[1] Goscelin, like Osbert of Clare, makes of his subject a hagiographical stereotype, whose sanctity is founded upon a conventional antithesis between the *uirgo regia* and the *sponsa summi regis*. And in so doing Goscelin, like Osbert, seriously obscures the historical role of a saint whose posthumous reputation was founded less upon the pleasant theory of royal piety than upon the hard fact of royal patronage.

I have suggested in my analysis of St Edburga's cult that the hagiographical model of Edburga's sanctity as derived from an ecclesiastical role both divorced from and antithetical to that implied by her royal birth tells only a part of the truth.[2] It breaks down because Edburga's life was spent in a religious community closely associated with the West Saxon royal house, predominantly aristocratic in composition and thoroughly *au fait* with the dealings of the royal and aristocratic world. Within that community there could be no real renunciation of secular status and no real antithesis between *uirgo regia* and *sponsa summi regis*: the path to the heavenly bridal chamber lay not through the renunciation of the attributes of royalty but through their redeployment within the monastic context. The same themes apply with equal force to the history of St Edith.

The abbey of Wilton, like Nunnaminster, was a creation of the

---

[1] *Vita Edithe*, p. 45. [2] See above, pp. 96–103.

West Saxon royal house. The original foundation can probably be dated to *c.* 830, when, according to the fifteenth-century *Chronicon Vilodunense*, a community of women was established by Alburga, widowed sister of King Egbert, in conjunction with the king and in or on the site of a church founded by her husband, Ealdorman Wulfstan.[3] The community seems to have been reconstituted under Alfredian influence late in the ninth century[4] and again during Edgar's reign in accordance with the principles of the tenth-century monastic reform.[5] The abbey's fourteenth-century cartulary preserves records of land grants by Athelstan, Edwy, Edgar, Æthelred and Edward the Confessor, and at the end of the Anglo-Saxon period Wilton was among the most prominent of England's nunneries, richly endowed, specially favoured by the Confessor's queen, and with royal and aristocratic connections which were to persist for some time after the conquest of 1066.[6]

Goscelin of Canterbury, when he sought at the beginning of the *Vita Edithe* to demonstrate the close connection between Wilton and the West Saxon royal house, did so not by reference to founders or citation of charters. Instead he emphasised a more immediate and

[3] *Chronicon Vilodunense*, p. 4. For the foundation and early history of Wilton see also Nightingale, *Memorials*, pp. 2–5; *VCH Wilts.*, III, 231–2; KH, p. 267; Meyer, 'Patronage of the West Saxon royal nunneries', pp. 334, 351–4.

[4] *Chronicon Vilodunense*, pp. 14–15; KH, p. 267.

[5] Wilton's history in the second half of the tenth century cannot be reconstructed in detail. In the MS of the *Chronicon Vilodunense* twelve folios are missing from the account of Edgar's reign and of Edith's career, and the surviving Wilton charters are of doubtful value: in particular S799, which purports to be a charter of refoundation, cannot be accepted as authentic in its present form (I am grateful to Dr Simon Keynes for his valuable comments on this and other Wilton charters). It is, however, most unlikely that Wilton could have remained isolated from the movement of reform. And the *Vita Edithe* itself contains a number of passages which strongly suggest that Wilton during the time of St Edith and her mother was a community in the process of reform. First, Goscelin asserts a close connection between Wilton and the leading reformers Dunstan and Æthelwold: see *Vita Edithe*, pp. 42, 57, 70–1, 74–5, 76, 87–8, 90–2, 95–6, 266–9. Second, he portrays the period as one of construction: St Edith built an *oratorium* in honour of St Denys (*ibid.*, pp. 86–7); a guest- or alms-house (*xenodochium*) was also constructed (*ibid.*, p. 96), and Wulfthryth is described as an important *edificatrix* (*ibid.*, p. 274). Third, Goscelin notes that one of Wulfthryth's major achievements was to surround her abbey with a stone wall (*ibid.*) – an activity which calls to mind the importance attached at Winchester to the enclosure of the newly reformed communities (see below, p. 110). Finally, Goscelin's work indicates that much importance was attached during this period to the acquisition of relics (*Vita Edithe*, pp. 73–5, 273–4): in this respect too Wilton's activities paralleled those of other reformed communities (see below, pp. 107–8).

[6] S424, 438, 582, 766–7, 799. The abbey's cartulary is preserved in London, BL, Harley MS 436 and is printed as *Registrum Wiltunense*, ed. R. C. Hoare (London, 1827). For the history of Wilton at the close of the Anglo-Saxon period see below, pp. 154, 172–3.

personal link between the saint's family and the religious community in which her life was to be spent. He notes that Wulfthryth, following the birth of her only child, renounced the pleasures of the flesh and withdrew from the royal court to Wilton, where she became abbess.[7] Wulfthryth's entry to Wilton must remain something of a historical mystery: it can be variously interpreted as the pious withdrawal of a virtuous wife, as the timely removal of an embarrassing concubine or perhaps as the no less timely removal of a wife who had outlived her political and dynastic usefulness.[8] Whatever the case, withdrawal did not imply disgrace. Wulfthryth's elevation to abbatial status in itself indicates that she received substantial royal backing in her new life. And one can perhaps go further. Wulfthryth seems to have presided over at least the greater part of Wilton's reform in Edgar's reign: she may well have been appointed by the king with this precise purpose in mind.[9]

About the composition of the community in the time of Wulfthryth and her daughter, and about its relationship with the outside world, Goscelin's account is particularly informative. The community had traditionally been, and continued to be, predominantly aristocratic in nature. Wulfthryth, whatever her relationship to the king, is described in her own right as 'offshoot of princes and noble child of a royal duke'.[10] The community included, in the person of a certain Wulfwen, at least one other representative of the royal family.[11] And, for the rest: 'The community of virgins and brides of Christ was at that time drawn, as is customary, from the highest ranks of society – from the most illustrious daughters of the princes, thegns and magnates of the realm.'[12] In the hagiographical theory, the saint was an exile, a waif awaiting rescue by Christ: 'with a prophetic voice she sang "My father and mother have forsaken me, but the Lord has taken me up."'[13] In reality, Edith was far from being forsaken: she remained under the direct care and supervision of her mother and, more generally, she continued to move within a royal and aristocratic society which was her natural milieu. With every page of Goscelin's narrative we are transported

[7] *Vita Edithe*, pp. 42–3.   [8] See above, pp. 37, 42–3.

[9] See above, n. 5. Goscelin's statement (*Vita Edithe*, pp. 42–3) that Wulfthryth was supported by St Æthelwold in her entry to the religious life perhaps lends some support to this suggestion.   [10] *Vita Edithe*, p. 40.

[11] *Ibid.*, p. 61: 'Regiam quoque consanguineam Vluennam ceteramque nobilium uirginum turbam suo emendabat exemplo.'   [12] *Ibid.*, pp. 61–2; cf. above, n. 11.

[13] *Vita Edithe*, p. 47, citing Ps. 26:10.

into a world where monasticism provided a respectable alternative career for those royal and aristocratic ladies who had failed to marry or who wished to extricate themselves from marriage. In theory those ladies had withdrawn from the world, and in practice the walls of their convents afforded some protection against the worst excesses of the world: but their seclusion was far from complete.

Wilton in the tenth century was the site of an important royal residence,[14] and several passages in Goscelin's *Vita* draw attention to the close and continuing connections between the royal court and the religious community. Thus the occasion of Edith's vocation, according to Goscelin, was a visit of her royal father to the abbey. Edgar, moreover, did not come alone. If the hagiographer is to be believed, Edith's formal commitment to the religious life was a public ceremony of some note: Edgar came to the nunnery 'with a stream of princes, clergy, members of the court and common people, as if to the court of Christ and a heavenly betrothal feast'.[15] Likewise the saint's death, in theory the culmination of a lifetime's withdrawal, was followed by a funeral which shows it to have been an event of national interest and importance.[16] Elsewhere it is made clear that the saint continued after her entry to the religious life to have access to her father[17] and, interestingly, that those whose political function was to honour the father found it prudent to honour the daughter likewise. Edith enjoyed the veneration of the dukes, magnates and matrons of her father's realm; greetings, letters and gifts poured in from foreign kingdoms and principalities; holy prelates begged for her intercession, and those envoys who were sent from Gaul or Germany, from Rome itself or even from the emperors to the court of King Edgar gloried in commending themselves to his saintly daughter.[18]

The community of Wilton, then, was a royal foundation, bound to the West Saxon royal house by the strongest ties of patronage and – though Goscelin's account may not be devoid of exaggeration – maintaining close connections with the royal and aristocratic world from which it had sprung. Within that community, the admiration felt for Edith, and likewise for her mother, may well

[14] *Life of King Edward*, ed. Barlow, pp. 94–5; Nightingale, *Memorials*, p. 1; *VCH Wilts.*, VI, 7–8. [15] *Vita Edithe*, p. 43.
[16] *Ibid.*, p. 95: 'Confluentibus autem turbis et eclesiasticis patribus ac proceribus regio funeri nobiles exsequie celebrantur; nec uero decuit maioris pompe comitatus, si terreni nupciis regis regia filia exhiberetur.' [17] See, for instance, *ibid.*, pp. 64–5.
[18] *Ibid.*, pp. 62–3.

have been a product less of exceptional piety than of exceptional social status: the nuns of Wilton, like those of Winchester, were unlikely to forget the special status of the *filia principis*. Nor were they likely to forget the special usefulness of the daughter and former wife or concubine of the king. That usefulness was, first, symbolic. Within the *sancta congregatio* the presence of Edith and her mother symbolised the traditionally close relationship between the religious house and the ruling dynasty: it was a status symbol in the world of monastic politics. And, second, the presence of the royal ladies had a practical value of the highest importance. As in the case of Edburga, it served further to cement that vital relationship: in the changing circumstances of the 960s and 970s it served to ensure continuing royal interest in and patronage of the abbey – to guarantee, in effect, a smooth and profitable transition from traditional to reformed community. Goscelin's narrative contains nothing to compare with the *Canaga* episode in the clarity and detail with which this delineates the saint's function as *mediatrix ad regem*.[19] It is, however, made clear from the outset that the community's expectations of the royal child were not to be disappointed. Goscelin's account of Edith's entry to the religious life at Wilton ends with a telling footnote:

The king gave lands; he bestowed royal gifts and increased pastures . . . So in the blessed Edith the abundant blessing of the Lord brought prosperity for ever to this house.[20]

Elsewhere, Goscelin provides some insight into the several forms which royal patronage, channelled through the *uirgo regia*, might take. He notes, for instance, in a chapter devoted to the saint's education and training, that King Edgar assumed responsibility for the appointment to Wilton of two priests of outstanding ability, Radbod of Rheims and Benno of Trier, the latter renowned for his skill as an artist: the context makes it plain that this 'intellectual patronage' was motivated by Edgar's desire to provide the best possible education for his daughter.[21] On other occasions, it seems, the royal goodwill needed a little deliberate prompting and the saint acted more directly as *mediatrix ad regem*: 'She obtained without difficulty', Goscelin writes, 'her father's indulgence.'[22] By her intercession with the king the saint seems to have obtained for the church and for her protégés benefits which were not only

---

[19] See above, pp. 99–101.   [20] *Vita Edithe*, p. 46.
[21] *Ibid.*, p. 50.   [22] *Ibid.*, p. 65.

financial but also judicial in nature: 'She tempered the stern decrees of the laws and the judges; she overcame by tears, prayers and offerings the furious hosts; she snatched the prey from the very jaws of death.' Whatever she demanded from her father he gladly gave, multiplying churches and other gifts and pardoning those under sentence.[23] For an indication of the type of concession which the royal lady might obtain we must look to an incident involving not Edith and her father but Wulfthryth and the later king Æthelred. When a thief fled to the monastic church in the hope of sanctuary Wulfthryth refused to ensure his safety by locking the doors against his pursuers. Instead, the royal servants who followed him into the church were blinded in punishment for their intrusion and, 'with the consent of King Æthelred, Wulfthryth let the robber depart in peace':[24] an essential adjunct of Wulfthryth's miraculous power was her ability to intercede with the king.

St Edith and her mother seem, moreover, to have provided for their community something more than intercession with the king – personal patronage based on continuing access to private wealth. Unlike Osbert of Clare, Goscelin nowhere explicitly states that his subject retained personal wealth following her entry to the religious life; such retention would have contravened the principles of the reformers; and it is unclear how in practice such wealth would have been administered. Goscelin does, however, make it clear that Edith and her mother had access to substantial financial resources, and he strongly implies that those resources, and the saints' rights of disposal over them, were of a personal nature; their deployment is portrayed as a series of acts of personal piety and generosity.[25]

Two such acts involved the acquisition of relics. In common with the heads of reformed communities elsewhere, Wulfthryth seems to have attached much importance to the acquisition of relics by which her community's prestige and corporate identity might be enhanced.[26] Goscelin explains that she conceived an ambitious scheme to procure for Wilton a relic of the Passion from the

[23] *Ibid.*, pp. 64–5.
[24] *Ibid.*, pp. 272–3, at p. 273. Cf. Æthelred's legislation on sanctuary: *EHD*, I, 411, no. 46, cc. 1–5 (VIII Æthelred, 1014).
[25] Since retention of personal wealth so evidently contradicted the principles of the reformers and their successors it is particularly striking that Goscelin implies the contraventions of his subject and that Osbert of Clare, writing of an earlier period, explicitly describes his saint's failure to conform to later ideals (see above, p. 102). But the point should not be too much laboured: few medieval princesses would have thought of renouncing their wealth if this meant the impoverishment of their communities. [26] See above, pp. 107–8.

community of St Paulinus at Trier. Her intermediary in this venture was Benno, the Wilton priest and former canon of Trier; her essential bargaining-counter lay in the wealth upon which she could draw: two thousand *solidi* changed hands before Benno was able to return to Wilton bearing a fragment of one of the nails of the Passion.[27] A similar story occurs elsewhere. In a chapter rather inauspiciously entitled 'Quomodo sanctum Iwium a suis non ualentem auferri optinuerit' Goscelin explains that, after Edith's death, a group of foreign clerks came to Wilton bearing relics of St Iwi: these were placed with those of Edith and, when the clerks prepared to leave the house, they had become immovably heavy.[28] The hagiographer here employs a common *topos* according to which relics, by becoming selectively immovable, express the will of the saint concerning his or her resting-place. In this case the implication was clear. St Iwi had judged the previous guardians of his relics unworthy: he had definitively allied himself with St Edith and her community.[29] Finally, after much wrangling and expression of grief, the unfortunate foreigners took the point. 'Wearied at last and despairing', they decided to cut their losses: they accepted two thousand *solidi* from Wulfthryth and 'went away, surrendering to those who held it the blessing of the incomparable treasure'.[30] The historical core underlying this miracle story is not easy to uncover. Very probably the element of the miraculous was adduced in order to make more edifying an essentially financial transaction. Alternatively, the miraculous expression of the saint's will may have been conceived in order to conceal a quarrel over relics or even a relic theft in which the losers had, quite literally, to be bought off. Whatever the case, the key to the success of the operation lay in the wealth which Wulfthryth so conveniently had to hand.

Goscelin's exposition of Edith's virtue culminates in an account

[27] *Vita Edithe*, pp. 73–4. The figure may be considerably exaggerated.
[28] *Ibid.*, pp. 273–4.
[29] *Ibid.* The relics had been placed 'in altari dormicionis beate Edithe' (p. 273); when the clerks came to leave, 'tanto sanctus Ywius affixus est pondere ut ab altari nullo modo leuari posset conamine, quatenus palam daretur intelligi illum sancte uirginis Edithe deuotarumque animarum eius loci amore teneri nec ultra inde uelle separari' (p. 274). The relics of St Iwi are located at Wilton by the *Secgan* (*Heiligen*, ed. Liebermann, p. 17). For a short Life of the saint see *NLA*, II, 91–2: according to this account Iwi was a disciple of St Cuthbert at Lindisfarne and subsequently travelled as an exile for Christ to Brittany, where he lived as a hermit. The feast of St Iwi on 8 October was commemorated in several eleventh-century English calendars: see Wormald (ed.), *Before 1100*, nos. 3, 9–12, 18.   [30] *Vita Edithe*, p. 274. Again the figure may be exaggerated.

of her construction at Wilton of an *oratorium* dedicated to St Denys. This narrative is skilfully juxtaposed with an account of Edith's rejection of an earthly kingdom and is intended to be a final and dramatic illustration of her commitment to the heavenly: central to the thematic structure of Goscelin's work is the statement that the church was built 'less by royal generosity than by heavenly devotion and charity'.[31] This statement, however, itself implies that royal generosity played a not insignificant part. Here as elsewhere, it seems, the purposes of the heavenly kingdom were most effectively served by the resources of the earthly: the construction of the *oratorium* of St Denys was Edith's last and most spectacular act of patronage.

The *oratorium*, according to Goscelin, was dedicated by Archbishop Dunstan. And the ceremony of dedication provided the occasion for that archbishop to make two prophecies of dramatic import. Towards the end of the ceremony the archbishop, weeping, foretold the imminent death of Edith. He also made a more significant prophecy. Observing how assiduously the saint made the sign of the cross, he clasped her right hand and exclaimed: '"Never shall this thumb which makes the sign of our salvation see corruption."'[32] In the highly emotive circumstances of the dedication of Edith's last and greatest gift to the church, Dunstan's prophecy takes on the appearance of a gesture of acknowledgement: there could be no clearer statement of the ease with which the royal patron might be transformed into the patron saint.

And so it came to pass. Edith died, as the archbishop had foreseen, shortly after the dedication of the church which she had provided and which she had designated to be her place of burial.[33] With the words of St Dunstan still ringing in their ears, it was only days before the nuns of Wilton – and foremost among them the saint's own mother – began to experience strange happenings at Edith's tomb. On the thirtieth day, according to Goscelin, the saint appeared in a vision to her mother and reported 'that she had been well received by her king in eternal grace'.[34] Thereafter, while 'Many mothers come near to death when they bury their children – but, once buried, soon forget them', Wulfthryth, 'long since converted from an earthly to a spiritual mother, sent a suppliant

[31] *Ibid.*, p. 86.   [32] *Ibid.*, p. 88.
[33] *Ibid.*, pp. 94–6; see esp. p. 96: 'in ecclesia beati Dionisii, quam tanto martiri fecerat domum, reconditur competenter, ipso prebente sepulcrum. Hunc locum presaga mente sepe uirgo notauerat, et "Hic locus requietionis mee est" dixerat, atque hunc frequentans assiduo imbre lacrimarum irrigauerat.'   [34] *Ibid.*, p. 98.

request for the salvation of her daughter whom she had, as it were, sent on before her, and knew by her pure faith was not dead but sleeping'.[35] The daughter of Edgar had paved the way to the heavenly bridal chamber with the resources of an earthly kingdom. And she had left behind her own mother – a lady with a shrewd appreciation of the usefulness of holy relics – to ensure that her contribution should not be forgotten. It was only a matter of time before the church which Edith had built became her own shrine.

EDITH THE PATRON SAINT

St Edith, then, lived on in the memory of the Wilton nuns: the earthly patron became the protector in heaven. And Goscelin provides a more detailed picture than does Osbert of his subject's posthumous role as patron of the house in which she had spent her life. The term 'patron saint' is one which in modern usage has been considerably debased; and yet the concept is one of infinite complexity. In essence, the function of the monastic patron saint of the Middle Ages was to provide for the individual community both a spiritual example and a powerful protector in heaven – a mediator between the community and the divine power. The relics of the saint formed the physical channel for the transmission of the divine power into the world of men. And, charged with this divine electricity, they became the essential and tangible symbol of the prestige, even the identity, of the community. The kinds of power transmitted through the saint – the kinds of protection or patronage exercised – took many forms: they may, however, be divided into two major categories. Of these, the first comprises protection from the vagaries of a natural world which could be neither controlled nor understood – protection, that is, from fire, from storm, from drought, from hunger, and, above all, from illness and injury. Miracles of this type form the common stock of hagiographical tradition: in various permutations they have a place in the *Vitae* of all respectable saints, and they were of central importance in attracting pilgrimage to any shrine. The second type of patronage is of more specific relevance to the cult of the monastic patron – protection within the world of men. The patron saint was in a real sense the proprietor of the community gathered about his or her shrine and, as such, the protector *par excellence* of its material status

[35] *Ibid.*, p. 99.

and political interests. In a world where no secular guarantee was absolute, and where royal charters might not exist or where their anathemas might be blatantly disregarded, the patron saint provided the surest protection that the time could devise.

Goscelin's account of the posthumous role of St Edith is wholly consistent with this definition of the functions of the monastic patron saint. His St Edith was a lady of two faces. Of these the first was that of the hard-headed businesswoman. And it is in the context of this function that the transition of royal patron into patron saint is most readily intelligible. The functions of the monastic saint as guardian of status and wealth were such that the community of Wilton, in looking to St Edith — and to a lesser extent to her mother — as its heavenly patron, quite understandably looked to a royal lady who in life had shown herself to be both dedicated to and effective in the protection of that community. St Edith as patron saint was called upon to fulfil after death by the exercise of miraculous powers functions closely analogous to those which in life she had fulfilled primarily through the use of wealth and influence.

St Edith was expected, in particular, to uphold the status of her abbey as an important local landowner; and, if her hagiographer is to be believed, she carried out her duties with the utmost diligence. Goscelin recounts, for instance, the fate of a certain Agamund, who is said to have seized an estate belonging to the nunnery and rather foolishly to have died impenitent. Thereafter, as he lay among his mourners, he rose and began to beseech his friends for aid: '"Behold, the terrible majesty and unbearable wrath of St Edith is shutting out this wretched soul from every region of heaven and earth; nowhere is the invader of her rights allowed to remain."' The saint's wrath threatened him — and, of course, his audience, which included no less a person than Queen Emma — with a particularly dreadful fate: '"With what severity, with what menacing power does she whom I, a lost soul, had lightly dared despise now confront me and drive my departing soul away, not allowing it to remain in this body, permitting me neither to live nor to die."'[36] The penitent duly appealed to his friends to make amends for his sin and to arrange for the restoration of the estate to St Edith and her community. Not until this was accomplished was he allowed to die in peace, finding in the saint, Goscelin is eager to point out, no longer an avenger but rather a helper.

[36] *Ibid.*, pp. 281–2, at p. 282.

Other offenders were less fortunate. A certain Brixius occupied land belonging to the church of St Edith and refused on his deathbed to make amends. But if the nuns lost their estate, one of their number, a relative of the said Brixius, at least had the satisfaction of witnessing in a vision the rough treatment which he subsequently received at the hands of the saint: 'she saw the rebellious Brixius howling unbearably . . . crouching down behind his little house and crying out to her with a horrible groan as she approached: "I implore you, my dearest kinswoman, make sure that St Edith does not catch sight of me; alas, where can I run to, where can I hide from her countenance?"'[37]

By such means as these St Edith terrorised those who were foolish enough to invade the lands of 'her' church and instilled fear in the hearts of those who might be tempted to emulate those invaders. But in addition to its landed endowment the church of Wilton had one further possession which was essential to its prestige, its prosperity and even its identity – the body of St Edith herself. Goscelin makes it quite clear that the saint was determined consistently, and on occasion even violently, to protect the right of the community to her own remains and to objects otherwise associated with her life and burial. First, a woman who attempted to steal the linen frontal from Edith's tomb was miraculously stopped in her tracks and rendered immobile.[38] On another occasion, apparently at or soon after the saint's translation, a Glastonbury monk who attempted to remove a fragment of her clothing was duly terrified when his knife slipped and touched the holy body: immediately 'a wave of blood gushed forth, as if drawn from a living vein, and spattered the snow-white garments and the floor with its rosy drops'.[39] By similar disconcerting methods, Edith even restrained the devotion of members of her own community when she considered that devotion to be inappropriately expressed. A Wilton nun who tried to remove a portion of the saint's head-band found that the head itself was menacingly raised against her, 'so that she would know with what fear and reverence for the saints who reign with God holy relics are to be treated'.[40] Finally, the saint's sensitivity as regards the proper treatment of her relics combined with her financial acumen in a dramatic incident concerning her shrine. According to Goscelin, King Cnut ordered

---

[37] *Ibid.*, pp. 283–4, at p. 284.   [38] *Ibid.*, pp. 100–1.
[39] *Ibid.*, pp. 270–1, at p. 271.   [40] *Ibid.*, p. 271.

the manufacture of a golden shrine to house the relics of St Edith. The workmen, however, with an eye to their own best interests, appropriated the king's gold and made the shrine instead from gilded silver. Divine vengeance followed quickly: 'they were punished with instant blindness of the eyes which had coveted the gold; those whose minds were dark were cast into outer darkness'.[41]

The purposes of the monastic patron, however, were not served exclusively by dire threats and dreadful punishments. On occasion St Edith was content to resort – apparently with greater effectiveness – to gentle persuasion. Goscelin writes that King Cnut, when imperilled by a storm at sea, was saved by the intercession of St Edith. His gratitude was expressed in the customary fashion – 'when after his return to England he came to Wilton he offered up to God, through the holy intercessor Edith, his thanks with solemn gifts'.[42] Edith's treatment of Cnut forms a convenient bridge between those miracles in which the saint appears first and foremost as vindicator of the material status and political interests of the house and those miracles, most commonly curative in nature, in which she appears rather as *adiutrix*. The two are of course closely connected, for it was on the performance of conventional curative miracles that any widespread or popular recognition of the cult depended; and widespread and popular recognition brought with it both prestige and wealth. The point is made explicit in the story of Cnut's rescue, but it must be remembered that even the lesser clients of Edith's shrine were each a part of an intricate pattern of spreading reputation. Even in the context of this kind of miracle, however, we are left in no doubt that the saint's first responsibility was to her own community of Wilton. Goscelin attributes to both Edith and her mother a number of 'domestic' cures; and in a particularly memorable incident he makes a group of Wilton nuns whose sufferings had *not* been alleviated express in no uncertain terms their doubts concerning St Edith's sense of priorities:

when the heavenly rod tested the Lord's flock, and the scourge of sickness consumed a great number of the sisters, they, sick in mind as well as in body, began to wonder and complain among themselves that St Edith, who so speedily came to the aid of any strangers . . . appeared deaf to the entreaties of her own household.[43]

---

[41] *Ibid.*, p. 280.
[42] *Ibid.*, p. 279. No documentary record has survived of Cnut's generosity to Wilton.
[43] *Ibid.*, p. 297.

THE ROYAL PROMOTION OF ST EDITH'S CULT

The cult of St Edith is primarily intelligible as that of a monastic patron. It was created by the nuns of Wilton in recognition of Edith's historical role as member and patron of their community, and its subsequent development was dictated by the spiritual and material requirements of that community. Likewise the secondary cult of Wulfthryth, the 'hidden treasure and light'[44] for whom Goscelin felt so much admiration, appears as a logical sequel to her historical role as abbess and patron. But the cult of St Edith was not, as that of St Edburga seems to have been, exclusively local and monastic in origin and implication:[45] it possessed a further dimension of the highest importance.

It seems clear from Goscelin's narrative that there was at the time of Edith's death an atmosphere favourable to the transition of Edith the royal patron into Edith the patron saint. Edith's miracles commenced within days of her death; and her own mother became a zealous guardian of her memory: the scene seems set for the smooth and rapid development of Edith's cult. Instead, however, there follows in the recorded history of that cult an unexplained hiatus of thirteen years. And when the cult finally re-emerged, control of its promotion seems to have been removed entirely from the nuns of Wilton. In the thirteenth year after Edith's death, according to her hagiographer, it pleased God to make known her sanctity. The mechanism of this divine revelation was the saint's appearance in visions to a number of prominent individuals, each of whom was urged to undertake the elevation of her remains. She appeared to her half-brother King Æthelred, to the *princeps* Ordwulf, whose position is described as second only to the king, and to a further, unnamed secular magnate; finally, she approached St Dunstan, who was tactfully reminded of his prophecy concerning her incorruption and was ordered to travel to Wilton, where he would find the body not only incorrupt but also raised up, 'as though already prepared to leave the tomb'.[46] Encouraged by this and by a further vision in which Edith's claim to sanctity was warmly recommended by her personal patron, St Denys, the archbishop made his way to Wilton and there performed that translation which is portrayed as setting the seal on the development of Edith's cult.

[44] *Ibid.*, p. 278.   [45] See above, p. 121.   [46] *Vita Edithe*, pp. 265–9, at p. 267.

Goscelin's account of this translation raises a number of extremely difficult problems. The first concerns the actual occasion of the translation. It is unlikely that St Dunstan could have translated Edith thirteen years after her death: we cannot know, however, whether the hagiographer had mistaken the date of the translation or, perhaps more likely, the identity of the archbishop who carried it out.[47] Second, it is unclear how real was the thirteen-year hiatus in the history of the cult which Goscelin's account implies. Third, we cannot know what was the role of the Wilton nuns, omitted entirely from Goscelin's account, in arranging the translation of their patron saint. Nor, finally, do we know what was the relative importance of the several persons whom Goscelin *does* associate with the event. One point, however, does emerge with some clarity – that the translation of the monastic patron was carried out, at least in part, on the initiative of King Æthelred and a number of his leading magnates.

Æthelred, moreover, seems not to have been the only pre-Conquest ruler with an interest in the promotion of St Edith's cult. Cnut, if Goscelin is to be believed, also had a hand in the process. The hagiographer dwells at some length upon that king's devotion to the saint. Whenever he came to Wilton, 'he did not presume to ride within the monastic precinct but would dismount before the gate and with his companions proceed on foot to the church, so that he might teach the distinction between the sacred and the public, between the church of God and the stable'. His mild and generous conduct was determined by 'his reverence for the virgin and for the holy place'.[48] Goscelin goes on to note that it was to St Edith that Cnut prayed when in danger at sea and that it was his gratitude and devotion to the saint which prompted him to reward her community and even to provide a richly decorated shrine to house her relics.[49] Emma, wife of Æthelred and subsequently of Cnut, also

[47] See above, pp. 40–1.
[48] *Vita Edithe*, pp. 278–9. William of Malmesbury preserves (*GP*, p. 190) a rather different tradition concerning Cnut's attitude to the saint. He notes that one Pentecost, at Wilton, the king 'in ipsam virginem solennes cachinnos effudit: "Nunquam se crediturum filiam regis Edgari sanctam esse, qui vitiis deditus maximeque libidinis servus in subjectos propior tiranno fuisset."' Cnut, having been contradicted by Eadnoth, archbishop of Canterbury, angrily ordered the opening of Edith's tomb: 'Effracto ergo mausoleo, defuncta, oppanso ante faciem velo, cingulotenus assurgere, et in contumacem regem impetum facere visa. Hoc ille metu turbatus, longe reducto capite debilitatoque vigore genuum, lapsus humo concidit. Ruina corpus attrivit, adeo ut intercepto diutius anhelitu exanimis putaretur. Sed, redeunte paulatim vigore, letum erubuit, quod, quamvis severe castigatus, penitentiæ reservatus sit.'   [49] *Vita Edithe*, pp. 279, 280.

receives special mention for her devotion to the saint: she not only revered Edith for her holiness but also loved her as a kinswoman, translating her love for the brother into affection for the sister.[50] Elsewhere in the *Vita Edithe* Goscelin makes parenthetical reference to the construction of a new church at Wilton, in honour of Our Lord, the Blessed Virgin and St Edith.[51] Further light is shed upon this church by the anonymous *Vita Ædwardi regis*, where it is said that Edith, queen of the Confessor, emulated her husband's work at Westminster by building a stone church at Wilton: 'For at Wilton at that time, although there was a convent of the handmaidens of Christ, a choir, too, of the greatest antiquity, and her namesake saint, adequately housed, was worshipped there – Ædith, from whose stock King Edward himself was descended – the church was still of wood. And she judged no place more deserving of her devoted labour and zeal than that which, she recalled, had taken pains with her education, and where above all she had learned those virtues which deservedly made her seem suitable to become queen of the English.'[52]

This record of royal veneration of St Edith and royal concern for her church stands in marked contrast to the silence of the *Vita Edburge* concerning royal interest in Winchester's saintly princess. It strongly suggests that the cult of St Edith had political implications which transcended the local and the monastic. And those implications might be most effectively examined by a comparison of the cult of St Edith with the traditionally more controversial cult of her half-brother, Edward the Martyr.

ST EDITH AND ST EDWARD THE MARTYR: THEIR POLITICAL SIGNIFICANCE

Both St Edith of Wilton and St Edward the Martyr were products of King Edgar's complex marital history.[53] There, to all intents and purposes, the connection between the two saints ends. The *uirgo regia* whose life was conceived as a pilgrimage towards the heavenly bridal chamber and the child king whose claim to sanctity derived from his murder by fellow Christians for political ends belong to two quite distinct hagiological traditions,[54] their legends take

---

[50] *Ibid.*, p. 281.   [51] *Ibid.*, p. 300.
[52] *Life of King Edward*, ed. Barlow, pp. 46–7.   [53] See above, pp. 37, 42–3, 44.
[54] On the place of Edward within the Anglo-Saxon hagiological tradition see C. E. Fell,

wholly different forms, and their cults might be expected to have little in common.

But between the cults of Edgar's children there runs one highly significant connecting thread. It has been shown that, if the inception of Edith's cult at Wilton is primarily intelligible in terms of the transition of royal patron into patron saint, that cult nevertheless owed much to the interest and support of King Æthelred and his leading magnates: to Goscelin of Canterbury it was the translation performed *c.* 997 on royal and aristocratic initiative that set the seal upon the establishment of Edith's cult. In similar fashion, the Northern recension manuscripts of the *Chronicle* make it clear that the divine vindication of Edward the Martyr culminated in and was symbolised by the translation of that king's remains by Ealdorman Ælfhere to the abbey of Shaftesbury.[55] The *Vita Oswaldi* states that, one year after Edward's murder, 'the glorious ealdorman Ælfhere came with a crowd of people and commanded that his body be raised from the ground'; the body was found to be uncorrupt and was duly carried 'to the place where they gave him a worthy burial, where, at the command of the ealdorman, Masses and holy offerings were celebrated for the redemption of his soul'.[56] The *Passio Edwardi* tells a more complicated story. Between the initial disposal of the body and its ultimate removal to Shaftesbury it interposes a second concealment, this time in marshy ground, a revelation of the body by a miraculous column of fire, a burial at Wareham and a gradual spreading of Edward's fame.[57] Nevertheless, the real inception of the cult had to wait until 'A certain noble ealdorman, Ælfhere by name, hearing that the holy body had been revealed by so clear a sign, was filled with great joy and, wishing to render faithful service to his lord as if he were still alive, determined to translate the body to a more worthy resting-place.'[58] It is, moreover, important to note that, in this account as in that of the *Vita Oswaldi*, Ælfhere's translation of Edward is portrayed as a public gesture on a grand scale.[59] Ælfhere, ealdorman of Mercia, was until his death in 983 probably the most influential layman at Æthelred's

---

'Edward King and Martyr and the Anglo-Saxon hagiographic tradition', in Hill (ed.), *Ethelred the Unready*, pp. 1–13; Rollason, 'Cults of murdered royal saints'.
[55] See above, p. 46.   [56] *Vita Oswaldi*, pp. 450–1.   [57] *Passio Edwardi*, pp. 6–8.
[58] *Ibid.*, p. 8.
[59] *Ibid.*: 'Ad quod opus digne peragendum, episcopos et abbates cum optimatibus regni quos habere potuit inuitat, et ut in hoc sibi negotio consentiant et subueniant monet, precatur.'

court.[60] His ostentatious promotion of Edward's cult can only have taken place with the knowledge and consent of the young king: very probably it was an act less of private devotion than of royal policy.

This suggestion is corroborated by further evidence of Æthelred's interest in the relics of his murdered half-brother. The author of the *Passio Edwardi*, after making brief reference to his subject's miracles at Shaftesbury, goes on to describe a second translation which took place at that house in the year 1001. The saint's desire to be raised from his resting-place was made known by his appearance in a vision to 'a certain religious'.[61] This unnamed intermediary was ordered to go to Shaftesbury, to make known the saint's will to the abbess, and to urge her to pass on the information to the king. These instructions were duly followed and Æthelred, 'hearing how boundless was his brother's glory, was filled with great joy and, had he been granted the opportunity, would gladly have . . . been present at his elevation'.[62] The king, hemmed in by the Danes,[63] was unable to take any personal part in the proceedings, but he did the best that he could in the circumstances: he sent messengers to Wulfsige, bishop of Sherborne and to another prelate, named Ælfsige, 'instructing and commanding them to raise his brother's body from the ground and to lay it in a worthy resting-place'.[64] It is of course possible that Æthelred in thus ordering his half-brother's translation was responding to some skilful propaganda on the part of the Shaftesbury nuns.[65] More important, however, is the testimony which the hagiographer provides to the sincerity and the importance of the king's support of the enterprise: he leaves us in no doubt as to the fact that the translation was carried out 'in accordance with the royal command'.[66]

The testimony of the hagiographer, moreover, receives support from a somewhat unexpected quarter – a royal diploma issued in 1001 in favour of Shaftesbury abbey. The grant is specified as being to God and to 'his saint, my brother Edward, whom, drenched with his own blood, the Lord has seen fit to magnify in our time through many miracles'.[67] It gives to the community of Shaftes-

[60] See Keynes, *Diplomas*, p. 157; A. Williams, '*Princeps Merciorum gentis*: the family, career and connections of Ælfhere, ealdorman of Mercia, 956–83', *ASE* 10 (1982), 143–72; Stafford, 'Reign of Æthelred II', p. 17.   [61] *Passio Edwardi*, p. 12.

[62] *Ibid.*   [63] *Ibid.*; see *ASC*, A, C, D, E, *s.a.* 1001.   [64] *Passio Edwardi*, p. 12.

[65] See below, pp. 169–71.   [66] *Passio Edwardi*, p. 12.   [67] S899; K706.

bury jurisdiction over the Wiltshire *coenobium* of Bradford-on-Avon; and its express purpose is to provide for that community and its relics 'of the holy martyr and the other saints' a place of refuge in case of Danish invasion.[68] It seems, then, that the cult of his murdered half-brother was close to the forefront of Æthelred's mind in 1001: the king was not only closely involved in the translation of Edward's relics but was also responsible for a constructive and quite unparalleled measure to protect those relics from one of the principal dangers of the time.[69]

One further possible indication of Æthelred's interest in Edward's cult deserves mention. The law code V Æthelred, believed to derive from Æthelred's legislative session held at Enham in 1008, includes an instruction that the feast of St Edward the Martyr be observed throughout England on 18 March.[70] The dating of the clause, however, is a matter of some controversy. It finds no parallel in VI Æthelred, thought to derive from the same session, or in the Latin version of the Enham legislation, and it has been suggested by both Kenneth Sisam and Patrick Wormald that it was a pronouncement of a later council interpolated in the defective copy of V Æthelred from which the surviving manuscripts derive: Wormald has put forward the interesting hypothesis that it dates from the early years of Cnut's reign.[71]

Whatever the case, there remain strong indications that the making of Edward the Martyr – the transition of the earthly king into the heavenly saint – owed much to the intervention of Ed-

---

[68] K706: 'cum adiacente undique uilla humili deuotione offero coenobium quod uulgariter æt Bradeforda cognominatur, hoc mecum sub sapientum meorum testimonio tacite præiudicans, ut supradictum donum sancto semper subiaceat monasterio æt Sceftesbirio uocitato, ac ditioni uenerabilis familiæ sanctimonialium inibi degentium, quatenus aduersus barbarorum insidias ipsa religiosa congregatio cum beati martyris cæterorumque sanctorum reliquiis ibidem deo seruiendi impenetrabile optineat confugium.'

[69] See below, p. 229, n. 74, for the enforced exile of St Edmund's relics from Bury during the Danish invasions of the early eleventh century. Cf. also the wanderings of St Cuthbert's body occasioned by the invasions of the ninth century: *Symeonis monachi opera omnia*, I, 207–8.

[70] For the Enham legislation see *CS*, I, i, 338–73; the decree concerning Edward's festival is printed at pp. 353–4.

[71] K. Sisam, *Studies in the history of Old English literature* (Oxford, 1953), pp. 280–1; P. Wormald, 'Æthelred the lawmaker', in Hill (ed.), *Ethelred the Unready*, pp. 47–80, at pp. 53–4. See also *CS*, I, i, 353–4, where Dorothy Whitelock suggests that the omission of the clause from VI Æthelred could perhaps be explained by the fact that this version was intended for use in the north, where it might have been unrealistic to hope to enforce the veneration of a West Saxon king; Kennedy, 'Cnut's law code', p. 70; Keynes, *Diplomas*, p. 171 and note.

ward's successor on the English throne. The cult of St Edward, like that of St Edith, seems to have possessed a political relevance which transcended the local and monastic. It remains to consider what that relevance may have been.

The traditional interpretation of Edward's cult takes as its starting-point the historical mystery which surrounds the circumstances of Edward's death and Æthelred's accession. Edward had come to the throne only after considerable opposition from the supporters of his younger half-brother.[72] And both the *Vita Oswaldi* and the *Passio Edwardi* make it clear that Edward was murdered while on a goodwill visit to Æthelred, who was staying on an estate owned by his mother, Ælfthryth.[73] In the sequel, moreover, it became clear that the principal beneficiaries of the murder were Æthelred, who received the throne which fair means had denied him, and Ælfthryth, who as queen-mother became, for a time at least, an important power behind that throne. The interpretation of these events has been strongly conditioned by the tendency of historians to regard Æthelred's reign as an inexorable progression towards the king's exile in 1013 and the subsequent delivery of the Old English state into the hands of the Danes. Seeking an explanation for the ignominious end to the reign, writers from the eleventh century to the twentieth have looked back to the dark deed which marked its inception: Æthelred's failure has been portrayed as a direct consequence of that deed and of his own supposed complicity in it.[74] Hence Goscelin, in his *Vita Edithe*, wrote that Æthelred was judged unworthy to rule because 'his succession had been purchased with his brother's blood'.[75] The hagiographers of St Dunstan developed a tradition according to which that saint foretold the disasters of Æthelred's reign on the very day of his coronation.[76] And by the late eleventh century there had emerged, in the figure of the wicked step-mother, the perfect scapegoat for the crime. Goscelin wrote in the *Vita Edithe* that Edward's death was the result of 'his step-mother's treachery'; and the whole thematic structure of the *Passio Edwardi* is founded

---

[72] See above, pp. 44–5.
[73] *Vita Oswaldi*, p. 449; *Passio Edwardi*, pp. 4–5.
[74] For an important analysis of Æthelred historiography see S. Keynes, 'The declining reputation of King Æthelred the Unready', in Hill (ed.), *Ethelred the Unready*, pp. 227–53; cf. Keynes, *Diplomas*, pp. 228–31. [75] *Vita Edithe*, p. 84.
[76] *Memorials of St Dunstan*, pp. 114–15 (Osbern), 215 (Eadmer), 309–10 (William of Malmesbury; cf. *GR*, I, 185–7).

upon the assumption of Ælfthryth's guilt. Edward's reign, we are
told, was initially a happy and prosperous one, 'But the devil, the
enemy of all that is good . . . stirred up his step-mother, Ælfthryth,
to hatred of him . . . inflamed by the spirit of envy she began to
ponder how the man of God might be rooted out from the
kingdom and her own son Æthelred be raised unimpeded to the
throne in his place.'77 Ælfthryth did not herself strike the fatal
blow, but the initiative was undoubtedly hers. More recent historians, although reluctant to apportion the blame for the murder,
have likewise portrayed the disasters of the reign as directly related
to the circumstances of its inception. Thus Sir Frank Stenton:
'Æthelred, who was crowned a month after the murder, began to
reign in an atmosphere of suspicion which destroyed the prestige of
the Crown.'78 And Christopher Brooke writes that the murder
'cast a gloom over Ethelred's accession, and in a measure over his
whole reign'.79

The assumption that Æthelred commenced his reign under a
cloud of suspicion has suggested one explanation for his subsequent
interest in Edward's cult. That interest has been seen as a defensive
stratagem, an attempt to dispel the cloud: in the ever-worsening
political and military circumstances of Æthelred's reign it was an
act of political expiation. Christopher Brooke, for instance, has
seen Æthelred's acknowledgement of Edward's sanctity as a product less of royal initiative than of political coercion: 'The young
man's bones became holy relics; his brother was compelled to
acknowledge him a saint, and to pronounce the day of his death a
solemn festival . . . When the ealdorman translated the body to
Shaftesbury he seems to have been performing an act of reconciliation; by doing honour to the murdered king, he seems to have

---

77 *Vita Edithe*, p. 82; *Passio Edwardi*, pp. 3–4. For the evolution of the 'Ælfthryth legend' see
   also Keynes, *Diplomas*, pp. 168–9; Keynes, 'Declining reputation', p. 237; Wright,
   Cultivation of saga, pp. 161–71. The place of the wicked step-mother in the Anglo-Saxon
   hagiographical tradition is discussed by Fell, 'Edward King and Martyr and the Anglo-
   Saxon hagiographic tradition'; and for the role of female relatives in the murder of
   saintly kings see Rollason, 'Cults of murdered royal saints'.
78 Stenton, *ASE*, p. 373. Stenton goes on to note that 'Much that has brought the
   condemnation of historians on King Æthelred may well be due in the last resort to the
   circumstances under which he became king' (*ibid.*, p. 374). His behaviour suggests 'the
   reaction of a weak king to the consciousness that he had come to power through what his
   subjects regarded as the worst crime committed among the English peoples since their
   first coming to Britain' (*ibid.*).
79 C. N. L. Brooke, *The Saxon and Norman kings*, 2nd edn (London, 1978), p. 126.

hoped to rally Edward's supporters to Ethelred.'[80] A corollary of this statement is the belief that Edward's cult in fact
originated among those of his erstwhile supporters who were
reluctant to accept the rule of Æthelred. In the circumstances of
external defeat and internal disaffection which characterised
Æthelred's reign 'The rapid growth of Edward's cult is very likely
in part a reflection of growing political unrest . . . one cannot help
suspecting that Edward's bones became a rallying point for disloyalty and opposition.'[81] In these circumstances, Æthelred's promotion of Edward's cult, if it is accorded any significance at all, seems
to have been not merely an attempt to atone for a crime and to rally
supporters: it was also an attempt to draw the political poison from
what was, in origin, a cult of rebels. More recently, a similar
interpretation has been advanced by David Rollason. Edward's cult
is designated as one of a type in which 'The enemies of the killers or
of those on whose behalf they had acted may have regarded the
cults of their victims as a means of expressing and focusing opposition to them.'[82] Æthelred's own acknowledgement of Edward's
sanctity is explained as an attempt to diminish the effectiveness of
the cult 'for focusing the forces of social tension and political
opposition'.[83]

This interpretation of the early history of Edward's cult is
persuasive. But it cannot be accepted without reservation. It seems,
first, to underestimate the evidence for Æthelred's early, continuing and considerable interest in the relics of his murdered half-
brother. That evidence seems to suggest rather a positive
commitment to the promotion of Edward's cult than a half-
hearted, defensive or even coerced acknowledgement of his sanctity. Second, if Edward's cult indeed originated as a cult of rebels, it
is curious that no early source gives us the slightest indication of
who those rebels might have been. The only possible reference to
the interest of rebels in the fate of Edward's relics occurs in the
Passio's ambiguous and conventional account of the finding of the
body by 'certain faithful men who zealously sought it' and of its
burial at Wareham by the 'faithful men' of that town.[84] These
unnamed benefactors apart, the only recorded promoters of Edward's cult were men and women of the highest political respect-

---

[80] *Ibid.*, pp. 125–6.   [81] *Ibid.*, p. 126.
[82] Rollason, 'Cults of murdered royal saints', p. 17.   [83] *Ibid.*, p. 21.
[84] *Passio Edwardi*, p. 7. The 'certain religious' to whom the saint's will was revealed in 1001
(*ibid.*, p. 12) is unlikely to have been of rebellious disposition.

ability – Ealdorman Ælfhere, the king himself, Bishop Wulfsige, the prelate Ælfsige and the nuns of Shaftesbury and Wilton.[85] Third, if indeed Æthelred bore the odium for Edward's death, and if indeed a group of elusive rebels accordingly decided to turn Edward's cult into a political weapon, it is difficult to see how Æthelred's acknowledgement of that cult would have helped him: surely it could only have underlined his guilt and increased his political vulnerability.[86] Fourth, if we accept this interpretation of Edward's cult, some thought must be given to the implications of Æthelred's similar promotion of the cult of St Edith. Is this to be dismissed as a pious fiction invented by Goscelin for some now obscure hagiographical purpose? Or was Æthelred's promotion of the two royal cults perhaps quite fortuitous and motivated by wholly different concerns? Or are we to assume that the cult of Edith, like that of Edward, was in origin a cult of rebels from which a reluctant Æthelred was forced to draw the political sting? Certainly Goscelin intimates that Edith during her lifetime formed an alternative focus of loyalty for those who found the yoke of Æthelred difficult to bear. So much is suggested by the lengthy story in which Goscelin makes the magnates, under the unlikely leadership of Ælfhere of Mercia, come to Wilton and offer their own daughters in fulfilment of Edith's monastic vow if only she will leave the nunnery and rule in place of the unworthy Æthelred. But that story can almost certainly be dismissed as a product of an eleventh-century hagiographical imagination prepared to go to considerable lengths to illustrate the other-worldliness of its subject.[87] And, that story apart, the history of Edith's cult is one of promotion by the cream of the political cream – by the nuns of Wilton, by King Æthelred and by the king's uncle, Ordwulf.[88]

Taken together, these points strongly suggest that historians should begin to look elsewhere for an explanation of Æthelred's interest in the cults of Edward and Edith. And the recent work of Simon Keynes has both further exposed the cracks in the traditional structure and opened the way for a reappraisal of the political relevance of the cults. The theory that Æthelred sought either to

---

[85] *Ibid.*, pp. 8–9, 11–13.
[86] For this point see also Keynes, *Diplomas*, p. 171, where it is pointed out that if Æthelred was held responsible for the murder 'the glorification of the victim as a martyr could serve only to diminish the security of Æthelred's own position, by drawing attention to the circumstances of Edward's martyrdom'.
[87] *Vita Edithe*, pp. 84–6; see above, p. 41. [88] See above, p. 152.

disarm a cult of rebels or, more simply, to repair a tarnished image, is founded upon the assumption that contemporaries believed that image to be tarnished and therefore that it was feasible for the king's enemies to make political mileage out of Edward's relics. But, Keynes argues, it is far from clear that contemporaries held any such belief.[89] Among the early sources for Edward's murder and cult, no version of the *Chronicle* names Edward's murderer or murderers, although its Northern recension manuscripts indicate that the crime was perpetrated by men who had refused to submit to Edward's earthly rule and who presumably therefore had supported Æthelred's claim to the throne.[90] The *Vita Oswaldi* is more specific. The murder, which took place at Ælfthryth's house, was the outcome of a conspiracy among 'the thegns who supported his brother': neither Æthelred nor his mother is implicated in the crime, and the author is at some pains to point out the affection which existed between the two brothers.[91] Perhaps most significant is the testimony of the *Sermo*. Wulfstan's catalogue of the sins of the English culminates in his indictment of disloyalty to the monarchy: Edward had been murdered and subsequently burned; Æthelred had been driven from his kingdom.[92] The inference here is clear – if Edward's murder was the worst sin committed by the English since first they came to Britain, then Æthelred's exile came a close second. It is hard to believe that Wulfstan would thus have juxtaposed the two brothers, writing with equal distaste of their sufferings, had the fate of the elder been generally associated with the activities of the younger. It was not, it seems, until the late eleventh century that Æthelred came to be associated with the death of his brother – and even here, in the major account of the *Passio Edwardi*, he appears only as the somewhat reluctant beneficiary of his mother's crime.[93]

There is, moreover, no early evidence for that unholy alliance postulated by D. J. V. Fisher, in which Edward's murder becomes a product of a conspiracy between the queen-mother and a so-called

---

[89] Keynes, *Diplomas*, pp. 163–74.   [90] See above, p. 46.
[91] *Vita Oswaldi*, p. 449.   [92] See above, p. 46.
[93] The author of the *Passio* digresses from his main account to emphasise Æthelred's affection for his murdered half-brother and to note that his distress following Edward's death was so great that his understandably frustrated mother was driven to beat him with the first thing that came to hand: 'candelis quia aliud ad manus non habebat, atrociter eum uerberauit, ut ita ululatum eius per multa uerbera tandem compesceret. Hinc ut fertur postea toto uitae suae tempore candelas ita exosas habuit, ut uix eas aliquando coram se lucere permitteret' (*Passio Edwardi*, p. 7).

anti-monastic party under the leadership of Ealdorman Ælfhere.[94] Keynes has pointed out that Ælfthryth, designated in the *Regularis concordia* as the special protector of England's nunneries, 'fits badly in anti-monastic clothes' and that there is no evidence for Ealdorman Ælfhere's involvement in the murder.[95] There is, in short, no early evidence that Edward's murder resulted from a plot hatched within the royal family itself: there is accordingly no reason to assume that King Æthelred and his followers had any need to perform an act of political expiation.

In a further, equally important, way Keynes's work has cast doubt on the traditional interpretation of Æthelred's reign and of the place of Edward's cult within it. Keynes has demonstrated that our principal narrative source for the reign – the account extending from 983 until 1016 in manuscripts C, D, E and F of the *Anglo-Saxon Chronicle* – was itself written retrospectively.[96] As the product of a single author, working probably between 1016 and 1023, its story is strongly influenced by that author's knowledge of the reign's ignominious end: its tone of gloomy pessimism cannot be held accurately to reflect the unchanging mood of a particularly long and eventful reign.[97] By a careful analysis of alternative sources, and especially of Æthelred's diplomas, Keynes has shown that the reign can no longer be dismissed as a relentless cycle of political betrayal and military defeat significant only as a prelude to the destruction of the Old English state. Instead, he suggests, the reign may be divided into four periods quite distinct in character.[98] In the first of these, the young king probably remained under the close supervision of his mother, of Ælfhere of Mercia and of St Æthelwold.[99] The latter's death in 984 seems to have heralded a 'period of youthful indiscretions' (984–*c.* 993), which saw the temporary eclipse of Ælfthryth and which was characterised by a series of misdeeds, especially against the church, encouraged by a group of unscrupulous lay advisers.[100] Between this and the disas-

---

[94] Fisher, 'Anti-monastic reaction'.   [95] Keynes, *Diplomas*, pp. 171–3.
[96] Keynes, 'Declining reputation', pp. 229–36. Keynes does note, however, that the compiler of the *Chronicle* very probably made use of some earlier annalistic material (*ibid.*, p. 233).   [97] *Ibid.*, p. 235.   [98] Keynes, *Diplomas*, ch. 4.
[99] *Ibid.*, pp. 157, 174–5; Williams, '*Princeps Merciorum gentis*', p. 170.
[100] Keynes, *Diplomas*, pp. 176–86. It is however possible that it was during this decade that Æthelred established his own foundation of Cholsey and Ælfthryth the nunneries of Amesbury and Wherwell. The foundation of Cholsey is dated by KH to *c.* 986 (p. 62) and those of Amesbury and Wherwell to *c.* 979 and *c.* 986 respectively (pp. 104, 267). According to William of Malmesbury the two nunneries were founded by 'Elfrida Sancti Eduuardi interfectrice . . . causa penitentiae' (*GP*, p. 188).

trous final decade, and despite a worsening military situation, the years 993 to 1006 are designated 'a period when the internal affairs of Æthelred's kingdom prospered, under the guidance of the king acting with the assistance and advice of a group of distinguished ecclesiastics and laymen'.[101] The queen-mother returns to the witness lists and is joined by her brother Ordwulf, by Æthelweard of the Western provinces and his son Æthelmaer, kinsmen of the king, and by a second group of secular magnates, Wulfric, Wulfgeat and Wulfheah. Æthelred's ecclesiastical advisers included Sigeric, archbishop of Canterbury from 990 until 994, and Wulfstan II, bishop of London and later archbishop of York. The period was characterised by a strong currency, by important legislative and administrative developments,[102] and by a renewed royal and aristocratic interest in the patronage of the church. Of Æthelred's closest advisers, Ordwulf was the founder of Tavistock abbey, Æthelmaer founded the houses of Cerne and Eynsham, and Wulfric can probably be identified with the Wulfric Spot who founded the Staffordshire abbey of Burton-on-Trent.[103] The religious establishments which tasted the fruits of royal patronage during this period included Abingdon, Muchelney, Old Minster, St Albans, Sherborne, Westminster, Burton, St Frideswide's, Eynsham, the sees of Cornwall and Rochester and the nunneries of Wilton, Shaftesbury and Wherwell.[104] 'One might even', writes Keynes, 'consider the possibility that the period was one of the most prosperous for the advancement of the ecclesiastical cause before the Norman Conquest.'[105]

Against the background of this four-fold periodisation of Æthelred's reign, the chronology of St Edward's cult becomes particularly interesting. The first sign of royal interest in Edward's relics came right at the beginning of Æthelred's reign, while the young king's affairs were still strongly influenced by his mother and St Æthelwold. And Edward's cult received its second major

---

[101] Keynes, *Diplomas*, p. 193.
[102] For further analysis of the numismatic, administrative and legal developments of Æthelred's reign see R. H. M. Dolley, 'An introduction to the coinage of Ethelred II', in Hill (ed.), *Ethelred the Unready*, pp. 115–34; D. Hill, 'Trends in the development of towns during the reign of Æthelred II', in *ibid.*, pp. 213–26; Stafford, 'Reign of Æthelred II'; Wormald, 'Æthelred the lawmaker'.
[103] For these foundations see Keynes, *Diplomas*, pp. 192–3; KH, pp. 77, 62, 65, 61. For the foundation of Tavistock see also H. P. R. Finberg, 'The house of Ordgar and the foundation of Tavistock abbey', *EHR* 58 (1943), 190–201; Finberg, *Tavistock abbey*, Cambridge Studies in Medieval Life and Thought, New Series 2 (Cambridge, 1951).
[104] See Keynes, *Diplomas*, p. 198.   [105] *Ibid.*, p. 199.

impetus in 1001, in a period when Æthelred, again working with advisers sympathetic to monasticism, seems to have made a genuine effort to follow the example of his father in the patronage of the church. This chronology becomes even more interesting when it is remembered that, if Goscelin's account is correct, Æthelred's involvement in the translation of St Edith fell squarely within this same period, and was associated with the activities of Ordwulf, royal adviser and founder of Tavistock abbey.[106] It seems, then, that Edward's cult, and very probably also that of Edith, was fostered by Æthelred at a time when he was working with advisers who had a well-attested interest in the patronage of the church and when, despite the continuing threat from the Danes, the internal affairs of the kingdom were smoothly and constructively run. This strongly suggests that it may be a mistake to consider the cult of Edward in isolation and to see Æthelred's promotion of this as the defensive reaction of an ever-weakening king. Perhaps instead we should consider the cults of Edward and Edith in association, as closely related parts of a cogent policy devised by a king in reasonable control of his affairs: what did the promotion of those cults contribute to the power of the king?

Simon Keynes has suggested that, if indeed Æthelred was not held responsible for Edward's murder, he 'would naturally profit materially from the cult of a royal saint so closely related to him'.[107] The ways in which Æthelred 'naturally profited' are both diverse and difficult to define. At their heart there lies a fact so fundamental that it rarely receives explicit mention in the sources: a saintly ancestor or relative was an exceptionally valuable status symbol. Æthelred, in making saints of the children of Edgar, surrounded himself with saintly siblings: a ruler with both a brother and a sister so firmly ensconced in the kingdom of heaven could not but find his own prestige on earth increased accordingly. And in the political circumstances of Æthelred's reign, such an increase in prestige was particularly important. The renewed Danish invasions presented to Æthelred's kingdom a threat far more real than a cloud of suspicion and the guilty conscience of its ruler. Recent research, moreover, has shown that, despite his ultimate failure to counter the Danish threat, Æthelred – together with his traditionally discredited counsellors – never ceased to try. A central theme of their trying seems to have been a consistent effort to

---

[106] See above, p. 152.   [107] Keynes, *Diplomas*, p. 171.

create, for the more effective pursuit of war and the attainment of *pax* at home, a society purged of its sins and securely ordered 'under one God and one king'.[108] Of this crucial but often neglected theme of Æthelred's reign the glorification of the king through his saintly family may have been an important *leitmotiv*.

Æthelred's promotion of the cults of Edward and Edith appears, then, to be intelligible in general terms as part of an important, if ultimately abortive, movement to enhance the prestige of the king in order more effectively to meet the challenge of the Danes. It may be further suggested that the promotion of those cults, and especially of that of St Edward, was the medium through which Æthelred chose to make a number of specific political statements, each of which was important in its own right, and each of which contributed something to the overall design.

Of these the first may have concerned the vindication of his brother. The Northern recension manuscripts of the *Chronicle* emphasise the fact that Edward's murder was not avenged by his earthly kinsmen,[109] and Æthelred's failure to carry out his responsibilities in this respect might seem at first sight to be indicative of his complicity in the murder. But there may well have been good reasons for Æthelred's failure to avenge his half-brother. He may not have known who Edward's killers were; or, more likely, he may have been subject to their political control:[110] it would take a quite exceptionally *unraed* king to attempt to divest himself at once of those supporters to whom he owed his succession. It is, however, interesting to note that the *Chronicle* goes on to state that vengeance was carried out instead by Edward's heavenly father and that it

---

[108] Cf. *CS*, I, i, 338 (V Æthelred, 1008). An interesting study could be made of the royal propaganda and political ideology developed during Æthelred's reign in order to equip the nation for war; it is beyond the scope of the present study to do more than touch the tip of the iceberg. The *Sermo* itself is of the highest importance, preaching moral reform and a respect for social order as prerequisites for the successful defence of the kingdom. These themes are echoed in Wulfstan's homilies (see *The homilies of Wulfstan*, ed. D. Bethurum (Oxford, 1957)), in the *Institutes of polity* and in the law codes drafted under Wulfstan's influence. Particularly interesting is Æthelred's so-called seventh code, probably issued in 1009, which opens with the proposition that 'all of us have need eagerly to labour that we may attain God's mercy and his compassion and that we may through his help withstand our enemies'. The code stated that every priest was to say mass for the king and his people on the three days before Michaelmas and that a mass which referred in particular to the need of the times was to be said daily in every minster until things should improve (see Keynes, *Diplomas*, pp. 217–19). For the career and influence of Wulfstan see especially D. Whitelock, 'Archbishop Wulfstan, homilist and statesman', *Transactions of the Royal Historical Society*, Fourth Series 24 (1942), 25–45.
[109] See above, p. 46.
[110] For some treatment of this point see Keynes, *Diplomas*, p. 173.

received its expression in the development of his cult. Æthelred, in promoting that cult, was thus acting as the instrument of the 'divine feud'.[111] His purpose, I would suggest, was not to expiate his role in the crime but rather to dissociate himself from it and to express in the most forceful way available to him his disapproval of its perpetrators.

Æthelred's second political statement may have concerned the nature of kingship. The disputed succession which followed the death of Edgar was far from unusual in tenth-century England; but the assassination after a short reign of the successful contender was quite unparalleled. It is important not to underestimate the shock to which that assassination gave rise. To the compiler of the *Chronicle* it was the worst deed in the history of the English; to Wulfstan it was the culminating sin which formed the thematic centre of the *Sermo*. The cult of St Edward was a product of that shock: it was a categoric and spectacular statement that kings should not be treated thus. Both David Rollason and Simon Keynes have drawn attention to the possible connection between the cults of murdered royal saints and the history of legislation concerning royal murder.[112] Rollason in particular has suggested that a resurgence of interest in saints of this type in the late eighth and early ninth centuries may have been connected with the promulgation by the papal legates in 786 of 'one of the strongest condemnations of royal murder ever made in England'.[113] Edward's cult, although a product of a much later age, may have owed something to this tradition. And the promotion of that cult by Edward's successor on the English throne was particularly appropriate. For if Æthelred was the principal beneficiary of Edward's murder he was also above all men the one most directly threatened by it. Edward had been removed after a short reign because he proved unacceptable to the magnates of his kingdom. Once the precedent had been set, was there any reason why his successor should not be similarly removed? Edward's cult went some way towards supplying that reason. The murdered king would become a heavenly saint; and his cause would be vindicated by God: the cult of Edward the Martyr was to be his brother's insurance policy.

---

[111] For the concept of the 'divine feud' see Rollason, 'Cults of murdered royal saints', p. 14.
[112] *Ibid.*, pp. 16–17; Keynes, *Diplomas*, p. 171, n. 68.
[113] Rollason, 'Cults of murdered royal saints', p. 17. For a printed version of the condemnation see *Councils and ecclesiastical documents relating to Great Britain and Ireland*, ed. A. W. Haddan and W. Stubbs, 3 vols. (Oxford, 1869–78), III (1878), 447–62.

Æthelred's promotion of the royal cults may have had a further political implication. Æthelred had come to the throne after a protracted conflict concerning his right of succession. Very probably, however, that conflict was conducted rather on Æthelred's behalf than by Æthelred: we have no evidence that Æthelred himself questioned his half-brother's right to rule or that he was involved in Edward's murder, and there is accordingly no reason to assume that Æthelred's reign was clouded with guilt. It may, however, have been tinged with insecurity, and it is possible that, by posing as the vindicator of his murdered half-brother and by promoting the cult of his half-sister, Æthelred sought to emphasise his own status among the children of Edgar and thus to establish as securely as possible his own right of succession. The possibility is interesting, for a similarly direct connection between insecurity of succession and the promotion of royal cults seems to have existed elsewhere. Most striking is the case of Cnut. Goscelin notes that the 'foreign king' Cnut, 'enthralled by the piety and abundant miracles of St Edith, was bound to her by so much love and affection that he might have been her own brother Æthelred or nephew Edmund'.[114] The words are telling: Cnut was a 'foreign king' who venerated St Edith as if he belonged to her own family. The inference is that he hoped, by venerating the saint as by marrying the widow of his defeated predecessor, to create connections with that family where none had previously existed and, by so doing, to establish as clearly as possible the legitimacy of his rule. It is possible too that Cnut's attentions were not limited to St Edith: he may have been responsible for the decree ordering the observance of Edward's festival throughout England.[115] If so, Rollason suggests, he may have intended thereby to heap dishonour upon the man whose kingdom he had 'usurped':[116] more likely he was attempting, by flaunting his veneration for a saint of the house of Cerdic, to secure his own position within that royal line.[117]

The foregoing provides some analysis of the political advantages which rulers in general could hope to reap from the promotion of royal cults and of those which Æthelred and Cnut in particular could hope to reap from their promotion of the cults of Edward and Edith. The result is a theory neither as neat nor as monolithic as the

[114] *Vita Edithe*, p. 278.   [115] See above, p. 157.
[116] Rollason, 'Cults of murdered royal saints', p. 18.
[117] For a suggestion that the West Saxon kings were interested for similar reasons in the promotion of the cults of Æthelthryth and, more important, Edmund, see below, pp. 195–6, 225–6.

traditional 'negative' interpretation of Æthelred's interest in the relics of his murdered half-brother: but it may well approximate more closely to the historical reality. The royal cult becomes an infinitely flexible instrument of royal propaganda. At the most superficial level it enhances the prestige of the promoting ruler; at its most sophisticated it becomes the medium through which that ruler makes, in a public and often spectacular way, a number of highly important political statements.

This analysis of the political significance of the royal cults, moreover, allows one further dimension to be added to our understanding of the attitudes of the religious communities which guarded the relics. Both Edburga and Edith, I have suggested, stimulated during their lifetime royal patronage of the community to which they belonged.[118] I have also suggested that royal patronage of Nunnaminster throughout the late tenth and eleventh centuries may have been encouraged by royal interest in the cult of the *uirgo regia*:[119] the available evidence, however, permits no certainty on this point. The history of St Edith's cult, in contrast, makes that postulated connection quite explicit. Both Æthelred and Cnut seem to have shown considerable interest in the relics of St Edith; in each case that interest seems to have been stimulated at least in part by important political considerations; and in each case it may have been expressed in the form of generous patronage:[120] the cult of St Edith clearly had political implications which could be of much value to the abbey which housed her relics. The Wilton nuns must have been aware from the outset of at least some of those political implications and of their potential usefulness: when they made a saint of the daughter of Edgar they very probably did so not simply in recognition of services rendered but also in the hope that the royal child would continue, in death as in life, to act as *mediatrix ad regem*.

This point in turn raises an important question about the cult of St Edward. What was the role of the Shaftesbury nuns in the creation of Edward the Martyr? Shaftesbury, like Wilton, was an important royal foundation,[121] and its members must have been

---

[118] See above, pp. 99–101, 103, 144–5.   [119] See above, p. 120.

[120] Æthelred, in a charter dated 994, grants an estate at Fovant, Hants., to the church of St Mary at Wilton (S881). Goscelin describes in some detail Cnut's patronage of Wilton, but no documentary record survives to support the hagiographer's account.

[121] The author of the *Passio Edwardi* notes that the convent of Shaftesbury was founded by Alfred, who made his daughter its abbess and whose gifts to the community included 100 hides of land. Alfred's alleged foundation charter, condemned as spurious by

aware both of the political symbolism of the royal relics which came into their possession and of their own ability to trade upon that symbolism. Indeed it seems that they already had one royal cult. The *Secgan* locates at Shaftesbury a certain Ælfgyfa, to be identified possibly with Alfred's daughter, the first abbess, or, perhaps more likely, with the wife of Edmund I who according to William of Malmesbury established (presumably refounded) a community of nuns at Shaftesbury and was buried there.[122] The feast of this rather elusive lady is entered in several calendars of the eleventh century.[123] Against this background there is a very strong possibility that the Shaftesbury nuns came to regard the body of King Edward as an important focus around which might be worked out their relationship with his successor: his role, paralleling that of his saintly sister at Wilton, was that of *mediator ad regem*. And his usefulness as such is made clear by Æthelred's Shaftesbury charter of 1001. The background to that charter, I would suggest, is not simply that, to a rather harassed ruler, it seemed like a good idea at the time. Very probably the nuns had tactfully pointed out to the ruler that it might prove embarrassing if the relics of his brother were to be destroyed by the Danes and that the problem might be solved by an extension of the abbey's landowning rights to include the *coenobium* of Bradford-on-Avon. It might therefore be suggested that the cult of Edward the Martyr was not exclusively a royal creation: it was a product of mutual convenience on the part of the king and an acquisitive religious community. It is difficult, moreover, to be certain as to which of the partners came first. The sources without exception describe Edward's burial at Shaftesbury as a translation of a ruler already regarded as a saint. But the sources were written with hindsight, if only of a few years, and there is at least a possibility that to contemporaries that burial appeared merely as an attempt to provide for a murdered ruler an appropriate resting-place: Shaftesbury abbey, in view both of its

Dorothy Whitelock, is preserved on fols. 21v–22 of BL, MS Harley 61; it is listed as S357 and is printed as B531–2 (English and Latin versions). On the foundation of Shaftesbury see also KH, p. 265; *VCH Dorset*, II, 73. For its endowment see Meyer, 'Patronage of the West Saxon royal nunneries', p. 350.

[122] *Heiligen*, ed. Liebermann, p. 17; for Alfred's daughter see above, n. 121; for Edmund's wife see *GP*, pp. 186–7. William discusses at some length the benevolence of Edmund's consort, records her gift of prophecy and mentions her posthumous miracles; he concludes with some admiring but uninformative verses in her honour.

[123] Wormald (ed.), *Before 1100*, nos. 5, 9, ?10 (*Sancte* followed by an erasure), 11, 12, 14–16, 18. For the date and provenance of these calendars see Wormald's introduction to each calendar.

proximity to Wareham and of its royal associations, was eminently suitable. Thereafter, Edward's recorded miracles took place entirely within the precinct of the abbey and his translation in 1001 was the result of heavenly messages relayed first to the abbess and subsequently to the king. It is at least possible that the idea of Edward the Martyr was conceived by the nuns of Shaftesbury and subsequently sold, attractively packaged, to a receptive king.

THE HAGIOGRAPHY OF WILTON AND SHAFTESBURY: A RESPONSE TO CONQUEST?

For each of Edgar's saintly children there survives a major hagiographical source which dates from the decades immediately following the Norman Conquest[124] and which traces the history of the cult, albeit with some omissions, from its inception to the time of writing. These sources, like the *Vita Edburge*, provide by their very existence important testimony to the continuity of cult in the aftermath of conquest. They seem also to suggest that there was, in the immediate post-Conquest period, a revival of interest in the cults of Edgar's saintly children. But they tell us little of the circumstances in which that revival of interest took place. It is possible, for instance, that the community of Wilton – and perhaps also that of Shaftesbury – simply took advantage of the presence of an itinerant professional hagiographer to secure for posterity a record of the traditions concerning its patron saint. Conversely, the causes of that revival may have been more deeply rooted in the history of the religious communities in the years following 1066. Perhaps those communities were concerned to advertise the virtues and the powers of their saintly patrons in order to forestall the scepticism and hostility of the Normans. Perhaps even, in producing Lives of their patron saints, they were already responding to a Norman offensive.

Of these suggestions the last is the least plausible. If the nuns of Wilton and Shaftesbury had been prompted by a Norman offensive to commit to writing the deeds of their saintly patrons, one might expect to find within their hagiographies some reference to that offensive. But the most immediately striking feature of these post-Conquest hagiographies is the silence which they maintain on the events of 1066. The *Passio Edwardi* makes not a single reference

---

[124] For the dates of the *Vita Edithe* and the *Passio Edwardi* see above, pp. 38, 48.

to those events. And the *Vita Edithe* is likewise a work of the old world. On only three occasions does Goscelin refer to the reign of William I, and in each case he does so only in order to establish a chronological framework for his narrative:[125] the new Norman ruler was, to Goscelin, precisely what he claimed to be – the man to whom Edward had bequeathed the kingdom.[126] The reader both of the *Vita Edithe* and of the *Passio Edwardi* is left with the overriding impression that the Norman Conquest had made not the slightest impact upon the day-to-day existence of either Wilton or Shaftesbury and that in each case the hagiographer had failed entirely to appreciate the significance of that conquest as a political phenomenon.[127]

Nor is this surprising. Goscelin, together with the house or houses for which he wrote, had led a sheltered life. It is impossible to reconstruct in detail the history of either Wilton or Shaftesbury in the immediate post-Conquest period, but it is important to note that both houses were in the diocese of Goscelin's patron, Bishop Herman, whose episcopate lasted until 1078.[128] Herman, although a Lotharingian by birth, seems to have felt some sympathy for the traditions of the English:[129] very probably his longevity cushioned the houses of his diocese against the immediate effects of conquest. At Wilton this cushioning must have been aided by the succession of a new abbess of native birth *c.* 1067: this lady, Godgifu, was still alive when Goscelin was writing the *Vita Edithe* and may have continued in office until the 1090s.[130] More than this, it may have

[125] *Vita Edithe*, pp. 36, 278, 296.

[126] *Ibid.*, p. 36: Goscelin describes St Edith's relationship to Edward, 'qui hodierno Willelmo reliquit imperium'.

[127] See also Wilmart, 'Eve et Goscelin', p. 284, where it is suggested that although Goscelin's work may have done much to facilitate reconciliation between churchmen of the English and Norman traditions he made no judgement concerning the importance of the Norman Conquest as a political event.

[128] For Herman's career, and for the religious houses of his diocese, see *GP*, pp. 182–93.

[129] For Herman's Lotharingian origin see *Vita Edithe*, p. 37, n. 4. Herman's respect for the traditions of the English is suggested by his role in commissioning Goscelin's *Vita Edithe* (*ibid.*, p. 37) and his Life of St Wulfsige of Sherborne ('Life of Wulsin', ed. Talbot, p. 73). See also the prominent role accorded to Herman in one of the miracles of Edward the Martyr (*Passio Edwardi*, pp. 14–15).

[130] *Vita Edithe*, pp. 36, 36–7n, 295–6; the next recorded abbess, Matilda, occurs 1093 × 9 (*Heads*, p. 222). At Shaftesbury an Abbess *Leveva* (? Leofgifu) is recorded prior to 1066 (*ibid.*, p. 219): her abbacy may have continued until the appointment of Eulalia in 1074 (*ibid.*, citing *Annales de Wintonia*, p. 30). The abbey church of Shaftesbury seems to have been rebuilt at the turn of the eleventh and twelfth centuries, the work probably commencing during the abbacy of Eulalia (Royal Commission on Historical Monu-

been to Wilton, the place of her upbringing, that the Confessor's widow retired following the political disaster of 1066, and it may be significant that it was to Wilton that another Edith, great-great-granddaughter of King Æthelred and future bride of Henry I, was sent for her education.[131] The community seems successfully to have retained both its English character and its royal connections.

More difficult to gauge is the fear that might have been. The communities of Wilton and Shaftesbury had suffered no catastrophe in the aftermath of conquest. But it is unlikely that they were not profoundly worried by the turn which political events had taken. Very probably they had already suffered some territorial losses, making it clear that a term had been set to their Peter Pan existence; and the replacement of Herman by William's erstwhile chancellor, Osmund, can only have strengthened that same impression.[132] The nuns' problem was many-sided. Both Wilton and Shaftesbury were important foundations of the West Saxon royal dynasty and throughout the late Saxon period had been heavily dependent upon the protection and patronage of that dynasty.[133]

---

ments (England), *Inventory of historical monuments in Dorset*, IV, *North Dorset* (London, 1972), 58–9).

[131] For the most useful discussion of these points see *Life of King Edward*, ed. Barlow, pp. 100, 121.

[132] By 1086 at the latest Wilton had lost two hides at Ditchampton (Wilts.) to the bishop of Bayeux (*VCH Wilts.*, II, 80; *DB*, I, 66b, 68a) and half a hide of its estate at Watchingwell (Isle of Wight) to the king's park (*DB*, I, 62d). Seven and a half hides at Chalke (Wilts.), apparently leased from Wilton before the Conquest, were held by Richard Poynant of the king and claimed by the abbess of Wilton (*DB*, I, 68a); and the same Richard also held the manor of Trow (Wilts.) (*DB*, I, 73b). And Ugford (Wilts.), abstracted from Wilton by Earl Godwin and allegedly 'recovered' by Ednoth, was in 1086 held by Osbern Giffard (*VCH Wilts.*, II, 79; *DB*, I, 72d). In Sussex the abbey had lost the large manor of West Firle, assessed at forty-eight hides in 1066, and that of Falmer (*DB*, I, 21a; 19a, 19b, 19d; 26b): these, however, may initially have been confiscated by Harold Godwinson or one of his lay magnates in order to ensure effective control of the Sussex shore. For the history of Wilton's endowment in the late eleventh century see Meyer, 'Patronage of the West Saxon royal nunneries', pp. 355–6. Shaftesbury's losses had been more limited. The manor of Farnham had passed to a certain Aiulf and the wife of the former sheriff Hugh fitz Grip (*DB*, I, 78d), and a virgate in Kingston had passed to William de Briouze (*VCH Dorset*, III, 37; *DB*, I, 78d). On the other hand two of four manors taken from the abbey by Earl Harold had been restored by William I in accordance with a writ of the Confessor (*DB*, I, 78d); and the abbey had gained the estate of Kilmington which it held of Serlo de Burcy for his daughter who was a nun at Shaftesbury (*DB*, I, 98a).

For the succession of Osmund see *GP*, pp. 183–4; *Life of King Edward*, ed. Barlow, p. 101. The *Vita Edithe* was certainly composed or completed after Herman's death in 1078; it is less clear that this was the case with the *Passio Edwardi*; see above, pp. 38, 48.

[133] For royal grants in favour of Wilton see S424, 438, 582, 766–7, 799, 881, 1811; for grants in favour of Shaftesbury see S357, 419, 429, 630, 744, 850, 899, 1868.

How, then, were they to fare under a new Norman ruler whose connections with the house of Cerdic were tenuous in the extreme and for whom patronage of the English religious houses must have been a poor second best when compared with patronage of the ducal foundations of Normandy? How were they to maintain their position *vis-à-vis* a new and acquisitive local aristocracy who shared their ruler's cross-channel interests and whose interest in the English religious houses may have taken the form rather of plunder than of patronage?[134] And how, finally, were the spiritual, liturgical and political traditions of their houses to withstand the potentially innovative activities of a new Norman bishop?

With such concerns as these at the forefront of their minds, it is unlikely that the nuns of these two communities had to wait for a Norman offensive before experiencing a sense of corporate unease. Thomas Hamilton has suggested that Norman hostility towards the English saints was generally a product of Norman disdain for English hagiography: accordingly it was the aim of the post-Conquest hagiographers, and of Goscelin in particular, by rewriting in more acceptable style the legends of the saints, to persuade the Normans that the obscure saints with outlandish names were worthy of veneration.[135] This, at the most superficial level, may have been the purpose – or one of the purposes – of the post-Conquest hagiography of Wilton and Shaftesbury. The *Vita Edithe*, commissioned by the Wilton nuns and Bishop Herman, was dedicated to Archbishop Lanfranc, and Goscelin's prologue provides elaborate acknowledgement of Lanfranc's importance in the inauguration of a new era.[136] More than this, Goscelin went to some lengths to point out the rather tenuous links between St Edith and Lanfranc's own see of Canterbury. He notes, for instance, that the saint was born at the royal vill of Kemsing, near Canterbury, and he emphasises the close connection of his subject with Lanfranc's distant predecessor, Archbishop Dunstan.[137] Quite clearly Goscelin hoped to provide for the new archbishop an impressive and relevant introduction to one of the royal saints of

---

[134] For discussion of the 'plundering' of the English church for the benefit of the Norman monasteries see Le Patourel, *Norman empire*, pp. 37–8. It is interesting to note that by 1086 the effects of this plundering had already been felt at Wilton: the manor of Falmer and two and a half hides at West Firle had passed to William of Warenne's foundation of St Pancras at Lewes and half a virgate at West Firle had passed to the monks of Tréport (*DB*, I, 26b, 21a, 19d).

[135] Hamilton, 'Goscelin', pp. 255–71. For general criticism of this approach see Ridyard, 'Condigna ueneratio', pp. 205–6.   [136] *Vita Edithe*, pp. 34–6.   [137] *Ibid*., pp. 38, 41.

Anglo-Saxon England: St Edith's feasts were not to be deleted from the calendars or her relics to be tested by fire.[138]

But if the post-Conquest hagiography of the two houses was indeed prompted by a desire to forestall the scepticism of the Normans, its significance was greater than this. The symbolism of the patron saint was such that Norman disdain for the English cults, if it existed at all, was more deeply rooted than in literary criticism and that the testing of relics by fire was far more than an act of profound irreverence: it was a deliberate insult to the history, the traditions and even the identity of the community which 'owned' those relics. Defensive hagiography, accordingly, was an attempt to vindicate not only the status of a saint but also the history, the traditions and the political status of the religious community with which that saint was associated: it was an act of monastic propaganda on a grand scale.

[138] The feast of St Edith's deposition (16 September) is commemorated in only five of the tenth- and eleventh-century calendars printed by Wormald – *Before 1100*, nos. 2 (West Country; St Edith's feast was added in the twelfth century), 6 (Wells), 12 (Winchester), 14 (Sherborne), 20 (Crowland). The feast of Edith's translation (3 November) is commemorated only in nos. 12 (Winchester) and 19 (Bury). Her cult seems to have acquired no wider popularity in the post-Conquest centuries, the feast of her deposition only being commemorated in just five of the calendars printed by Wormald – *After 1100*, I, 10, 92, 157; II, 87, 100. For a reconstructed calendar of Wilton itself, in which the saint continues to receive high veneration, see G. Benoît-Castelli, 'Un Processional anglais du XIVe siècle', *Ephemerides Liturgicae* 75 (1961), 281–326, at 286–8.

   The feast of St Edward (18 March), no doubt as a result of its legal enforcement, attained greater popularity in the eleventh century than did that of St Edith: it occurs in Wormald (ed.), *Before 1100*, nos. 2 (added s. xi) – 20. In the post-Conquest period likewise, St Edward was one of the most commonly venerated English saints: see Wormald (ed.), *After 1100*, I, 4, 21, 36 (added s. xv), 70 (added s. xv), 86, 102, 119, 151; II, 29, 46, 65, 94. For detailed comments on the date and provenance of these sources see Wormald's introductions to the individual calendars. A sixteenth-century calendar of Shaftesbury abbey survives in Cambridge, Fitzwilliam Museum, MS 2–1957, fols. 2–8v (see Morgan, 'Notes', p. 156; Ker, *Medieval libraries*, p. 177). Here Edward, Ælfgyfa and Edith all receive high veneration, and it is interesting to note that the calendar includes an *obit* for King Æthelred, brother of Edward. The same saints are dominant also in the litany which occupies fols. 58–60v.

Chapter 6

THE ROYAL CULTS OF ELY

The cult of the royal patron received its clearest expression in the veneration at Ely of St Æthelthryth. To Bede, as to the hagiographers of St Edburga and St Edith, the essence of his subject's sanctity lay in her preservation of *uirginitas* and in the replacement of secular by monastic goals which this both implied and symbolised.[1] But to Bede as to the later writers virtue depended for its effectiveness upon the resources of an earthly kingdom. In the kingdom of the East Angles the Christian faith had been received with some hesitancy in the early decades of the seventh century. The attitude of Redwald, the first East Anglian ruler to receive baptism, had been ambivalent, if not downright cavalier: 'After the manner of the ancient Samaritans', Bede wrote with some distaste, 'he seemed to be serving both Christ and the gods whom he had previously served; in the same temple he had one altar for the Christian sacrifice and another smaller altar on which to offer victims to devils.'[2] A second attempt to convert the East Angles had proved abortive when Redwald's son, Eorpwald, was killed by a heathen almost immediately after receiving the faith.[3] It was not until the 630s, when King Sigebert joined forces with the Burgundian bishop Felix, that any real progress was made towards the establishment of the church. Felix is said to have 'reaped an abundant harvest of believers'; an episcopal see was established at Dunwich; the earliest monastic foundations were made.[4] But the process was far from complete: Bede's account of Sigebert's unfortunate end makes it quite clear that not everybody had come to terms with the new religion and with its social and political implications.[5]

---

[1] *HE*, IV, 19–20.   [2] *Ibid.*, II, 15.   [3] *Ibid.*
[4] *Ibid.*; III, 18–19.   [5] See above, p. 92.

It was, therefore, to a kingdom in which the Christian faith was only recently introduced, and in which its tenets were far from universally appreciated, that there succeeded, probably in the late 630s, 'a very religious man and noble both in mind and deed' – King Anna, from whom there sprang that dynasty of royal ladies who came to be venerated as 'the Ely saints'.[6] Anna is a shadowy figure. We know from Bede that he too met his end at the hands of the ubiquitous Penda: like Sigebert, he seems to have been regarded in some quarters as a martyr.[7] We know too that he continued his predecessor's patronage of the newly established church, and in particular of the monastery of *Cnobheresburg*.[8] In the matter of monasticism, however, it seems that here as elsewhere demand must have outrun supply. Bede writes of this period that 'because there were not yet many monasteries founded in England, numbers of people from Britain used to enter the monasteries of the Franks or Gauls to practise the monastic life; they also sent their daughters to be taught in them and to be wedded to the heavenly bridegroom'.[9] Anna's daughter Æthelburga, his step-daughter Saethryth and his granddaughter Eorcengota each joined in this movement of religious emigration.[10] But Æthelthryth did something rather different: she was among the pioneers in the establishment of the religious life, and in particular of the religious life for women, in England itself.

More significant therefore in Bede's account of the saint than her initial decision to leave her husband for the religious life at Coldingham was the sequel to that decision: 'A year afterwards she was herself appointed abbess in the district called Ely, where she built a monastery and became, by the example of her heavenly life and teaching, the virgin mother of many virgins dedicated to God.'[11] To Bede the site of Æthelthryth's foundation was a *regio* 'of about 600 hides in the kingdom of the East Angles' where the saint 'wished to have her monastery, because . . . she sprang from the race of the East Angles'.[12] To the compiler of the *Liber Eliensis*, in

---

[6] *HE*, iv, 19.

[7] *Ibid.*, iii, 18. The *Vita Sexburge* notes that Anna 'in defensione Christiane religionis insudaret, a quodam gentili et sacrilego Merciorum duce Penda nomine interemptus est, et a bonorum remuneratore Deo glorioso in celis martyrio coronatus' (TCC O.2.1, fol. 217; Calig. A. viii, fol. 110). The *Vita Withburge*, whose account is incorporated almost verbatim in the *LE*, describes Anna's death at the hands of Penda and adds that the king's body rests at *Blyðeburch* (Blythburgh) 'et usque ad diem hanc pia fidelium deuotione ueneratur' (TCC O.2.1, fol. 238v; *LE*, i, 7).   [8] *HE*, iii, 19.   [9] *Ibid.*, c. 8.

[10] *Ibid.*   [11] *Ibid.*, iv, 19.   [12] *Ibid.*

contrast, it was the territory given to Æthelthryth as a dower by her first husband, Tonbert, *princeps* of the South Gyrwe.[13] The truth of the matter cannot now be recovered;[14] whatever the case, it was from her status as *filia principis* that Æthelthryth's powers over the site were ultimately derived. In her subsequent disposition of the site, the attributes of royalty had not been relinquished: they had simply been redeployed. The virgin queen had created her own *Eigenkloster*, a double foundation for monks and nuns; she had been established as ruler over it; and she had retained those proprietary rights which enabled her to name her own sister, Sexburga, as her successor.[15] She had founded one of the first religious houses – perhaps *the* first – to make provision for women in eastern England between the Thames and the Humber.[16]

[13] *LE*, I, 4: 'insulam Elge ab eodem sponso eius [Tonbert] accepit in dotem'. The written source claimed by the compiler for this statement has not been identified. See also *ibid.*, p. 3 (*De situ*) and *ibid.*, I, 16, where Bede's view is also cited.

[14] The political status of Ely in this period has been the subject of much discussion not only in the context of the abbey's history but also in that of the political evolution of eastern England. Two major issues are involved. First, was Ely a *regio* of the East Anglian kingdom, as claimed by Bede, or did it belong to the territory of the South Gyrwe, as alleged by the *LE*? Second, if the latter was the case, did Ely (the geographical unit described below, n. 50 and some outlying islands, as distinct from the later administrative Isle) represent the *whole* of the territory of the South Gyrwe, as seems to be indicated by the correspondence between the 600 hides ascribed by Bede to the *regio* of Ely and the 600 hides at which the South Gyrwe are assessed in the Tribal Hidage? For discussion of these problems, and of related issues of political geography, see especially H. C. Darby, 'The Fenland frontier in Anglo-Saxon England', *Antiquity* 8 (1934), 185–201; E. Miller, *The abbey and bishopric of Ely: the social history of an ecclesiastical estate from the tenth century to the early fourteenth century*, Cambridge Studies in Medieval Life and Thought, New Series I (1951), pp. 8–15; W. Davies and H. Vierck, 'The contexts of Tribal Hidage: social aggregates and settlement patterns', *Frühmittelalterliche Studien* 8 (1974), 223–93; W. T. W. Potts, 'The Pre-Danish estate of Peterborough abbey', *Proceedings of the Cambridgeshire Antiquarian Society* 65 (1974), 13–27. In the present state of knowledge firm conclusions remain impossible: Miller's reservations (*Ely*, p. 11) about jettisoning Bede in favour of a tradition written down at Ely in the twelfth century remain valid, as does his suggestion (*ibid.*, n. 1) that 'The fact . . . that the early abbesses of Ely followed in some sort of hereditary line may suggest a proprietary right which originated in the East Anglian royal house rather than in St Etheldreda personally.' It is, however, difficult to divorce Ely entirely from the South Gyrwe, and the most plausible solution to the problem may well be that which in some measure reconciles the two traditions – that Ely was the centre of (not necessarily coterminous with) an independent *regio* of the South Gyrwe, situated on the frontier of East Anglia and Mercia and in the time of Æthelthryth politically under the influence of the former (see Darby, 'Fenland frontier', pp. 195–6; cf. Miller, *Ely*, pp. 11–12).

[15] *HE*, IV, 19; KH, p. 64. Æthelthryth's foundation at Ely is dated to 673 by the *ASC* (A, E, *s.a.*). For further discussion of Æthelthryth's career and of the early history of her church see Bentham, *History of Ely*, pp. 45–63; *Monasticon*, I (1817), 457–8; Stewart, *Ely cathedral*, pp. 1–12 and especially Miller, *Ely*, pp. 8–14.

[16] Two such communities which were probably founded almost contemporaneously with

Æthelthryth died after an abbacy of seven years, and the initial promotion of her cult seems to have been something of a family affair. Just as Wulfthryth ensured that her daughter should not be forgotten by the Wilton nuns, so Sexburga decided to translate her sister's remains from the common graveyard to a prestigious position within the church. In the process, Æthelthryth's body was found to be uncorrupt, both the coffin and the clothes in which she had first been buried were found to possess miraculous powers, and a marble sarcophagus discovered near the deserted fortress of *Grantacaestir* miraculously proved to be the right size for the body. The sisters accordingly washed the holy body, 'wrapped it in new robes, carried it into the church, and placed it in the sarcophagus which they had brought, where it is held in great veneration to this day'.[17] Sixteen years after her death, the church which St Æthelthryth had built became her own shrine: the commemoration of benefactors was complete.

Royal proprietorship and royal patronage seem likewise to have been of central importance to the subsidiary cults of Ely. St Æthelthryth designated her sister to succeed her as abbess; Sexburga in turn seems to have designated her daughter Eormenilda;[18] and, if the *Liber Eliensis* is to be believed, Eormenilda was succeeded by her daughter, Werburga:[19] along with the role of abbess was bequeathed that of proprietor, patron and protector. The extant sources reveal virtually nothing about the early history of Ely's subsidiary cults and indeed provide us with no certain means of dating their inception.[20] It is however probable that of

Æthelthryth's Ely were East Dereham in Norfolk, founded by Æthelthryth's sister, Withburga, and Barking in Essex, founded for St Æthelburga by her brother Eorcenwold prior to his appointment to the bishopric of London in 675 (*HE*, IV, 6).

[17] *HE*, IV, 19.

[18] TCC O.2.1, fol. 226; Calig. A. viii, fol. 119 (*Vita Sexburge*); *LE*, I, 36. The *lectiones* for the feast of Eormenilda describe her entry to the religious life at Ely but do not state that she became abbess (TCC O.2.1, fol. 229v; Calig. A. viii, fol. 97; CCC 393, fols. 73v–74).

[19] *LE*, I, 37. The *Vita Werburge* describes its subject as a nun at Ely but not as abbess (col. 102).

[20] The *Vita Sexburge* follows its account of the saint's death with stories of two posthumous miracles, at least one of which concerns Sheppey rather than Ely and neither of which can be precisely dated (TCC O.2.1, fols. 226v–227v; Calig. A. viii, fols. 119v–120v). The *lectiones* for the feast of Eormenilda record the saint's death and burial at Ely but tantalisingly fail to describe the development of her cult (TCC O.2.1, fol. 229v; CCC 393, fols. 74–74v; Calig. A. viii, fols. 97–97v). Neither of the two miracles which are supplied can be precisely dated: one is described as 'recent' and concerns the miraculous release of a Saxon bound in chains; the other concerns the 'magister puerorum scole' and is said to have happened 'in oculis omnium fratrum ibidem commanentium' (TCC

these ladies the two former at least were remembered and honoured by their immediate successors, and it is reasonable to infer that there was a direct connection between hereditary proprietorship, hereditary abbatial status and subsequent veneration: a dynasty of royal patrons produced a dynasty of patron saints.

The descendants of Anna, moreover, were far from inactive elsewhere. In East Anglia itself another daughter, Withburga, founded and ruled a religious community at East Dereham in Norfolk and seems to have been venerated there prior to her translation to Ely in the tenth century.[21] More interesting are those ladies with wide-ranging dynastic connections whose activities provide an insight into the workings of the royal patron/patron saint model in kingdoms not otherwise covered by this study. Sexburga, prior to her departure for Ely, had played in Kent a role closely analogous to that of Æthelthryth in the Fens. She had been married to Eorcenbert, described by Bede as 'the first English king to order idols to be abandoned and destroyed throughout the whole kingdom', and according to her *Vita* had given vital support to his work of Christianisation.[22] After his death she had entered the religious life at *Middeltona*; she had subsequently founded and ruled her own community at Sheppey; *mediatrix ad regem*, she had secured for that community the protection and support of her sons Lothar and Egbert; and very probably she had designated her own daughter to succeed her as abbess.[23] Eormenilda came to Kent from Mercia, where she had been married to the Christianising king Wulfhere and where she had apparently more than fulfilled the

---

O.2.1, fol. 230; CCC 393, fol. 74v–75; Calig. A. viii, fol. 97v). The earliest direct evidence for the veneration of Sexburga and her daughter at Ely refers to the late tenth · century, when Abbot Brihtnoth is said to have provided images of four saints (probably Æthelthryth, Sexburga, Eormenilda and Withburga; see below, n. 45). The *Vita Werburge* likewise sheds no light upon the inception of its subject's cult at Ely: it is impossible to establish with any certainty whether that cult was a product of the eighth century, of the period of the monastic reform, from which date the feast of Werburga appears in a number of English calendars (see below, n. 46), or of the twelfth century.

21   *Vita Withburge, passim*; on the saint's translation at Dereham *c*. 798 and on the possible existence of an early hagiographical tradition see above, p. 57, n. 192 and p. 58.

22   *HE*, III, 8; TCC O.2.1, fols. 217v–218; Caligula A. viii, fols. 110v–111v (*Vita Sexburge*); cf. CCC 393, fols. 70–71; Caligula A. viii, fols. 94v–95 (*lectiones* for the feast of Sexburga).

23   *Heiligen*, ed. Liebermann, p. 5; Lambeth 427, fol. 211 ('A fragmentary life of St Mildred', ed. Swanton, p. 27); TCC O.2.1, fols. 219v–223v; Calig. A. viii, fols. 113–116v (*Vita Sexburge*). On the foundation and history of Minster-in-Sheppey see also KH, pp. 261, 478.

supportive function of the believing wife.[24] Perhaps less innovative than her mother, perhaps constrained by political circumstance, she worked not as a founder of religious institutions in her husband's kingdom but rather as consolidator of work already begun in Kent and in the Fens.[25] For her daughter Werburga, in contrast, the Mercian connection proved all-important: she returned from Ely to her father's land and was chiefly remembered as abbess of the Mercian houses founded by her uncle, King Æthelred.[26] The short lives or the later obscurity of such houses as Sheppey, Dereham or the Mercian Hanbury and Weedon should not blind us to the scale in its own time of the achievement of the 'daughters of Anna'. Over three generations and in three kingdoms where 'there were not yet many monasteries' they had dedicated – in whole or in part – their lives, their wealth and their influence to the establishment and protection of the religious life: they had richly deserved their reward in heaven.

THE TENTH-CENTURY REFORM: THE RELICS AND CONTINUITY AT ELY

Three centuries of obscurity separate St Æthelthryth's foundation at Ely from the abbey established by St Æthelwold in 970.[27] A review of the evidence for these three centuries is of some impor-

---

[24] TCC O.2.1, fols. 228v–229; CCC 393, fols. 72–73v; Calig. A. viii, fols. 96–96v (*lectiones* for the feast of Eormenilda).

[25] The several accounts of Eormenilda's monastic career show some variation in detail. The *lectiones* for the saint's feast, written for Ely use, state simply that the saint, following Wulfhere's death (674), 'Extimplo ad precellentissimum Elig monasterium confugit' (TCC O.2.1, fol. 229v; CCC 393, fol. 73v; Calig. A. viii, fol. 97). The Lambeth Fragment (fol. 211; Swanton, 'A fragmentary Life of St Mildred', p. 27) and the *Vita Sexburge* (TCC O.2.1, fols. 218v–219; Calig. A. viii, fols. 111–112) in contrast assert that Eormenilda, like her mother, took the veil at Milton in Kent; and the latter source adds that Eormenilda succeeded Sexburga as abbess of Sheppey (TCC O.2.1, fols. 222, 223v; Calig. A. viii, fols. 115v, 116v).

[26] *Vita Werburge*, cols. 103–7. The Life notes that Werburga died at the *cenobium* of *Tricengeham*, that her body was subsequently stolen and, in fulfilment of her wishes, taken for burial to Hanbury, and that after nine years it was elevated, and found to be uncorrupt, by the *Heanburgenses* and with the consent of King Ceolred. On the Mercian houses of Weedon, Hanbury and *Tricengeham* mentioned in the Life see KH, pp. 474, 484.

[27] The tenth-century refoundation of Ely forms the subject of *LE*, II, 1–5: the remainder of Book II up to c. 99 concerns the subsequent development of Ely's landed endowment and prestige up to 1066. Cc. 1–49 are mainly derived from the *Libellus* (see above, p. 51 and n. 170), borrowings from which are fully documented in the notes to Blake's edition. On the refoundation of Ely see also *ASC*, E, s.a. 963; *Three Lives*, ed. Winterbottom, pp. 24 (Ælfric), 47 (Wulfstan); Miller, *Ely*, ch. 2 and *passim*; KH, p. 64.

tance for the history of St Æthelthryth's cult. To later generations of Ely monks the assertion of continuity between the two founda- tions on St Æthelthryth's isle was a central point both of faith and of propaganda. Thus, according to the compiler of the *Liber Eliensis*, Sexburga was succeeded as abbess by Eormenilda and Werburga;[28] the community subsequently flourished under a succession of unnamed abbesses until its destruction by the pagan *Inguar* and *Ubba*;[29] and thereafter a small group of priests returned to guard the relics of St Æthelthryth – with varying degrees of diligence – until expelled by Æthelwold.[30] This twelfth-century tradition of continuity was emphatically rejected by Edward Miller in his study of the origins of the Ely estate and liberty: 'Between St Etheldreda's abbey and the abbey which St Ethelwold refounded there had been a break at least of a century.'[31] Miller's analysis, however, cannot be accepted without reservation. It is founded upon the apparent conflict between the *Liber Eliensis* and the earlier accounts of the *Libellus*, the Lives of St Æthelwold and King Edgar's Ely charter of 970, each of which asserts that it was from the king that Æthelwold obtained the site of the monastery which he wished to refound.[32]

---

[28] *LE*, I, 36–7.

[29] *Ibid.*, c. 37: 'At quippe post ipsius decessum [Werburga's] beate femine, quarum nomina solius Dei novit scientia, nobis autem incognita, sub vite regularis observantia locum Elge in honore et sanctificatione usque ad vastationem a Danis gestam servaverunt.' For the Danish invasions see also *ibid.*, cc. 38–42, especially c. 39, where the destruction of Ely is associated with the activities of *Inguar* and *Ubba*; *ibid.*, II, I.

[30] *Ibid.*, II, I: Æthelwold refounded Ely, 'quod non ut cenobium sed ut publicum monasterium sine cultu et reverentia omni transeunti patebat'. Cf. *ibid.*, c. 3, where it is noted that some of the clerks were expelled and that others were converted to the monastic life. Blake notes (*ibid.*, p. 75, n. 1) that the compiler's language here is modelled upon Wulfstan's account of the expulsion of the clerks from Winchester (*Three Lives*, ed. Winterbottom, p. 45) and warns that as such it may be founded less upon Ely tradition than upon the compiler's misinterpretation of a source which itself makes no reference to the expulsion of clerks from Ely.

A similar outline for the history of Ely is preserved in the Corpus/Dublin Life of St Æthelthryth (CCC 393, fols. 13–14v; cf. TCD 172, pp. 267–8; cf. also CCC 393, fols. 42v–44 (verse Life)). These sources describe the continuance of the religious life until the Danish invasions and the subsequent establishment of a community of priests, which survived until the reign of Edgar.

[31] Miller, *Ely*, pp. 14–15, at p. 15.

[32] *Ibid.*, pp. 14–15. For the *Libellus* account see *LE*, App. A, pp. 395–7, especially p. 396 (c. 1): 'Sicque postea per destitutionem regie sorti sive fisco idem locus additus erat.' Cf. *Three Lives*, ed. Winterbottom, pp. 24 (Ælfric), 47 (Wulfstan). King Edgar's alleged charter of refoundation (S779) is incorporated into the *LE* as Book II, c. 5 and is also printed as B1266–7 (Latin and Old English versions) and K563 (Latin and Old English versions). The charter is accepted as authentic by Miller (*Ely*, p. 15 and *passim*) but is seriously questioned by Whitelock ('The dealings of the kings of England with Northumbria in the tenth and eleventh centuries', in Clemoes (ed.), *Anglo-Saxons*,

But it fails adequately to differentiate between the tenth- and twelfth-century layers of tradition incorporated into the *Liber Eliensis*. This is particularly important for an understanding of the century between the Danish invasions and the time of St Æthelwold. The major *Liber Eliensis* account of 'the time of the priests' forms a self-contained narrative concerning the plan of an *archipresbiter* during Edred's reign to check on the contents of Æthelthryth's tomb: it is said to be derived from the narrative of a certain Ælfhelm, an associate of the *archipresbiter*,[33] and, if this ascription is correct, it must be dated to the second half of the tenth century and its statements concerning the existence of the community of priests must be treated with respect. It seems clear, moreover, that one of the principal purposes of that narrative was to demonstrate the unworthiness of the priests to act as guardians of St Æthelthryth's relics:[34] such propaganda would scarcely have been necessary had there been no priests. The statements of the Ælfhelm narrative, moreover, seem to be corroborated by a number of passages within the *Libellus* which point to the existence of a landholding religious community at Ely prior to the refoundation by Æthelwold.[35] And the existence of such a community is in no sense incompatible with King Edgar's subsequent grant of the site for a different purpose: when he sanctioned Æthelwold's establishment of monks in his own cathedral he sanctioned precisely such a displacement of a pre-existing community.[36] Perhaps less reliable,

---

pp. 70–88, at p. 77n.) and Blake (*LE*, App. D, pp. 414–15). The Old English and Latin versions of the charter seem to tell two slightly different stories. In the former the king notes that the place had been neglected in his time and with less service than was pleasing to him; the latter states 'locus denique predictus deficiente servitio Dei nostra etate regali fisco deditus erat'.

[33] *LE*, I, 43–9. At c. 42 the narrative is introduced by the statement that, in the reign of Edred (947–55), 'mirum et audientibus valde stupendum apud Ely de sacerdotibus ibidem degentibus contigit quod unus illorum Alfelmus nomine sub persona alterius de se, qui errori et facinori eorum consenserat, asseruit et scripsit, quod hic sub silentio non preterimus'. Cf. *ibid.*, c. 49, where 'prelibatus presbiter Alfhelmus' is described as one of four participants in the *archipresbiter*'s scheme. The Corpus/Dublin Life of Æthelthryth incorporates this narrative in a differently organised form (CCC 393, fols. 19v–22v; cf. TCD 172, pp. 269–75; cf. also CCC 393, fols. 48–50v (verse Life)). The relationship between the two versions of the narrative is discussed by Blake (*LE*, p. xxxii).

[34] *LE*, I, 43–9 *passim* and especially c. 49: 'Sed nec quidem ecclesia sic ab iniquorum cessavit presbiterorum dominio, verum sub eorum naufragosa gubernatione usque ad decimum regni gloriosi regis Ædgari annum fluctuabat.'

[35] *LE*, II, 18, 24 (from *Libellus*, cc. 27–8, 34). These passages, together with the more difficult *LE*, II, 28, seem to indicate both that there was a landholding religious community at Ely by 955 at the latest and that St Æthelwold's foundation succeeded to at least a part of the endowment of that community.   [36] See above p. 106.

but none the less interesting, is the apparent corroboration both by the Ælfhelm narrative and by the *Libellus* of the tradition that the religious life was maintained at Ely until the Danish invasions.[37]

But if the evidence for Ely's missing centuries is more complex than previous writers have allowed, it is far from providing proof of 'continuity'. The community allegedly destroyed by the Danes cannot with any confidence be placed in a direct line of succession from the seventh-century foundation of St Æthelthryth;[38] the extent of the havoc subsequently wrought by the Danes cannot be accurately assessed;[39] the establishment of the priests cannot be precisely dated; and we can only dimly perceive the tenurial and political changes brought by the conquest of the Eastern Danelaw by the tenth-century West Saxon kings.[40] Finally, it is of central importance to note that, even if Æthelwold's monks were the

---

[37] *LE*, I, 49; App. A, p. 396 (*Libellus*, c. 1).

[38] It has been noted above (p. 178) that St Æthelthryth's foundation was a double house for monks and nuns. The community displaced by the Danes is variously described by later writers who may well have been more concerned to establish a continuing ecclesiastical presence at Ely than to define the precise nature of that ecclesiastical presence. According to the *Libellus* the community was one of nuns (*LE*, App. A, p. 396 (c. 1)). *LE*, I, 38 describes the continuance of the religious life after the abbacy of Werburga 'sub beatarum regimine feminarum, non tepescente sed magis ac magis in ea fervescente fervore discipline regularis ac custodia monastice professionis'. *Ibid.*, c. 40 speaks of a 'cenobium . . . virginum' and notes that 'Mactatur, ut victima innocua, sanctimonialium caterva et, quoscumque repperit sacri desiderii fratres et sorores, absque ulla humanitatis consideratione precipiti peremit strage.' C. 41 notes that 'Totus pene trucidatur clerus, abducitur in captivitatem quisque residuus' and refers to the 'clerici, qui depredati sunt'. And c. 49 (Ælfhelm) speaks of both clerks and nuns and echoes c. 41 in its description of clerks 'qui ex Elgico depredati sunt cenobio'. The Corpus/Dublin Life of St Æthelthryth describes the community in terms closely analogous to *LE*, I, 38 and 40 (CCC 393, fols. 13–14v; cf. TCD 172, pp. 267–8). If any credence whatever can be attached to these varied accounts, it seems that the community of the ninth century may have been one of nuns with an associated group of priests: the mechanism by which this organisation had evolved from St Æthelthryth's foundation is nowhere elucidated, and it would be dangerous to assume that the process was one of direct descent.

[39] Little credence can be given to the conventional and exaggerated descriptions of Danish devastation preserved by the *LE* (especially Book I, cc. 39–40) and by the Corpus/Dublin Life of Æthelthryth (CCC 393, fols. 13v–14v; cf. TCD 172, p. 268; cf. also CCC 393, fols. 43v–44 (verse Life)). For modern analysis of the social, political and ecclesiastical consequences of the Danish invasions and conquest of eastern England, see below, pp. 217–18 and notes.

[40] For the West Saxon conquest of the Eastern Danelaw see especially Stenton, *ASE*, pp. 325–38; Miller, *Ely*, p. 14; D. Whitelock, 'The conversion of the Eastern Danelaw', *Saga-Book of the Viking Society* 12 (1937–45), 159–76, at 161–2. Both Stenton, *ASE*, and Miller, *Ely*, emphasise the modification of local administrative patterns which took place between the Danish invasions and the mid tenth century, and Miller notes in particular that the administrative unit of the Isle of Ely may have been a product of the West Saxon reconquest of the region from the Danes.

direct successors to a community of priests, their arrival marked, both spiritually and institutionally, a complete break with the recent past. The spiritual core of the tenth-century reform was the strict observance of regular Benedictine monasticism; its institutional implications included the communalisation of an endowment which may previously have been in the 'ownership' of individual members of the community; and its secular guarantee was a close alliance with the royal family in order to defeat *secularium prioratus* – the lordship of the local notables.[41] Between the seventh and the tenth century there may have been very few years in which St Æthelthryth's isle lacked its church and her relics their guardians: but in terms both spiritual and institutional the history of Ely abbey began with the advent of St Æthelwold.

But St Æthelthryth, it appears, did make one bequest of the highest importance to St Æthelwold's foundation – that of her own remains. The *Liber Eliensis* records that Æthelwold, apparently at the time of the reconstruction of the abbey church, found beside the high altar the body of the holy virgin and queen Æthelthryth.[42] In another context the same source informs us that the bishop found and translated the remains of Æthelthryth's successors, Sexburga and Eormenilda.[43] The first abbot, Brihtnoth, was likewise remembered for his interest in the saintly daughters of Anna. He took steps to increase his abbey's investment in sanctity by bringing – apparently by means which were far from fair – the relics of St Withburga to join those of Æthelthryth, Sexburga and Eormenilda at Ely.[44] And he provided four richly decorated images of the saints to be placed on either side of the high altar.[45] Nor were the monks of the new community content with private devotion: the surviving calendars of the late tenth and eleventh centuries provide ample testimony to their active promotion of the cults of Ely's royal saints.[46] St Æthelthryth, it is clear, was no less useful to the

---

[41] See above, p. 107 and n. 40.   [42] *LE*, II, 52.

[43] *Ibid.*, c. 145. Æthelwold's translation of these saints is not recorded elsewhere.

[44] CCC 393, fols. 63v–66 (*Vita Withburge*); *LE*, II, 53.

[45] *LE*, II, 6: 'Fecit namque beatarum virginum imagines easque auro et argento gemmisque pretiosissime texuit et iuxta altare maius duas a dextris et duas a sinistris statuit.' The four saints in question were presumably Æthelthryth, Sexburga, Eormenilda and Withburga. As Werburga was not buried at Ely it is unlikely that her image would have been associated with the high altar of that church.

[46] The incidence of the feasts of the Ely saints in the calendars printed in Wormald (ed.), *Before 1100*, is as follows:

Æthelthryth	*dep.*	23 June	nos. 2–20
	tr.	17 Oct.	nos. 3, 7, 9, 10, 12, 14–16, 18–20

successor community of the tenth century than she had been to her own foundation of the seventh. For an explanation of that continuing usefulness the *Libellus* and *Liber Eliensis*, especially the latter, are our most valuable tools.[47] Each is of course concerned less with miracles and pilgrims than with the history of Ely's landed endowment and liberty. The compiler of the *Liber Eliensis* intersperses this with short accounts of the abbots and locates the whole within a framework of national history.[48] Together these sources provide an unparalleled insight into the workings of the tenth-century reform, not only as a spiritual movement, but also as a social and political phenomenon with a profound impact upon local society. Within their account St Æthelthryth occupies – together with her saintly family – a place of some importance: that she does so permits some analysis of the importance of her cult, not simply in enhancing the spiritual prestige of the new foundation, but also as one of several tools used by the monks to secure their assimilation into a local society which had every reason to regard their activities with some distrust.

The refoundation of Ely did not begin and end with the installation of monks on a desolate island in the Fens. Monks, once

Sexburga	*dep.*	6 *July*	nos. 2, 3, 5, 6, 10–20
Eormenilda	*dep.*	13 *Feb.*	nos. 4 (add. s. xi)–6, 9–20
Withburga	*dep.*	17 *Mar.*	nos. 15–17
	tr.	8 *July*	nos. 5, 14, 20
Werburga	*dep.*	3 *Feb.*	nos. 3, 5, 6, 14 (add. s. xi), 16, 20
Æthelburga	*dep.*	7 *July*	nos. 5, 14, 20
Eorcengota	*dep.*	21 *Feb.*	—

For the date and provenance of the calendars cited see Wormald's introductions to the individual calendars. The calendar of the Missal of Robert of Jumièges (no. 15) is attributed to Ely by Tolhurst ('Examination of two Anglo-Saxon manuscripts') and to Thorney by Atkins ('Investigation of two Anglo-Saxon kalendars'). The Ely monks clearly gave priority to the cults of the three early abbesses. The cult of Withburga was of secondary importance. The feast of Werburga likewise had not yet gained widespread popularity. Moreover, in the absence of any corroborative evidence for the veneration of Werburga at Ely in the Anglo-Saxon period, it is possible that the appearance of her feast in the calendars was a product of the promotion of the cult not by the Ely monks but by the clerks of Chester, into whose possession the saint's relics had passed. Æthelburga and Eorcengota were never of more than peripheral interest to the church of Ely and, so far as I have been able to ascertain, the only English sources to record the feast of the latter are the post-Conquest calendars of Ely itself (Wormald (ed.), *After 1100*, II, 9, 14).

[47] For the period between the tenth-century reform and the Norman Conquest the hagiographical sources are disappointingly barren. The Life of St Withburga includes (CCC 393, fols. 63v–66) an account of that saint's translation to Ely which closely parallels that incorporated into *LE*, II, 53. This apart, no other hagiographical source contains material which can be shown to refer to this period.

[48] For his sources see *LE*, pp. ix–xi, xxxiv.

installed, had to be provided for; and that provision fell into two distinct phases – the first, lasting until the early 980s, a period of rapid and systematic acquisition carried out by Æthelwold in conjunction with Abbot Brihtnoth and, initially, with the support of King Edgar; and the second, continuing until the 1020s, a period of consolidation, in which gift replaced purchase as the principal means of acquisition.[49] Of these, the former is by far the more interesting. Æthelwold evidently pursued a deliberate policy of providing for the new community an adequate and territorially compact landed endowment;[50] there are indications that that provision was not always effected by the most scrupulous means;[51] and it was effected only at the cost of a significant revolution in the local tenurial structure.[52] The result was a severe, if short-lived,

[49] Of these the former is the period covered by the *Libellus quorundam insignium operum beati Æthelwoldi episcopi* and by those chapters of the *LE* derived from it – Book II, cc. 1–49 (except cc. 5, 6, 9, 16, 28, 29, part of 39, 40). The following cc. 50–7 of *LE*, Book II concern such aspects of monastic history as King Edgar's gifts to Ely (c. 50), the dedication of the new church (c. 52) and the 'martyrdom' and replacement of Abbot Brihtnoth (cc. 56–7). The account of the second period of expansion occupies Book II, cc. 58–97, which (with the exception of a number of historical chapters) seem to be largely based upon vernacular documents of the house. For discussion of the development of the Ely endowment between the tenth-century refoundation and the Norman Conquest see Miller, *Ely*, pp. 16–25; on the origins in this period of the liberty of Ely see *ibid.*, pp. 25–35.

[50] Miller notes that it was the achievement of this period 'to consolidate, more or less, the abbey's ownership over the "island of Ely"' (*Ely*, p. 17). This 'island of Ely' comprised an area quite distinct (though not always clearly distinguished by the Ely historian) from the administrative 'Isle of Ely'. It is defined thus by the compiler of the *LE*: 'Restat autem insula in longitudine miliaribus vii a Cotingelade usque ad Litleporte vel ad Abbotesdelf, nunc vero Biscopesdelf vocitatum, et in latitudine iiii^{or}, hoc est a Cherchewere usque ad mare de Straham' (*LE*, p. 3 (*De situ*); cf. *ibid.*, II, 54). For discussion of these bounds see *ibid.*, p. 3, n. 1 and Miller, *Ely*, pp. 12–13.

[51] See, for instance, *LE*, II, 10 (from *Libellus*, cc. 7–9), where it is claimed that the transfer of land via Æthelwold to the monks had been the result of a forced bargain, and *LE*, II, 12 (from *Libellus*, cc. 15–17), where a similar accusation is made concerning an estate acquired by Abbot Brihtnoth. A particularly interesting case is that of a certain Oslac (*LE*, II, 19; from *Libellus*, c. 29), who had been sentenced by King Edgar to forfeiture of all his possessions. Through Æthelwold's intercession this penalty was commuted to a fine of 100 pounds. Oslac, however, was unable to produce this sum and was forced to give a part of his estate to Æthelwold (and thence to the monks) in return for forty pounds. In each of these cases the value of the evidence is difficult to assess, for in each case unfair treatment meted out by Æthelwold was being used as an excuse for the repudiation after Edgar's death of arrangements made with the bishop. None the less the nature of these complaints does strongly suggest that Æthelwold was, at the very least, a shrewd and forceful businessman with few qualms about pressing home an economic advantage.

[52] The full extent of this 'tenurial revolution' could be appreciated only by minute analysis of the transactions recorded in the *Libellus* and the *LE*: nevertheless, a few examples may be cited. *LE*, II, 8 (from *Libellus*, c. 6) records Æthelwold's purchase from Leofric of

crisis on the death of Æthelwold's royal patron. The 'anti-monastic reaction' of Edward's reign has stimulated much controversy.[53] It is clear, however, that in so far as it affected Ely that reaction had its roots in the tenurial and political problems attendant upon the assimilation of the monks into local society. It was directed against the emergence of the abbey of Ely as a great landowner and against the incursions into the local pattern of landholding and privilege which that emergence entailed. Hence its most common manifestation seems to have been the repudiation of a sale or grant of land either by the original vendor or grantor or by his descendants.[54] Very probably conflicts of this kind were exacerbated by uncer-

Brandon of *Lindune* with its appurtenances of Hill, Witcham and Wilburton. *LE*, II, 10 (from *Libellus*, cc. 7–9) records the bishop's purchase of eight hides at Stretham, perhaps from the same family, and his subsequent acquisition of further land at Stretham from a certain Ælfwold of *Merthamlege* and from a widow, Wulfled. *LE*, II, 12 (from *Libellus*, cc. 15–17) describes Abbot Brihtnoth's purchase from Sumerlede of 200 acres at Witchford and the augmentation of this by two minor transactions. In the same area a bequest brought 100 acres at Wold (*LE*, II, 13; from *Libellus*, c. 18) and a further transaction brought fifty acres at Witcham: 'His acris simul collectis, sancta Æðelðriða habet iii hydas integras in Wicceford et Walde et Wiceham.' (*LE*, II, 14; from *Libellus*, c. 19). *LE*, II, 16 and 17 (from *Libellus*, cc. 20–6) provide detailed accounts of the several minor transactions which went to build up the Ely estates at Hill and Haddenham and at Wilburton. For some insight into the consequences of this monastic intrusion into the local tenurial structure see below, n. 54.

53 See especially Stenton, *ASE*, p. 455, where it is noted that 'The anti-monastic reaction which followed Edgar's death was due to political rather than religious feeling.' Fisher, in his detailed study of the reaction, argued that attitudes towards monasticism were determined by political rivalries engendered by the disputed succession which followed Edgar's death: 'There was, strictly speaking, no anti-monastic reaction. The forces opposed to monasticism were used in support of one party in a primarily political dispute' ('Anti-monastic reaction', p. 255). Edward Miller, in his analysis of the Ely material, was struck by the fact that 'there is nothing in the *Historia Eliensis* to suggest that any political motive or any genuinely anti-monastic issues were involved. On the contrary, the real problems seem to have been at root problems of land-title' (*Ely*, p. 18). Other writers have likewise related the reaction which followed Edgar's death to the profound social and political effects of the monastic revival as it was worked out at the local level. See especially John, 'The king and the monks', pp. 178–80, where the opposition of Ealdorman Ælfhere to the monasteries is explained by reference to the erosion of his powers by the royally appointed abbots of Oswald's Mercian monasteries.

54 See, for instance, *LE*, II, 8 (from *Libellus*, c. 6; Leofric of Brandon's original sale of land to Æthelwold is described above, n. 52): 'Postea vero evoluto tempore et defuncto rege Ædgaro, nisus est idem Leovricus subdola calliditate omnem conventionem quam cum episcopo fecerat annullare, si posset.' *LE*, II, 11 (from *Libellus*, cc. 10–13) records an agreement negotiated between Æthelwold and a certain Leofsige. King Edgar, however, died before the transaction was complete: 'Quo mortuo, predictus Lefsius, Dei inimicus deceptorque hominum, et uxor eius omne pactum habitum cum episcopo irritum fecerunt et aliquando optulerunt ei x libras quas ab eo acceperant, aliquando vero se ei aliquid debere omnino denegabant.' Cf. also similar accounts preserved in *LE*, II, 7, 10, 12, 18, 19, 24, 27, 30, 35.

tainties in custom and in conveyancing procedure: Miller points out, for instance, that some of the disputes of this period suggest that the right of a man to disinherit his heirs by selling his land to the church 'was not fully conceded in the custom of the time'.[55] Certainly these conflicts resulted in complex litigation centring upon the establishment of title to land: a number of estates seem to have slipped permanently from the possession of the abbey;[56] and where the monks were successful in retaining their estates, they often did so only at a price.[57]

Two further issues may have complicated at Ely a reaction which was essentially tenurial in nature. The first was that of regional particularism. By the 970s the West Saxon conquest of the Eastern Danelaw had long been completed and the Fenland region assimilated with some success into a new, Wessex-dominated, England.[58] Nevertheless, it is striking that St Æthelwold's Ely was to all intents and purposes a West Saxon institution, its foundation the result of an alliance between West Saxon bishop and West Saxon king, and its first abbot, Brihtnoth, a former prior of Winchester cathedral.[59] King Edgar, of course, was well aware of the usefulness of a landowning religious community, closely associated both with the church of Winchester and with the West Saxon royal house, in consolidating the achievements of political conquest: the refoundation and re-endowment of Ely was both instrument and symbol of the deliberate expansion of West Saxon royal power.[60] And it is

---

[55] For discussion of the 'transitional state' of conveyancing procedure see Miller, *Ely*, pp. 19–20.

[56] See, for instance, *LE*, II, 42 (from *Libellus*, c. 53): 'Thurverðus abstulit cum rapina Deo et sancte Æðelðreðe xii hydas apud Norðwalde; nam hec terra erat pars terrarum quas beatus Æðelwoldus comparavit a rege Ædgaro, dans ei pro hiis Eartingan.' *LE*, II, 43 (from *Libellus*, c. 54) notes that the same man 'Diripuit etiam Deo et sancte Æðelðreðe Pulham, quam Æðelwoldus episcopus emerat a rege Ædgaro pro xl libris . . . Hec igitur duo maneria [Norðwalde and Pulham] predictus Thurverðus vi cepit et optinuit.' Elsewhere the compiler is less explicit about the manner in which estates came to be lost: see, for instance, *LE*, II, 45, 46, 49a and b.

[57] See, for instance, *LE*, II, 12 (from *Libellus*, cc. 15–17). The abbot obtained an estate at Witchford from Sumerlede, who subsequently repudiated his agreement. The result was a plea held before Ealdorman Æthelwine: 'abbas dedit . . . Sumerlede xxx solidos sicque persolvit ei xii libras pro cc acris'. Cf. also *LE*, II, 19, 27.

[58] See the references cited above, n. 40.

[59] *LE*, II, 3: Æthelwold establishes monks at Ely and installs as abbot 'virum . . . religiosum nomine Brihtnodum, suum prepositum'. Brihtnoth succeeded in 970 and died 996 × 9 (*ibid.*, App. D, p. 413; *Heads*, p. 44). For the extraordinary story of Brihtnoth's death at the hands of Queen Ælfthryth see *LE*, II, 56; also Wright, *Cultivation of saga*, pp. 158–61.

[60] For discussion of the relationship between the establishment of the new monasticism and the extension of West Saxon royal power see especially John, 'The king and the monks'

at least possible that the political implications of this West Saxon monastic plantation went some way towards compounding the irritation of those whose tenurial rights that plantation eroded.

The second issue was that of local politics. According to Ely tradition, the principal despoiler of the house was Æthelwine, ealdorman of East Anglia – a man who was remembered at nearby Ramsey as principal benefactor and *advocatus noster*.[61] Ely found its own protector in the person of Brihtnoth, ealdorman of Essex, who with his family provided a large proportion of the abbey's landed wealth.[62] It is clear that these were not two men who can neatly be labelled either 'pro-' or 'anti-monastic'. Rather their attitudes towards individual monasteries seem to have been determined by concerns of a local and political nature. The local status of aristocratic families might be enhanced, and their spheres of influence might be both broadened and defined, by the establishment of patronage relationships with individual houses. And in these circumstances the less-than-reverent treatment of one monastery by the principal benefactor of another might be just one element in the working out of local social and political relationships. It was the problem of the monks that, because they could not be established without significantly changing the face of local society, they were dependent for their successful assimilation into that society not only upon royal support but also upon the goodwill of a local aristocracy whose interests might be far removed from a straightforward respect for monasticism.

Within this process of assimilation the relics of St Æthelthryth were of central importance. So much was clearly understood by the compiler of the *Libellus*, who commenced his work with a short

and N. Banton, 'Monastic reform and the unification of tenth-century England', in *Religion and national identity*, ed. S. Mews, *Studies in Church History* 18 (Oxford, 1982), 71–85.

[61] *LE*, II, 55, entitled 'De his qui bona ecclesie de Ely fecerunt et qui mala.' The list of evil-doers commences: 'Maxime Ælwinus, Rameseiensis cenobii fundator, monasterium de Ely lacessere calumpniis ac rebus minuere, contempta Dei reverentia et sanctarum illic quiescentium, sicut in libro terrarum, quem librum sancti Æðelwoldi vocant, legitur, ut sibi de rapina oblationem aptaret, presumpsit.' The Ely writer goes on to make clear the reason for his condemnation of Æthelwine: following the death of King Edgar the ealdorman and his brothers had seized the estate of Hatfield from the Ely monks. For Æthelwine's reputation at Ramsey see *Chronicon abbatiæ Rameseiensis*, ed. W. D. Macray, RS 83 (London, 1886), pp. 26–7, 29–37, 103–6; *Vita Oswaldi*, pp. 428–30, 445, 465–7.

[62] See *LE*, II, 55 (where Brihtnoth receives acknowledgement in conjunction with Wulfstan of Dalham), 62–4, 67, 88–9. For discussion of these gifts see *LE*, App. D., pp. 422–3; Miller, *Ely*, p. 22; *Wills*, ed. Whitelock, pp. 189–93.

prehistory of the establishment of the monks at Ely. He explains that the island of Ely was claimed during Edgar's reign by two magnates of the royal court. Wulfstan of Dalham, however, by pointing out to the king all that there was to know 'about the dignity of the house and the fame of its relics',[63] was able to persuade Edgar to reject each of these claims. Instead the king, moved by Wulfstan's narration, asked Æthelwold to found a religious community on the island, 'stating that he did not wish such important relics to remain any longer without worshippers and without due veneration'.[64] These passages, whatever their value as a detailed foundation history, constitute an important policy statement on behalf of the new community. They announce that the principal *raison d'être* of that community was to guard the relics of St Æthelthryth. In so doing, they establish a single and vital thread of continuity between the community of the seventh century and that of the tenth: they provide for the successor foundation a respectability born of antiquity.

But the continuity symbolised by the relics of St Æthelthryth seems to have conferred more than a rather vague respectability: it provided also title to land. It seems clear that St Æthelthryth in her lifetime exercised proprietary rights over the land on which her community was founded:[65] her translation into a patron saint had perpetuated that proprietorship and had provided it with a tangible symbol – the uncorrupt body of the saint. The tenth-century monks, in publicising their veneration for St Æthelthryth's relics, publicised also their right and intention to inherit the proprietorship vested in those relics. Possession of the church and lands of Ely was vested in St Æthelthryth: 'guardianship' of her relics conferred 'guardianship' of the same church and lands. The close association between title to property and the guardianship of relics is further underlined by two translations which allegedly took place shortly after the tenth-century refoundation of the house – Abbot Brihtnoth's thinly disguised theft of St Withburga from her original resting-place at Dereham,[66] and Abbot Ælfsige's translation of the mysterious St Wendreda from March.[67] In each case the translation of relics seems to have been associated with the acquisi-

---

[63] *LE*, App. A, p. 396 (*Libellus*, c. 2); cf. *LE*, II, 2.

[64] *LE*, App. A, p. 397 (*Libellus*, c. 3); cf. *LE*, II, 3.   [65] See above, p. 178.

[66] CCC 393, fols. 63v–66 (*Vita Withburge*); cf. *LE*, II, 53.

[67] *LE*, II, 76. The relics of St Wendreda were subsequently lost in the Battle of Ashingdon (1016), to which they had been carried by the Ely monks (*ibid.*, c. 79).

tion of land:[68] as such it served not only to increase the spiritual prestige of Ely but also to strengthen the abbey's title to the estate which it had acquired and to symbolise the wide extent of its territorial power.

'Guardianship' of St Æthelthryth's relics had a further implication. It meant that, just as the church and lands of Ely became the church and lands of the saint, so the monks of Ely became significant only as members of an undying community whose function was to serve the saint. And this had the highly desirable effect of distancing their activities from the sordid affairs of men. St Æthelwold and his associates laboured not to enrich the monks of Ely but for the greater glory of St Æthelthryth; the tenurial revolution of the tenth-century reform was justified as an act of devotion. Hence, for instance, Æthelwold, having completed his initial purchases of estates from Edgar, 'offered these lands, with all royal customs, and strengthened by a privilege of eternal liberty, to God and St Æthelthryth'.[69] And elsewhere the Ely tradition is more specific: a total of sixty hides had been obtained by Æthelwold 'within the waters and fens and marshes of Ely' and given 'to God and St Æthelthryth'.[70] The *Libellus* and the *Liber Eliensis* preserve a vivid and not altogether attractive picture of St Æthelwold as a shrewd and successful businessman who worked with the backing of an acquiescent king and an acquisitive saint. The royal charter provided the most effective earthly protection that the time could devise; the patron saint provided both a superior moral right and a powerful protector in heaven. Thefts of land from the church constituted thefts from St Æthelthryth, to whose service the land had been dedicated.[71] And although the *Libellus* and *Liber Eliensis* are concerned less with divine vengeance than with the judgements of men, it is made quite clear that thefts from the saint would receive fitting punishment. A certain Ingulf 'by force and against justice took Brandon from God and St Æthelthryth' and did not long survive his crime:

---

[68] *LE*, ii, 40: Æthelwold 'a rege Ædgaro Dyrham cum omnibus que ad eandem villam pertinebant ecclesie de Ely adiecit et sancte Æðeldreðe gratanter optulit'. Cf. *ibid.*, c. 53: the account of Withburga's translation to Ely is introduced by the statement that 'Inter alia vero magnifica expetitum a rege Æðgaro monasterium in Dyrham cum pretiosissimo thesauro suo Withburga adiecit, cui nimirum in omnibus his gratia transferendi parabatur.' For the abbey's acquisition of land at March see *ibid.*, c. 67.
[69] *LE*, II, 4 (from *Libellus*, c. 4).   [70] *LE*, II, 23; cf. *ibid.*, c. 24.
[71] See for instance *ibid.*, cc. 35, 42 (cited above, n. 56).

from the very day on which he thus invaded the possession of the church he tasted neither food nor drink. Indeed without delay his heart burst open. And so it came about that he who living had unjustly seized those things which belonged to God meeting with death was not able to retain them, but lost at the same time both life and lands.[72]

One further function of the Ely saints should not be overlooked. It has been suggested that the community depended for its successful assimilation into local society upon the support – most effectively expressed by gifts of land such as those made by Ealdorman Brihtnoth and his family – of the local aristocracy. It has been suggested too that the map of aristocratic patronage was generally drawn in accordance with political considerations.[73] But it is important to remember also that the age was one of lay piety. The monks, in committing to writing their stories of divine vengeance, would have been wasting their time had there not been a very real belief in the ability of the saint, as intermediary with the other-worldly, to call down that vengeance. And, by the same token, there was a very real belief, both in the ability of the saint to intercede on the day of Judgement for one's own soul and for those of one's nearest and dearest, and in the ability of the individual to secure that intercession by an appropriate gift to the religious community whose function was to guard the property of the saint. That belief, as well as political considerations of a more 'cynical' nature, underlay every gift made to the church in the Anglo-Saxon period. Its implication was that a skilfully developed cult could be one of the most valuable assets of a church in its struggle for local influence. There can be little doubt that the potency of this aspect of lay spirituality is reflected in the *Liber Eliensis* records of gifts such as that of Æðeric, who gave Chedburgh to St Æthelthryth, 'so that both he and his wife, together with their offspring, might earn God's blessing':[74] the monks of Ely had not been slow to advertise the intercessory powers of their royal ladies.

In the aftermath of the tenth-century reform, therefore, the cults of the East Anglian monastic patrons had been taken over by a religious community which bore no discernible relationship to St Æthelthryth's foundation and had been adapted in accordance with

---

[72] *Ibid.*, c. 35; repeated *ibid.*, III, 120 (from *Libellus*, c. 46). The incident has an equally daunting sequel: 'Uxor quoque et filii eius eo mortuo invaserunt eandem terram similiter, sed quemadmodum honorem Deo non dederunt nec anime sue pepercerunt, sic ultio divina exarsit super eos et infra unum annum omnes miserabiliter interierunt.'
[73] See above, p. 190.   [74] *LE*, II, 68.

the principal requirements of that community. The relics of St Æthelthryth – and to a lesser degree those of her supporting cast of saintly 'sisters' – were utilised to provide for Æthelwold's foundation a link with the seventh-century past, to strengthen its claims to land, to justify its acquisitiveness and to encourage the patronage of an aristocracy acutely conscious of status in this world and of judgement in the next. It remains to consider whether the Ely cults in this period had any significance other than the local and monastic.

The *Libellus* and the *Liber Eliensis* have preserved evidence of consistent and considerable royal patronage of the abbey of Ely throughout the late tenth and eleventh centuries. The refoundation of Ely is said to have taken place on royal initiative;[75] King Edgar, with St Æthelwold, heads the *Liber Eliensis* list of benefactors of the house;[76] and records survive of grants made to the community by Æthelred, Cnut and Edward the Confessor.[77] Both Cnut and Edward, moreover, are said to have possessed a special interest in Ely. Cnut allegedly made it his custom to celebrate the feast of the Purification there and even composed a song in honour of the place and its monks,[78] and Edward was said to have spent part of his childhood at Ely and to have expressed his gratitude by liberal patronage.[79] Perhaps behind the devotion of the kings we can detect the influence of Emma, mother of Edward and, after Æthelred's death, consort of Cnut, whose own generosity to Ely receives special acknowledgement in the *Liber Eliensis*.[80] There are isolated suggestions too of specific royal interest in the Ely saints. Edgar was said to have been prompted to refound the abbey by his great, if new-found, reverence for its saints[81] and to have given his support to Abbot Brihtnoth's 'kidnapping' of St Withburga.[82] Æthelred, according to the *Liber Eliensis*, visited Ely with his mother during the reign of Edward the Martyr and thereafter

[75] *LE*, App. A, pp. 396–7 (*Libellus*, cc. 1–3); cf. *LE*, II, 1–3.

[76] *LE*, II, 55. See also *ibid*., c. 50, entitled 'Que ornamenta rex Ædgarus dedit ecclesie de Ely'.

[77] *Ibid*., cc. 58 (S907), 77 (S919), 82 (S958), 92 (S1051), 95–95a (S1100). For discussion of the authenticity of these documents see *ibid*., App. D, pp. 417–19. [78] *Ibid*., II, 85.

[79] *Ibid*., c. 91: 'Iamque sullimatus in regno, beneficiorum que puer in Ely habuerat nequaquam est oblitus, digna enim recompendere premia studuit.' The chapter serves as an introduction to Edward's charter in favour of Ely (*ibid*., c. 92 (S1051); discussed *ibid*., App. D, p. 417). For discussion of Edward's alleged sojourn at Ely see Barlow, *Edward the Confessor*, pp. 32–4. [80] *LE*, II, 79.

[81] *Ibid*., App. A, p. 397 (*Libellus*, c. 3), cited above, p. 191.

[82] *LE*, II, 53; CCC 393, fols. 63v–66 (*Vita Withburge*).

professed a special reverence for St Æthelthryth.[83] Less remark-
ably, the royal charters of the late Anglo-Saxon kings almost
without exception express grants to the abbey as given to God, St
Æthelthryth and, in various permutations, her saintly 'sisters'.[84]

This evidence is difficult to interpret. Royal patronage of a
religious community does not in itself constitute evidence of active
royal promotion of that community's cults, and the few specific
references to royal interest in the Ely cults are conventional in tone
and may reflect monastic propaganda more accurately than royal
policy. Quite clearly there is nothing here to compare with the
surviving evidence of direct royal intervention in the cults of St
Edith and St Edward; at most there may have been a rather low-key
royal interest in St Æthelthryth and her family. That interest is no
doubt to be explained primarily by the prestige factor. The most
fundamental attraction of a royal cult lay in its value as a status
symbol: a royal saint in heaven brought prestige to those who
exercised the royal office on earth. There are signs, moreover, that
such a status symbol was particularly sought-after where there had
been a change of dynasty: thus Cnut, if Goscelin is to be believed,
proved in his veneration of St Edith to be almost more West Saxon
than the West Saxons.[85] In the Fenlands the political situation was
more complicated:[86] it is impossible now to ascertain the degree of
authority, if any, exercised by the East Anglian dynasty over Ely
and its region in the seventh century; it is impossible also to
ascertain what the monks and rulers of the tenth and eleventh
centuries believed that degree of authority to have been; and a
much longer period had elapsed between the lifetime of the saints
and the adoption of their cults by rulers of a 'foreign' dynasty. If,
however, the churchmen and rulers of the tenth century believed
Ely to have been in the pre-Viking period a *regio* within the
prouincia Orientalium Anglorum – and it is worth noting that
Wulfstan in his *Vita Æthelwoldi* accepted the Bedan view – then it is

[83] *LE*, II, cc. 11, 78. At c. 78 it is noted that 'Adiecit itaque gloriosus rex gloria et honore
Elyensem decorare ecclesiam, sicut pollicitus fuerat quando eum illic cum matre et
nobilibus regni sanctus Ædelwoldus adduxerat tempore fratris sui Ædwardi regis, ubi
coram multitudine plebis ad sepulchrum beate virginis, cui affectu et multa dilectione
deditus erat, se servum deinceps illius fore spopondit.'
[84] *Ibid.*, cc. 58, 77, 82, 92, 95–95a. Cnut's privilege (c. 82) does not specify the grant as being
to the saint, but the document is dated 'Die festivitatis sancte Æðeldreðe regine et
virginis, que sanctis suis meritis cum sororibus suis, videlicet Withburga, Sexburga et
filie Sexburge Ærmenilda, illud monasterium patrocinatur et regit.'
[85] See above, pp. 153, 168.   [86] For what follows see above, n. 14.

possible that the cult of St Æthelthryth may have had for the West
Saxon rulers a specific significance analogous to that which led
Cnut to venerate the daughter of Edgar. They may have hoped by
demonstrating their reverence for saints of the East Anglian royal
dynasty to ease their own acceptance as legitimate successors to that
dynasty. Even if the rulers did not subscribe to this view of Ely's
political past, they certainly had nothing to lose by adopting the
cults of those East Anglian royal ladies in whom and in whose relics
proprietorship of the church and lands of Ely was vested: by joining
with the monks in veneration of those saints they joined also in
publicising the West Saxon right of 'guardianship' over relics,
church and lands; their own lordship was enhanced accordingly.
The tenth-century adoption of the Ely cults both by West Saxon
monks and by the West Saxon monarchy might be interpreted on
two levels. It was, first, conciliatory – an attempt to ease an
important political transition by demonstrating continuity with
and respect for the past. It was also declaratory: it was an
unambiguous statement that Ely and her cults were under new
management.

ELY AND THE NORMAN CONQUEST

The advent of the Normans hit the church of St Æthelthryth hard.
The island in the Fens, remote, inaccessible, a natural fortress
against the incursions of the world, had provided an ideal retreat for
the seventh-century queen who sought only to live 'as if in the
wilderness'.[87] But in the aftermath of conquest that inaccessibility
and those natural fortifications very nearly proved fatal to the
prosperity and the prestige of the abbey of Ely. The island became a
stronghold of rebels – a basis for the military operations of those
'nobles of the country', prominent among them a Lincolnshire
thegn called Hereward, who were determined to hold out against
the rule of the Normans.[88] And the monks of Ely could hardly

---

[87] *LE*, I, 8; cf. *ibid.*, II, 105.
[88] *Ibid.*, II, 102, 104–7, 109–11. The rebellion is probably to be dated to the year 1070/1: in
1070 the rebels, in alliance with the Danish king Sweyn, used Ely as their base for an
attack on Peterborough, and thereafter, following the Danish withdrawal, Hereward
returned to Ely until successfully besieged by William (*ASC*, E, *s.a.* 1070, 1071; D, *s.a.*
1072). For general accounts of Hereward's rebellion see Stenton, *ASE*, pp. 605–6; D. C.
Douglas, *William the Conqueror: the Norman impact upon England* (London, 1964; repr.
1977), pp. 221–2; C. Hart, 'Hereward "the Wake"', *Proceedings of the Cambridgeshire
Antiquarian Society* 65 (1974), 28–40.

avoid implication in the seditious activity which centred upon St Æthelthryth's isle. The local tradition, although difficult to reconstruct in detail,[89] asserts a close connection between the monks and the rebels in the island — encouraged perhaps by stories of the Normans' plundering of the English monasteries and by rumours threatening the deposition of Abbot Thurstan.[90] The rebels, according to the *Liber Eliensis*, would admit nobody to their company 'unless first by swearing faithful service over the body of the most holy virgin Æthelthryth they had pledged themselves to labour with them body and soul'.[91] And one of the king's men captured by Hereward is made to return to the royal camp with a striking description of the political situation in the island:

Always the soldiers ate with the monks at lunch and at dinner, and shields and spears hung from the wall beside them, and in the middle of the building, from end to end, hauberks, helmets and other vital arms had been placed on seats, so that if the need arose they could quickly complete their preparations for battle. At the high table the most respected and devout abbot sat together with the three companions I have mentioned and with those two noble men, Hereward and Thurkill, the one on his right hand and the other on his left.[92]

But if the monks of Ely were initially tempted to throw in their lot with the rebels, it seems that they came rapidly to regret their choice. The king, according to the Ely historian, 'as soon as he learned . . . that the most courageous warrior Hereward was there,

---

[89] The *LE* account of this period is described by its editor as the 'outstanding example' of the compiler's tendency to present his materials 'in such disorder as to deprive them almost completely of their intrinsic value' (*LE*, p. liv). The account of the rebellion and of William's siege of Ely is presented 'as a consecutive narrative which protracts the siege from 1069 to 1075' (*ibid.*, pp. liv–lv). The whole is 'clearly untrustworthy' (*ibid.*, p. lv), as it cannot be reconciled either with the *ASC* and 'Florence', which describe the siege and capture of Ely *s.a.* 1071 (see above, n. 88) or with the death of Abbot Thurstan in 1072 or 1073 (see below, n. 116). Blake notes (*LE*, p. lv) that the *LE* account of the circumstances leading to William's attack on Ely is derived from 'Florence' and that the rest of the story seems to be drawn from three local sources, each describing from different viewpoints the same siege. The compiler however seems to have regarded these several accounts of the same siege as describing a number of different operations taking place between 1069 and the rebellion of Ralph Waher in 1075: a valiant attempt to disentangle his narrative is made by Blake, *LE*, pp. lv–lvii.

[90] See *LE*, II, 101–2, 112. In Book II, c. 107 it is made clear that a number of the abbey's estates had been 'invaded' by William's followers and that those invasions were subsequently sanctioned by the king. The compiler does not make clear at what stage these 'invasions' had occurred, but it is possible that some of them had taken place at an early date and were therefore among the factors which prompted the monks to side with the rebels. [91] *LE*, II, 102. [92] *Ibid.*, c. 105.

and strong men with him, assembled a mighty power to fight against them, and pondered evil against the holy place'.[93] And the *Liber Eliensis* preserves a vivid picture of a community which went in fear of the royal wrath. The monks' implication in the rebel cause seems to have prompted William officially to sanction his followers' invasions of the abbey lands.[94] And that royal decision may well have brought home to the monks the seriousness of their position. The *Liber Eliensis* account, although chronologically vague, suggests that it may have been in the aftermath of that decision, and of the seizure of St Neots (Eynesbury) by Gilbert de Clare,[95] that the monks, recognising that they lived in evil times, concluded with the king that peace which formed the prelude to his victorious entry into the island.[96]

In some respects, however, it was already too late. King William's anger had been aroused; and the price for reconciliation was high. According to the Ely historian, the king, following his entry into the island, treacherously repudiated the peace which he had made with the monks, who eventually had to appear before him at Witchford and to purchase their pardon, promising a payment of seven hundred marks of silver. There follows a graphic description of the difficulty which the monks experienced in raising the sum, of increasing royal demands and continuing threats of royal vengeance, and of the ultimate satisfaction of the king at the cost of despoiling the richly decorated images of the Blessed Virgin and of the Ely saints.[97]

Perhaps more important, however, was the fact that the early years of Norman rule had seen a severe crisis in the abbey's position as holder of lands and lordships: both the Domesday survey and the *Liber Eliensis* preserve a dismal record of 'invasions' of the lands of St Æthelthryth.[98] Some of these 'invasions' may have preceded the

93 *Ibid.*, c. 102.   94 *Ibid.*, c. 107.
95 *Ibid.*, c. 108 (cf. *ibid.*, c. 29 for the monks' acquisition of St Neots). According to this account, the Ely monks were ousted from their estate at St Neots and replaced by monks from Bec. The *LE* implies that the usurpation took place prior to the end of the rebellion, but as elsewhere its account is chronologically vague. M. Morgan (Dr Chibnall) notes that the new foundation was probably established *c.* 1079 (*The English lands of the abbey of Bec* (Oxford, 1946), p. 11).   96 *LE*, II, 109–11.
97 *Ibid.*, c. 111. Allowance must of course be made for the fact that the historian's partisanship may have led him to exaggerate the extent of the sufferings thus inflicted upon the church. Cf. *ibid.*, c. 112, where it is noted that as long as Abbot Thurstan lived, William 'gravissimis illum semper lacessivit iniuriis'.
98 See especially *ibid.*, cc. 107–8, 119, 131–2, 134. For the best general account of the tenurial effects of the Norman Conquest on the abbey of Ely see Miller, *Ely*, pp. 66–74.

rebellion in the island; others were doubtless encouraged by it.[99] Some seem to have been direct usurpations of demesne lands; others were more complicated – Miller cites, for instance, the crisis of lordship created when lands held of the abbey by Anglo-Saxon notables passed into the hands of their Norman successors.[100] The result was prolonged and complex litigation: 'Many questions were still undecided in Henry I's time, perhaps in Henry II's; and in 1086 the abbey's losses were still far more striking than property regained. It retained only about a quarter of the dependants who had been subject to its lordship on the day that King Edward was alive and dead.'[101] More than this, Miller points out, the reclamation of lands and lordships seems to have been complicated by the additional problem of adjustment to the abbey's new role as provider of feudal military service.[102]

The problems posed by a foreign ruler and a new and acquisitive military aristocracy were compounded in the decades following 1066 by problems within the church. In 1081 or 1082 Simeon, brother of Bishop Walkelin and former prior of Winchester cathedral, was appointed abbot of Ely by King William.[103] There followed a bitter quarrel as Remigius, Norman bishop of Lincoln, claimed the right to bless Simeon, while the monks sought exemption from episcopal jurisdiction.[104] The dispute, to the disgust of the monks, was eventually solved by compromise:[105] but it was

---

See also *Inquisitio comitatus Cantabrigiensis, subjicitur Inquisitio Eliensis*, ed. N. E. S. A. Hamilton, Royal Society of Literature (London, 1876); W. Farrer, *Feudal Cambridgeshire* (Cambridge, 1920), especially pp. 42–5, 150–2, 219–20.

99   See above, n. 90.

100 *Ely*, p. 66. A further problem also receives emphasis here – that 'the confusion of pre-conquest dependent relationships tended to give rise after 1066 to a multiplicity of claims to the land of a great many of the abbots' men; and the abbots did not always manage to assert their rights "propter commendationem"'.

101 *Ibid.*, pp. 66–7. On the Ely litigation see especially E. Miller, 'The Ely land pleas in the reign of William I', *EHR* 62 (1947), 438–56; *LE*, App. D, pp. 426–32.

102 *Ely*, pp. 67–8, citing especially *LE*, II, 134, chronologically confused but probably a reference to the tradition that the *servitium debitum* was exacted for the Scottish campaign of 1072 (see *LE*, p. 216, n. 1). See also H. M. Chew, *English ecclesiastical tenants-in-chief and knight service* (Oxford, 1932), pp. 2–3, 114–15.

103 *LE*, II, 118. On the dates of the abbots of Ely see *ibid.*, App. D, pp. 410–14 and *Heads*, pp. 44–5. Blake suggests that Simeon's term of office may have been calculated at Ely from 1081 (*LE*, App. D, p. 413); the editors of *Heads* favour 1082 for his succession (p. 45).   104 For details of this quarrel see *LE*, II, 118, 124–7.

105 *Ibid.*, c. 118. The Ely historian notes that Simeon, afraid of dying without benediction, accepted this from Remigius on condition that 'episcopus hoc ius non diffinita discussione contra sequentem abbatem vindicaret, sed esset ceterorum post eum tam plena renitendi libertas, ut unquam ante eum alicui liberior extitit'. The monks, hearing

reopened on the succession of Abbot Richard in 1100;[106] and its final resolution in 1108/9 brought only a further series of problems. In the latter year, after protracted negotiations, a new episcopal see was established at Ely and Hervey, exiled bishop of Bangor and former *procurator* of Ely, consecrated as its first bishop.[107]

The creation of the bishopric marked a watershed in the history of St Æthelthryth's church. The monks remained as the inhabitants of the cathedral priory, with the new bishop as their titular head, but the prior and convent gradually achieved a degree of institutional independence. The process was marked by conflict on two major scores. First, it was necessary to divide the landed endowment of the old abbey in order to provide for the distinct needs of the bishop and the cathedral community: that division resulted in wranglings between bishop and convent which may not have been fully resolved until early in the reign of Henry II.[108] And, second, the establishment of the bishopric brought the threat of episcopal control to the monks' own doorstep: the monks of the twelfth century fought a hard battle 'to prevent the new bishops from assuming, by right of succession to the abbots of Ely, the exercise of powers in the isle which had been denied to their predecessors in their episcopal capacity, the bishops of Lincoln'.[109] Finally, the conflicts of ecclesiastical politics were not helped to an easy solution by the involvement of Bishop Nigel in the civil war of Stephen's reign: the island in the Fens once again became a fortress held against the king.[110]

There can, then, be little doubt that, for the community of St Æthelthryth, the decades following 1066 constituted a period of

---

of this solution, 'portas ei offirmant, ostia claudunt, non ut patrem, non ut fratrem, non salutem ut hospitem suscipiunt, sed ut hostem repellunt'.

[106] For Richard's succession, and his refusal of blessing from Remigius's successor, Robert Bloet (1093/4–1123), see *LE*, II, 140–1. On the dates of Richard's abbacy see *ibid.*, App. D, p. 413 (succeeded 1100 after a seven-year vacancy; deposed 1102; restored probably in or soon after 1103; d. 1107) and *Heads*, p. 45.   [107] *LE*, II, 141; III, 1–7.

[108] The conflict between bishop and prior and convent is a dominant theme of *LE*, Book III; the creation of the distinct estates is discussed by Miller (*Ely*, pp. 75–80) and some of the documents are examined by Blake (*LE*, pp. l–li).   [109] *LE*, p. l.

[110] For the events of Stephen's reign, and for the involvement of Bishop Nigel in the civil war, see *LE*, III, 62–78. Blake notes (*ibid.*, App. E, p. 433) that the compiler 'has used a narrative account which is credible and authentic documents, but in dividing the narrative into chapters and attaching the documents at seemingly appropriate points he has confused the sequence of events'. For an attempt to reconstruct the activities of Bishop Nigel between 1139 and 1144 see *ibid.*, App. E, pp. 433–6; R. H. C. Davis, *King Stephen 1135–1154* (London, 1967), pp. 31–2, 43, 56, 80–1, 85, 91, 145.

crisis. Even allowing for a measure of monastic exaggeration, it seems clear that the monks' involvement in Hereward's revolt went some way towards making that community 'the special prey of the Norman spoiler';[111] and the political embarrassment of the house was compounded by ecclesiastical conflicts which, if not a direct result of the setting of Norman against Saxon, nevertheless had their roots in the Norman conquest of the English church. It remains to consider the fate of Ely's royal saints in this period of crisis and transition. The editor of the *Liber Eliensis* saw the post-Conquest hagiographical tradition of Ely mainly as the product of a defensive policy intended to forestall or to counter the scepticism of the Normans: 'the production of a *Life* and miracles of St Etheldreda are testimony less of a lively cult of the saint than of the doubts and disrespect of the generations of monks and laymen in the century after the Norman invasion'.[112] It is my purpose in the following pages to demonstrate that this dismissal of the post-Conquest tradition underestimates the very considerable body of evidence which quite definitely points to a continuing 'lively cult' of St Æthelthryth within the Anglo-Norman community of Ely. More than this, I shall argue, the Ely traditions – and in particular that fascinating blend of historiography, hagiography and propaganda which constitutes the *Liber Eliensis* – allow the historian to do far more than simply assert the continuity of cult: they provide a rare and exceptionally valuable insight into the mechanism by which the Anglo-Saxon cults might be adapted in accordance with the crises of post-Conquest monastic politics.

The first adaptation of St Æthelthryth's cult took place in the most unfavourable circumstances. In 1070/1 the monks of Ely were implicated in the most famous of the 'native' revolts of the post-Conquest era. And, if the local tradition is to be accorded any credence whatever, the role of St Æthelthryth in that revolt was far from negligible. The rebels were said to have admitted no man to their company unless he had first sworn an oath of loyalty on the relics of St Æthelthryth.[113] And the captured royal soldier was made to report that the island was defended not only by its natural inaccessibility but also by the patronage of 'the saintly ladies Æthelthryth, Withburga, Sexburga and Eormenilda'.[114] Finally, the Ely historian notes that William, on successfully entering the

[111] *VCH Essex*, II, 340–1 (J. H. Round).   [112] *LE*, p. xlix.
[113] *Ibid.*, II, 102, cited above, p. 197.   [114] *LE*, II, 105.

island, came to the monastery and, 'standing far from the holy body of the virgin, flung a mark of gold onto the altar, not daring to come any closer; he feared that the judgement of God might come upon him because of the wicked deeds which his followers had perpetrated in the house'.[115] In two ways, I would suggest, this account is of central importance. First, it seems to point – beneath a number of semi-legendary anecdotes – to a reality in which, during the troubled years after 1066, the monastic patron of Ely came to be regarded also as the patron of the political cause which the monks espoused. For a brief – but perhaps not inglorious – period, St Æthelthryth became the champion of the 'native' cause: her shrine became a rallying point of rebellion. Second, it suggests also that the relevance of the cult was not limited to the period of rebellion. It should be noted in this context that the historical truth of whether or not the events happened is considerably less important than the fact that a writer of the twelfth century believed them either to have happened or to be worth inventing. Their incorporation into the *Liber Eliensis* provides eloquent testimony to the fact that St Æthelthryth the protector of Ely and vindicator of its rights was no less important to the monks of the twelfth century than to those of the seventh or the tenth.

The continuity – albeit rather precarious – of Thurstan's abbacy until 1072 or 1073[116] precluded any immediate assault from within the church upon the customs and the cults of the Anglo-Saxon community of Ely. But even after the abbacy passed into the hands of the Normans there is little sign of the 'doubts and disrespect' of generations of monks. Thurstan's successor, Theodwine, a former monk of Jumièges, was remembered primarily as a hard-headed vindicator of the abbey's rights and as an important patron whose only fault lay in his death after an abbacy of no more than two and a half years.[117] Neither he nor Godfrey, the monk and *procurator* who administered the abbey in the long vacancy following his

---

[115] *Ibid.*, c. 111.

[116] For Thurstan's abbacy see *LE*, App. D, pp. 412–13, where the year 1072 for Thurstan's death is preferred; *Heads*, p. 45. For a summary of Thurstan's career, and for William's threat to depose him, see *LE*, II, 112.

[117] On Theodwine's appointment see *LE*, II, 112–13; *ibid.*, App. D, p. 412; *Heads*, p. 45. The compiler of the *LE* notes that Theodwine 'priusquam abbatiam intraret, ad eam revocavit totum quod in auro et argento et lapidibus ante illius promotionem rex inde abstulerat, nolens eam ullo modo suscipere, nisi rex que iusserat auferri iuberet referri' (*LE*, II, 113). The chapter continues with a brief account of the abbot's gifts to the church and a note that 'Multoque pretiosiora gessisset abbas predictus, si tempus proximum de vita illum non demeret.'

death, 'serving its interests no less than if he had been abbot',[118] make convincing adversaries of the Anglo-Saxon saints. Abbot Simeon seems to have given his monks a more difficult time. He was condemned by the Ely historian for his acceptance of abbatial blessing from Bishop Remigius, for a number of 'invasions' which took place during his abbacy, and for the introduction to Ely of a group of his supporters from among the Winchester monks.[119] These Winchester monks seem to have shown scant respect for the church of Ely: there is, however, not a shred of evidence to suggest that their lack of respect was conditioned by – or expressed in – hostility towards the Anglo-Saxon saints.[120] And, more generally, it was pointed out that Simeon's failings were the product less of Norman arrogance than of some loss of control due to advancing age.[121] He was remembered also as the abbot who began the construction of a new abbey church[122] and as a man who regarded the Ely saints with more than a minimum of reverence. The *Liber Eliensis* incorporates a tradition that, during Simeon's time, Goscelin of Canterbury was resident at Ely and was composing a *prosa* on St Æthelthryth.[123] It includes a series of miracles, two of which are definitely dated to Simeon's time, and all of which may have been committed to writing at his behest.[124] And it makes the abbot give the following instruction when one of his monks is smitten with madness: 'we do not know who could better assist

---

[118] *LE*, II, 115. For Godfrey's dates see *ibid*., App. D, p. 413 (1075–81) and *Heads*, p. 45 (1075/6–1082).

[119] *LE*, II, 137. These three misdeeds and their consequences are recounted in greater detail in *ibid*., cc. 118 (cited above, n. 105), 135, and 138 (see also *ibid*., cc. 129 and 133 for further references to the Winchester monks).

[120] *Ibid*., c. 138, concerning the theft of Ely property by these monks following Simeon's death and their miraculous punishment. The stolen goods included relics, but not, apparently, those of the royal ladies of Ely: the compiler refers only to 'philacteria cum sanctorum multorum reliquiis irreverenter de feretris extractis, insuper capud beatissimi confessoris domini Botulphi simul et maiora ipsius ossa'. We have, moreover, no evidence of what proportion of these Winchester monks installed by Simeon were Norman. And one of their number, a certain Godric, is said to have possessed a special reverence for St Æthelthryth and to have been the favoured recipient of visions of the Ely saints (*ibid*., cc. 129, 133).   [121] *Ibid*., cc. 135, 137.   [122] *Ibid*., c. 143.

[123] *Ibid*., c. 133. Goscelin's *prosa* cannot be identified with any of the extant Lives of the saint (see above, pp. 54–6).

[124] *LE*, II, 129–33. These concern respectively the cure of a monk, Edwin, suffering from madness; the cure of two mutes; two instances of the punishment of 'invaders' of the abbey's lands (see below, pp. 204–6 and notes); and the liberation of the community from an epidemic. Of these only cc. 129 and 133 are specifically dated to Simeon's abbacy: but the placing of the others between these strongly suggests that they were believed to belong to the same period.

him than that mistress whose servant he is; if he is placed before her, he will, we believe, speedily recover his health. Go, therefore, and, leading him under a strict guard, diligently keep watch at the tomb of our mistress and ask for her intercession.'[125]

Simeon's successor, Richard, formerly a monk of Bec,[126] clearly shared his views. He completed the reconstruction of the abbey church and, on 17 October 1106, 'The royal lady Æthelthryth was . . . translated into the new church, untouched and without inspection, and with most fitting praise was placed behind the high altar in her bridal shrine.'[127] The bodies of Sexburga, Eormenilda and Withburga were likewise laid to rest in the new church,[128] and the history of the Norman conquest of Ely ends with a poignant illustration of the continued importance of the daughters of Anna: Abbot Richard, on his deathbed,

saw the virgin most dear to him, the most holy Withburga, standing nearby. At once he fixed his gaze upon her and with a great cry addressed those who were standing by: 'Go away', he said, 'brothers, go away. Behold, my lady Withburga comes; behold, she stands here. Do you not see her? Can you not see her standing here? Oh . . . mistress have pity upon me.'[129]

Hostility to St Æthelthryth, if it existed at all during this period, came not from within the church but from those aristocratic companions of the Conqueror who had the most to gain from undermining the power of that church. For such hostility the most direct evidence is found in the *Liber Eliensis* account of Picot, Norman sheriff of Cambridgeshire and one of the most notorious despoilers of the community of Ely. When rebuked for his seizure of Ely lands and for his failure to show the respect due to the saint, Picot allegedly replied: 'Who is that Æthelthryth whom you prate about – that I have usurped her lands? I know her not, and I will not release her lands.'[130] But this evidence is both isolated and difficult

---

[125] *LE*, II, 129.
[126] *Ibid.*, c. 140. Richard was appointed after a seven-year vacancy (*ibid.*, c. 137); for the dates of his abbacy see above, n. 106.
[127] *LE*, II, 144. Cf. CCC 393, fols. 66–67 (*Vita Withburge*).
[128] *LE*, II, 145–8. For the translation of Withburga cf. CCC 393, fols. 67–69 (*Vita Withburge*).   [129] *LE*, II, 150.
[130] *Ibid.*, c. 131, entitled 'De Picoto vicecomite, qui multa incommoda huic iessit ecclesie'. The incident is probably to be dated to the abbacy of Simeon; see above, n. 124. For a very different view of Picot see *Liber memorandorum ecclesie de Bernewelle*, ed. J. W. Clark (Cambridge, 1907), pp. 38–40: Picot and his wife were remembered as pious founders of this house.

to interpret. Its context strongly suggests not a climate of disrespect for the Anglo-Saxon saint *per se* but rather a situation in which such disrespect was a by-product of – at most perhaps an excuse for – a conflict with the church of Ely which was essentially political and tenurial in nature. Picot's 'I know her not' was significant less as a statement of ignorance of or disrespect for the saint than as a refusal to acknowledge the landowning rights of her church.[131] And the Picot episode, when viewed in this light, becomes of central importance not as an illustration of the demise of the Anglo-Saxon cults but rather as the key to an understanding of the well-attested adoption of those cults by the Norman abbots of Ely. Those abbots, like their precursors in the tenth century, found their political and tenurial position open to challenge and, like those precursors, they met that challenge by recourse not only to litigation and to royal privilege but also to the local patron saint. Blake's proposed alignment of Norman monk and Norman layman against Anglo-Saxon saint therefore mistakes the temper of the post-Conquest decades. At Ely during those decades the issue of nationality was reduced almost to irrelevance. The Norman abbots, it seems, regarded themselves primarily as abbots of Ely and only secondarily as Norman conquerors. Their reputation depended upon the effectiveness with which they were able to defend and enhance the status of their church, and in pursuit of that priority they were prepared to utilise any tool which came to hand. In the period of the 'invasions' the Norman abbots and the Anglo-Saxon saints presented a united front against Picot and his kind.

This interpretation of abbatial policy is wholly corroborated by the other evidence concerning the period of the 'invasions' and its aftermath. As in the earlier period of crisis, thefts of the abbey's lands are described as thefts from St Æthelthryth,[132] and that saint was made to go to some lengths in order to vindicate the rights of her church. Picot himself, it seems, did not escape unscathed from the wrath of the saint.[133] And one of the compiler's most telling stories – intentionally so – concerns a Norman, Gervase, who

---

[131] The suggestion that Picot's hostility to the church of Ely was determined rather by tenurial considerations than by contempt for St Æthelthryth *per se* is supported by the fact that the abbey was far from being the only landowner to suffer from his territorial ambitions: see *DB*, I, fols. 189a (the burgesses of Cambridge complain that Picot has invaded the common pasture and that three mills built by Picot have diminished the pasture and destroyed homes), 190a, c, 199d. I am grateful to Katharin Mack for pointing out to me this more general pattern.

[132] See *LE*, II, cc. 108, 131, 135.   [133] *Ibid.*, c. 131.

showed himself 'a mighty enemy of St Æthelthryth and, as if he waged a special war against her, attacked and oppressed her possessions whenever and wherever he could'. The abbot, wearied by continual conflict, decided to draw St Æthelthryth's attention to his plight: he instructed his monks to seek the saint's mercy by singing the seven penitential psalms at her tomb. At once he was summoned to a lawsuit against Gervase; but before he could reach the appointed place he learned to his relief that his litigious opponent was dead. Gervase's death, it appears, was occasioned by a quite unremarkable heart attack: but that was not how the Ely monks wished to remember it. Instead we are told that St Æthelthryth had appeared before him in the company of her saintly sisters and had vented upon him the full force of her wrath: 'Are you not the man who in contempt of me has so often harried my men, whose patron I am, and who still persists in infesting my church? Take this as your reward, so that others will learn by your example not to plague the followers of Christ.' Thereupon she raised her staff and, 'as if to transfix him', drove its point into his heart; her sisters Sexburga and Withburga followed suit; and Gervase survived just long enough to explain to his servants precisely what was happening to him. And in case the reader should remain in any doubt as to the import of the story, the compiler adds a warning footnote: the story of Gervase's end was rapidly publicised, so that 'Fear of the saint spread through all her neighbours, and for many years no noble, judge, thegn or man of any note dared seize any possession of the church of Ely – so manfully did the holy virgin everywhere protect her properties.'[134]

The Norman abbots of Ely, it is clear, inherited and utilised the cults of St Æthelthryth and her saintly 'sisters' in a manner closely analogous to that adopted by their West Saxon predecessors in the tenth century. In 1109 the abbey of Ely was transformed into an episcopal see and a new era inaugurated which saw the institutional separation of monastic community and bishop's *familia*. What, if anything, was the effect of this separation on the cults of the Ely saints?

The most striking feature of 'the time of the bishops' is the contrast in tone between Hervey's episcopate (1109–31) and that of Nigel (1133–69). Of these the former was remembered as a period

---

[134] *Ibid.*, c. 132. This account appears, like the story of Picot which precedes it, to refer to the time of Abbot Simeon; see above, n. 124.

of regeneration and growth marred only by the first rumblings of the grand quarrel concerning the respective rights of monks and bishop.[135] The period seems to have witnessed a major drive to promote the Ely cults, and there are strong indications that Hervey's personal role in that promotion was of some importance. The Corpus Life of St Æthelthryth includes four miracles attributed to Bishop Hervey's time;[136] these are incorporated into the *Liber Eliensis* along with several other miracles assigned to Hervey's time:[137] very probably Hervey himself encouraged this up-dating of the Æthelthryth legend.[138] More than this, it is clear that the Corpus/Dublin Life of Æthelthryth was completed prior to the death in 1135 of Henry I and that the hagiography of Sexburga and Withburga was re-written following the translations of 1106.[139] As Abbot Richard died in 1107, it is tempting to see Hervey as the instigator of a large-scale programme of hagiographical work – a programme perhaps conceived as the logical sequel to the events of 1106 and perhaps intended to establish as clearly as possible the continuity between the new bishopric and the old abbey. St Æthelthryth appears throughout the miracles of Hervey's time in her traditional guise of protector of the church of Ely and vindicator of its rights. Her activities range from the preservation of the tower following a lightning strike[140] to the miraculous liberation of a certain Brihtstan who, having vowed himself to St Æthelthryth, was imprisoned by the officials of King Henry:[141] the miracle is a spectacular statement of the inviolability of those under St Æthelthryth's protection. Three further points are of

---

[135] The career of Hervey (with accounts of miracles performed during his episcopate) forms the subject matter of *LE*, III, 1–41. Of these, cc. 1–8 concern the establishment of the bishopric; c. 9 is entitled 'Quam viriliter Herveus episcopus ecclesiam suam de Ely et res ipsius ab iniusta oppressione eripuit'; cc. 10–24 and 40 comprise various royal documents concerning the restitution or augmentation of Ely lands and privileges (full references to printed versions and discussions of these documents are found in the notes to Blake's edition).   [136] See above, p. 54.

[137] Together the miracles of Hervey's time occupy Book III, cc. 27–36. Of these chapters the first is a general introduction entitled 'Laus auctoris de miraculis sancte Æðeldreðe que contigerunt temporibus Hervei episcopi'. The Corpus miracles are incorporated as cc. 33–6.

[138] The miracle incorporated as Book III, c. 33 was used in a slightly different version by Orderic Vitalis. Here it is said to have been written up by Abbot Warin of Saint-Evroul at the request of the bishop and convent of Ely; it takes the form of a letter, addressed generally, by Bishop Hervey (Orderic Vitalis, *Historia ecclesiastica*, ed. M. Chibnall, 6 vols., Oxford Medieval Texts (1968–80), III (1972), 347–61).

[139] See above, pp. 54–5, 57–8, 59.   [140] *LE*, III, 28.   [141] *Ibid*., c. 33.

some interest. The miracles indicate that the festival of St Æthelthryth was being regularly and appropriately celebrated.[142] The fact that the beneficiaries of Æthelthryth's miracles included a certain Baldwin and a 'master Ralph'[143] perhaps suggests that the clientele of the shrine included persons of continental origin as well as those of native birth: it is, however, equally possible that these were men of native stock who had been endowed with names more common among the conquerors than among the conquered. Finally, one of the miracles attributed to St Æthelthryth concerned the cure of an inhabitant of Barningham, 'not far from the monastery of St Edmund'.[144] Although there is no reference here to the rejection or failure of a supplication at the shrine of St Edmund it is possible that this miracle bears witness to a degree of local rivalry between the churches and the cults of St Æthelthryth and St Edmund.

Following the accession of Nigel the situation at Ely was less happy. Generalisations concerning the nature of Nigel's long episcopate are fraught with difficulty. None the less, it does seem clear that the overall tone of that episcopate was one of conflict – conflict between bishop and monks exacerbated by Nigel's costly and dangerous involvement in the high politics of Stephen's reign.[145] St Æthelthryth, as was her custom, was infinitely adaptable. In the hands of a highly partisan monastic historian, she became the powerful vindicator of the monks in their struggle against the bishop and his advisers. Thus one of Nigel's associates, a certain 'master Ralph', who was foolish enough both to oppress the Ely monks and to institute a conspiracy against the king, was finally betrayed by the merits of St Æthelthryth: Nigel, duly impressed, was persuaded for a while at least to treat his monks with more respect.[146] And elsewhere the Ely historian notes in a matter-of-fact way that Nigel, against the wishes of the monks, 'had set up a powerful castle of stone and plaster in Ely, which he held against the king and which was quickly reduced by the power of St Æthelthryth'.[147]

---

[142] See *ibid.*, c. 31, a cure which is said to have taken place on the festival of St Æthelthryth. The post-Conquest liturgical sources amply corroborate the impression of continuity of cult provided by the *Liber Eliensis* and by the hagiographical material. For the post-Conquest Ely calendar see Wormald (ed.), *After 1100*, II, 1–19.

[143] *LE*, III, 30, 35.   [144] *Ibid.*, c. 36.

[145] For the history of Nigel's episcopate see the references cited above, n. 110.

[146] *LE*, III, 51–3.   [147] *Ibid.*, c. 62.

In the late eleventh and twelfth centuries therefore the Norman leaders and community of Ely took over the cult of St Æthelthryth, adapted that cult to the changing purposes of the new age and recorded that adaptation by the production of hagiography and by the incorporation of that hagiography into an official and highly biased monastic history. But they did more than this. A comparison of his work with the other extant sources strongly suggests that the compiler of the *Liber Eliensis*, when incorporating the legend of St Æthelthryth into his monastic history, re-wrote that legend in a number of significant ways. He noted, first, that St Æthelthryth's community at Ely was established on the site of an earlier foundation of St Augustine.[148] He emphasised the personal nature of Æthelthryth's association with Ely by stating that she received the island as a dower from her first husband, Tonbert.[149] And he went on to note that, following Tonbert's death, the saint withdrew to the religious life at Ely for a short while prior to her marriage to Ecgfrith.[150] Thus, in accordance with the twelfth-century preoccupation with continuity, he established as firmly as possible both the antiquity of the religious life at Ely and the continuity of St Æthelthryth's own association with the isle.[151] And the compiler

---

[148] *Ibid.*, I, 15; cf. *ibid.*, p. 4 (*De situ*).

[149] *Ibid.*, I, 15; cf. *ibid.*, p. 4 (*De situ*). For discussion of this point see Miller, *Ely*, pp. 8ff; above, n. 14.   [150] *LE*, I, 8.

[151] It is not impossible that the compiler of the *LE* was also the originator of the tradition that Ely's dynasty of royal abbesses included not only Sexburga and Eormenilda but also Werburga. This would be wholly consistent with what seems to have been an attempt on the part of the twelfth-century community to emphasise the place in Ely's history of those royal ladies who had hitherto been accorded little, if any, importance. In those sources which derive from or relate to the tenth and eleventh centuries importance is accorded above all to Æthelthryth and then to those saints whose relics were located at Ely – Sexburga, Eormenilda and Withburga. There is no narrative or documentary evidence that Werburga was venerated at Ely in this period, and the liturgical evidence (see above, n. 46) suggests that her cult was of relatively little importance: it may indeed have been promoted in this period rather by the clerks of Chester than by the Ely monks. Æthelburga appears in only three extant pre-Conquest calendars (Wormald (ed.), *Before 1100*, nos. 5, 14, 20) and Eorcengota appears in neither liturgical nor narrative material. This situation seems to have changed by the twelfth century. The twelfth-century Ely hagiographical compilations, which include the *Vita Werburge* and the albeit brief and unoriginal materials on Æthelburga and Eorcengota, seem to bear witness to an attempt to integrate these figures more closely into Ely historiography. And although the absence of pre-Conquest calendars which can with certainty be attributed to Ely makes firm conclusions impossible, it seems that this trend may be reflected also in the appearance of Eorcengota, and in the importance generally accorded to Werburga and Æthelburga, in the post-Conquest calendar of Ely (Wormald (ed.), *After 1100*, II, 1–19; see also above, n. 46). That a degree of uncertainty continued to surround the status of Werburga's cult at Ely is perhaps indicated by the fact that, while TCC O.2.1 includes

of the *Liber Eliensis* went further: he provided a new analysis of St Æthelthryth's role as abbess. He stated that she was consecrated abbess by the Northumbrian bishop Wilfrid – perhaps hoping in this way to justify the claim of the twelfth-century community to exemption from the jurisdiction of the diocesan.[152] And he was at pains to emphasise that St Æthelthryth was able with the help of the same bishop to obtain a papal privilege for her community. Wilfrid, he claims, brought back from Rome 'a privilege for the monastery of Ely as the glorious abbess Æthelthryth had wished and had requested of him, so that the house might stand more securely against the incursions of the wicked'.[153] The abbess of the seventh century had been most effectively re-created in the image of the twelfth.

a copy of the *Vita Werburge*, the feast of Werburga is omitted from the calendar of *c.* 1170–89 incorporated in that MS.

[152] *Ibid.*, c. 16. This may of course be nothing more than an unsubstantiated inference from Bede's statement that St Æthelthryth initially received the veil from Wilfrid (*HE*, IV, 19).

[153] *LE*, I, 19. There is no corroborating evidence that a privilege was issued in this period on behalf of Ely (see *ibid.*, p. 37, n. 5).

Chapter 7

THE CULT OF ST EDMUND

ORIGINS: 'REX ORIENTALIUM ANGLORUM'

Edmund, *rex Christianissimus*, fell victim to the heathen Ivarr on 20 November 869.[1] The king's body, according to Abbo, was left where it had fallen; the head was tossed into the undergrowth of the wood of *Haegilisdun* in order to prevent a proper burial:[2] thus was the humiliation of the Christian king complete. But Ivarr, it seems, did little to follow up his victory. The history of East Anglia in the years following Edmund's martyrdom is extremely obscure, but it seems that the great army which Ivarr had brought into the kingdom moved in the year following Edmund's death to Reading; Ivarr himself may have left England for Dublin.[3] In 871, the *Anglo-Saxon Chronicle* records, the great army was joined in Wessex by a further force, a 'great summer army', and until 874 these armies acted in unison against Wessex, Mercia and a rebellious Northumbria. In the latter year the forces divided – the one, under Halfdan, going to Northumbria, and the second, 'summer army', under Guthrum, Oscetel and Anwend, moving from Repton to Cambridge.[4] Cambridge seems thereafter to have been used as a base for an intensified attack upon an ever-weakening Wessex: King Alfred was forced to withdraw to the marshes of Athelney in order to avoid the fate of his East Anglian counterpart. But the tables were soon to be turned. Alfred defeated the Danes at Edington in 878; Guthrum, together with thirty of his foremost warriors, accepted Christianity, Alfred standing as sponsor at the war-leader's baptism; and a newly Christianised Guthrum-Athelstan returned to East Anglia to make the best of an unfortunate

---

[1] For Edmund's martyrdom see above, pp. 61–9.   [2] *Passio Edmundi*, pp. 79–80.
[3] See Smyth, *Scandinavian kings*, ch. 18.
[4] *ASC*, A, E, *s.a.* 871–5; Stenton, *ASE*, pp. 248–52; Smyth, *Scandinavian kings*, pp. 240–3.

situation.[5] It seems that it is to this period rather than to 869 that the creation of Danish East Anglia is to be dated. The *Chronicle* notes that, following its West Saxon defeat, the host went from Cirencester into East Anglia 'and occupied that land and divided it up'.[6] Guthrum the war-leader, having failed to win the greater prize, became Guthrum the settler, and as such he was to rule St Edmund's kingdom until his death in 890.[7] His reign, it appears, was followed by that of Eric, who was killed at the Battle of the Holme in 903, and thereafter by that gradual extension of West Saxon power which brought the final demise of independent East Anglia.[8]

It was in these circumstances of conflict and political change that the cult of St Edmund was created, and by them that it was shaped. Abbo tells us that, despite the machinations of the Danes, the body of the fallen ruler did not remain neglected for long. As soon as a measure of peace was restored to the churches, the Christians began to emerge from hiding and to search for Edmund's head, hoping to join this with the body and to give the king as honourable a burial as the circumstances allowed. A large-scale search was instituted, and before long the East Angles were rewarded for their labours. To their anxious cries of 'Where are you?' the severed head responded by calling 'Here, here, here!'; it was found lying between the protective paws of an enormous wolf. The searchers took up the head with some trepidation, carried it to an unspecified destination, and buried it along with the body in a humble chapel erected for the purpose. Here the king remained 'for many years' until the time of war and persecution was over and the Christian community could breathe freely again. At this point miracles at Edmund's tomb prompted a translation to the royal vill of *Bedricesgueord* (later Bury St Edmunds); a church was built to house the body; and a tentative examination revealed that the royal corpse was not only uncorrupt but also whole, bearing only a fine red scar as testimony to Edmund's beheading.[9]

Abbo's account of the origin of Edmund's cult is a minefield of

---

[5] *ASC*, A, E, *s.a.* 876–8; Stenton, *ASE*, pp. 253–7; Smyth, *Scandinavian kings*, pp. 243–53.
[6] *ASC*, A, E, *s.a.* 880.
[7] *Ibid.*, *s.a.* 890; see also Smyth, *Scandinavian kings*, p. 253.
[8] For Eric's death at the Battle of the Holme see *ASC*, A, D, *s.a.* 905; C, *s.a.* 902. For the West Saxon conquest of the Eastern Danelaw see Stenton, *ASE*, pp. 321–9; and for more detailed discussion of the nature and history of the Eastern Danelaw see the references cited below, n. 29. [9] *Passio Edmundi*, pp. 80–2.

hagiographical *topoi*;[10] it is also chronologically vague. Particularly disappointing is its failure to indicate a date either for Edmund's initial burial or for his translation to *Bedricesgueord*. It might, however, be conjectured that the Danish withdrawal immediately following Edmund's death provides the most plausible context for the former event;[11] and Abbo fortunately makes it clear that Edmund's relics were at *Bedricesgueord* by the time of Theodred, who attests as bishop of London from 926 until *c.* 951.[12] Hermann, writing more than a century after Abbo, supplies the information that the place of Edmund's initial burial was *Suthtune*.[13] He also, in a rather difficult passage, indicates that the translation to *Bedricesgueord* had taken place by the reign of Athelstan (924–39); his Latin, however, is obscure and the passage cannot be taken to imply that the translation actually took place during Athelstan's reign.[14] A late-fourteenth-century account in MS Bodley 240 assigns the translation either to *c.* 900 or to 906, and the fifteenth-century Curteys Register supplies the date of 903.[15] This apart, the later sources add nothing to our understanding of the early history of St Edmund's cult: the hagiographers seem to have been content simply to embellish Abbo's elegant and uncluttered narrative with an ever-increasing repertoire of miracle stories. From the *Passio* itself, two themes of fundamental importance emerge. First, the

[10] See Gransden, 'Legends and traditions', pp. 6–7.

[11] See *Passio Edmundi*, p. 80. The search for the martyred king is said to have taken place when, 'quantulacumque reddita aecclesiis pace, coeperunt Christiani de latibulis consurgere'. Abbo goes on to note that 'Siquidem paganis abeuntibus et depopulationi quoquo locorum operam dantibus, illud corpus sanctissimum, adhuc sub diuo positum, facillime est repertum in eodem campo ubi rex occubuit, conpleto cursu sui certaminis.' This description of the pagans' activities seems to accord well with what is known of their doings in 869 and 870 (see above, p. 211); it is less easy to see how it could refer to any later period.

[12] *Passio Edmundi*, pp. 83–5: a miracle concerning the punishment of eight thieves who attempt to break into the church at *Bedricesgueord* is dated to Theodred's time. For the career of Theodred, who seems to have controlled not only the bishopric of London but also a see in East Anglia, see especially *Wills*, ed. Whitelock, pp. 99–102 and Whitelock, 'Conversion', p. 171; M. A. O'Donovan, 'An interim revision of episcopal dates for the province of Canterbury, 850–950: part II', *ASE* 2 (1973), 91–113, at 98.

[13] *De miraculis*, ed. Arnold, p. 27: Edmund was buried in the *villula* of *Suthtune*, close by the site of his martyrdom, fear of the Danes preventing his burial in a more important place.

[14] *Ibid.*, pp. 28–9: 'Praefato itaque Ædelstano regna moderante, Deique gratia condonante, orientalis rex et martyr [Eadmundus] in Beodrici villa pausans sibi propria, jamjam declaratur sanctus, virtute signorum splendescens, usquequaque notificatus'.

[15] See Whitelock, 'Fact and fiction', p. 222; *VCH Suffolk*, II, 57, n. 1, citing London, BL, Add. MS 14848, fol. 211. Neither MS Bodley 240 nor the Curteys Register indicates a source for its information.

hagiographer clearly believed that Edmund's cult originated among the people of his own kingdom. The king's initial burial was carried out by those of his followers who had been forced into hiding by the Danes and who, remembering his good deeds and mercy, sought as soon as possible to give their dead ruler a decent burial.[16] And those responsible for the translation, which marked the real inception of cult are said to have been drawn from both the common people and the nobles 'of the same province' – of, that is, the province of the East Angles.[17] Second, it can be inferred that, in the East Anglia of the late ninth and early tenth centuries, the cult of St Edmund was born of political and religious conflict: the veneration of the fallen ruler by his erstwhile subjects is intelligible only in terms of their opposition to the Danes.

The hagiographical account of the origin of Edmund's cult can be supplemented by reference to a contemporary source of unique value – the 'St Edmund memorial coinage'.[18] This comprises around two thousand extant specimens of the same general type, bearing on the obverse a central *A*, surrounded by the legend *Sce Eadmund rex*, within two circles; the reverse bears a central cross surrounded by an inscription, usually with the name of the moneyer. Over the date, circulation and provenance of the coins there has been much debate. Nevertheless, several points do emerge with some clarity. Over ninety per cent of the extant specimens were found in the great Viking hoard at Cuerdale, Lancashire; the date of this hoard is now generally placed at *c.* 905.[19] Clearly, therefore, the St Edmund coinage was in circulation by the opening years of the tenth century. There is, moreover, a strong probability that the date of the earliest coins can be pushed back to *c.* 895 – to,

---

16 *Passio Edmundi*, p. 80.   17 *Ibid.*, p. 82.
18 For the St Edmund coins see C. F. Keary, *A catalogue of English coins in the British Museum, Anglo-Saxon series*, 2 vols. (London, 1887–93), I (1887), 97–137; P. Grierson and M. Blackburn, *Medieval European coinage, with a catalogue of the coins in the Fitzwilliam Museum, Cambridge*, I, *The early Middle Ages (5th to 10th centuries)* (Cambridge, 1986), pp. 319–20; C. E. Blunt, 'The St Edmund memorial coinage', *Proceedings of the Suffolk Institute of Archaeology* 31 (1967–9), 234–55; Whitelock, 'Conversion', pp. 164–6; Whitelock, 'Fact and fiction', p. 218. The recent work of Grierson and Blackburn suggests some modification of the conclusions reached by Blunt and accepted by Whitelock. I am grateful to Mark Blackburn for his helpful advice on the St Edmund coinage.
19 Blunt, 'St Edmund memorial coinage', p. 236; Grierson and Blackburn, *Medieval European coinage*, p. 318; M. Blackburn and H. Pagan, 'A revised check-list of coin hoards from the British Isles, *c.* 500–1100', in M. Blackburn (ed.), *Anglo-Saxon monetary history: essays in memory of Michael Dolley* (Leicester, 1986), pp. 291–313, at p. 294.

that is, little more than twenty-five years after the martyrdom which they commemorate. The coinage was not represented in the Ashdon and Stamford hoards, each deposited *c.* 893/5; but one specimen was overstruck by Archbishop Plegmund towards the end of Alfred's reign.[20] The coins continued in use, it appears, until the second decade of the tenth century – perhaps until the 'reconquest' of East Anglia and Eastern Mercia in 917/18.[21] They are found in hoards deposited at Harkirk, Lancs. (*c.* 910); Dysart Island (no. 4), Co. Westmeath (*c.* 910); Dean, Cumberland (*c.* 915); York, Walmgate (*c.* 915); Chester, St John's (*c.* 917); Leggagh, Co. Meath (*c.* 920); Morley St Peter, Norfolk (*c.* 925); Glasnevin, Co. Dublin (*c.* 927).[22] The evidence of these hoards, together with a number of single finds, strongly suggests that the coins were circulated primarily in areas under Danish control; and the single finds in particular have been concentrated in East Anglia and the East Midlands.[23] It is generally assumed that they were minted in East Anglia. Much significance, for instance, has been attached to the inscription *NORDVICO* found on the obverse of one specimen, this being interpreted as the mint-name Norwich; it is however possible that it is rather the personal name of a moneyer, Nordvic.[24] Recent work suggests that the search for a single place of provenance may well be misleading: a number of mints are likely to have been involved, some perhaps in the Five Boroughs.[25] Uncertainties regarding provenance, however, should not obscure the general picture: there can be little doubt that the coins were

---

[20] Grierson and Blackburn, *Medieval European coinage*, p. 320.   [21] *Ibid.*

[22] Blunt, 'St Edmund memorial coinage', pp. 237–8; Mark Blackburn, personal communication. For the dating of these hoards see now Blackburn and Pagan, 'Revised check-list of coin hoards', p. 295. For the Dysart Island hoard see also M. Ryan *et al.*, 'Six silver finds of the Viking period from the vicinity of Lough Ennell, Co. Westmeath', *Peritia* 3 (1984), 334–81.

[23] Of the single finds noted by Blunt ('St Edmund memorial coinage', p. 238), two are recorded from English territory, from Long Wittenham and Cholsey, both in Berkshire. The remainder come without exception from the Danelaw – from Norwich; East Kirby, Lincs.; Bowbeck Heath, Suffolk; Narford, Norfolk, and Thetford, Norfolk. Blunt's list can now be expanded, particularly in the Five Boroughs: notably there are now seven specimens from Northampton, two from Lincoln, two from Cambridge and two from near Royston, Herts.: Mark Blackburn, personal communication; M. Blackburn, C. Colyer and M. Dolley, *Early medieval coins from Lincoln and its shire c. 700–1100* (London, 1983), p. 12.

[24] For the identification of *NORDVICO* with Norwich see Blunt, 'St Edmund memorial coinage', pp. 245–6, 252; for the suggestion that it could be a personal name see V. Smart, 'The moneyers of St Edmund', *Hikuin* 11 (1985), 83–90, at 86.

[25] Grierson and Blackburn, *Medieval European coinage*, p. 320.

minted and circulated in the Eastern Danelaw of which Edmund's kingdom formed a part, under the auspices of its Danish rulers, and for the use of its mixed Danish and indigenous population.[26]

For the history of St Edmund's cult the memorial coinage has two implications of the highest importance. It demonstrates, first, that the murdered king was honoured as a saint within little more than twenty-five years of his death. And, second, it indicates that veneration of the new saint was officially sanctioned by those Danish successors of his slayer who had 'inherited' Edmund's kingdom. This in turn raises a fascinating problem. For what reasons and in what circumstances had the Danes of East Anglia adopted St Edmund 'the Martyr'? What was in the minds of those newly converted warlords when they officially recognised their political victim as 'saint'?

To this problem the most immediately obvious solution lies in the conversion of the Danes. Edington must have demonstrated to all but the least observant Dane that the Christian God was a protector at least as effective as Oðinn; and it is not beyond the bounds of possibility that the subsequent conversion of the Danish high command, initially no more than a political expedient, was by the mid 890s so thoroughgoing as to induce them to venerate the Christian saints even at the expense of their own political pride. Conversely – and very much more plausibly – the Danish rulers may have had a more utilitarian approach to Edmund's cult. Their adoption of St Edmund may have been a move shrewdly calculated to enhance their political position within Edmund's kingdom. That position was from the outset open to challenge, and the cult of St Edmund, created by the East Angles, is most readily understood as a potent symbol of that challenge. Perhaps the Danish rulers, in acknowledging Edmund's status as 'saint', sought to perform an act of expiation and political reconciliation similar to that commonly attributed to the slayers of Edward the Martyr; perhaps even they sought to draw the sting from a cult of rebels.[27] Each of these ideas suggests a Danish reaction to a perceived threat. But they may have been acting under a different kind of political pressure: their adoption of St Edmund may have been, like their conversion to

---

[26] See *ibid.*, pp. 319–20; Blunt, 'St Edmund memorial coinage', p. 253. For similar conclusions see also C. W. C. Oman, *The coinage of England* (Oxford, 1931), p. 46; G. C. Brooke, *English coins from the seventh century to the present day* (London, 1932), p. 30; R. H. M. Dolley, *Viking coins of the Danelaw and of Dublin* (London, 1965), p. 17; Whitelock, 'Conversion', p. 168.   [27] See above, pp. 159–60.

Christianity, a product of diplomacy, a negotiated, perhaps enforced, concession which might help to stabilise their political power. They were no doubt aware, moreover, that the cult of St Edmund offered benefits of a more positive nature. Edmund seems to have been the last reigning monarch, and perhaps even the last surviving representative, of the ancient ruling dynasty of the East Angles.[28] Quite possibly his Danish 'successors' hoped that by showing themselves to be patrons of his cult they might suggest their own legitimate succession to the kingdom and might accordingly buttress their somewhat anomalous political position.

Each of these explanations for Danish acknowledgement of Edmund's sanctity — and they are not perhaps mutually exclusive — centres on the function of St Edmund as mediator, spiritual or political, between East Angles and Danes. Each carries the straightforward but sometimes neglected implication that by c. 895 the cult of St Edmund was sufficiently established for news about it to reach the Danes and sufficiently important for that news to matter. This in turn suggests that it was promoted by men whose influence was such that their hostility would be dangerous to the Danes, their marketing would be effective with the Danes and their political cooperation would be useful to the Danes. It invites a more detailed consideration of precisely who the early promoters of Edmund's cult might have been and of what might have been their role in the years following Edmund's martyrdom. Those promoters, it seems, may not have been simply the few cowering survivors of the Danish onslaught implied by the hagiographers: they may have been rather a sizeable local population with political and religious leaders of some importance. The point is consistent with the

---

[28] The obscurity of ninth-century East Anglian history is such that Edmund's place within the ruling dynasty cannot be traced with any certainty. Numismatic evidence suggests that he may have succeeded a King Æthelweard (see above, p. 61, n. 213), and Abbo notes that he was 'ex antiquorum Saxonum nobili prosapia oriundus' (*Passio Edmundi*, p. 70). Very probably this is simply Abbo's rather verbose way of saying that Edmund was descended from the ancient nobility of his race, but by the mid twelfth century, in the *De infantia*, it had become the starting-point for an intriguing, if implausible, legend concerning the saint's descent from the continental Saxons. Edmund's childlessness was an important theme of his hagiographical legend (see especially *Passio Edmundi*, pp. 86–7). By the post-Conquest period, however, he had been endowed with an improbable entourage of saintly relatives. William of Malmesbury was familiar with a tradition that Edmund had a brother Edwold, who became a hermit at Cerne in Dorset (*GP*, p. 185); TCD MS 172 preserves (pp. 226–30) a Life of Ragener, said to have been a nephew of Edmund martyred by the Danes; and a substantial hagiographical tradition survives concerning Fremund, allegedly a relative both of Edmund and of Offa of Mercia (see Hardy, *Descriptive catalogue*, nos. 1091–4; BHL, nos. 3145–7).

research of recent decades, which indicates that the traditional cataclysmic interpretation of the social and political effects of the Danish conquest of East Anglia may have been seriously exaggerated.[29] It receives support from Professor Whitelock's analysis of the ecclesiastical evidence, which points to a fairly rapid Christianisation of the Eastern Danelaw.[30] And, most interesting, it seems to be corroborated by such conclusions as can tentatively be drawn concerning the geographical area of Edmund's martyrdom and subsequent veneration.

Abbo notes that Edmund was staying, at the time of his martyrdom, at *Haegilisdun* (or *Haeglesdun*), that he was captured *in palatio*, and that his head was concealed in the nearby wood of *Haegilisdun*; the site of his initial burial is identified by Hermann as *Suthtune*.[31] Abbo's *Haegilisdun* has traditionally been identified with Hoxne in Suffolk.[32] More recently, it has been suggested by Whitelock that *Haegilisdun* is 'the correct form for Hellesdon, Norfolk, and for no other surviving name'.[33] In 1978, however, Dr Stanley West noted that there exists in the parish of Bradfield St Clare, only five miles from modern Bury St Edmunds, a field-name Hellesden; a mile to the south is Sutton Hall; and about two miles to the north, in Rougham parish, are Kingshall Farm, Kingshall Street and Kingshall Green.[34] The names Hellesden and Sutton Hall uniquely

---

[29] For general discussion of the social and political effects of the Danish conquest of East Anglia see especially E. Ekwall, 'The proportion of Scandinavian settlers in the Danelaw', *Saga-Book of the Viking Society* 12 (1937–45), 19–34; R. H. C. Davis, 'East Anglia and the Danelaw', *Transactions of the Royal Historical Society*, Fifth Series 5 (1955), 23–39; P. H. Sawyer, 'The density of the Danish settlement in England', *University of Birmingham Historical Journal* 6 (1958); Sawyer, *The age of the Vikings*, 2nd edn (London, 1971); G. Fellows Jensen, 'The Vikings in England: a review', *ASE* 4 (1975), 185–206. The suggestion that a substantial local population may have survived the events of 869/70 is not incompatible with the emphasis placed by Abbo upon the pagans' slaughter of Edmund's followers. Whether this took the form of a battle or, as seems more likely, of a massacre planned to forestall the formation of an army (see above, pp. 66–8), it is unlikely that wholesale slaughter of the East Angles took place. Indeed, if such a massacre as that described by Abbo took place, it seems likely that the slaughter would have been limited to the unnamed town at which the invaders first arrived and to the countryside between there and the site of Edmund's capture (*Passio Edmundi*, pp. 72–3).

[30] Whitelock, 'Conversion'. For continuity of ecclesiastical organisation see also M. J. Franklin, 'Minsters and parishes: Northamptonshire studies', unpublished Ph.D. thesis (University of Cambridge, 1982), pp. 8–11.

[31] *Passio Edmundi*, pp. 73, 78, 79–80; Hermann, *De miraculis*, ed. Arnold, p. 27.

[32] For the genesis of this tradition, which makes its first appearance in the charter granted by Herbert Losinga to Norwich cathedral priory *c.* 1100 (pr. *Monasticon*, IV, 15–17), see Gransden, 'Legends and traditions', p. 9; Gransden, 'Baldwin', p. 70.

[33] Whitelock, 'Fact and fiction', p. 220.

[34] I am indebted for this information to the kind advice of Dr West; for a published report

correspond to those preserved in the early St Edmund literature; the Kingshall place-names call to mind Abbo's implication that there was a royal estate and residence close to the site of Edmund's martyrdom. Together these names provide by far the most plausible site for the martyrdom of St Edmund, and they place that site very much closer than has hitherto been supposed to the centre of his subsequent veneration.

If this identification is correct, the Kingshall place-names, in conjunction with Abbo's statement that the king was captured *in palatio*, strongly suggest that there may have been, in the immediate pre-Danish period, a royal estate and residence within five miles of *Bedricesgueord*. There are indications too that *Bedricesgueord* itself bore a distinctively royal stamp. It is described by Abbo as a *uilla regia*.[35] And an isolated reference in the *Liber Eliensis* suggests that its royal association may be traced back to the seventh century. Here *Betrichesworde* is named as the site of the *monasterium* which was founded by King Sigebert and to which he subsequently

see S. E. West, 'A new site for the martyrdom of St Edmund?', *Proceedings of the Suffolk Institute of Archaeology and History* 35 (1981–4), 223–4. For the field-name Hellesden the earliest evidence seems to be the Tithe Map of 1840, but this should not detract from the value of this unusual and highly significant name. The earliest reference to the Kingshall place-names (in the forms *Kingeshae, Kingshal'*, perhaps meaning king's water meadow or corner of land) is found in an early thirteenth-century document of Bury St Edmunds: see *The kalendar of Abbot Samson of Bury St Edmunds and related documents*, ed. R. H. C. Davis, Royal Historical Society, Camden Third Series 84 (London, 1954), p. 97. Dr West has also noted that there exist in Rougham parish a number of field-names with a St Edmund element: these names may indicate no more than that the lands in question formed part of the estate of St Edmund's abbey; conversely they may be indicative of a local tradition which placed the site of Edmund's martyrdom in the area between Rougham and Bradfield St Clare. Also of interest is a note 'Coincidence or corroboration?', a note from D. P. Dymond, *Proceedings of the Suffolk Institute of Archaeology and History* 35 (1981–4), 225. Here it is pointed out that the 1535 *Valor ecclesiasticus* records that the cellarer of Bury St Edmunds paid small rents for *Aule de Saint Clarisbradfeld* and *Suttonhal*: 'These two manors or "halls" are, of course, close geographically but their striking juxtaposition in the list of rents may have another significance. It could mean that the abbey traditionally rented, through a major officer, two small pieces of land which were connected with St Edmund: one at Bradfield St Clare being the place of his martyrdom, and the other at Sutton Hall being the earliest resting-place of his revered body.'

35 *Passio Edmundi*, p. 82. Antonia Gransden has suggested that the designation *uilla regia* in the extant MSS of Abbo's work may be a late-eleventh-century interpolation. For discussion of this point see below, n. 80. The *Passio* does not explicitly state that *Bedricesgueord* was a *uilla regia* in Edmund's own time, although this is surely its implication. Hermann, in an account probably derived from local tradition, does make the point explicit: he describes the arrival of Sweyn's tax-collectors 'ad sancti . . . mansiunculam, Beodrici villam nuncupatam, sibi, dum vixerat, suorumque antecessorum regum orientalium, a quodam, ut dicitur, rege Beodrico proprie nominatam' (*De miraculis*, ed. Arnold, p. 33).

retired; the identification, although late, may be founded upon reliable local tradition.[36] It is impossible to reconstruct the history of Sigebert's foundation, but – particularly if *Bedricesgueord* already had the status of a *uilla regia* – the continuity of some kind of religious community until the Danish invasions is not improbable. Indeed it is perhaps suggested by the St Edmund legend itself. Abbo notes that Edmund was translated to *Bedricesgueord* and a church built to house his relics.[37] But this conventional 'saint-centred' account of the translation may well obscure a reality in which Edmund was taken to *Bedricesgueord* for the very good reason that there was already a church there. Abbo's description of the building of a church does not necessarily refer to the inception of the religious life at *Bedricesgueord*: it may equally plausibly refer either to the construction within an existing ecclesiastical precinct of a new church to house the relics or to the reconstruction of a church only recently destroyed by the Danes.

Taken together, therefore, the historical and place-name evidence suggests both that the site of Edmund's martyrdom was very close to that of his subsequent veneration and that the area as a whole possessed a highly distinctive character. For that character the most striking, if indirect, evidence is found in the history of St Edmund. One might wonder why, when the time came to translate the king from his humble, perhaps intentionally temporary, burial place to a more honourable location, *Bedricesgueord* was chosen. It is unlikely that the East Angles would simply have moved the king's body a few miles down the road from one insignificant place to another. Their actions make sense only if *Bedricesgueord* was already a political and religious centre of some importance.[38]

For the history of St Edmund's cult the point may be crucial.

---

[36] *LE*, I, I (p. II, n. e). The site of Sigebert's foundation is interlined in a later hand in the Ely Dean and Chapter MS of the *LE* and is included (in the form *Betrichesuurðe*) in the text of MS Cotton Domitian xv, TCC O.2.1. and Bodl. MS Laud Misc. 647. For Sigebert's career see above, pp. 92, 176, and *HE*, III, 18, where the site of his monastic foundation is not named. The *LE* tradition is accepted by Knowles and Hadcock (p. 61); cf. also D. Whitelock, 'The pre-Viking age church in East Anglia', *ASE* I (1971), 1–19, at p. 4, n. 4.

[37] *Passio Edmundi*, p. 82.

[38] I am grateful to Dr Stanley West and to Mrs Glenys Putnam for pointing out that recent archaeological work tends to corroborate my tentative conclusions concerning the distinctive character in this period of modern Bury St Edmunds and its region. As regards Bury itself, Dr West has drawn my attention to the fact that recent excavations have revealed traces of middle and late Saxon occupation in the vicinity of the abbey's west front. At Brandon, about sixteen miles north of Bury, excavation has revealed a series of post-holed buildings with associated finds of a Christian and royal or aristocratic character. The precise function of the site cannot at present be determined, but Dr West suggests that it may have been a royal or monastic site.

Between the martyrdom of St Edmund and the establishment of Danish rule under Guthrum-Athelstan there elapsed a decade in which the history of East Anglia seems lost beyond recall. At the postulated royal and ecclesiastical centre of *Bedricesgueord*, if anywhere, local society may have been able to reorganise itself following the withdrawal of the invader. In this context two further points are of special interest. First, Abbo accords an important part in his narrative to a bishop who advised the king during his negotiations with the Danes.[39] This bishop cannot be identified with any certainty. East Anglia in the pre-Viking period was divided into two dioceses, based at Elmham and *Dommoc*, usually identified with Dunwich. The last recorded ninth-century bishop of Elmham was Hunbert, who occurs in 845 but whose episcopate cannot be precisely dated. A profession of obedience exists for a Bishop Æthelwald of *Dommoc* to Archbishop Ceolnoth (833–70).[40] A number of later writers identify Edmund's bishop with Hunbert, but this may be no more than an assumption based on the fact that Hunbert's name is the last to occur in the episcopal lists.[41] There is, however, no reason to doubt Abbo's statement concerning the role of a bishop in the negotiations,[42] and it would be interesting to know what happened to the bishop after Edmund's death.[43] Did he perhaps arrange for the burial – and did he perhaps encourage the cult – of the fallen ruler? Second, we know from the *Anglo-Saxon Chronicle* that in both Mercia and Northumbria the Danish conquest was followed initially by the establishment of a native 'sub-king', who seems to have governed with some autonomy until the Danes returned to colonise.[44] It is tempting to

---

[39] *Passio Edmundi*, pp. 74–5.

[40] For discussion of the diocesan organisation of pre-Viking East Anglia see Whitelock, 'Pre-Viking age church', pp. 1–4. For Æthelwald's profession see *Canterbury professions*, ed. M. Richter, with a palaeographical note by T. J. Brown, Canterbury and York Society 67 (Torquay, 1973), no. 28.

[41] See Whitelock, 'Pre-Viking age church', pp. 18–19.

[42] Indeed, Abbo may have been well informed about the diocesan organisation of Edmund's kingdom, for he notes that Edmund consulted not simply with 'his bishop' but with 'uno ex suis episcopis' (*Passio Edmundi*, p. 74). Cf. Dorothy Whitelock's suggestion ('Pre-Viking age church', p. 19) that, despite William of Malmesbury's statement that the see of *Dommoc* was suppressed early in the ninth century (*GP*, p. 148), the two sees seem to have continued in existence until the Danish invasions.

[43] For a tradition that he too was martyred see *Symeonis monachi opera omnia*, I, 55; II, 107. But, as Whitelock points out ('Pre-Viking age church', p. 18), it is most unlikely that such a dual martyrdom would have escaped the attention of Abbo and of the later Bury hagiographers.

[44] See above, p. 69. Smyth notes (*Scandinavian kings*, p. 207) that in each case the native ruler may have controlled substantial areas until the final Danish settlement took place.

suggest that the key to East Anglia's missing decade may be found in the establishment of precisely such a native ruler – a man who was acutely conscious of the fate of his predecessor, who fully appreciated the symbolic and political value of a cult of that predecessor, and who, with his secular and ecclesiastical advisers, may well have been in a position to exert some influence over the later Danish rulers of East Anglia.

The point may be carried further and this attempted reconstruction of East Anglian history in the years immediately following Edmund's death be used to suggest a tentative revision of the chronology of St Edmund's cult and St Edmund's community. It is clear that by the time of King Athelstan and Bishop Theodred St Edmund's body had been translated to *Bedricesgueord* and a small religious community established around his shrine; Hermann's narrative perhaps implies, but is far from proving, that the translation and the establishment of the community took place during that reign; still later sources date the translation to *c.* 900.[45] If, however, we accept both the probable existence of a religious community at *Bedricesgueord* prior to the Danish invasions and a significant survival of local society following those invasions, it is surely unnecessary to wait until the 920s, or even until *c.* 900, for the translation and for the establishment of an Edmund-centred community. The most plausible context for these events seems rather to be the years immediately following Edmund's martyrdom – the

Thereafter, Egbert's rule was confined to 'the Northumbrians beyond the Tyne' (citing *Symeonis monachi opera omnia*, I, 55) and the Mercian Ceolwulf was allocated certain lands in the eastern part of the kingdom (citing *ASC*, A, E, *s.a.* 877).

[45] For the difficulty of dating Edmund's translation see above, p. 213. Abbo makes it clear (*Passio Edmundi*, pp. 83–4) that a religious community of some kind had been established around Edmund's shrine by the time of Theodred's episcopate. His account, moreover, is corroborated by Theodred's will, which is dated by Whitelock to *c.* 942 × *c.* 951 and which includes bequests of land to *sce Eadmundes kirke* (*Wills*, ed. Whitelock, pp. 4, 99). Hermann supplies more precise information on the nature of St Edmund's community. He notes (*De miraculis*, ed. Arnold, p. 30) that in the reign of Athelstan 'clericorum aggregantur personæ paucorum servientium inibi, quorum nomina prælibamus pro veraci testimonio, quæque sine testibus dantes exterminio. Fuerunt quippe diaconus Leofricus, et alter presbyter ejus æquivocus; Alfricus sacerdos, Bomfild quoque, ipsius ordinis compos; Kenelmus levita, ac Eilmund vivens sacerdotii vita.' This passage is difficult to interpret, but it cannot be taken to imply that the initial foundation of the community took place during Athelstan's reign. The importance accorded to that reign as a starting-point for Hermann's narrative does perhaps indicate that it was perceived as a turning-point in the history of St Edmund's community, and Abbo's statement (*Passio Edmundi*, p. 67) that Edmund's story had been related at the court of King Athelstan does suggest that the king took an interest in Edmund's shrine: but that interest may well have taken the form of endowment, perhaps with some reorganisation, rather than of initial foundation. Cf. KH, p. 61, where this interpretation is favoured.

period when the political message of his cult would carry its greatest force and relevance. One further consideration tends in support of this view. Abbo, it is important to note, clearly differentiates between Edmund's initial burial at an unnamed site and his subsequent removal to *Bedricesgueord*. The former was inspired by the desire to give a proper Christian burial to a much-respected ruler; the latter, accompanied by an examination of the relics, was the translation of a saint. It is clear, moreover, that Edmund was recognised as a saint by the time the first St Edmund coins were issued, probably *c.* 895. It seems likely therefore that the translation which marked the transition of Edmund the king into Edmund the saint took place prior to the issue of the memorial coins. And it might be further suggested that the translation was to a religious community which either had survived more or less intact the Danish invasions or had been re-established almost immediately thereafter. There is a strong probability that the establishment of both the cult and the community of St Edmund was a *fait accompli* by the mid 890s; very likely that cult and that community were among the achievements of local society during East Anglia's lost decade.[46]

The cult of St Edmund seems therefore to have originated among the East Angles, very probably in the years between Edmund's martyrdom and the establishment of Danish rule. Subsequently recognised by the Danes in their production of the St Edmund coins, it seems to have formed in the late ninth and early tenth centuries a focus for the working out of political relations between the East Angles and their Danish conquerors. It appears, however, that interest in the cult was not limited to East Angles and Danes: the West Saxons also had a hand in its development. The origin of West Saxon interest cannot be precisely dated. I have suggested elsewhere that it commenced with King Alfred, and that the Danes in acknowledging the veneration of Edmund may have been responding to political pressure not only from the East Angles but also from the West Saxon king.[47] This view was founded,

---

[46] For a different view see Folz, 'Saint Edmond', pp. 227–8: 'Si ces monnaies très nombreuses maintinrent le souvenir d'un roi qui n'était encore qu'un nom – mais le nom d'un martyr –, la translation de sa dépouille du lieu ou elle avait été inhumée dans la villa royale de Beodricsworth fut le point de départ de la reconnaissance officielle de la sainteté d'Edmond.' Folz notes that the translation cannot be precisely dated: 'Peu importe après tout: c'est dans le premier tiers du Xe siècle que l'idée de la sainteté d'Edmond, d'abord diffuse, se précise et trouve à Beodricsworth son lieu de fixation.'

[47] 'Royal saints', ch. 7.

however, on numismatic evidence which has since been shown to be misleading. A group of three St Edmund coins, among the earliest and finest of the issue, bear on the reverse not the usual moneyer's name but the legend + *AELFRED REX DO* (for Dorovernia).[48] This has been taken to indicate that the coinage originated at Canterbury and was produced under the aegis of King Alfred.[49] And from this it seems reasonable to infer that when the Danes adopted the coinage they were following a West Saxon model in response to West Saxon political pressure. Recent research however suggests that these three coins have been accorded too much significance. The Danes of East Anglia and the East Midlands had been accustomed before 895 to producing a large two-line coinage imitating that of Alfred and bearing his name – without any apparent political significance attaching to it. The three early St Edmund coins seem likewise to have been imitations: they differ both in style and in weight from the official products of the Canterbury mint. Very probably they represent an experiment by the die-cutter accustomed to placing Alfred's name on his coins and continuing to do so for the new St Edmund coinage.[50] They cannot be used as evidence of Alfredian interest in the cult of St Edmund.

With the reign of Athelstan we are on firmer ground. It was at Athelstan's court, according to Abbo, that an ageing armour-bearer related in the presence of the young Dunstan the story of Edmund's martyrdom. And indeed it is striking that Abbo's work, the earliest written version of the St Edmund legend, made no claim to be a product of local hagiography but rather was mediated through the court of King Athelstan and the circle of Archbishop Dunstan.[51] It seems likely that Athelstan, even if not responsible for the translation of Edmund and the establishment of the community of *Bedricesgueord*, at least endowed and perhaps reconstituted the community.[52] His half-brother and successor may likewise have endowed the house;[53] and it is perhaps more than coincidence that

---

[48] Grierson and Blackburn, *Medieval European coinage*, p. 320; Blunt, 'St Edmund memorial coinage', p. 242.

[49] Blunt, 'St Edmund memorial coinage', pp. 242, 252–3.

[50] Mark Blackburn, personal communication; cf. Grierson and Blackburn, *Medieval European coinage*, p. 320. The three coins in question were struck from a single pair of dies.

[51] See above, pp. 63–5.   [52] See above, n. 45.

[53] S507 (B808), a grant 'ad monasterium quod situm est in loco qui dicitur aet BAEDERICESPIRDE in quo sanctus Ædmundus rex quiescit corpore', believed to be spurious by Lobel and Harmer, accepted as authentic by Hart.

he bore the name Edmund.[54] It has traditionally been believed that
it was the Danish king Cnut who, *c.* 1020, sanctioned the replacement by monks of the clerks who served St Edmund's shrine.
Antonia Gransden, however, has recently and persuasively argued
that the Bury monks 'adopted Canute as their putative founder late
in the eleventh century' and that the establishment of Benedictine
monks may in fact have taken place under the influence of Ramsey
abbey in the time of St Oswald or his successor Eadnoth.[55] Whatever the case, Cnut does seem to have acted as benefactor to the
house, and his wife Emma certainly did so; there may be some truth
in Hermann's statement that Cnut's generosity was a product of his
devotion to St Edmund.[56] Edward the Confessor is likewise
accredited with a special devotion to the saint;[57] the point seems to
be supported by two of Edward's extant writs, in which he refers to
Edmund as 'my kinsman';[58] and Edward was without doubt the
greatest royal benefactor of St Edmund's abbey.[59]

This record of royal devotion to St Edmund and of royal
patronage of his church seems to suggest that in the tenth and
eleventh centuries successive rulers of Wessex and England felt an
interest in the saint which went beyond the merely conventional.
The nature of this interest can be understood, in part at least, by
analysis of the St Edmund created, under the influence of the West
Saxon court, by Abbo of Fleury. That Edmund is the personifica-

[54] See R. Folz, *Les saints Rois du Moyen Age en Occident (VIe–XIIIe siècles)*, Subsidia Hagiographica 68 (Brussels, 1984), p. 138.
[55] Gransden, 'Legends and traditions', especially pp. 11–12.
[56] For Cnut's devotion and generosity see Hermann, *De miraculis*, ed. Arnold, p. 46: 'protectorem suum post Deum invisens sanctum [Eadmundum], actu regali xeniavit locum donis ac redditibus propriis munificavit, liberumque omni consuetudine chyrographizavit'. The extant diploma of Cnut in favour of the community of Bury (S980) is generally acknowledged to be a late-eleventh-century forgery but was probably copied in part from a genuine document: see Gransden, 'Legends and traditions', pp. 10–11, citing F. E. Harmer, *Anglo-Saxon writs* (Manchester, 1952), pp. 140–1 and notes. For Emma's patronage of the community see S980 and Harmer, *Writs*, pp. 148, 159–60.
[57] Hermann, *De miraculis*, ed. Arnold, p. 48: 'adiens sanctum [Eadmundum], vix effari potest cum qua veneratione descenderit ad illum. Eques rex imperialis fit modo pedes, via miliarii adventans cum optimatibus suis, venerando martyrem sanctum, tum impetrans regni gubernationis suffragium.'
[58] Harmer, *Writs*, pp. 160–1, 164–5; see also Gransden, 'Legends and traditions', p. 12.
[59] Hermann, *De miraculis*, ed. Arnold, p. 48, describing Edward's grant to the community of the eight and a half hundreds of Mildenhall which formed the basis of its later liberty; cf. the Morgan and Titus *Miracula*. For documents of King Edward relating to St Edmund's abbey see S1045–6, 1068–75, 1077–85, and for discussion of Edward's relations with the abbey see especially Gransden, 'Baldwin', p. 66; Gransden, 'Legends and traditions', p. 12.

tion of an idealised Christian kingship; and the development of his cult symbolises the vindication of his cause and the ultimate victory of Christian over pagan. To Athelstan and his successors in the tenth century, whose power had grown out of their conflict with the heathen, the message of St Edmund must have been clear and compelling: to the West Saxons as to the East Angles Edmund's cult may have had profound importance as a symbol of religious and political defiance and survival. Whether Athelstan was the first West Saxon ruler to take an interest in Edmund's story we cannot now know; but it is worth remarking that the significance of that story – if it was known – would not have been lost on Alfred, who so narrowly escaped a comparable fate, or on his son and successor Edward the Elder: it is at least possible that vindication of St Edmund may have been both the banner behind which the West Saxons rode to do battle with the Danes and a point of some importance in subsequent attempts to establish a *modus vivendi* with them. But West Saxon dealings with St Edmund had a further dimension. When Edward the Elder and his successors established West Saxon political dominance over the Eastern counties, it was not only the Danes who lost out: it was also the possibly substantial remnants of an independent East Anglia. Against this background it is possible that the cult of St Edmund became one of the tools or foci for the working out of relations between the East Angles and their West Saxon overlords. Vindication of St Edmund may have been the propaganda which justified the West Saxon venture into Danish–controlled East Anglia. Respect for the cult of the martyred ruler may in general terms have been perceived as easing West Saxon assimilation into local society: the parallel with the West Saxon promotion of the cult of St Æthelthryth is striking. And, more specifically, veneration of St Edmund may have been an important way of claiming and proclaiming a right of legitimate succession to his kingdom. It is perhaps significant that the Wessex-influenced legend of St Edmund created a virgin king:[60] St Edmund was to be allowed no successor whose claim to rule in East Anglia might be more watertight than that of the house of Cerdic.

THE MONASTIC SAINT AND THE NORMAN CONQUEST

The cult of St Edmund was primarily – perhaps exclusively – political in origin. It cannot be satisfactorily explained as a sponta-

[60] *Passio Edmundi*, pp. 86–7.

neous popular movement originating among a few helpless survivors of the Danish onslaught and being sanctioned by the Danes simply because they considered themselves Christians. More complex forces and more powerful influences seem to have been at work. The circumstances of Edmund's death were such that his cult became a potent symbol of Christian victory, and in the troubled decades which followed it became an important focus around which could be worked out the ever-changing relationship between East Angle, West Saxon and Dane.

But Edmund's cult possessed, perhaps from a very early date and certainly from the mid tenth century, a further dimension of fundamental importance. The relics of St Edmund provided the focal point first for a community of clerks and subsequently for a great Benedictine abbey. Abbo's *Passio* ends with an account of two miracles performed through the saint's intercession at the church of *Bedricesgueord*. In the first of these St Edmund appears as the vindicator of the material status of 'his' community; he strikes immobile a group of eight thieves who attempt to break into the church.[61] And in the second he appears as the jealous guardian of his own relics – and hence, by implication, of the church's claim to possess those relics: an unfortunate noble, after arrogantly demanding to see the contents of the shrine, is immediately smitten with madness and suffers a miserable end *uermibus consumptus*.[62] The hagiographers of the later eleventh and twelfth centuries brought Abbo's work up to date, but the tone of Edmund's cult was already set: St Edmund the political symbol had been absorbed into St Edmund the monastic patron.

For the community of St Edmund the Anglo-Saxon period ended in 1065. In that year King Edward appointed as abbot of Bury his own physician, Baldwin, a Frenchman by birth, formerly a monk of Saint-Denis and prior of the abbey's dependency of Leberaw in Alsace.[63] Baldwin became in turn physician to the Conqueror, and the abbey of Bury St Edmunds entered the Norman era in a political position diametrically opposed to that of rebellious Ely: it remained quite securely in favour.[64] Indeed it seems to have profited from the shortcomings of its Fenland neighbour and from the political uncertainties of the post-Con-

---

[61] *Ibid.*, pp. 83–4.   [62] *Ibid.*, pp. 85–6.
[63] Hermann, *De miraculis*, ed. Arnold, pp. 56–7, followed in the Morgan and Titus *Miracula*; Heads, p. 32.
[64] Hermann, *De miraculis*, ed. Arnold, p. 58; Gransden, 'Baldwin', p. 66.

quest years. Antonia Gransden has pointed out that the liberty of Bury, 'as a loyal bloc under its French abbot, was an invaluable asset to the Norman monarch': it might serve not only to counterbalance the insurrection at Ely but also, more generally, as a buffer against threatened Danish incursions into Eastern England.[65] The abbey was accordingly given all the support necessary to ensure its continuing loyalty and usefulness to the king. Baldwin's abbacy witnessed the recognition by William I of the abbey's landholding and legal rights,[66] the expansion of the town of Bury,[67] and the construction of a new and impressive abbey church: 'the abbey emerged from the post-Conquest period richer and more powerful than it had ever been before'.[68]

But the years following the Norman Conquest brought problems to even the most favoured community. Bury, like Ely, suffered a number of invasions of its properties. Hermann tells us, for instance, that an unnamed follower of the Conqueror invaded one of the abbey's estates and that Robert 'de Curzon' and his followers tried to seize the manor of Southwold.[69] A second problem came, as at Ely, from within the church. Herfast, bishop of East Anglia from 1070 until 1084, attempted to move the see to St Edmund's abbey, a measure which threatened both the wealth of the community and the status of its head. In 1081, after more than a decade of conflict, the royal court ruled in the abbey's favour, but Bishops Herfast and Herbert Losinga continued to press the case until the see was finally moved to Norwich in 1094/5. This brought not an end to the argument but a redefinition of its terms: Losinga sought to exercise authority over the abbey, the monks in turn fighting for exemption from episcopal jurisdiction. The quarrel dominated Bury politics at the turn of the century and had a crucial and enduring influence on the formulation of the abbey's hagiography and historiography.[70]

[65] Gransden, 'Baldwin', p. 67; also Gransden, 'The Domesday inquest and the abbey of Bury St Edmunds', paper presented at the Fifth Annual Conference of the Charles Homer Haskins Society for Viking, Anglo-Saxon, Anglo-Norman and Angevin History, University of Houston, November 1986.

[66] Hermann, *De miraculis*, p. 67; Gransden, 'Baldwin', p. 67.

[67] See '*De infantia*', ed. Thomson, pp. 25–6 and references therein cited; R. H. C. Davis, 'The monks of St Edmund, 1021–1148', *History* 40 (1955), 227–39.

[68] Gransden, 'Baldwin', p. 67; cf. '*De infantia*', ed. Thomson, pp. 25–6; Folz, 'Saint Edmond', pp. 231–2.

[69] Hermann, *De miraculis*, ed. Arnold, pp. 58–9, 78–80.

[70] For Baldwin's struggle against the claims of Herfast see *ibid.*, pp. 60–7; for the history and importance of the dispute with Herfast and Losinga see especially Gransden, 'Baldwin', pp. 67–72; Gransden, 'Legends and traditions', pp. 8–9 and *passim*.

In the aftermath of conquest, therefore, the community of Bury, although in a politically more advantageous position, faced a series of problems closely analogous to those experienced by that of Ely. It seems moreover to have adopted analogous methods in order to secure their resolution. Those methods comprised a two-fold recourse to law and to propaganda.[71] And the value of the local saint as material for monastic propaganda was not lost on Bury's foreign abbot. At Bury, as at Ely, there was no clear alignment of conquering monks and laymen against Anglo-Saxon saint; at Bury, as at Ely, an abbot of foreign extraction quite plainly regarded the cult of the local saint as one of several tools which might be utilised in order to defend the rights and to further the interests of the church committed to his care. Baldwin's grasp of the situation is shown by his commissioning of Hermann's *De miraculis sancti Edmundi*.[72] Here a series of punitive miracles forcibly demonstrates the inability of the unnamed 'invader', of Robert 'de Curzon' and his misguided followers and even of Bishop Herfast to escape from the wrath of St Edmund.[73] And, perhaps to emphasise the point, the decades between St Edmund's arrival at *Bedricesgueord* and the Norman Conquest are filled in with a series of similarly telling stories. The death of King Sweyn is presented as a punishment for his imposition of tribute on the lands and men of St Edmund; the shire-reeve Leofstan goes mad after challenging a woman's right to seek asylum with the saint; and the Dane Osgod Clapa is similarly punished for his failure to show due respect to Bury's patron.[74] Hermann's stories were probably drawn from traditions already current at Bury; but there can be little doubt that his presentation of those traditions was conditioned by his acute awareness of the problems of his own time.

One theme of the *De miraculis* is particularly interesting: the monastic patron created by Hermann remained a thoroughly kingly saint. Thus he notes at the beginning of his work that

---

[71] At Bury St Edmunds as elsewhere litigation, propaganda and forgery seem to have been closely connected. For discussion of Baldwin's probable responsibility for the forged privileges on which the abbey's case against Herfast was founded see Gransden, 'Baldwin', pp. 71–2.   [72] See above, p. 70.

[73] Hermann, *De miraculis*, ed. Arnold, pp. 58–9, 78–80, 62–3.

[74] *Ibid.*, pp. 32–9, 30–2, 54–6. Cf. a series of stories concerning the proper treatment of the saint's body: *ibid.*, pp. 40–2 (the punishment of a priest who refuses to give hospitality to the saint as he is taken to London to escape the Danish invasion of 1010), 44 (the punishment in London of an arrogant Dane who seeks to examine the saint's body), 55 (the punishment of Abbot Leofstan for rough handling of the saint). Each of these stories appears also in the Morgan *Miracula* and in the *Miracula* of Titus A. viii.

Edmund remained after death 'the patron of the East Anglian region
. . . winning from the Almighty the reward that no king after him,
save God himself, should rule in those regions'.[75] Elsewhere in the
De miraculis Edmund is presented as 'protector of the East Angles',
as 'glory and shield of the East Angles' and, in the context of Bury's
dispute with Bishop Herfast, as patron of the area in which Herfast
held office.[76] For Hermann and for the community of Bury, it
appears, the local importance, the popular appeal and the political
usefulness of the monastic saint were enhanced by Edmund's royal
status and by his consequent portrayal as patron not just of a
religious house but rather of the whole province of the East Angles.

And perhaps Edmund's royal status had a further, more specific,
significance which the late-eleventh-century community found
useful. St Edmund's abbey, whose *raison d'être* was guardianship of
the martyr's body, succeeded not only to the special protection but
also in some measure to the political status of the saint: there could
be no clearer statement of the political dominance and consequent
inviolability within East Anglia of the abbey of Bury St Edmunds.
Again it can be inferred that Hermann was drawing upon traditions
current at Bury at an earlier date, and the theme of inviolability
receives its clearest expression in the story of the exactions and
death of King Sweyn; but its relevance to Bury's position in the late
eleventh century would not have been lost on a contemporary
audience.

The Bury monks however did not press the point too far. A
regional protector was always useful, but a separatist saint might be
self-defeating. For the monks wished to use the asset of their saint's
royal status in two quite distinct ways. Hermann, while emphasising Edmund's role as ruler and patron of the East Angles, showed
no hesitation in making him also kinsman of Edward the Confessor.[77] Elsewhere, with comparable ambiguity, he explains that
fifteen kings have reigned between Edmund and the Norman
Conquest, without the slightest acknowledgement that there has
been at least one change of dynasty.[78] Edmund's role as patron of
the East Angles was paralleled, in short, by his role as patron of the
English. That role had its origin in the early tenth century, in the
West Saxon adoption of Edmund's cult; it continued after 1066.
Indeed the late eleventh century may have marked the beginning of
a period of transition, in which St Edmund of England came

[75] Hermann, *De miraculis*, ed. Arnold, p. 28.   [76] *Ibid.*, pp. 46, 51, 63.
[77] *Ibid.*, p. 57.   [78] *Ibid.*, p. 58.

gradually to attain dominance over St Edmund of East Anglia. Such a transition may have owed something to the political events of 1066, which perhaps reduced still further what little relevance remained in the old distinctions between the various English kingdoms. More likely it was hastened by the desire of Abbot Baldwin and his monks both to retain royal favour and to establish their abbey as a pilgrimage centre with more than local appeal. By the 1120s the process may have been well advanced: it is perhaps indicative of·propaganda rather than confusion that in the final illustration of Morgan 736 St Edmund appears, enthroned and wearing not the martyr's crown but the crown of England.[79]

Under the guidance of Abbot Baldwin therefore the legend of St Edmund was brought up to date and adapted in accordance with the requirements of the post-Conquest era. And, as at Ely, new circumstances may have prompted the re-writing of the past: there is some evidence that Baldwin was responsible for the interpolation of Abbo's *Passio Edmundi* in such a way as to support the interests of the abbey in its quarrel with the bishops of East Anglia.[80] Nor was Baldwin's interest in St Edmund limited to the updating and perhaps refurbishing of his legend as an instrument of monastic propaganda. He adopted a quite·deliberate policy of enhancing the prestige of his church by the promotion of Edmund's cult. Thus

[79] This point was brought to my attention by Cynthia Hahn in her paper '*Peregrinatio et natio*: the Life of Edmund King and Martyr', presented at the Fifth Annual Conference of the Charles Homer Haskins Society for Viking, Anglo-Saxon, Anglo-Norman and Angevin History, University of Houston, November 1986. For the transition of Edmund protector of the East Angles into Edmund protector of the English see also Folz, *Les saints Rois*, pp. 215–16.

[80] Gransden, 'Baldwin', p. 72. Here it is noted that the three earliest extant MSS of the *Passio* date from the late eleventh century and contain a number of variations from the text as this is preserved in Ælfric's English translation. Two of these variations may be of some importance in the light of the anti-episcopal propaganda current at Bury in Baldwin's time. First, the statement that Edmund's body was removed from its original resting-place to the *uilla regia* of *Bedricesgueord* is absent from Ælfric's account, and Dr Gransden suggests that this may have been added late in the eleventh century in order to emphasise 'not only St Edmund's burial at Beodricesworth but also Bury's royal connection, in contradistinction to any episcopal one'. This suggestion is not entirely convincing, for Ælfric's version of the *Passio* omits all place-names, locating the events which he describes simply within East Anglia. It is perhaps the case that he was adapting the text for use by an audience to whom the local place-names would be meaningless and hence that no special significance should be accorded to his omission of the crucial phrase. Second, and more convincing, is the fact that the extant text of Abbo accords no part in the endowment of the church at *Bedricesgueord* to Bishop Theodred. Ælfric, in contrast, specifically states that Theodred was responsible for the enrichment of the church (*Lives of saints*, II, 329), and his statement seems to be corroborated by Theodred's bequest to *Bedricesgueord* (see above, n. 45).

when Baldwin heard of a local miracle, the cure of a certain Wulmar, he ensured that the event was announced in the church and publicly celebrated.[81] He also had more grandiose plans, attaching special importance to the dissemination of Edmund's relics and cult on the continent. Abbot Warner of Rebaix, while receiving Baldwin's hospitality, composed four antiphons in honour of St Edmund; he returned home bearing a relic of the saint.[82] Hermann tells us that on another occasion Baldwin while in Normandy sent to Bury for a reliquary;[83] perhaps this was intended as a gift to some Norman church or individual. And the abbot's policy receives its most striking illustration in Hermann's moving story of the cure of a young Italian boy by a relic of St Edmund which Baldwin, *en route* to Rome, had placed in the church of St Martin at Lucca.[84]

The post-Conquest promotion of Edmund's cult reached a spectacular climax in 1095, when the martyred king's body was solemnly translated to Baldwin's new abbey church.[85] The translation was not without hitches. It seems to have taken place in a rare atmosphere of hostility between king and abbey: Hermann provides a rather puzzling account in which William II is said to have agreed to the translation but to have refused Baldwin's further request for the dedication of the new church.[86] There were also, it appears, those who opposed the translation: the hagiographer goes on to explain that there arose among William's courtiers a rumour that St Edmund's uncorrupt body did not in fact rest at Bury.[87] Is this perhaps an example of Norman scepticism towards the saints of the Anglo-Saxons? At first sight it appears to be so. But Hermann makes no reference to the existence of doubts concerning Edmund's sanctity; rather the point at issue is quite explicitly said to have been the location of the body. And Hermann goes on to provide a crucial clue to an understanding of the incident. As the

[81] Hermann, *De miraculis*, ed. Arnold, pp. 80–3, at 83; also in the Morgan and Titus *Miracula*.   [82] *Ibid.*, p. 70; also in the Morgan and Titus *Miracula*.

[83] *Ibid.*, p. 72; also in the Morgan and Titus *Miracula*.

[84] *Ibid.*, pp. 67–9; also in the Morgan and Titus *Miracula*.

[85] Hermann, *De miraculis*, ed. Arnold, pp. 84–91.

[86] *Ibid.*, p. 85. It is not clear why William's consent to either translation or dedication was felt to be necessary.

[87] *Ibid.*, p. 86: 'inter quosdam palatinos oritur malus ac invidiosus murmur male ruminans, dicendo in Beodryci villa non, ut dicebatur, incorruptibiliter manente martyre [Eadmundo] . . . Rumor quippe malus extitit, qui lingua venenifera sanctum inibi non esse præsentialem dixit, opusque fabrile suo scrinio consertum consiliatus est ad militare rapi stipendium. Verum Deus, judex justus, mutabit consilium Achitofel in melius.'

abbey did not possess the body, the courtiers argued, surely Edmund's shrine should be stripped and its precious metals put to military service.[88] What was under attack was not the veneration of St Edmund but the wealth of his church. By denying the presence of the saint the courtiers struck at the very foundation of Bury's wealth and prestige; the saint was merely a pawn in a game of power.[89] The incident had no serious consequences; the translation was performed in due course by Bishop Walkelin of Winchester.[90] That such an incident arose at all however is striking testimony to the success with which the martyred king of the East Angles had continued to serve the interests of his people in the decades following 1066. Well before the year 1100, when Bury acquired its first abbot of Norman birth,[91] the survival of St Edmund was assured[92] and his function within the post-Conquest community both clearly defined and widely acknowledged.

[88] *Ibid.*; cited above, n. 87.

[89] For discussion of a similar incident which took place prior to the translation of St Cuthbert in 1104, and for some general comments, see Ridyard, '*Condigna veneratio*', pp. 198–200, 204.

[90] Hermann tells us (*De miraculis*, ed. Arnold, p. 87) that further opposition to the translation came from the East Anglian bishop, Herbert Losinga. The bishop's hostility seems to have originated not in any scepticism concerning St Edmund but in his own exclusion from the proceedings; it is best understood in the context of his continuing conflict with St Edmund's abbey: 'Grave fert Herbertus episcopus dioceseus, qui non ad hoc interpellatur ut sit ex eis unus; vetitum vult inferre, sed cassatur inde, velut nomen Sathanæ de libro vitæ. Viget enim eadem abbatia privilegio regali fulcita; sed et corroboratur auctoritate privilegii domni et apostolicæ sedis papæ Alexandri secundi, non debere eam subigi sub ditione alicujus diocesiani, nisi quo libuerit abbatem prædicti loci, vel sub metropolitano Cantuariensi.'

Hermann goes on to note that Edmund was accompanied to the new church by the relics of saints Botulf and Jurminus (*ibid.*, pp. 88–9; cf. *GP*, p. 156). Neither of these saints is located at Bury by the *Secgan*; the deposition of Botulf (17 June) is commemorated in the Bury calendar of *c.* 1050 (Wormald (ed.), *Before 1100*, no. 19), but no feast of Jurminus occurs here. The *LE* preserves a tradition (I, 7) that Jurminus was a son of King Anna and that he was buried with his father at Blythburgh prior to his translation to *Betricheswrde*; and a note, probably of the twelfth century, in MS Bodley 297 (pr. Arnold (ed.), *Memorials of St Edmund's abbey*, I, 352; cf. p. lxviii) states that Botulf and Jurminus were each translated to Bury in the time of Abbot Leofstan (1044–65).

[91] Robert, son of Hugh, earl of Chester, and formerly a monk of Saint-Evroul; see *Heads*, p. 32.

[92] It is worth noting that the liturgical sources demonstrate that both before and after the Conquest Edmund was among the most popular of the English saints. His feast on 20 November appears in Wormald (ed.), *Before 1100*, nos. 6–20 (no. 19 is a Bury calendar of *c.* 1050) and in Wormald (ed.), *After 1100*, I, 29, 44, 61, 78, 110, 127, 143, 159, 178; II, 18, 37, 54, 73, 89, 102, 117; for the date and provenance of these sources see Wormald's introductions to the individual calendars. For more detailed discussion of the liturgical sources for the veneration of St Edmund see Folz, 'Saint Edmond', pp. 235–6.

Chapter 8

PIETY, PATRONAGE AND POLITICS: TOWARDS AN UNDERSTANDING OF THE ANGLO-SAXON ROYAL CULTS

Close to the heart of medieval Christianity stood the cult of the saints. As real presence and potent symbol, the saints occupied a central place within both church and community. Their cults, in theory founded upon divine acknowledgement, in fact created by man, fulfilled a complex series of functions, spiritual, social and political. The creators of those cults were men and women of great power: theirs was the ability to create the saints, if not in their own image at least in accordance with their own interests, and thereafter to pursue those interests through the manipulation of legend and cult. The present study has sought, by analysis of the identity, the beliefs and the actions of such creators – and of those who continued and adapted their work – to recover the history and function of a group of West Saxon and East Anglian royal cults. Focussing upon the three major problems of theoretical interpretation, historical explanation and continuity of cult, it has attempted to arrive at a new understanding of the place of the Anglo-Saxon royal saint not only in pre-Conquest society but also in that of the Anglo-Norman realm.

At no point in the history of Anglo-Saxon England was it possible to expect or to assume royal sanctity. The Lives of the royal saints combine with the broader traditions of medieval political theory to demonstrate the weakness of the Chaney thesis which, portraying the saint king as the lineal descendant of the sacral king, makes sanctity an almost inevitable adjunct of birth into the ruling dynasties of Anglo-Saxon England. That thesis breaks down because it fails to distinguish either sacral kingship from Christian kingship or sacrality from sanctity. Sacrality, an ascribed status, was wholly incompatible with the concept of useful, 'official' kingship formulated and promulgated by the Christian church; sanctity, an achieved status, could be controlled by that church and utilised in support of its theory of useful rulership. Sanctity therefore had no place among the assumed attributes of the Christian Anglo-Saxon ruler or among those of his female kinsfolk; sanctity had to be earned.

The hagiographers of the royal saints went further; they wrote with much care and more than a little skill of the means of its earning. Their first concern was to locate their subjects within the recognised categories of Christian sainthood. Thereafter, in almost all cases, the theoretical interpretation of individual sanctity was filled out not only by conventional description of conventional virtues but also by careful analysis of the relationship of those virtues to inherited royal status. To the hagiographers upon whose work this study has been founded royal sanctity might be attained either by manner of life or by nature of death, more specifically by monasticism or by martyrdom. Of these two paths to sanctity the former was followed without exception by the royal ladies. For Edburga and Edith, Æthelthryth and her saintly 'sisters' sanctity was founded upon the virtues of *uirginitas* or *castitas* practised and perfected within the context of the monastic life. As such their attainment of sanctity stood in a negative relationship to the royal state. Sanctity was founded upon the renunciation of royal status, upon commitment to the alternative goal of the religious life and upon the adoption in pursuit of that goal of conduct antithetical to that implied by royal birth: from *filia principis* was created *sponsa Christi*. For Edmund and Edward in contrast sanctity was earned at the moment of death, in the suffering of martyrdom. The hagiographers of the two saints offered quite different interpretations of martyrdom. Abbo of Fleury provided a detailed theoretical statement, in which Edmund's death, deriving from his refusal to submit to pagan overlordship, was presented as the fulfilment of his duty not just as an individual Christian but more specifically as a Christian king. The *Passio Edwardi* stands apart from the other hagiographical works reviewed here: it has little theoretical content and concerns itself not at all with the relationship of royal birth to the attainment of sanctity; its subject is located instead within the distinct hagiological tradition of the martyred innocent.

Those who made it their business to write about kingship and about the lives of the saints distinguished clearly between sanctity and sacrality and were able when necessary to propose a detailed definition of the relationship between royal birth and the attainment of sanctity. They were, however, a clerical elite; and their theoretical subtleties may well have been beyond the reach of the lay society within which the cults of the royal saints were received – of the *folc* who might expect God to honour the *stirps regia* and of the rulers who might expect to be thus honoured. It is accordingly important to recognise that there may have existed, especially but not exclusively in the earlier centuries, two quite different levels of understanding of the cults of the royal saints – that of the church, characterised by careful definition of the grounds for an individual's veneration, and that of secular society, which perhaps needed no greater justification for honouring royalty than the fact that it had always done so. But it is equally important to establish the relative importance of these two levels of understanding in the creation of the royal cults. One of the weaknesses of the Chaney thesis is its designation of the English royal cults as 'popular'.[1] It is apparent from any detailed study of those cults that, while they may have been readily accepted by the *folc*, it was to an ecclesiastical and political elite that they owed their making.

In the creation of the royal cults two distinct traditions strikingly reflect the distinct roles and career-patterns of the royal ladies and the martyred kings. The cults whose story I have sought to tell were without exception political in origin: far from growing out of spontaneous popular devotion, they were deliberate creations of a specific group or specific groups of people who perceived the cult of the royal saint as an important means to a specific end. They owed their inception, however, to two very different kinds of politics. The cults of the royal ladies were products of the monastic world; those of the martyred rulers originated in the high politics of their former kingdoms.

St Edburga's reputation for sanctity first took root among, and was fostered by, the Winchester nuns; the daughter of Edgar seems similarly to have been elevated to sainthood by her colleagues, and indeed by her mother, at Wilton; St Æthelthryth was translated at Ely by her sister, who succeeded her as abbess. In each case the cult of the *uirgo regia* was created by the religious community within which her life had in whole or in part been spent and which in death provided her final resting-place. As such that cult was a direct

---

[1] Chaney, *Cult of kingship*, p. 77, noting that many kings 'who died unjust and violent deaths became popular saints'; p. 79, referring to 'a canonization by the folk'.

product and an appropriate culmination of her historical role within the community. Its creation was both a gesture of acknowledgement and an investment for the future. There was much to acknowledge. If the hagiographical theory presents a starkly defined picture of an ecclesiastical role divorced from and antithetical to that implied by royal birth, the hagiographical narrative amply demonstrates that in practice such antithesis between *filia principis* and *sponsa summi regis* was neither attainable nor desirable. The role of the royal lady within the religious community was founded not upon the renunciation of the attributes of royalty but rather upon the redeployment of those attributes in the service of the church. Her presence alone was an act of patronage: within the aristocratic and highly politicised world of the *sancta congregatio* she was a status symbol of the highest importance. She brought, or perhaps reinforced, a prestige whose institutional benefits, though rarely defined, were doubtless considerable. Very probably such prestige, born of new or continuing alliance with the royal house, served to enhance the internal cohesiveness of the community while externally raising its profile in such a way as to stimulate both patronage and recruitment. More than this, the royal lady was a crucial focus for the definition and conduct of relations between religious house and royal dynasty: *mediatrix ad regem*, she provided for her community access to information, influence and patronage. Finally, she brought wealth. Such wealth might, as in the case of St Æthelthryth, be essential to the foundation and survival of the community; or it might represent a valuable addition to adequate but limited resources. It might take the form of a gift on entry to the religious life, of personal wealth retained and used in building projects, relic-acquisition or charitable work, or of precious objects such as St Edburga's gospel-book which contributed something both to the wealth of the house and to its corporate myth. Not only was there much to acknowledge; there was also much to hope for. The religious community had every reason to believe that, by honouring the *uirgo regia*, it might ensure the continuing interest and patronage of future generations of kings and their consorts. Thus, in commemoration of the past and with an eye to the future, the nuns of Winchester, Wilton and Ely were assiduous in translating the remains and in publicising the miracles of their saintly sisters: from the royal patron was created the patron saint.

There may, and indeed should, be those who on reading this analysis will be provoked to ask 'But were not these royal ladies also

237

pious individuals?' and 'Was there no piety involved in the creation of their cults?' In seeking to weigh the relative importance of piety and patronage in the lives of the saints, piety and politics in those of their contemporaries, we approach one of the great intangibles of religious history. In the creation of the cults there can be little doubt that several motives, not always acknowledged or clearly defined, went hand in hand. Considerations of future gain might combine with desire to honour an associate, with recognition or even exaggeration of holiness and with a deep-rooted spiritual and social need for a local patron saint. Above all, perhaps, there was a real and potent belief that an individual who in life had effectively served the interests of the community might be expected after death to intercede with like effectiveness both among future generations on earth and in heaven. Of the lives of the saints it must first be said that hagiography is not always as helpful as we might wish. The sections of the *Vitae* which purport to record those of the saint's actions which were of lasting importance to her community might be rooted more firmly in objective reality than those sections which, extolling her monastic-ascetic virtues, form part of, and might be strongly influenced by, the common stock of hagiographical tradition. The royal ladies, it appears, each attained a standard of piety acceptable to the monasticism of the time. Beyond this, there was doubtless much variety. St Æthelthryth, for instance, seems to have combined in perfect balance the skills of the institution builder and the virtues of the ascetic; St Edith, in contrast, may have earned rather easily her reputation for holiness. From the foregoing case-studies, however, one fact emerges with startling clarity: the distinction between 'piety' and 'patronage' is one which means far more to the twentieth-century observer than it did to the men and women of the Anglo-Saxon period. The piety which these cults commemorate was not defined exclusively in monastic-ascetic terms; it included also a strong element of community-oriented *utilitas*. Patronage did not stand apart from piety; it was subsumed within it. By the exercise of patronage virtue was rendered effective; there is no evidence that it was rendered redundant.

In striking contrast to the cults of the royal ladies those of St Edmund and St Edward were a product less of the saint's actions in life than of the nature of his death and the symbolic value of his memory. Each seems to have been created as an instrument for the pursuit of political interests in the decades following – and in political circumstances created or exacerbated by – the death of its object. The killing of Edmund left his kingdom open to conquest by the Danes and to the eastward expansion of West Saxon royal power. In the late ninth and tenth centuries the cult of the fallen ruler seems to have been an important focus for the working out within Edmund's kingdom of political relations between the East Angles, their immediate conquerors the Danes and their ultimate conquerors the West Saxons. By the murder of Edward, his half-brother Æthelred succeeded to the thone. Edward's cult has traditionally been interpreted as a creation of rebels which a reluctant Æthelred was forced to acknowledge. More detailed analysis of the historical and hagiographical record suggests rather that the cult was promoted by Æthelred and his supporters as a vehicle for a number of important political statements. By his promotion of that cult the king dissociated himself from Edward's murder, condemned its perpetrators, emphasised his own legitimate status among the children of Edgar, and issued a spectacular statement of the inviolability of kingship.

In the decades and centuries between their inception and 1066 the cults of the royal saints developed in different directions in response to different stimuli. The process was always complex and can in no case be fully reconstructed. It was not unusual for a cult to be promoted by two or more different interest-groups in pursuit of two or more distinct goals. Thus, for instance, the cult of St Edmund appears to have aroused the interest simultaneously or in rapid succession of East Angles, West Saxons and Danes, each group seeking by adoption of the cult to enhance its own position *vis-à-vis* one or both of the others. Three general patterns of evolution can, however, be distinguished. First, the cult of the martyred ruler as instrument of high politics came to be absorbed into, and to be dominated by, the cult of that ruler as patron of the religious community which gained possession of his relics. St Edmund, by the mid tenth century at the latest, was the potent domestic patron of the clerks of *Bedricesgueord*. And well before the end of Æthelred's reign St Edward had proved of no little value to the Shaftesbury nuns. In each case, I have suggested, the monastic interest may have been present from the earliest days and may indeed have been at least partially responsible for marketing to the rulers the usefulness of the royal cult; in neither case can the rise to dominance of that interest be precisely dated. Second, the cults of the royal ladies, originating in local and monastic interests, might on occasion become involved in more far-reaching political issues.

St Edith, for instance, appears to have been briefly implicated, with her murdered half-brother, in the high politics of Æthelred's reign. And the adoption by West Saxon monks and West Saxon monarchy of the Ely saints may have played some part in the establishment of West Saxon dominance over the Fenland. Finally, there is scattered but substantial evidence to suggest that the cults of the royal saints, both male and female, attracted the interest and patronage of successive generations of rulers and consorts. Such interest and patronage came not only – perhaps not even primarily – from rulers of the saint's own dynasty. West Saxon rulers showed much interest in Æthelthryth and Edmund; the Scandinavian Cnut adopted both West Saxon and East Anglian saints. This widespread and continuing tradition suggests that, quite apart from those occasions when they could be used in pursuit of specific and short-term political goals, the royal cults possessed a general significance which rendered them attractive to rulers. To members of the same dynasty their appeal was founded upon the value of the saintly relative or ancestor as status symbol. A royal saint in heaven brought prestige to a royal house on earth; and the promotion of such a cult by the saint's successors in the royal dynasty might serve as a symbol of respect for and adherence to the traditions of that dynasty. To the *externus rex*, the cult of a royal saint, like the laws of his predecessors, formed a channel for the public assertion of his relationship, real or fictive, to the dynasty which he supplanted. Veneration of such a saint was a statement of respect for and of legitimate succession to that dynasty; it was also an unambiguous statement that the new ruler was now monarch of all he surveyed.

The case-studies developed in the preceding chapters concern only a small proportion of the royal saints of Anglo-Saxon England. They do, however, suggest a pattern, or a series of patterns, from which may be derived a tentative model for the more general understanding of Anglo-Saxon royal sanctity. That model distinguishes sharply between the legends and cults of the royal ladies, both virgins and widows, and those of the martyred kings – perhaps also those of other males of the royal stock. It can be summarised as follows. The royal ladies attained sanctity by their role within the religious life. This role, in theory divorced from and antithetical to that implied by the royal state, in practice was made possible by royal status and connections. The subsequent creation of cult was the achievement of the religious community to which the saint had belonged; it marked the transition of royal patron into patron saint. For the martyred kings, in contrast, the attainment of sanctity came with the moment of death, and the inception of cult was a product of the political conditions attendant upon or created by that death. In the hagiographical theory martyrdom might stand in a positive relation to the royal state, being associated with fulfilment of the ecclesiastically defined duties of the Christian king; or the relationship between royal birth and sanctity might be accorded little, if any, importance, the saint being located instead within the distinct tradition of the martyred innocent. The nature and function of each cult might be expected to change over time in accordance with changing political circumstances and with the changing requirements or even identity of its promoters. Some general patterns of evolution have been highlighted; further study will doubtless reveal others.

Preliminary investigation suggests that this model can usefully be employed to describe the cults of a high proportion of those royal saints whose presence in the *Secgan* and in the associated 'Kentish royal legend' attests to their veneration in the pre-Conquest period. In the Lives of the royal ladies the dominant themes are the renunciation of the world and the attainment of sanctity by commitment to the religious life; the inception of their cults is most readily intelligible in terms of the royal patron–patron saint transition. Thus in Kent the community of Minster-in-Thanet was founded by King Egbert, probably in conjunction with the royal lady Domne Eafe, who ruled as its first abbess.[2] Her daughter Mildrith succeeded her and was quickly recognised as a saint, being translated by her successor Edburga.[3] Elsewhere in Kent likewise, as Rollason points out, 'it was princess-abbesses of royally founded abbeys who were regarded as the real saints'.[4] Of the princess-abbesses Æthelburga and Eanswith we know only that they were venerated by the communities which they had founded or ruled.[5]

---

[2] *Heiligen*, ed. Liebermann, p. 3. The foundation story preserved in the various versions of the Mildrith legend makes Domne Eafe receive the land for the foundation from Egbert as compensation or *wergild* for the death of her brothers Æthelred and Æthelbert, which he had ordered. For the foundation and for Domne Eafe's career see Rollason, *Mildrith legend*, especially pp. 11, 34–5.

[3] *Heiligen*, ed. Liebermann, p. 5; Goscelin's *Vita Deo dilectae uirginis Mildrethae*, in Rollason, *Mildrith legend*, pp. 108–43.   [4] Rollason, *Mildrith legend*, p. 47.

[5] *Heiligen*, ed. Liebermann, p. 1, where Æthelburga is associated with Lyminge, Eanswith with Folkestone; Rollason, *Mildrith legend*, especially p. 9. It is unclear whether the Edburga with whom Æthelburga is here associated also belonged to the Kentish royal house. Mildrith's aunt Eormengith, to whom miracles are attributed (*Heiligen*, ed.

This however is perhaps sufficient to suggest that their cults evolved in circumstances and for reasons closely analogous to those which gave rise to the royal cults of Winchester, Wilton and Ely. The cults of the Kentish royal ladies, it seems, were created by individual religious communities in recognition of their historical roles as leaders and patrons of those communities and with the intention of ensuring continuing good relations between religious community and royal house. More than this, it seems that together those communities created a legend which emphasised not only their own royal foundation and glorious history but also the spiritual and political distinction of the royal dynasty of Kent.[6] In that legend are incorporated also those royal ladies whom I have designated the 'Ely' saints[7] and two sisters of Mildrith, Mildgith and Milburga, of whom the latter renounced the secular life to found and rule a monastery at Much Wenlock.[8]

Of the other royal ladies who appear in the *Secgan*, St Frideswide, allegedly the daughter of a *subregulus*, 'having renounced everything . . . by the king's generosity built a monastery' at Oxford, where she was subsequently venerated.[9] Cuthburga and Cwenburga, sisters of the West Saxon king Ine, were venerated at the monastery of Wimborne: Cuthburga was remembered as founder and abbess; Cwenburga may have followed her example in the patronage and leadership of the community.[10] Other saints are more obscure; but, as in the case of Æthelburga and Eanswith, the little information that we have about their lives and cults at least suggests that they were created in the same mould. Cyneburga and Cyneswitha, of the Mercian royal house, were translated to Peterborough in the late tenth century;[11] the former seems to have founded a religious house at Castor, the latter to have married but remained a virgin; she may

---

Liebermann, p. 1), seems to have been a member of the community at Minster-in-Thanet but never its abbess.   [6] Rollason, *Mildrith legend*, ch. 4.   [7] See above, pp. 50–1.

[8] *Heiligen*, ed. Liebermann, pp. 3, 11. A Life of Milburga, which is probably drawn from the tradition of Much Wenlock and which can be dated *c.* 1080, is preserved in London, BL, Add. MS 34,633, fols. 206–216v (see Rollason, *Mildrith legend*, pp. 25–6).

[9] *GP*, pp. 315–16; *Heiligen*, ed. Liebermann, p. 19; *ASC, s.a.* 718. For this saint see F. M. Stenton, 'St Frideswide and her times' (1935), in D. M. Stenton (ed.), *Preparatory to Anglo-Saxon England: being the collected papers of Frank Merry Stenton* (Oxford, 1970), pp. 224–33, where William of Malmesbury's account is accepted in outline and the antiquity of the cult accepted.

[10] *Heiligen*, ed. Liebermann, p. 19; *GR*, I, 35, n. 1; *AASS*, Aug. VI (1743), 696–700.

[11] *ASC*, E, *s.a.* 963; *Heiligen*, ed. Liebermann, p. 13; *GP*, p. 317.

eventually have joined her sister at Castor.[12] The Edith located by the *Secgan* at Polesworth seems to have been a sister of King Athelstan and founder of a nunnery there; and Ælfgyfa was a member of the West Saxon royal house associated with the nunnery of Shaftesbury.[13] Of Osthryth we know only that with her husband Æthelred of Mercia she enriched (perhaps founded) the monastery of Bardney, that she was murdered by the Mercian nobles and that she was venerated at Bardney.[14] No liturgical or hagiographical source survives to define the grounds for her veneration. It is possible that her murder was interpreted as martyrdom; but if, as seems probable, the King Æthelred located by the *Secgan* at Bardney was her husband, who seems to have become a monk and abbot there,[15] it is perhaps more likely that the two were venerated together in recognition of their importance in the early history of the house. This in itself would make them a somewhat unusual couple, for Osthryth seems never to have entered the religious life and Æthelred would be the only monk-king to appear in the *Secgan*.[16]

The kings and princes of the *Secgan* almost without exception attained sanctity by martyrdom.[17] Oswald, *rex Christianissimus*, was killed in battle by the forces of the heathen Penda. For the Northumbrian prince Ealhmund, the East Anglian Æthelbert, the

---

[12] *Vita Mildrethae*, in Rollason, *Mildrith legend*, p. 115.

[13] For Edith see *Heiligen*, ed. Liebermann, p. 13; Matthew Paris, *Chronica majora*, ed. H. R. Luard, 7 vols., RS 57 (London, 1872–83), I (1872), 446–7; for Ælfgyfa of Shaftesbury see above, p. 170.   [14] *HE*, III, 11; v, 24; *Heiligen*, ed. Liebermann, p. 11.

[15] *Heiligen*, ed. Liebermann, p. 11; *HE*, v, 19, 24. Colgrave notes (p. 246, n. 1) that Æthelred became a monk at Bardney, but the name of the house to which he withdrew is not given by Bede.

[16] Wigstan (see below, pp. 244–5) allegedly refused for religious reasons to accept the Northumbrian throne and may have entered the religious life; he was venerated however not as a monk-king but as a martyr.

A further somewhat puzzling case is that of St Osyth, located by the *Secgan* at Chich in Essex (*Heiligen*, ed. Liebermann, p. 13), and allegedly a daughter of Penda of Mercia, wife of Sighere of Essex, founder and ruler of a religious community at Chich and martyr at the hands of a pagan. For this saint see Hohler, 'St Osyth', and Bethell, 'Lives of St Osyth of Essex and St Osyth of Aylesbury', pp. 75–127. Her career is particularly difficult to reconstruct for, as Bethell notes (p. 107), all the extant hagiographical texts 'show a confusion between two saints Osyth, of Aylesbury and Essex'. The Mercian royal origin attributed to Osyth of Essex in each of those Lives is in fact derived from the legend of Osyth of Aylesbury. It is however probable that the story of her marriage to King Sighere and her work at Chich has some basis in fact. She seems to have been remembered both as patron of Chich and as a virgin martyr.

[17] The only exceptions are the infant prince Rumwold – whose legend asserts that he died when only three days old after making a confession of faith and giving detailed

---

Kentish princes Æthelred and Æthelbert and the Mercians Wigstan
and Kenelm martyrdom took a different form, analogous rather to
that of Edward than to that of Edmund: each was murdered for
political reasons by fellow-Christians. The hagiographers of these
saints wrote with varying degrees of skill of the interpretation of
individual sanctity. For Oswald, as for Edmund, martyrdom followed directly from defiance of the heathen; the king, in going to
his death, accordingly fulfilled the last and greatest duty of the
Christian king.[18] Æthelbert of the East Angles met his death in 794
at the hands of Offa of Mercia.[19] His earliest extant *Passio*, although
written after the Conquest, very probably incorporates some
earlier material from the cult centre at Hereford; it locates its
subject firmly within the hagiographical tradition of martyred
innocent.[20] Æthelred and Æthelbert, sons of Eormenred of Kent,
were committed to the care of their cousin King Egbert and put to
death by his servant Thunor; by their hagiographers they were
portrayed as martyred *innocentes*.[21] Of Kenelm little is known. His
Passio, probably composed in the mid eleventh century and of
doubtful reliability, makes him a child king murdered at the
instigation of a jealous sister; as such he fits naturally into the
innocent victim tradition.[22] Wigstan, according to a *Vita* of the
twelfth or early thirteenth century, was a son of Wigmund, king of
Mercia. He refused for religious reasons to accept the throne on his
father's death, and he was subsequently murdered by a kinsman

instructions for his burial – the hermit prince Guthlac, and the Mercian Æthelred,
apparently the only monk-king to appear in the *Secgan* (*Heiligen*, ed. Liebermann, pp. 13,
11).

[18] See above, pp. 92–3.   [19] *ASC*, *s.a.* 792 (correctly 794).

[20] M. R. James, 'Two Lives of St Ethelbert, king and martyr', *EHR* 32 (1917), 214–44, at
236–44, from CCC MS 308. Æthelbert is 'rex innocens'; he goes to Offa 'in innocentia
sua'; and 'Sic innocenter peremptus in terris rex et martyr gaudia regni celestis conscendit'
(*ibid.*, pp. 240, 239). The same themes dominate the somewhat later Life by Gerald of
Wales (printed *ibid.*, pp. 222–36). For discussion of the hagiography of Æthelbert see *ibid.*,
pp. 214–21 and Rollason, 'Cults of murdered royal saints', p. 9.

[21] For these saints see *Heiligen*, ed. Liebermann, pp. 1, 13; Rollason, 'Cults of murdered
royal saints', p. 5; Rollason, *Mildrith legend*, pp. 14–20. A *Passio* now preserved in the
Durham *Historia regum* perhaps derives from the early eighth century (*Symeonis monachi
opera omnia*, II, 3–13; Rollason, 'Cults of murdered royal saints', p. 5 and n. 19). Of the
martyrdom its author exclaims (p. 7): 'O quam immitis fraudulentorum in innocentes
saevitia! . . . Quid plura? mortifera idem in se ipsum armatur pestifer turbo nequitia, qua
absente regis praesentia manus nisus est extendere in Deo cernua innocentium colla.'

[22] Kenelm *cynebearn* is located at Winchcombe by the *Secgan* (*Heiligen*, ed. Liebermann,
pp. 17, 19). For the history and hagiography of this saint see Rollason, 'Cults of murdered
royal saints', pp. 9–10. The fullest version of the *Passio* is contained in a thirteenth-century
MS, Oxford, Bodleian Library, Douce 368, fols. 80–83; an abbreviated version is in
NLA, II, 110–13.

whose suit he had persuaded his mother to reject; he too was portrayed as a martyred innocent.[23] The case of Eahlmund is more complex. He is described in an early annal as a prince killed *c.* 800 by order of King Eardwulf.[24] We might expect a martyred innocent; but this is not what Ealhmund's post-Conquest hagiographer provides. Instead he makes his subject a Northumbrian king slain in a battle which he enters to support the men of Wiltshire against the Mercians; martyrdom, because suffered in defence of a just cause, is presented as the fulfilment of royal duty.[25] The anomaly, it appears, derives from nothing more than hagiographical confusion. The author of the *Vita* seems, by misreading a crucial passage in the Worcester Chronicle, to have believed that he was dealing with a king killed in battle;[26] he went on to interpret that king's sanctity in the conventional way.

The distinct theoretical traditions encountered in the hagiogra-

[23] For Wigstan see Rollason, 'Cults of murdered royal saints', pp. 5–9. The saint is located at Repton by the *Secgan* (*Heiligen*, ed. Liebermann, p. 11). The *Vita* survives in three closely related versions, which, although late, may be founded upon the traditions current at Repton in the ninth century. The three versions are contained in the thirteenth-century MS Oxford, Bodleian Library, Rawlinson A. 287, in Gotha, Landesbibliothek, MS I. 81 and in London, BL, MS Harley 2253, of the fourteenth century. Of these the former, by Thomas of Marlborough, prior and later abbot of Evesham (d. 1236), is printed in *Chronicon abbatiae de Evesham*, ed. W. D. Macray, RS 29 (London, 1863), pp. 325–37.

[24] For this saint see Rollason, 'Cults of murdered royal saints', pp. 3–5; he is probably to be identified with the Ealhmund whose burial at Derby is recorded in the *Secgan* (*Heiligen*, ed. Liebermann, p. 11). His murder on the order of King Eardwulf is noted in an early annal incorporated into the Durham *Historia regum* (*Symeonis monachi opera omnia*, II, 30–68, at 45).

[25] The *Vita S. Aelkmundi regis* is contained in Gotha, Landesbibliothek, MS I. 81 and is printed by P. Grosjean, 'Codicis Gothani appendix', *AB* 58 (1940), 177–204, at 178–83. The saint's guiding principle, like that attributed by Abbo of Fleury to St Edmund (see above, p. 93) was the Biblical 'Ducem te constituerunt; noli extolli, sed esto in illis quasi unus ex illis.' The hagiographer explains (p. 181) that the *Wyltonienses* sought Ealhmund's support against the unjust incursions of the Mercians: 'Quod idem rex Northanimbrorum sanctissimus Aelcmundus libenter annuens et opus diu optatum votumque diucius cupitum implere desiderans, videlicet animam suam dare pro Christo, illud dominicum ante mentis sue oculos superduxerat quod in evangelio legitur: "Qui perdiderit animam suam propter me, salvam faciet eam." Unde in fide Christi Iesu ad pugnam letus accessit, gloriosum et super omnia desiderandum existimans et lucrum perhenne si contigerit pro fidelium tuicione illum occumbere'.

[26] See Rollason, 'Cults of murdered royal saints', p. 4, n. 13. The episode seems to be based on the account of the Battle of Kempsford given *s.a.* 800 in the Worcester Chronicle ('Florence of Worcester', *Chronicon ex chronicis*, I, 64). Here there is no reference to Ealhmund's participation in the battle, but the account is followed in the same entry by a sentence stating that Ealhmund, son of the Northumbrian king Alcred, was killed: 'Whereas the writer of the Worcester Chronicle does not seem to have connected this event with the battle, the writer of Ealhmund's *Vita* may have thought incorrectly that this was what was intended.'

phy of Edmund and Edward were therefore wholly typical of the Lives of England's saintly kings and princes. The theme in each case was selected in accordance with the actual or perceived circumstances of the saint's death. Martyrdom might be interpreted in a positive relation to the royal state if the saint died in battle against the heathen or in some activity which could be described as the pursuit of Christian royal duty against other, more delinquent Christians. If he died as the victim of political machinations over which he had no control, and in particular if he was politically handicapped by extreme youth, he would be located within the alternative tradition described here as that of the martyred innocent.[27]

The origin and early history of the cults of the *Secgan*'s men is more difficult to reconstruct. There is, however, a strong probability that each had its origin in the high politics of Anglo-Saxon England. The hands and arms of Oswald were taken by his brother and successor Oswiu to the Northumbrian *urbs regia* of Bamburgh, the head to Lindisfarne. The body was translated, apparently more than thirty years after the martyrdom, by Oswald's niece Osthryth, wife of Æthelred of Mercia, to the monastery of Bardney in Lindsey, where it was received with some reluctance by the monks, who quite reasonably pointed out that Oswald 'belonged to another kingdom and had once conquered them'.[28] More study is needed to place this cult within its historical and political context. It can however tentatively be suggested that within Oswald's own kingdom his relics may have formed an important symbol of Northumbrian identity and prestige; and it is unlikely that Osthryth's translation of the body to Bardney was without significance in the context of Northumbrian relations with Mercia and its satellite Lindsey.[29] For the cults of the murdered kings and prince political contexts have been cautiously suggested by David Rollason. The cult of Ealhmund at Derby may have been o

---

[27] For further interesting comment on this tradition, designated that of the 'boy victim cults', see Fell, 'Edward King and Martyr and the Anglo-Saxon hagiographic tradition pp. 8–11.   [28] *HE*, III, 6, 11, 24.

[29] For discussion of Oswald's cult in Northumbria see Folz, 'Saint Oswald', pp. 51–6 Osthryth's translation of her uncle to Bardney, a community which she founded i conjunction with her husband Æthelred of Mercia, might be interpreted as a gestu intended to smooth over old differences between the kingdoms of her father and h husband. Equally plausibly, it may have been intended to keep alive the memory Northumbrian heroism and Mercian misdeeds; Osthryth's eventual murder by th Mercian nobles indicates that some at least of her actions had been less than conciliator

significance in the context of political conflict between Cenwulf of
Mercia and Eardwulf of Northumbria, by whose order Ealhmund
had been slain: it may have emphasised 'the guilt of his killer and
may thus have helped Cenwulf to undermine Eardwulf's power'.[30]
The cult of Æthelbert of East Anglia at Hereford, if it originated in
the ninth century, 'is likely to have been injurious to the prestige of
Offa, who instigated the killing'.[31] Those of Wigstan and Kenelm,
particularly the former, may have been connected with the dynastic turmoil of Mercia in the ninth century.[32] More generally,
Rollason has suggested, the cults of the murdered royal saints may
have been connected with an ecclesiastically directed – and surely
also royally supported – campaign to condemn, and to limit the
consequences of, royal murder.[33]

The patterns suggested by the cults studied in the preceding
chapters were, then, by no means limited to those cults; rather they
dominated Anglo-Saxon royal hagiology in so far as this is represented by the saints who appear in the *Secgan* and in *þa halgan*. The
model of Anglo-Saxon royal sanctity which I have proposed has
not been fully tested and refined. The *Secgan*, although a
convenient tool for the isolation of individuals venerated as saints in
Anglo-Saxon England, is far from comprehensive. Many more
cults remain to be explored – and the analysis of each must begin
with the crucial and often difficult question 'Was this person
regarded as a saint by the Anglo-Saxons?' In particular a number of
cults which appear to stand outside the proposed model, and which
may require some modification of it, deserve special attention –
those of the infant prince Rumwold, the hermit prince Guthlac and
the elusive Osthryth and Æthelred spring most readily to mind.
The place of the monk-king within the Anglo-Saxon tradition is
likewise of special interest. The absence of monk-kings from the
English calendars and the apparent inclusion of Æthelred alone in
the *Secgan* suggests that saints of this type were not popular among
the Anglo-Saxons, and they accordingly find no place in the
proposed model; further study may necessitate some revision.

[30] Rollason, 'Cults of murdered royal saints'. p. 20; *Heiligen*, ed. Liebermann, p. 11.
[31] Rollason, 'Cults of murdered royal saints', p. 21; *Heiligen*, ed. Liebermann, p. 11.
[32] Rollason, 'Cults of murdered royal saints', pp. 19–20, 21. The cult of Æthelred and
   Æthelbert is particularly obscure. Rollason suggests (*ibid.*, p. 21) that it 'reflected badly on
   their murderer's master, King Egbert' but suggests no context for the utilisation of the
   cult in opposition to that king. In view of the fact that the cult was initially centred in the
   monastery of Wakering in Essex, it may have been of significance in political relations
   between Kent and the East Saxons.   [33] *Ibid.*, pp. 16–17.

More than this, the range of motives for cult-creation might be expanded; and more patterns of change over time may emerge. None the less the suggested model does seem to provide a useful instrument for the description of Anglo-Saxon royal sanctity. It enables the location of individual cults within a broader tradition. It may be of value in enhancing our understanding of those cults which can never be fully documented but about which at least a number of significant clues survive. And in revealing something of the general pattern which underlies the rich variety of the individual cults it adds depth to our understanding of the place of the royal saint within Anglo-Saxon society.

What, if anything, do the cults of the royal saints tell us about the place of the monarchy within that society? It was suggested by Górski in respect of Scandinavia and Eastern Europe that the cult of the saint king was created by the church only in those countries where the power of the monarchy was severely limited and specifically in order to bolster royal authority. The presence of saint kings accordingly implies a weak monarchy, their absence a strong and centralised royal power. The present study has been concerned with the relationships within Anglo-Saxon England of royal persons, living and dead, with each other and with the men and women of the church. From it has emerged a picture of a society quite different from that of the Górski model.

It would be at best misleading to describe the English royal cults as created by 'the church'. They were created by individual religious communities or by specific lay interest-groups or on occasion by both. In so far as they were sanctioned by bishops or archbishops, and in so far as they gained widespread popularity, they attained a place within the broader structure of the English church; but the interests which created them were essentially local or partisan – or both. Nor is it necessarily helpful to study the origin and use of those cults in terms of the 'strength' or 'weakness' of the monarchy. Certainly the cults of the Anglo-Saxon royal saints were used to further the political interests and to enhance the prestige of rulers. But it does not follow from this that the individual rulers in question were otherwise 'weak', still less that 'the monarchy' was so. What the royal cults most strikingly and consistently reveal is neither the 'strength' nor the 'weakness' of 'the monarchy': it is the social dominance within Anglo-Saxon England of kings and of royal dynasties.

The cults of the royal ladies were created in acknowledgement of their role in the church – more specifically in the monastic movement. As such they demonstrate the central importance of these women in the establishment, leadership and patronage of the religious life in England. More than this, these cults were created in the hope – perhaps, after the earliest generations, in the knowledge – that they would cement relationships between religious community and royal house, thus stimulating the patronage of successive generations of rulers and consorts. Royal involvement in and patronage of the religious life was, in short, important. The point is not new: it is apparent from Bede's account of the establishment of the church in England and from the provisions of the *Regularis concordia* for the royal oversight of England's religious houses. But it deserves emphasis. The preponderance of royal women among the female saints of Anglo-Saxon England is testimony to the social dominance within England of the royal dynasties;[34] in particular it is testimony to their dominance over the sources of patronage.

Kings Edmund and Edward remained after death as in life potent figures in the high politics of their former kingdoms; so too, it appears, did the other martyred kings and princes whose veneration is attested by the *Secgan*. The creation and utilisation of their cults reveals much of the dynamics of Anglo-Saxon history. The power of kings and royal dynasties was recurrently destabilised by conflict between kingdoms, by unsettled succession practices and by external invasion. None the less that power was the central fact of Anglo-Saxon society: political relations within and between kingdoms centred upon the succession to and expansion of royal power. The point is highlighted by reference to the general tradition of English sanctity. The Anglo-Saxons did not, to my knowledge, create a single martyred aristocrat; nor did they seek the sanctification of 'opposition to the king'.[35] Or, perhaps more accurately and more significantly, the cults of, for instance, Wigstan and Kenelm may suggest that when they did so that opposition was personified not in secular magnate or in rebellious churchman but in another former or 'potential' king – a representa-

---

34 Of the female saints listed in the *Secgan* only Edburga of Sout! .ell, Æthelburga of Barking, Æthelflaed and Maerwyn of Romsey, and perhaps Os th (see above, n. 16) seem not to have been of royal birth.

35 For the somewhat different tradition of a later age see J. C. Russell, 'The canonization of opposition to the king in Angevin England', in C. H. Taylor (ed.), *Anniversary essays in mediaeval history . . . presented to C. H. Haskins* (Boston, Mass., and New York, 1929), pp. 279–90.

tive of or symbol for one party in a political dispute which was dynastic in character. The power of Anglo-Saxon kingship was limited; its importance was not.

There can be little doubt that the creation of a royal saint might further the immediate political objectives of a ruler, might enhance the prestige of a dynasty and might go some way towards conferring legitimacy upon a fictive successor.[36] And there can be little doubt that the church sanctioned this political use of the royal cult. It did so not in order to shore up an otherwise feeble monarchy but in recognition of the centrality of royal power. Royal power, by which I mean kingly authority in conjunction with the resources of royal dynasties, had been shown to be essential to the foundation and prosperity of the church in England; what the church contributed to that power it accordingly contributed with a shrewd awareness of where its own best interests lay.

The church in promoting or sanctioning the cults of the royal saints not only acknowledged and reinforced the social dominance of kings and royal dynasties. It also gave voice to its own interpretation of kingship and society. Most obviously it was able through the Lives of the royal saints to promulgate ecclesiastically defined concepts of good rulership. Thus the martyred kings became models of an idealised Christian kingship, and the Lives of the royal ladies might sketch in some detail the correct role of the royal female within the world as well as dwelling upon her withdrawal from it. More than this, the Lives and cults of these royal ladies, in glorifying such withdrawal, emphasised the desirability of monasticism as an influential career choice or second career. This naturally redounded to the advantage of the church, which sought to benefit from royal involvement in the monastic movement. It also may have contributed something to political stability. There came a time in the career of many royal ladies when withdrawal from the world was not only virtuous but also politically desirable; ecclesiastical glorification of such withdrawal could only have reinforced this traditional way of solving potentially destabilising

---

[36] A recent article by David Rollason offers a wider view of the political advantages which the Anglo-Saxon kings were able to derive from their promotion of the cults of saints both English and other: 'Relic-cults as an instrument of royal policy *c.* 900–*c.* 1050', *ASE* 15 (1986), 91–103. See also Rollason, 'The shrines of saints in later Anglo-Saxon England: distribution and significance', in R. Morris (ed.), *The Anglo-Saxon church: papers on history, architecture and archaeology in honour of Dr H. M. Taylor*, Council for British Archaeology, Research Report 60 (London, 1986), pp. 32–43.

dynastic problems. If the withdrawal of royal ladies tended to avert political crises, the abdication of kings was likely to create them. The reluctance of the church to encourage such abdication may perhaps underlie the apparent reluctance of the Anglo-Saxons to make saints of their monk- or pilgrim-kings. Finally, the murder of kings or potential kings might likewise generate or exacerbate political instability; ecclesiastical promotion of the cults of murdered royal saints may accordingly have formed part of a programme to condemn royal murder and to limit its social consequences.

In the centuries between the conversion and the coming of the Normans the royal saint was a familiar and important figure in English church and English society. The relics and the cults of men and women of royal birth brought prestige both to religious communities and to royal dynasties; they also formed important foci for the working out of relations between those communities and dynasties and between the several kingdoms and dynasties of Anglo-Saxon England. The Norman invasion of 1066 destroyed for ever the political context within which those cults had been formed. But it did not destroy, or even attempt to destroy, the cults themselves.

We cannot begin to understand the relationship of Norman churchman and Anglo-Saxon saint unless first we divest ourselves of what, on examination, dissolves into a myth of Norman scepticism. The royal cults with which this study has been concerned – like those of other saints throughout England – survived and even prospered in the decades following 1066.[37] Only rarely is it possible to trace in any detail the mechanism of their survival. Where it is, the most striking attribute of the Norman churchmen is not their scepticism towards, their contempt of or their hostility to the English saints: rather it is their businesslike readiness to make the heroes of the past serve the politics of the present.

At Ely and Bury St Edmunds the churchmen of the Norman era accepted the cults of the Anglo-Saxon saints, adapted those cults in accordance with the changing requirements of a new age, recorded that adaptation in new Lives and miracle collections, and actively encouraged the diffusion of cult. They were not alone in this. The

---

[37] For more general treatment of this subject see Ridyard, *'Condigna ueneratio'*.

cults of the West Saxon royal saints seem to have been similarly acknowledged, if less assiduously promoted, following 1066. And, more generally, the northern saint Cuthbert was of central importance in Norman Durham;[38] possession of St Mildrith's relics was hotly disputed between two of the religious communities of post-Conquest Canterbury;[39] and Archbishop Lanfranc himself, whatever his initial reservations, seems to have been an important promoter of the cults of saints Ælfheah and Dunstan.[40] The Norman adoption of the Anglo-Saxon saints cannot be explained simply as a public relations exercise intended to diminish tensions between Normans and English within the post-Conquest religious communities – though this may well have been among its consequences. Nor is there any evidence that these saints were foisted upon the Norman ecclesiastical leaders by aggressively English factions among their subjects. Nor indeed does it appear that the cults of the English royal saints were accorded any specific value in the high politics of the Anglo-Norman realm. The key lies rather in the status and function of the saint as monastic patron. As such that saint was a crucial part of the equipment used by the religious community in the definition both of its internal relations and of its relations with external secular and ecclesiastical powers. The legend and cult of the saint were essential to the proper functioning of the religious community; and the Norman churchmen had nothing to gain by rendering their communities incapable of functioning properly. Accordingly there was created in the years following 1066 a powerful coalition of continental churchman and Anglo-Saxon saint in opposition to the threats posed variously by Norman aristocrat, by English layman, by Norman bishop, by rival religious house and on occasion by rebellious monk.[41] There was no place in the Anglo-Norman realm for the alignment of Norman monk and Norman layman against Anglo-Saxon saint.

[38] See *ibid.*, pp. 196–200.
[39] See Rollason, *Mildrith legend*, pp. 21–2, 62–8. The quarrel was between the community of St Augustine's and the canons of St Gregory's priory, which had been founded in 1084 by Archbishop Lanfranc: it is interesting to note that it seems to have been started by the latter community.
[40] See Ridyard, '*Condigna veneratio*', pp. 200–4.
[41] For the latter see the Life of St Dunstan by Osbern (*Memorials of Saint Dunstan*, ed. Stubbs, pp. 144–53, 155–6): a monk Egelward goes mad, threatens to spread scandal about the community and is finally cured through the intercession of St Dunstan, Lanfranc himself being among those who advise supplication at the saint's tomb; a monk Edward seeks to return to the world and is prevented from doing so by St Dunstan.

THE LIFE OF ST EDBURGA OF WINCHESTER BY OSBERT OF CLARE, PRIOR OF WESTMINSTER

(Oxford, Bodleian Library, MS Laud Misc. 114, fols. 85–120)

INTRODUCTION

The manuscript

The earliest extant *Vita* of St Edburga of Winchester, composed in the twelfth century by Osbert of Clare, is preserved in Oxford, Bodleian Library, MS Laud Misc. 114 (fols. 85–120).[1] The manuscript comprises 170 leaves;[2] its collation is as follows: 1^8–4^8, 5^8 (7 cancelled), 6^8–11^8, 12^8 (wants 1), 13^8–14^8, 15^6 (wants 6), 16^8–21^8, 22^8 (3, 4, 8 cancelled). Its average page size is 260×165 mm., although quires 20 and 21 average about 259×160 mm. The size of the written space varies considerably.[3] Quires 1–3, containing Augustine's *De doctrina Christiana*, have thirty lines to the page; elsewhere thirty-one is general.

The manuscript, containing in addition to the Augustine work a series of hagiographical texts,[4] seems to be of Pershore provenance.

---

[1] For description of the MS see *SC*, no. 1547; H. O. Coxe, *Catalogi codicum manuscriptorum Bibliothecáe Bodleianae*, II (Laudian MSS) (Oxford, 1858; repr. 1973), 122, no. 114; O. Pächt and J. J. G. Alexander, *Illuminated manuscripts in the Bodleian Library Oxford*, 3 vols. (Oxford, 1966–73), III (1973), 18, no. 151; Ker, *Medieval libraries*, p. 150. The card list from which *Medieval libraries* was compiled is available for consultation in the Bodleian Library. I am indebted for help in the following analysis of the MS to the kind advice of Dr Martin Brett and Dr Michael Franklin.

[2] The MS is wrongly foliated to give a total of 186 numbered folios. Of these, fols. 23, 49, and 65 are doubled and fols. 98v, 99v, 111–19 and 121–9 are omitted; fols. i, ii, 185 and 186 are flyleaves.

[3] The average size of the written space in the *Vita Edburge* (fols. 85–120) is approximately 195×126 mm.

[4] The contents of the MS are as follows (each item starts a new quire, except items 4, 5, 7, 9, 11):

1 Augustine, *De doctrina Christiana* (fols. 1v–23v bis); the work ends incomplete.

2 Incipiunt miracula in vita sancti Andree apostoli' (fols. 24–37v; fol. 38 is blank).

3 'Incipit passio sancti Vincentii martiris' (fols. 39–61v).

4 'Incipit vita siue passio sancti Ignacii episcopi. Quod est kalendas Februarii' (fols. 61v–65v).

5 'Incipit passio sancti Blassii [sic] episcopi et martiris' (fols. 65v–68v).

6 'Incipit vita sancti Willelmi confessoris' (fols. 69–81v). This is followed on fol. 81v by two short prayers to the saint.

7 An unfinished Life of St Audoen. Coxe (*Quarto catalogues*, II, 122, no. 114) identifies this item as containing two Lives, the first of St Audoen, the second of saints Ado, Rado and Dado. The identification is complicated by the absence of rubrication in this part of the MS, but it seems that we have rather a general prologue to a Life of St Audoen, followed by a list of contents (in which reference is made to two brothers of the saint, Rado and Dado), the first chapter described in this list and an unfinished second chapter. The item occupies fols. 82–84.

8 'Incipit epistola in vita et translatione et miraculis beate uirginis Ædburge premissa' (fols. 85–120).

9 A fragment on St Thomas of Canterbury (fol. 120v). The two remaining folios of this quire, numbered 130 and 131, are blank.

10 'Incipit prologus in uita sancte Frideswide uirginis' (fols. 132–140).

11 'Incipit prologus in uita sancte Wenefrede uirginis et martyris' (fols. 140–163v). The *Vita* was written by 'Rotbertus ... cenobii Salopesberiensis prior' and was dedicated to Warin, dean or prior of Worcester (fol. 140).

12 'Incipit prologus in vita sancte Katerine uirginis' (fols. 164–184).

N. R. Ker attributes it to that house on palaeographical grounds, and notes that the list of contents is in the same hand as that of Oxford, St John's College, MS 96, a manuscript known to have connections with Pershore.[5] A late medieval hand has scribbled 'Pershor' on fol. 23. These indications of Pershore origin are of course corroborated by the inclusion of the *Vita Edburge*, composed specifically for the Pershore monks.[6]

The manuscript is written in several hands of the second half of the twelfth century,[7] changes occurring, for instance, at fols. 24, 39, 55 and 69. Nor are these changes, together with the variations in line numbers and page size noted above, the only indications of discontinuity within the manuscript. Variations occur also in the method of ruling[8] and especially in the system of rubrication. For instance, the account of St Andrew is rubricated throughout in red, the items concerning saints Vincent, Ignatius, Blaise and William have no rubricated capitula, and the account of St Audoen has spaces for an elaborate scheme of colour which was never carried out. The Life of St Edburga is characterised by unusually elaborate initials in red, blue and green[9] and by a consistent system of rubrication in red as far as chapter 11 (fol. 95v).[10]

The list of contents indicates that the hagiographical portion of the manuscript formed a united whole in the second half of the twelfth century; and the several hands in the manuscript appear to be closely related. There are three clear units within the manuscript – that of the Vincent/Ignatius/Blaise material, that concerning saints William and Audoen, and that of the Frideswide/Wenefred Lives. Within each of these units, the Lives are presented in the

---

5 Ker, *Medieval libraries*, p. 150; also Ker, 'Sir John Prise', *The Library*, Fifth Series 10 (1955), 1–24, at 20.   6 See above, pp. 21–37 *passim*.

7 The Becket fragment on fol. 120v must have been written after Becket's martyrdom in December 1170. It appears, however, to be in a different hand from the Edburga material which precedes it and it may have been added to the 'spare' leaf at a slightly later date; it cannot be used to demonstrate that the MS as a whole was produced after 1170. The fragment cannot be identified with any of the extant Lives of St Thomas, although it shares a prologue with an anonymous Life contained in London, Lambeth Palace Library, MS 135: see *Materials for the history of Thomas Becket*, ed. Robertson, IV (1879), xiv, 80.

8 The Augustine section is ruled on the skin side only in dry point and has two long lines at top and bottom; St Andrew is ruled on both sides with a coloured implement and has only one line top and bottom; subsequent sections follow varying practice.

9 On the initials of this MS see Pächt and Alexander, *Illuminated manuscripts*, III, 18, no. 151.

10 Thereafter only chapter 17 (fol. 101) is rubricated, although spaces have been left throughout for continued rubrication.

natural order of the *sanctorale* – 22 January, 1 and 3 February; 28 May and 24 August; 19 October and 3 November.[11] One further point is of some interest. Osbert of Clare cites 'pridie Idus Octobris' as the date for the feast of St Edburga's translation to Pershore.[12] Osbert's *Vita Edburge*, although forming an independent unit within the manuscript, is incorporated immediately before the Frideswide/Wenefred material – in, that is, the correct *sanctorale* order for the Pershore feast of the saint.[13] Throughout the manuscript therefore the saints follow a possible pattern of the church's year, starting with St Andrew on 30 November and working through to St Katherine on 25 November. Together these points strongly suggest that the manuscript may comprise fragments of a martyrology undertaken by a group of scribes working in a single scriptorium. The positioning of the *Vita Edburge* within the compilation, moreover, provides important corroboration of the suggestion that those scribes were working at or for the community of Pershore.

The manuscript seems to have remained at Pershore until the Dissolution, when it passed into the hands of Sir John Prise.[14] Prise was related by marriage to Thomas Cromwell and was one of the men appointed by him to visit the monasteries in 1535 and 1539. Ker notes that most of his theological manuscripts were probably obtained 'from the monastic libraries at the moment of the Dissolution, since nearly all of them seem to have come from the West of England houses which the commissioners visited in December 1539 and January 1540, and from St Guthlac's, Hereford, the buildings of which Prise himself leased and then purchased'.[15] Prise be-

---

[11] Together the Vincent/Ignatius/Blaise items occupy quires 6–9: the fact that neither the Ignatius nor the Blaise material commences at the beginning of a new quire suggests that the three items were conceived and committed to writing as a unit. It is likely that each of these three items was intended specifically for use on the feast day of the saint concerned. Hence the prayer which follows the Life of St Vincent commences with reference to the celebration of the saint's festival (fol. 54v), the Life of Ignatius includes the date of the saint's festival in its rubric (see above, n. 4) and concludes with a reference to the celebration of the festival (fol. 65v) and the Life of Blaise likewise ends with reference to the saint's festival (fol. 68v). The William/Audoen and Frideswide/Wenefred materials form comparable units, occupying quires 10–11 and 16–19 respectively.

[12] Bodl. Laud Misc. 114, fol. 110v.

[13] It is worth noting too that the Life of St Katherine (of Alexandria), although likewise an independent unit, is incorporated immediately following the Frideswide/Wenefred material and therefore in the correct *sanctorale* order for the observance of her feast on 25 November.

[14] Ker, 'Sir John Prise', p. 14.   [15] *Ibid.*, p. 5.

queathed his theological manuscripts to Hereford cathedral, and from there many of them found their way to Jesus College, Oxford. A list of these manuscripts was copied, probably in 1621 or 1622, into a memorandum book of College affairs; it includes a volume entitled *Miracula sancti Andreae et aliorum* — the present Laud Misc. 114.[16] An inscription, 'Liber Guilielmi Laud. Archiepi'. Cantuar'. et Cancellarii Universitatis Oxon' 1635', testifies to the archbishop's acquisition of the manuscript, probably in that year:[17] it was among a large collection of manuscripts donated by him to the Bodleian Library on 16 June 1636.[18]

The present edition

In the present edition of the *Vita Edburge* the spelling has been retained throughout in the forms appearing in the manuscript. However, the forms 'e' and 'ę', which are very inconsistently used, are without exception rendered 'e'. Capitalisation and punctuation have been modernised. The chapter divisions are those of the manuscript; the chapter numbers have been added for ease of reference. The notes include references to Osbert's most direct quotations from or allusions to the Bible; those passages where Osbert employs Biblical diction indirectly have not been noted.

---

[16] *Ibid.*, p. 12. The list occupies fols. 42–43 of a volume entitled *Register 1602*, a memorandum book written mainly between 1602 and 1630. Ker notes that the list is probably in the hand of Eubule Thelwall, Principal of the College from 1621 until 1630.

[17] See Coxe, *Quarto catalogues*, II, ix.   [18] *Ibid.*, pp. xii, xxxvi.

Incipit epistola[1] *in vita et translatione et miraculis beate uirginis
Ædburge premissa*

Fidelibus sancte matris ecclesie filiis[2] in Anglorum regno per loca
dispersis, conciuis et cooperator eorum per eam que in Spiritu
Sancto est adoptionem et fidem, Osbertus municipii Clarensis
appellatus indigena,[a][3] utriusque uite felicitatem et pacem.

Dedi nouis studiis operam nouam Deo inspirante complexus
phylosophiam, ut de beate uirginis Eadburge angelica
conuersatione purpuram conficerem, unde in passionibus Christi
efficaciter appetendis, integritatem castarum mentium toga sancte
mortificationis ornarem. Imitabile autem prebetur in eius uita
cunctis audientibus documentum, quanto amoris desiderio flagrare
debeat anima fidelis ad celum. Regia namque uirgo decorata
egregie puritatis titulo, sic per diuersas partes orbis diuersis
choruscat in Christo miraculis, ut admiretur mundus ipsius radios
claritatis.[4] Quia uero[5] illius gesta confuso uidebantur sermone
contexta, nec in eis ordo uenustus radiabat insertus, precibus
deuinctus seniorum Persorensis ecclesie, inculta studui diligentius
elimare. Ut enim Seneca Cordubensis ait, 'sepe bona materia cessat
sine artifice',[6] oratoris igitur color rethoricus hac maiestate debet
excellere, ut in elegantia uerborum puritas sit aperta, et in
compositione constructio respondeat equaliter perpolita, et in
dignitate refloreat sententia pulchra uarietate distincta. Et cum tria
sint orationis genera, grauis figura scilicet mediocris et attenuata, sic
medium terere penes me decretum est tramitem, ut ad locutionis
infimum non decurram sermonem. Artifex siquidem nouus in hac

---

[a] *marginal note in later hand adds* Claruit sub rege Stephano
[1] This introductory *epistola* is printed in *Letters*, pp. 179–82 (no. 43).
[2] For the possibility that Osbert's work was put out in two versions, or at least with two
introductions, see above, p. 37, n. 101.
[3] Osbert was a native of Clare in Suffolk. Aspects of his career are discussed above, pp. 20–5
and full references are provided at p. 17, n. 19. Osbert describes his origin in similar terms
in a letter to the monks of Ely: 'Excellentissimi senatus Elyensis ecclesiæ ingenuis patribus,
municipii Clarensis indigena, consenator capitolii eorum, Osbertus' (*Letters*, p. 116, lines
5–7 (no.33)). This letter, which concerns a Shropshire miracle of St Æthelthryth, is
incorporated into the *Liber Eliensis* as Bk III, c. 43.
[4] Cf. notes 118 and 138 below. Cf. also *Letters*, p. 116, lines 8–12 (no. 33), with reference to
the miracles of St Æthelthryth.
[5] 'Quia uero . . . post triumphum': this passage strongly suggests that Osbert's *Vita Edburge*
was conceived as a re-working of an earlier hagiographical source. For this source, and
for Osbert's association with the Worcestershire community of Pershore, see above,
pp. 21–2.
[6] Seneca, *Ep.* XLVII, c. 16. For Osbert's use of Seneca see *Letters*, p. 228; L. D. Reynolds, *The
medieval tradition of Seneca's letters* (Oxford, 1965), p. 117.

suscepi constitutione cum beniuolentia persuadere, ut opus recens legentes non fastidient, nec facta diuisione erga insolita animosius insolescant. Quod namque prius ueteres protulerunt sub uno, modernis a me temporibus / sectum est in duo, ut uite uirginalis opera que gessit in corpore, luculenter resplendeant insigni nouitate; sicque sequatur secundo iocunda translatio, ut ad scribendi concitum recurrant articulum, que per illam miracula Deus operatus est post triumphum.

Licet enim per partes in suis sit diuisa reliquiis, uirtus tamen eius tota abundat in singulis. Wintoniensibus prebet in maiore sui corporis portione presidium, Persorenses exornat gloria celestium frequentata signorum. Nec succensere decet sacras uirgines prerogatiua castitatis insignes, que in dotali uirginis arce uersantur Wintonie, quod alibi prefulget densa miraculorum[b] claritate. Ibi namque illarum magnificatur excellentia, ubi precellentis Eadburge laus est magnificata; eoque honoris et glorie eis cumulatur Deo operante solatium, quo incorruptibilis uirgo et celebris in suis uirtutibus accepit incrementum.[c] Ea de causa dignum non estimo quiddam pretermittere, quod disposita ratione sacratis Deo uirginibus debet complacere. Sicut caritas ignita Persorensis ecclesie coegit ut scriberem, sic familiaris dulcedo et singularis dilectio sanctarum Wintoniensium feminarum compulit ut dictarem.[7]

Nec[8] in hoc anime sepulchro me Lethei fluminis inebriauit obliuio, quin uobis reuelem que ante annos quindecim felix et egregia uirgo mihi contulit, dum adhuc incognita festiua me apparitione insigniuit. Videbatur mihi eoquidem temporis spatio extra fines uirtutis in secularibus negotiis constituto, quod in oratorio Persorensis cenobii quod nunquam introieram, ante maius altare in deuotis precibus peruigil excubabam. Cum erectus in pedibus lacrimisque madens uberibus, choruscho splendore uernantem Eadburgam aspexi Dei sponsam uirginem, in illo quo sua imago constituta est loco, meque familiari inuisere dignatam oraculo. Ornata stabat undique in fimbriis aureis diuersa gemmarum uarietate respersis,[9] togaque qua uestiebatur erat purpurea, et sandalia preferebat diuersitate artificiosa / ultra quod usus habet intexta. Tantaque leticie conuenientia radiabat in uultu,

---

[b] miraraculorum *MS*   [c] *erasure MS; corr. in margin*
[7] For discussion of Osbert's association with the Winchester nuns see above, pp. 22–3.
[8] 'Nec . . . excubabam': on this passage see above, p. 17, n. 19.
[9] Cf. Ps. 44:14; cf. also *Vita Edwardi*, p. 75, line 27.

tamque honesta maturitas disponebatur in gestu, ut scribenti mihi sit inexplicabilis pars maior et celebrior illius beate uisionis. Meminisse tamen iuuat quod dextro pede coturnum eruit deauratum, quem inuiolata uirgo alacriter protulit, et ad me usque in pauimento proiecit. 'Accipe', inquit, 'hoc donatiuum quod hodie cedit in premium, aliud iterum tribuam quod potiorem tibi cedet ad profectum.' His dictis a sompno expergefactus euigilo, miroque et ineffabili modo sacram mihi apparuisse obstupesco uirginem, cuius uitam prius nusquam habueram familiarem. Interpretentur igitur alii quod estimant, ego uero de sompnio dicam quod sencio. Prescierat fortasse me in laboribus uite sue debere manus extendere, et cum qua communicare debere sudores in scribendo, miserationibus Domini per eam communicandum esset in premio.

Dirigere proinde oportet cotidiana operationis mee uestigia, et ex precedentium patrum exemplis tanquam ex mortuorum animalium coriis actus meos circumdare, ut inter pulchros pedes euangelizantium pacem,[10] pedum meorum gressus ualeam premunire. Confido autem in Domino, quod agenti in extremis gloriosa uirgo et felix stratam mihi Eadburga preparabit auream, ubi sanctorum agmina plateas Ierusalem[11] possident pretiosis lapidibus auroque constratas. In illa namque plenitudine gaudiorum serenam eius faciem concupisco cernere, que tam preclara uisione mihi solempniter dignata est apparere. Hoc itaque oro ut inuiolate uirginis iocunda promissio, sic spiritualis glorie mihi tribuat excellentiam, ut pro temporalis commodi felicitate transitoria, gloriam superne[d] beatitudinis non amittam.

Sed quid dico? Vulturis enim aspera et infesta crudelitas, iecur in me misere rodit conscientie, et interiora mentis admissi sceleris recordatio laniat, quem per seculares curas peccatrix conscientia terribiliter accusat. Ipsa contra huiusmodi insidiantes adhibeat presidium, que se castitatis iuge prebet exemplum. Nec opponat mihi quisquam / me tante non existere auctoritatis hominem, ut uitam describere debeam uirginalem, cum in ecclesia nec extulerit cathedra, nec fasces in re publica consulares dignitas patricia per me sit assecuta. Respondeo insolentie huiusmodi uoce philosophi,[e] quod patricius Socrates non fuit, et Cleantes undas extrahens rigandis holeribus manus prebuit, quodque Platonem non accepit nobilem

---

[d] superni *MS*   [e] *corr. from* philosophie *MS*
[10] Cf. Rom. 10:15.   [11] Cf. Ier. 7:17, 34; 44:6, 17.

phylosophyam^f sed fecit.[12] Quanuis et inter ingenuous aui mei numerati sint et proaui, et adhuc qui uidentur in carne superstites, generosi resplendeant inter uiros illustres. Suscipite itaque epistolam et in capite libri prefigite illam, cuius cum superficies grata Minerue pinguedine non eluceat, accepta dulcedine celestis sponse sapidius innotescat. Orationum ergo uestrarum suffragia pretendite, meque merita beate et gloriose uirginis Eadburge una cum redemptis, participem faciat felicitatis eterne. Opus itaque presens distinctum est capitulis, quemadmodum uita eius uirtutibus distincta est pretiosis. *Explicit epistola.*

Incipit prologus in uita beate et gloriose uirginis Ædburge

Apud Albanos[13] in templo Veste legimus ueterem uirgines tenuisse consuetudinem, ut ante dee simulachrum obseruarent ignem perpetuum mechanica arte confictum, castaque corpora in iuuentute gererent, et cum maturescent uirorum amplexibus se se copularent. Si uero aliqua clam uirginitate priuata nesciretur esse corrupta, extincto igne celari non poterat, cuius infesta adulterio ne hanc quidem conspiceret, Vesta suis oculis manus proprias opponebat. Unde et Rea uirgo uestalis que et aliis Ilia uel Siluia dicta est nominibus, coloratis poetarum mendaciis in sompno a Marte uiolata describitur, sicque Remum pariter et conditorem urbis Romulum dum ad diluenda sacra aquas hausisset, uno concubitu concepisse memoratur. In cuius reditu oculis dea manum opposuit, et ignem in momento totum extinxit. Non est igitur alienum si ex urtica lilium prodeat, cum de spina rubens rosa excellenter erumpat,[14] quia et in luto aurum queritur, et / pretiosa margarita in uilibus conchis et arena maris inuenitur. Faciamus proinde quod in exitu Israel de Egypto Domino precipiente legimus accidisse, et ex spoliis gentium catholice nostras adornemus historias, sicut mulieres Israhelitas mulieres spoliasse docemur Egyptias.[15]

Gloriosam enim ciuitatem Dei Eadburgam suscepimus temporaliter adornandam, quam in celestibus castris eternaliter a Christo non dubitamus ornatam. Hoc enim nominis eius ethimologia resonat, quod felix uel beata ciuitas Anglice dicitur, de

fol. 87

---

^f phylosophya *MS*

[12] Cf. Seneca, *Ep.* xliv, c. 3.

[13] 'Apud Albanos . . . totum extinxit': cf. Ovid, *Fasti*, iii, 1–48. Cf. also *Letters*, pp. 157–61 (no. 42), to Alice (or Adelildis), abbess of Barking (d. 1166; *Heads*, p. 208). On the use of Ovid by writers of the eleventh and twelfth centuries see *Letters*, p. 226 and references therein cited.   [14] Cf. Is. 34:13; Cant. 2:2.   [15] Exod. 12:35–6.

qua mille clipei dependent omnis armatura fortium,[16] proposita scilicet fidelibus omnia propugnacula uel munimenta uirtutum. Que ignem Sancti Spiritus in templo pectoris sui obseruauit eternum, nec ulla eum extincxit impudicicia, dum cum Dina non consensit ut fieret impudica.[17] Ab infantia didicit uirginitatem colere, quam uirgo mater misericorditer respexit, nec pro aliquo uiolati pudoris atramento, oculos ab ea misericordes auertit. Affirmare et enim autentico ueritatis possumus argumento, quod Christo uirginis filio et uirginum sponso uirginitas ualde displicet impudenter amissa, quando fabulosis commentis gentilium, dee etiam Veste ministra sua displicuit a Marte corrupta. Hoc itaque Christianas et sanctas uirgines decet imitari, ut quod ad uirtutis formam ab ethnicis tractum feminis auditur, ad correctionem morum subtilius transferatur. In hac enim unica phenice nostra que se in passione Christi celestibus cum illo aromatibus incendit, et iuuentutem suam uelut aquila apud fontem ueri luminis immortaliter renouauit,[18] pura intentione dicendi constituamus initium, ut finis redoleat aromatum floribus eternorum. Obseruandum tamen quod apud ethnicos iuuencule uirgines ministrabant, et dum circa senectutem deberent proficere, ad carnales amplexus cogebantur animos inclinare. Sed que celorum dominam et terrarum reginam Christianis temporibus sacre uirgines insecuntur, sic a bono uirginitatis proposito humiliter inchoant, ut in melius proficientes, diem sue uocationis optimo fine uite concludant. Igitur ignis ille celestis qui in anima beate uirginis Eadburge serenus illuxit, ita fulgore suo mentem dictantis illuminet, ut per eum gloriosam eius uitam audientes, ad amorem sponse celestis inflammet. *Explicit prologus.*

fol. 87v

[1] *Incipit uita sancte Ædburge uirginis*

Imperante populo Anglorum Dei prouidentia cultore eius Aluredo Aðulfi regis filio,[19] religionis per hunc disciplina in mentibus fidelium disseminata conualuit, et tanquam noui solis[20] claritas doctrina ueritatis infusa reluxit. Cuius in Scripturis tanta legitur extitisse scientia, ut in phylosophie[g] studiis ad unguem usque perfecte disertus orator existeret, et facundus interpres totum fere

---

[g] phylophie *MS*

[16] Cf. Cant. 4:4.   [17] Cf. Gen. 34.   [18] Cf. Ps. 102:5.

[19] Alfred, king of Wessex (871–99), son of King Æthelwulf (839–58).

[20] Cf. *Letters*, p. 64, line 27 (no. 6), to Anselm, abbot of Bury St Edmunds (1121–38, 1138–48; *Heads*, p. 32).

Appendix 1

testamentum in idioma lingue paterne transferret.[21] Inter cetera
uero pietatis que consueuit exercere negotia, gratia ei inspirante
diuina, nouum Wintonie incepit monasterium, quod nunc extra
muros urbis amplioribus spatiis constat collocatum.[22] Emulata est
etiam regia coniunx Alhswiða Dei emulatione bonum opus uiri, ut
sacrarum uirginum felicibus auspiciis prouideret sanctimonie,
fieretque deuota Deo in noua edificatione laudabilis structure.[23]
Cui loco mire sanctitatis feminam prefecit Eðeldridam,[24] rusque
possessionis amplissime arcis fundum contulit, et sanctimoniales
feminas in monasterio collocauit.

Sed neuter amborum prohibentibus fatis potuit perficere quod
deuota ante Deum proposuerant intentione complere. Quorum
predicande filius excellens memorie senior Eduuardus, cum sceptro
post patrem premineret in regno, finem nouis imposuit
fundamentis, et compleuit opus paterne deuotionis.[25] Hic stabili et
sancto precellentis regine donatus conubio, filiam in ea ex carne sua
genuit, quam Eadburgam uocari facta natiuitate imperauit. Sacro
uero baptismate perfusa, in etate tenera cum ethymologia gloriosi
nominis, concinnant dona gratie omnipotentie creatricis. Eadburga
autem felix uel beata ciuitas lingua Anglorum dicitur, in qua
sanctarum uirtutum exercitus triumphali maiestate collocatur.

[2] *De preciosis ornamentis ecclesie, que secularibus pretulit
ornamentis*

Educatur uirgo regia parentis utriusque diligenti sollicitudine, et
claritas Dei illam illuminat, et ad profectum uite mores eius

---

[21] The twelfth-century *Liber Eliensis* states (i, 39) that Æthelred was succeeded by Alfred,
'Qui acer ingenii per Grimbaldum et Iohannem doctissimos monachos tantum instructus
est ut in brevi librorum omnium notitiam haberet totumque Novum et Vetus
Testamentum in eulogiam Anglice gentis transmutaret.' This statement is probably the
result of a false reading of William of Malmesbury's statement that 'plurimam partem
Romanæ Bibliothecæ Anglorum auribus dedit' (*GR*, i, 132; see C. Plummer, *The life and
times of Alfred the Great* (Oxford, 1902), pp. 150–1). A translation of the Scriptures is not
conventionally included among the literary works ascribed to Alfred (see Stenton, *ASE*,
pp. 270–6, especially pp. 272–5).

[22] New Minster, Winchester; the community moved from its city-centre site to Hyde
in 1110 (*Annales de Wintonia*, p. 43; KH, p. 81). For the foundation of this house see above,
p. 31 and n. 78; for aspects of the community's history see above, pp. 97, 106, 111–12,
115–19, 124, 125–6.

[23] St Mary's abbey, or Nunnaminster, Winchester. The abbey was apparently founded on
an urban estate belonging to Alfred's consort, Ealhswith. For its foundation and history
see above, pp. 31–5, ch. 4.

[24] Osbert's treatment of the abbatial succession to Nunnaminster is discussed above,
pp. 33–5.

[25] Edward the Elder, king of Wessex (899–924). For his role in the foundation and
endowment of the religious houses of Winchester see above, pp. 31–3, 97–8, 99–101.

informat. Procedente itaque tempore paternus in eam declinat affectus omnino, nec recordatur sullimitatis regie, dum consuescit infantule frequenter assidere. Applaudit puellule / in regali residens solio, quiddamque in illa sanctum presagit ac diuinum, uelud eum celeste edocuisset oraculum.

fol. 88

Cumque trima esset etate et infantia cresceret, in ea dignatur[h] experiri spiritus Domini, cuius frons anime eius caractere debuisset insigniri.[26] Imperat igitur rex hinc indumenta consterni regalia, illinc ecclesiastica componi citius ornamenta, textum uidelicet euangelicum, et patenam et calicem, secusque consistere precepit infantem. Edoceri gestit pater utrum suspirare delectetur ad seculum, an spiritualiter anhelare contendat ad Christum. Que coniectis infans oculis cum presens attenderet, omisit instrumenta attrectare feminea, ecclesiastica per Spiritum Sanctum edocta discernere sacramenta. Appositis autem ecclesiasticis Eadburga felix incumbit ornamentis, et quod tenera per etatem discernere non ualebat infantia, instruebat efficaciter Spiritus Sancti disciplina.[27]

Gratulatur itaque princeps quod quasi celesti filia sua informatur oraculo, eiusque ad amorem Dei cuncti circumstantes animantur exemplo. Venerantur in illa et amplexantur indolem sacram cernentibus amabilem, magnamque futuris temporibus opinantur et predicant eius religionem. Laudat pater Dei onmipotentiam, benedicit ineffabilem eius gratuitam gratiam, que dono largitatis sue etatem teneram preuenit, et infantiles medullas ad ardorem diuine seruitutis accendit. Mandat exin conseruanda monastice rex insignis ornamenta familie, ut cum ablactationis tempus occurreret, in huiusmodi studiis animos puellares ante Dei oculos oblectaret.

Subtractis uero in modico nutricis uberibus, deuote Deo femine Edeldrithe committitur, cuius instantia sacris litterarum apicibus informatur. Ebibit nectar ethereum uirgo regia, et crescit cotidie proficiens in doctrina. Codex autem ille euangelicus de quo premisi superius, auro et argento furentibus per Angliam Danis exuitur,[28] sed diuturno postmodum tempore per Alfgheuam Coloniensem abbatissam[29] in decus pristinum excellentius reparatur. Cui uir

---

[h] *corr. from* dignetur *MS*

[26] Cf. Apoc. 7:3; 9:4; 14:9; 20:4. Cf. also *Vita Edwardi*, p. 68, line 16.

[27] Cf. Sap. 1:5. Cf. also *Letters*, p. 129, line 26 (no. 37); p. 176, lines 4–5 (no. 42); *Vita Edwardi*, p. 72, lines 1–2. Osbert's account of Edburga's vocation closely resembles Goscelin of Canterbury's account of the vocation of St Edith of Wilton (*Vita Edithe*, pp. 43–6; above, pp. 83–4). For the possibility that Goscelin was the author of an earlier version of the Edburga legend see above, p. 29, n. 69.

[28] This must refer to the series of Danish raids on England which commenced *c.* 980.

[29] For the abbesses of Nunnaminster see above, pp. 33–5.

religiosus Wintoniensis episcopus domnus Alwinus[30] prestitit
solatium, ut opus Dei melius claresceret nouo decore renuo
restauratum. / Ecclesiam uero beatissime Dei genitricis Marie
perpetue uirginis[31] quam auia sancte Eadburge regina Alsuuithis
incepit, et morte intercedente consummare non potuit, perfectam a
prefato rege Edwardo et deuota eius coniuge,[32] Wintoniensis
antistes Elphegus senior dedicauit.[33] Ipsa quoque intra beati Petri
principis apostolorum nouam basilicam, defuncta seculo, dignam
meruit sepulturam.[34]

fol. 88v

[3] *De inuicta eius fortitudine patientie*

Proficit splendida uirgo sub Spiritus Sancti disciplina,[35] languet
amore celestis sponsi caritate uulnerata. Dyaspis in ipsa candoris
uirginei texitur, et purpura sacre mortificationis spiritualiter
innouatur. Pullulat lilium uitalem germinans et spirans odorem,
proferens flores integerrimi corporis, in estatem eternam perpetua
gratia uirescentis. Talibus namque celestis sponsus delectatur
odoramentis, thalamumque casti pectoris eius inhabitat, magisque
ac magis ad desiderium superne glorificationis inflammet. Ad
insigne presertim sancte deuotionis testimonium, et ad cumulum
amoris intimi feruentius ostendendum, psalterium Dauid nusquam
manibus uirgineis excidit, nusquam decacordum legis diuine ab
eius intentione recedit. Purpurea uero tunica que passiones Christi
presignabat in ea futuras, cuius induuiis tempore sue oblationis
amiciri tenera consueuit infantia, in precipuis adhuc solenniis secus
altare suspenditur, et ad Dei gratiam et laudem uirginis aspectibus
intuentium publicis exhibetur. Cuius anima gladio amoris Christi
transuerberata, sanctarum uirtutum florebat exercitiis, fructificans
iugiter profectu patientie, humilitatis. Et cum sullimior ceteris esset
ex genere, inferiorem cunctis se reddebat obsequii dignatione.
Grandeuis matribus parebat ut filia, iunioribus et coeuis morum
honestate facta est forma, quin immo uniuersis ancillari con-

---

[30] Ælfwine, bishop of Winchester (1032–47).
[31] Nunnaminster; for the later inclusion of St Edburga in the dedication see above, p. 125.
[32] Osbert unfortunately does not make clear which of Edward's three wives is intended, although perhaps Edburga's mother, Edgiva, is implied.
[33] Ælfheah I, bishop of Winchester (934/5–51). The attribution of the dedication of Nunnaminster to this bishop is almost certainly erroneous; see above, p. 32, n. 82.
[34] This sentence most probably refers to Ealhswith, who was buried at New Minster (*LVH*, p. 5). [35] Cf. n. 27 above.

suetudine obsequebatur ut ministra. Precelsi sanguinis fastum premebat in illa iuge ieiunium, et animum eius dirigebat ad supera frequens sanctarum assiduitas lectionum. In orationibus sacris noctes agebat peruigiles, et siquid minus impletum in Dei laudibus diurna luce meminerat, nocturnis excubiis deuota sedulitate supplebat.

Unde cum tempore ut sibi uidebatur oportuno intra sacrum basilice domicilium lectioni diuine operam tribueret, hanc / loci preposita ex insperato ad lucernam offendens, grandis alapis percussione cohercet. Commouerat enim illam zelus discipline et domus Dei,[36] ut nulla earum priuatis in oratorio uacaret officiis, neque publicis abesset conuentibus eiusdem congregationis. Quam cum principis filiam esse cognosceret, toto in terram corpore prostrato postulans indulgentiam, accusat delictum et confitetur culpam. Ignorantie uero pressa caligine, quod in ipsa deliquerat se lamentatur deliquisse. Intuens equidem uirgo regia quanto humilitatis spiritu ante eam Christi suspirabat ancilla, reciproca uicissitudine uestigiis eius aduoluitur, et ut tanto misereri dignetur excessui, suppliciter deprecatur. De cetero spondet fines obedientie nec ultra transcurrere, nec instituta regule aliqua preuaricatione transire.

Eia uirgo regia insignis et decora, erumpe in iubilum et concine illud canticum, quod excellit et preminet inter omnia genera canticorum: 'Inuenerunt', inquit, 'me custodes qui circueunt ciuitatem, percusserunt me, et uulnerauerunt me.'[37] Ciuitas Dei que peregrinatur in terris sancta est ecclesia, cuius pastores et ministri sollerter inuigilant, ut animas subditorum ad gaudia eterna per custodiam sanctitatis et innocentie sustollant. Inde factum est, ut uirginei pudoris editua uirginem sacram in maxilla percuteret, dum uirtutum officinas sancta curiositate circumiret. Et dum intra lares obedientie domus preposita delictum confitetur, regis filia caritate mutua denuo uulneratur. Gratulatur itaque prouincia audita bona opinione quam de regia uirgine concipit, que in dies melior atque suauior innotescit. De eius plenitudine totius sanctitatis hauriunt dulcedinem, cum felix ipsa scientie salutaris eructuat ueritatem. Vita honestior et cultus abiectior, in illa exprimunt quod proponant ceteris, ut forme inprimantur tam egregie perfectionis. Quod euidentioribus approbabitur argu-

[36] Cf. Ioan. 2:17; Ps. 68:10. Cf. also *Vita Edwardi*, p. 98, line 11; p. 104, line 5.
[37] Cant. 5:7.

mentis, dum cognita fortitudine patientie, insigne occurrit humilitatis inuicte.

[4] *De humilitate uirginis gloriose*

fol. 89v

Dominici itaque pretiosa uirgo Eadburga assumens formam ministerii,[i] et signata caractere salutaris exempli, sicut Ipse discipulorum pedes lauit ad humilitatis imitan/de inuestigabile preconium,[38] sic ipsa sororibus suis facta est eiusdem uirtutis imitabile documentum. Calciamenta namque earum sola teste conscientia per singulas noctes clam solebat arripere, et liquido defecata elemento ad lumen uulcani aruine fluoribus emollire. Clamque reconsignabat[j] lectulis singularum singula, nec de aliquo uirtutis genere intumescebat elata. Sic longo tempore opus istud exercuit, ut in facto deprehendi non posset ab aliquo, auctorque tanti beneficii diu lateret in occulto. Sed lux eterna que omnem hominem in hunc mundum uenientem illuminat,[39] cuiusdam sanctimonialis femine lumine sue claritatis in mente resplenduit, et studii eius curam peruigilem, ad inuestigandum que in domo Dei latebat lucernam celitus arrexit. Frequenter enim mutuos inter se sermones conseruarent, et sollerter indagare tante pietatis auctorem satagebant. Explorat una attentius que cupiebat ardentius, et dum rex regum eius intuetur laudabile desiderium, idoneum desideranti largitur effectum.

Deprehensa est igitur uirgo sacra industria obseruantis in Dei tabernaculo femine, et diuulgatum exit exemplum in congregatione. Accersitur[k] deinde proles regia in congregatione sancta, et super huiusmodi negotio a singulis conuenitur, et publica correctione ut resipiscat arguitur. 'Dedecet', inquiunt, 'ut ad tam demisse seruitutis obsequium inclinet ceruicem genus regium, et opus aggrediatur uilis mancipii, faciatque preiudicium preclari germinis dignitati.' Consentit increpationi maiorum sanctarum uirtutum fecunda puerpera, et de reliquo huiusmodi correctionem profitetur, dum sibi talis obsequii sabbatum indicitur. Sacras agit uirgo ferias in Dei contemplatione sedula, cuius pudor dum Christo sanctitatis opera generat, in partu nec perit nec laborat.

Felix sponsa que dotales Dei filio uirginitatis tabulas optulit, canticum illud cantat quod non nouit uidua,[40] quod ignorat etiam

---

ⁱ misterii *MS* ^j *corr. from* recongsignabat *MS* ^k accessitur *MS*
[38] Cf. Ioan. 13:5–14. [39] Cf. Ioan. 1:9. [40] Cf. Iudith 16:1.

omnis coniugata. Que dum agno cohesit uirgo fuit, casta dum eum diligeret extitit, libera facta est quia seruiuit. Alloquenda est in huiusmodi negotio proles regia, et Salomonis epythalamio solemp / niter attollenda. 'Quam pulchri sunt', inquit, 'gressus tui in calciamentis, filia principis.'[41] Ecce quantum spectat ad mysticum anime proficientis intellectum, non de transitoria loquitur pulchritudine, nec monet gloriari de natalium splendore. Quanuis et ad litteram possit intelligi, et apte realiter ad uirginem referri. Cuius quanto humilior tanto pulchritudo lucidior, et quo uilioribus pro Christo incumbit officiis, eo apparet gloriosior in celsitudine superne dignitatis. Non auro intextis radiat ornamentis, quam sobria comitatur sufficientia, que prodire uisa est de paupertate Christiana. In hac sudat Eadburga ut pertingat ad premium, et uirtutum percolit in uirginitate principatum. fol. 90

[5] *De eo quod pater uirginis gratulatur approbatis insignibus eius humilitatis*

Inter hec dum generose indolis regia proles adolesceret, et diuine seruitutis exercitiis instaret, insignis pater uirginis Wintoniam ingreditur, et de moribus filie subtilius sciscitatur. Audit rex gratum a sanctimonialium conuentu responsum; puellares mores celebriter predicant et innatam regaliter illius mansuetudinem collaudant. In ambigue tamen posite nutant et trepidant, pauentes referre opus hoc dum taxat cunctis execrabile, ne regia percellerentur indignatione. Imperat princeps quod sentiunt eloqui, quicquid sciunt in uirgine celerius publicari. Fateantur ne diffidant, ne hesitent diffiniant, moras diutius uetat in silentio, propalant quod hactenus latuit in occulto. Ne formident, ne dubitent, scire gestit an uirginis opera eum reddant inglorium, an meritorum prerogatiua debeat efficere gloriosum. Tum pariter ab omnibus diuulgatur eius humilitas, predicatur eius sanctitas, insinuant auditui gloriosi principis, quibus per calceos uirginee manus infecte sunt atramentis. Gratulatur rex audita uirginee puritatis instantia, et ad humilitatis inuitat exercitium, et cohortatur ut talium fiat iugiter officina studiorum. Conditori seculorum deuote mentis immolat sacrificium, quam filia sua facta est ceteris sancte humilitatis insigne documentum.

41 Cant. 7:1.

[6] *De duobus militibus quorum offensa cesserunt regi hereditaria iura*

fol. 90v Eodem tempore sanctimoniales femine tenui Wintonie alebantur substantia[1] et uitam inopia transigebant copiosa. Sola eis ministrabat uilla subsidium, cuius uocabulum a nobis est superius designatum. Sapidiora cibantibus fercula deerant, sobriis tantum Christi stipendiis militabant;[42] et cum uix haberent panem hominum, confortabat eas assidue panis angelorum.[43] Tamen quia sine uictu carnis uita non geritur, spei sue anchora in Eadburgam obfirmatur. Exorant suppliciter ad quod inhiant pariter, ut liberalitatem regiam conueniat, et usibus ecclesie compendia quelibet profutura perquirat. Annuit egregie uirgo ad mensam admissa sapientie, et quam calix preclarus inebriabat ab ubertate domus Dei,[44] alimenta precibus a patre carnalia noluit extorquenda in augmentum diffiteri. Hec est occasio que se ultro intulit, qua ad regem uirgo regia mediatrix accessit.

Fuerant tempore diuturno in regis obsequio duo stipendiarii milites, Alla uidelicet et Muluca, nil nisi turgidum et insolens pro rerum abundantia sapientes. Qui, ut moribus erant incorrecti, ita frendebant seua barbarie leonis animositate permoti. His fortuitu prouenerat in ius hereditarium rus cui Canaga erat uocabulum,[45] terra frugibus opima conserendis, segetes cumulans tempore maturitatis. In curia principis mutuis inter se litibus seuiunt, et sullimes fastus incondite uulgariter indignationis ostendunt. Occasionem ut creditur iurgiorum, diuersarum administrabat copia suppellectilium, et adusque furias armauerat utrunque gladiorum. Et quia primo congredi manibus licuit, alter in alterum mucronem extendit. Fiunt ad ruinam utrique precipites, et forsan alteruter festinasset ad iugulum, si non eis obstitisset uirilis audacia satellitum regiorum. Dirimunt itaque litem qui diligunt pacem, et separantur procul ab inuicem, qui tueri nesciunt animi libertatem.

Sapientis enim est uti talibus instrumentis, ut priusquam suam regat domum, discat regere semet ipsum.[46] In salo autem naufragantis uite, nulla tempestas seuientis fortune, sapientem

---

[1] *corr. from* substantie *MS*
[42] Cf. 1 Cor. 9:7.
[43] Cf. Ps. 77:25. Cf. also *Letters*, p. 127, lines 27–9 (no. 36), to Theobald, archbishop of Canterbury (1138–61).
[44] Cf. Ps. 22:5; 35:9. Cf. also *Letters*, p. 167, lines 15–17 (no. 42), to Alice, abbess of Barking.
[45] The estate *Canaga* is probably to be identified with that of All Cannings in Wiltshire, which was in the possession of Nunnaminster at the time of the Domesday survey. For discussion of Osbert's account (cc. 6 and 7) of Edburga's acquisition of this estate for the nunnery see above, pp. 33, 88–9, 99–101.   [46] Cf. 1 Tim. 5:4.

sapienti preualet extorquere. Quidum / designata caruerit armatura, uiuendi legem libertas pertransibit amissa. Unde quia
cupiditas imperiosus est in orbe tyrannus, hos sibi miseros uiolenter
subiugat, et de ipsis facili congressione triumphat. Radix letifere
huius arboris profert ramos, furtis et homicidiis toxicatos; hominis
enim insolencia animalis, frigore congelata indurescit aquilonis.
Quod in Alla et Muluca impletum cognoscitur, dum uterque
preduce ratione uacuatur. Quin etiam consul ille Anichius^m in libro
de consolatione phylosophye scribit Boetius, 'fateor', inquiens,
'uitiosos tam et si humani corporis spetiem seruent, in beluas tamen
animorum qualitate mutari.'⁴⁷

Feruentis igitur ire rex in illos fulmina iaculat, et quid pro pena
tante debeatur incurie, curiali discutere precipit censure. Pax
namque uiolata et lese regie maiestatis iniuria, ad tantam
indignationem prouocant principem, ut pro preuaricatione patrie
legis condignam ex ambobus sortiatur ultionem.⁴⁸ Indicitur
proinde concilium, inter optimates uentilatur iudicium,
possessionibus priuantur ex lege, menbris indigni coram regia
maiestate. Sed regis gladius qui censura curie dicitur, horum
sanguinis atramento non inficitur, quippe quem et misericordia ab
eorum exitio reuocat, et iusticia comes propria eos spoliari facultate
dispensat. Adiudicatur itaque regi tota preuaricatorum substantia,
ne tam scelesta preuaricatio pertransiret impunita.

Hoc est quod in auribus uirginis immurmurat feminee
conglobatio plebis, ut considerata oportunitate temporis, impetret
a patre huius copiam facultatis. Terras enim affirmant usibus suis
congruas, et ex messe triticea uirginali familie maxime profuturas.
Virgo uero preclara rei necessitate premonita, uirginum prosequi
uoluntatem nititur, ut substantia monasterii per eam largius
augeatur.

[7] *De alleluia quod cecinit, et de rure Canaga quod sanctimonialibus
adquisiuit*

Interea heros egregius princeps Eduuardus recurrit ad urbem,
caram reuisurus in sancta congregatione progeniem. Facit moras

---

^m *the first* i *interlined MS*
⁴⁷ Boethius, *The consolation of philosophy*, ed. S. J. Tester, 2nd edn (London and Cambridge,
Mass., 1973), Bk IV, c. 4, lines 1–3. Cf. *Letters*, p. 55, line 34 (no. 3), to Henry, priest of
Westminster; here Boethius is described as 'inclitus consul ille Anicius'.
⁴⁸ The language 'lese . . . maiestatis iniuria . . . principem' derives from Roman law. On the
penalties for fighting in the king's house in Anglo-Saxon England see F. Liebermann

ibidem pro tempore, agitur res Dei dispositione.[n] Adducitur regis imperio filia lucis ad patrem carnis, et sicut in pectore gerebat scriptum[o] / digito Dei superne ueritatis euuangelium, sic genitorem exhylarat dulciter ingenita suauitate sermonum. Conuiue autem principis dum corporeas sumunt dapes, fauos Dei colligunt ex uirginis ore distillantes. Inde accidit quod in processu diei pater filie attentius imperat, ut aliquod celeste melos suaui modu-latione[p] concinat, alleluia uidelicet cuius uocali concordia celestis aula Dei terrestrisque resultat. Diffitetur uirgo facilitatem percurrere mandati quod precipitur, angelice dulcedinis coram cibantibus hymnus abnegatur. Suffunditur innato rubore uirginei pudoris, uincit uerecundia in conspectu populi conuiuantis. Metuebat sibi ne elatio cresceret, ne eam amor glorie secularis inflaret. Quia sicut uter uento distenditur sic cupiditate uanitatis animus etiam uirilis eneruatur. Insistit honesta regis improbitas, uirginalem precibus emollire constantiam, et lenire uerecundiam strepitu curie presentis innatam. Pollicetur condigna filia premia, inculcat plurimum, ut prorumpat in iubilum, et mulcere non differat animos auditorum. Quod cupit postulet ut citius impetret, celeste dum taxat inchoet canticum, et persoluto melo sue petitionis obtinebit effectum.

Tunc regina ueri Salomonis que tota uersabatur in eius deliciis,[49] nec cedere predonibus estuabat alienis, sponso suo cecinit 'alleluia, eripe me de inimicis meis'.[50] Que quia sibi de lignis Libani instituerat ferculum,[51] ut eam ferrent ad superos patrum exempla beatorum, inanem in cantico uitare gloriam didicit, et ad uirginalem reuerentiam oculos humiliter humi defixit. Preclara uero illa Spiritus Sancti fistula cum armonie celestis emisisset organum, omnium in se rapuit animos auditorum. Dyathessaron uero celeste[52] morum nobilitate concinum reddebat in illa decus nature, in qua prudentia iusticie sic sortita est copulam, ut fortitudini temperantia superne dulcedinis misceret armoniam.

---

[n] dispotione *MS*   [o] i *interlined MS*   [p] *corr. from* modullatione *MS*

(ed.), *Die Gezetse der Angelsachsen*, 3 vols. (Halle, 1903–16), I (1903), 90: laws of Ine, c. 6. For a brief introduction to Ine's laws and a translation of this passage see *English historical documents I*, ed. D. Whitelock, 2nd edn (London, 1979), pp. 398–407, at pp. 398–9. See also Sir F. Pollock and F. W. Maitland, *The history of English law before the time of Edward I*, 2nd edn, 2 vols. (Cambridge, 1898), I, 44–5.

[49] Cf. 3 Reg. 10:1–13. Cf. also *Letters*, p. 84, lines 32–4 (no. 15), to Henry of Blois, bishop of Winchester (1129–71).   [50] Cf. Ps. 17:18; 30:16; 68:19 and especially 58:2; 142:9.
[51] Cf. Cant. 3:9.
[52] 'Dyathessaron uero celeste': cf. *LE*, II, 148 (translation of St Withburga).

Approbat iste uocalem consonantiam, attollit ille uirginei pudoris reuerentiam, omnes communiter predicant tante formam honestatis sanctitatis brachiis amplectendam.

Quid multa? Exponit petitionem patri patris in palatio, deuincta tamen / eius imperio felix et gloriosa uirgo. Cumque secura esset fol. 92 quod ei rex postulata non negaret, in huiusmodi uerba orationis conseruit, et causam sanctimonialium luculenter perorauit: 'Audi rex pro uirginibus uirginem, pro sanctimonialibus sanctimonialem, attende pater filiam, ausculta genitor carnem tuam. Non a te peto diuersorum pondera metallorum, non flores argenteos alicuius artificis manu uariatos, non uestium cultus auri splendoribus et gemmis intexos. Aliud est quod mea poscit intentio, aliud quod effunditur a me in conspectu tuo. Presentem quem uirgines locum inhabitant, tua cepit genitrix regina construere, sed morte preuenta non potuit consummare. Quem nisi dierum suorum citius anticipasset cursum, omni cumulasset sufficientia commodorum. Verum quia tanta uirago uelocius quam expediret rapta est e medio et sancte uirgines Dei panis penuria deprimuntur in mundo, ad tuam confugiunt maiestatem regiam, ut eis releuare digneris hanc iacturam. Homo carens alimonia concitatur ad odia, nec potest Deo deuotus assurgere, qui famis inedia cogitur laborare. Sunt tamen aliqui in solitudinibus constituti, quos ex dolore peregrinationis sue et desiderio contemplandi uultum Dei, nec famis molestia, nec sitis impedit a speculatione diuina. Hi quia passiones superauerunt carnales, carnis execrant uoluptates. Et dum ministrare satagunt spiritui, abstinent facilius a delectatione corporalis cibi. Sed plebs infirmior et sexus inferior hac non sunt prediti fortitudine, ut queant subsistere sine corporali refectione. Hec est igitur causa qua ad tuam recurrunt munificentiam, que ecclesiasticam in domo Dei insequuntur disciplinam. Ambitiosam seculi respuere suppellectilem et diuinam frequentare meditantur lectionem. Suppleat ergo regalis auctoritas quod tue matris inchoauit largiflua caritas, et quod tibi satellitum cessit offensa, accipiat in stipendium puellaris turma.'

His Eadburga celebris finem faciens argumentis, responsum solenne prestolatur a patre. Et quam uoti uirginalis torquebat dilatio, metus decidendi cruciabat ex uoto. / Illuxit anime uirginis fol. 92v serena facies regis, et quibus in pectore gaudiis applaudit, uultus iocunditas indicauit. 'Opinor', ait, 'filia, multa uerberum te pertulisse supplicia, antequam didicisses uerba proferre tam luculenta uenustate polita. Quia uero integritas regia non debet deflecti a bona pollicitatione sua, proscriptorum arua in ius hereditarium cedant ecclesie, et hec perpetuo confirmentur ex tua petitione.'

Muniuntur igitur auctoritate regali priuilegia monasterii, et uirginee sanctitatis addicta collegio, adhuc hodie Canaga seruit sub tributo. De te uirgo insignis, uirgo celebris, canit in cantico, sponsi celestis mira et ineffabilis dulcedo. 'Sicut uitta', inquit, 'coccinea labia tua, et eloquium tuum dulce.'[53] Sparsos crines capitis consueuit uitta constringere, et fili splendoribus aurei ut ornetur splendide sponsa redimire.[q] Crinium uero nomine accipiuntur cogitationes, per illicita defluentes. Labia ergo tua felix Eadburga sunt sicut uitta coccinea, quia exhortatione tua diffusas cogitationes patris ad spiritualia applicasti negotia, ut usibus ancillarum Christi corporea ministraret alimenta. Coccinea etiam in te resplenduit, quia mentem tuam caritatis ardor conflagrauit. In cocco preterea significata est dominica passio, cuius sanguinis pretio regii generis proles ingenua, meministi quam copiosa dilectione es redempta. Et uere eloquium tuum dulce, quia celeste melos dum per te Spiritus Sancti sonuit organum, sua mulcet dulcedine aures auditorum. His hactenus habitis regrediamur ad ordinem, et oratio prosequatur materie uenustatem.

[8] *De operibus misericordie que Christi consueuit erogare pauperibus*

Celestibus itaque speciosa et precellens Eadburga flagrans desideriis, operum splendore bonorum ad tranquillitatem pacis interne suum preparat studium, in maceratione corporis minus apprecians quid caro posset, quam quid spiritus uellet. Virtutis satagit ministrare materiam, qua et integrum denuntiat mundi contemptum, et se ipsam Deo penitus immolat holocaustum. Sacras uigilias computat uirgo delicias, et psalmorum fauos in medullas / traicit, quibus uigor spiritualis ad profectum crescit. Succutit spiritum eius Dei timor et excitat, nocteque ac die horis insistens canonicis, deuota dominicis interest sacramentis. Sermo eruditus et abiectior cultus, et instituta Christiane seuerius retractata discipline, fulgoris radios in illa solent procreare.

fol. 93

Unde spetioso humane nature amicta celitus ornamento, misericordie operibus ita tota redolet, ut Christi pauperibus necessaria ministret. Qui pietatis expers est diffitetur hominem, et

q *corr. from* ?redimere MS
[53] Cant. 4:3.

inmitis in beluam declinat siluestrem. Argenteos autem triginta indigentibus erogare copiosius, purus et integer animus inclinabatur sedulo, idque in usum uerterat cotidiana consuetudo. Monete uero quolibet tempore cum precium deficit, rei familiaris grauis egestas cogit. In eminentioribus tamen uirgo solenniis assidue huiusmodi uacabat beneficio, ut innata largitas omnibus radiaretur pro exemplo. Quasi suggestum elicere poterat ex illa commonitorium, qui contemplabantur tam precellentis gratie imitabile documentum.

Licebat tunc temporis sanctimonialibus feminis, in eodem loco peculiaribus rerum abundare copiis, quoniam quicquid habebant in subsidium pertransibat religionis. Ordinis uiolati non inueniebatur ulla transgressio, dum non peperissent cum turpitudine federa, nec iniquitatis mercede quelibet esset obligata. Res sanctuarii exponuntur egentibus, et officinas morum[r] nulla inhabitat ad dispendium, ubi fratribus Christi singule earum administrant alimentum. Lex arctioris regule qua nunc in monasteriis Domino militatur, adhuc ea tempestate cunctis erat incognita, et beati patris Benedicti non instituebantur disciplina.[54] Inexorabile tamen uiciis indicitur odium, et perseuerantia custoditur Dei mandatorum.

[9] *De muliere ceca que uisum recepit ex sanctarum manuum lauatura*

Inter tot celebres uirginee integritatis cohortes preminet Eadburga ut luna inter sidera, quam solis fulgor irradiat, et diuersa miraculorum gloria diuinitus exornat. Algentibus amictum, infirmis obsequium, dapes prebet famelicis, occurrit cum remedio defectui sitientis. Dampnatos suppliciis in ergastulo carceris, suo releuat uirgo solatio, et ex odoris fragrantia suauiter emanat egrotis sospitas in munde. Ex ipsa siquidem aromatica sanctitatis cella, spirituale uirtu / tis Dei profluxit oleum, per quod cecis collatum est salutis incrementum.

fol. 93v

Mulier namque nota in eadem prouincia, oculorum lumen amiserat, quam Christus hoc modo et ordine reformat. Premonetur ceca uisione nocturna, ut aquas lotis Eadburge

---

[r] *corr. from* moras MS

[54] Osbert here refers to the changes in English religious life effected by the monastic reform movement of the later tenth century. The literature on the spiritual and political implications of the reform is extensive and is cited where appropriate in the preceding chapters. For measures to prevent property-holding by individual members of religious communities see especially *Regularis concordia*, pp. 96, xl; John, 'King and monks', pp. 164–73.

manibus exceptas inferat oculis, donatiuum denuo receptura sospitatis. Inuestigat ergo certius quod desideratur uberius, et iter pro negotio ad collegas uirginis applicat, eisque quam didicerat uisionem manifestat. Spes eius sita non est in ambiguo, neque enim falli formidat oraculo, que rore celi desuper sperat madefieri copioso.[55] Limphas subtrahunt comites uirgineis manibus excidentes, et occultari quod faciunt imperant, sicque liquidum mulieri elementum administrant. Ceca recipit donum, et reuertitur domum.

Inuocat propitiationem maiestatis diuine, ueneratur et exorat merita gloriose uirginis Eadburge. Noctis sue caliginem transferri poscit in diem, et tetras capitis tenebras[56] lucis radiis cedere, ut magnalia Dei sospes effecta ualeat predicare. Liquor itaque salutaris apponitur oculis, et dies temporalis irradiat candoris. Atri sanguinis sanies decidit, et albugo dispersa caliginem effugauit. Serena celi facies ostenditur, et mirabilis Deus a muliere collaudatur. Predicantur uirginis merita, et in ore mulieris semper uersantur Christus et Eadburga. Clara uirginalis glorie fama patentibus signis terras circumcirca transuerberat, et celis ingerit innocentie sanctitatisque dulcedinem, unde uirginitatis exhilaret auctorem. Copia gratie beata uirgo Eadburga que profluxit de te, ipsa redundauit super terram, et inebriauit eam. Surrexit aquilo et a muliere recessit, et mitissimus auster glaciem peccatricis anime instillata pinguedine pluuie salutaris dissoluit. Hec itaque tibi dona de paradiso Dei sunt allata. Quam suaue redolet ager ille tuus sponsus celestis ortus irriguus, odoribus uirtutum plenus, cui benedixit Dominus. De celi rore, et de terra uirgine, terra inquam que spinas et tribulos non germinat,[57] balsamum spiritualis antidoti creuit, quod lucis abundantiam / mulieri paupercule ministrauit. Pluit uenerabilis uirgo pro te Dominus, et rigauit aruum siccitatis de superioribus suis, ut infunderetur terra et germinaret spiritum salutis. Talem terra nostra fructum non baiulat, quam iniquitatis et malicie ariditas prefocat.

fol. 94

[10] *De insidiatoribus suis cecatis et per illam iterum sanatis*

Adiecit preterea Dominus his ampliora satis insignia, et miraculo solenniter addit miraculum, crescitque sanctorum triumphalis

---

[55] Cf. Gen. 27:39. [56] Cf. *Vita Edwardi*, p. 114, lines 5–6.
[57] Cf. Gen. 3:18. Cf. also *Letters*, p. 101, line 4 (no. 25); p. 133, line 3 (no. 39); p. 144, line 5 (no. 41); p. 154, line 27 (no. 42).

prerogatiua meritorum. Inoleuerat nanque uirginis animo diutina huiusmodi consuetudo, ut sub opace noctis tempore ad uicinum beati Petri apostolorum principis monasterium[58] pergeret, seque uiuentem hostiam Domino in precibus et lacrimis mactaret. Affinis autem et peruius ecclesie subter erat ortus, per quem uirgo sacra ad idem solebat officium diuertere, completisque spiritualis uite negotiis, eodem itinere ad cellam redire. Arctus teneros exquisitis non innutriebat deliciis, sed debilior sexus onus exceperat impar uiribus delicatis. Et cum mulier mixta carni deprimatur infirmitate duplici, uixque discat consortium dediscere uoluptatum, tanquam maturior etas felix Eadburga nociuum restrinxit incendium. Dum proles itaque regia se extenderet ad palmam per sobria et sancta pietatis exercitia, occursantium ex insidiis prorumpit uiolentia nebulonum, dum nocte qualibet iter aggrederetur ad sacras orationes totiens peruagatum. Arbor stabat in proximo spine pungentis feruida genitrix, sub cuius densis scurre latitantes foliis, gressus perscrutantur diuine contemplatricis. Cumque celestem rosam infernales tribuli lacerare contenderent, et obliquo sidere nudis eius uestigiis inuidentes inhyarent, suspicati sunt illam cuiuslibet macule notatam infamia, cuius uita celebris totius corruptionis erat aliena. Tellus namque nocturno rore irrigata fuerat, cuius guttas in restrictione uestium sponsa Dei pretiosa declinabat. Emuli autem eius quos mordaces cure cinici liuoris occupauerant, ad huiusmodi facinus applicuerant studium, ut eam quelibet fuscaret nebula uitiorum.

Ipsa quidem de ligno uite mala / sibi sine intermissione punica colligit, et inter sponsi brachia iuuencula Syon conquiescit. Contemplatur hec eadem regem Salomonem, de matre uirgine carnis induuias assumentem. Considerat eum cum diademate passionis sue, pro sceptro regni de cedris Libani, lignum superhumeros sibi portare supplicii. Cernit maiestatis Dominum flagellis cesum et sputis illitum, et auctorem uite cruci confixum clauis, et militis lancea uulneratum.[59] Speculatur mortuum et in sepulchro positum a mortuis resurgere, Christumque de mortis principe morte mortua triumphare. Intuetur eundem cum captiuitate carnis nostre celorum sullimia penetrantem, et per eum

fol. 94v

---

[58] This *monasterium* of St Peter was probably a small church or chapel in or near the garden of the nunnery; it may have been identical with the later parish church of St Peter in *Colobrochestret* (WS1, pp. 321–2 and 556, where it is noted that the word *monasterium* was frequently used in early medieval Winchester to denote a small church or chapel; WS2, 1, 112). For a less plausible identification of St Edburga's *monasterium* with a 'chapel of St Peter's monastery near by' see Braswell, 'St Edburga', p. 302.   [59] Cf. Ioan. 19:34.

celitus in pristinum decus humana refloruisse natura. Hec sunt mala punica que carpebat Eadburga de ligno uite, ex diuini floris amigdalo quod uirga Aaron sub sola nocte protulit, quando sine suco in testimonii tabernaculo germinauit.[60] In ortum igitur dilecti sui introducta hec summi principis sponsa,[61] diuini saporis dulcedinem mutuat, et fercula benedictionis eterne suis cibariis applicanda dispensat.

Donec enim talibus consuescit operibus, et malorum dulcescit degustatione punicorum, insidiatur predonum turba malig-nantium, et uergere eam gestiunt funditus ad occasum. Quo-rum reuerberat aciem uelud choruscatio fulguris uirtus excelsi principis, et in momento insolescentes fastus tante impietatis edomuit, eamque tetra caligine priuate lucis inuoluit. Fremunt infelices in orto miserabiliter oberrantes, et qui Dei sponse prius machinati sunt tendere muscipulam, calamitose cecitatis offenderunt erumpnam. Redit ad sanctarum uirginum uirgo beata domicilium, horasque noctis reliquas deputauit ad requiem, post expensum noctis preterite laborem. Deflent orbitatis tenebras uelud amentes proprie effecti iniquitatis iudices, et qui sine duce uenerant incogniti, per nouos ductores redeunt cognoscendi. Quesiti tandem ac reperti suorum rapiuntur manibus propinquorum, et per eos redditi laribus propriis, lamentabiles casus edunt exorte cecitatis. Cognita uero lenocinantis audacie graui contumelia, et Dei iudicio acrius[s] castigata, caro carni inten/dit assurgere, et sanguis sanguini opem remedii salutaris procurare.

Iuncto proinde plurimorum consortio adit sanctam uirginem uicina cognatio, orans per eam ut infelices redeant ad gratiam, pro cuius iniuriis meruerunt offensam. Verum serena illa facies uirginis que contemplata infinite solet esse dulcedinis, solito asperior aliquantum inhorruit, nec celeriter uultibus assistentium solennis illuxit. Cohercet illorum primo uesaniam, furentem tanti sceleris increpat audaciam, indignum protestans ancillas Dei liuore malicie persequi, quos merito earum deceret beneficiis gratulari. Profitentur non manicis ferreis obligati, sed ut eis uisum est tetra caligine perpetue calamitatis, profitentur erumpnam et lamentantur offensam, et pietatem qua redundat propinari sibi suspirant copiosam. Ex uasis ire uasa poscunt fieri misericordie, et se deinceps pollicentur ab omni prauitate corrigi, qui in huiusmodi passionibus didicerunt esse correcti. Tunc dolium clementie

---

[s] *marginal addition MS*
[60] Cf. Num. 17:7–11.   [61] Cf. Cant. 5:1.

balsamo caritatis insigne, nebulam non exhalauit liuoris et odii, sed effudit liquorem spiritualis unguenti. Secundum dominicum felix Eadburga non diffitetur operari mandatum, quo pro persequentibus orare precipimur,[62] et percutienti maxillam prebere alteram commonemur.

In orationibus igitur sanctimonialium confidens feminarum, innocens puella de Dei presumit auxilio, et demisse humilitatis sincereque dilectionis prefulget exemplo. Lauit itaque manus celebs uirgo celebes, lauit palam manus myrram misericordie distillantes, et sicut diuina bonitas sua per ipsam beneficia cumulat, ita salutares undas allegari patientibus ipsa dispensat. Datque mandatum ut in fide non hesitent, nec a Dei uoluntate ulterius discordent. Intingant hoc ordine oculos cecitatis sue lauachro salutari, dum exortam subito desiderant exuere caliginem, et rursus induere nouam lucem. Madefactis autem liquido oculis elemento, tota caligo eliminata disparuit, ortusque solis radius credentibus infulsit. Diei igitur claritas et noue lucis immensa iocunditas, illorum uoces in Dei laudibus excitat, et ad / amorem uirginis animos auditorum ardenter informat.

fol. 95v

O predicanda solenniter Eadburge ciuitatis Dei prerogatiua meritorum, que sic excecat insidiantes ut illuminet, sic corripit errantes ut emendet: 'Quem enim diligit Dominus corripit, flagellat autem omnem filium quem recipit.'[63] Ecce qui prius fuerant stipula gehenne, facti sunt utensilia gratie, et qui antea extiterant uasa furoris, ex ira constituuntur filii reconciliationis. Dies enim eadem que eis pro perfidia intulit caliginem, in noua confessione utriusque hominis exhibuit claritatem.

[11] *De confessione[t] eius sacra, et eius transitu ad celestia*

In tam solenni sabbato gloriose uirginitatis dum ferias ageret caro uirginis ab operibus carnis, et ad delicias suspiraret superne ciuitatis, mundi uictrix emerita ad diem supremam annis labentibus labitur, et a conciuibus regni Dei uirginibus sancta eius dissolutio postulatur. Iamque in debili corpore uires inualide, cum spiritus in dies accelerabat ad exitum, et sanctis exercitiis roborabatur ad profectum. Ea de causa uero priusquam inuitaretur a sponso uenire de Libano, ut coronari deberet incorruptibilis uirgo,[64] acceptum

---

[t] conffessione *MS*

[62] Cf. Matt. 5:44; Luc. 6:27, 35.

[63] Cf. Hebr. 12:6; Prov. 3:12. Cf. also *Letters*, p. 114, lines 11–12 (no. 31).

[64] Cf. Cant. 4:8.

Deo sue puritatis efficiebat studium, et pinguescebant cotidie apud superos suarum libamina uictimarum. Manu sancte sedulitatis excutiebat a cogitationibus suis maculas pulueris, nec aliqua eam nebula ualebat inficere, nec sancti constantiam propositi a statu bone mentis sufficiebat retardare. Semper ad omne opus bonum augebatur in illa spirituale gymnasium, et dum felix agitur cum celesti creditore negotiatio, debitori exsoluitur quod debetur in celo. Usuras parat quas summo feneratori Deo restituat, et ut ad eius tribunal reportet lucrum, ociosa non habet in negotiatione talentum.[65] Reminiscitur assidue uirgo sapiens et clara lampade prefulgens, quod in proximo celesti sponso occurret ad nuptias,[66] et ei de numero debitorum suorum oportet ut respondeat, qui solus

fol. 96 / arenam maris et pluuie guttas et dies seculi dinumerare non ignorat.[67] Unde et puritate[u] sancte confessionis innouata sic sui uirginei corporis defecat officinam, ut amaritudo penitentie omnem euacuet cum lacrimis offensam. Interea uero febre corripitur, et maxima inualitudine celerius aggrauatur. Attenuatur in dies infirmitate corporea uirgo regia, et quamuis languor uires carnis trahat ad defectum, uegetatior spiritus exhylarat animum diuinitus innouatum. Quamdiu autem potuit contra debiles arctus reluctari non destitit, nec strato decumbere hanc coegit iniuria, que minabatur occasum infirmitate contracta. Quia nimirum natura diu contra morbum rebellare non ualet humana, dum carnalis uigor decoquitur ad pernitiem, tandem strati cogitur ut transeat ad quietem.

Presagiebat ergo transitum suum ad superos sancta et uenerabilis heros, et dum deuotione sua esset sollicita, totis cordis medullis Deo erat intenta. Imminente uero diuisione corporis et anime,[68] conciuium feminarum sancta conuocat femina multitudinem, celeremque sui manifestat dissolutionem. Singulas earum pro ingruenti necessitate conuenit, et ut eam suis apud Deum iuuent suffragiis, pia sedulitate poscere non desistit. Inde secundum apostolum sacre Dei benedictionis efflagitat oleum, et salutaris corporis et sanguinis Christi premuniri uiatico, ut alteri uite innitatur tanto confederata sacramento.[69] Assunt officiosa sedulitate uocati sancti altaris ministri, accurrunt etiam sacre

---

[u] puritate . . . sic *added, partly in margin, after erasure of several words* MS
[65] Cf. Matt. 25:14–29.
[66] Cf. Matt. 25:1–13. Cf. also *Letters*, p. 139, lines 3–4 (no. 40), to Ida, a nun (possibly of Barking), and p. 146, lines 18–22, to Matilda of Darenth.
[67] Cf. Ecclus. 1:2.   [68] Cf. *Vita Edwardi*, p. 110, line 5.
[69] Cf. 1 Cor. 10:16–17; 11:23–34. Cf. also *Vita Edwardi*, p. 111, lines 4–11.

uirgines uirginis exequias prestolantes. Non emarcuit pudicitie lilium in conualle lacrimarum, quod sacra irrigauerunt stillicidia, et fluenta psalmorum inebriauerunt inundatione copiosa. Unde et ipsa^v in ecclesiastico se precentricem exhibebat officio,[70] et quandiu uitalis spiritus lingue^w loquentis habuit instrumentum, ad Dei semper mouebatur obsequium. Ceteras in antiphonis sorores preueniens inchoandis, Dauiticos ructabat fauos in psal/mis, horam sue imminentis prestolans migrationis. Flebant igitur filie Syon filiam Iuda, quibus in caritate disperserat que sibi fuerant peculiaria, ut huiusmodi beneficiis eis attentius esset commendata. Inuncta tandem uirgo sacra cum cruce dominice salutiferum pre oculis haberet uexillum, signum salutis nostre sibi iugiter pingebat in fronte, cuius mortificationem circumferre uiuens consueuit in corpore. Deficiente autem uoce pariter et uigore, serena facie decumbebat in lectulo, toto spiritu ligni salutaris intenta uexillo. Ita generosa uirgo et sponsa summi regis Eadburga uite subtracta presentis ergastulo, in confessione uere fidei et unius Dei cognitione migrauit ad celum, cum sacris coronanda uirginibus sanctorum subuecta^x presidiis angelorum.

fol. 96v

[12]^y

Tryumphauit uirgo felix corporalibus exonerata induuiis, et illius uirginis matris in celo dedita gratulatur obsequio, que salua uirginitate Deum et hominem generi profudit humano. Et quia uestibus auro textis que regio generi congruunt nullatenus gloriabatur, nec suorum splendore natalium insolescere uoluit, circumdata uarietate uirtutum,[71] agnum sponsum meruit uirgineo uellere candidatum. Ad cuius nuptias sapiens uirgo cum chorusca lampade oleo bone conscientie delibuta peruenit,[72] in illa etate mystico consecrata numero suum ad celestia faciens transitum, qua Saluator mundi in amne Iordanis Iohannis manibus baptizandus uenit ad baptismum.[73] Et in qua filius Dei in corpore proprio ueterem reformauit hominem,[74] in eiusdem typico salutaris

---

^{v} *addition MS* ^{w} lingui *MS with signs of emendation* ^{x} *corr. from* subiecta *MS*
   ^{y} *from this point on only chapter 17 is rubricated, though space has been left at the head of each chapter for addition of rubric*
[70] See above, p. 34, n. 89.
[71] Cf. Ps. 44:10. Cf. also *Letters*, p. 90, lines 21–2 (no. 21), to Osbert's niece, Margaret, nun of Barking; p. 138, lines 27–8 (no. 40), to the nun Ida; p. 155, line 21 (no. 42), to Alice, abbess of Barking. Cf. also notes 89 and 107 below.
[72] Cf. Matt. 25:1–13.   [73] Cf. Matt. 3:13; Marc. 1–9.
[74] Cf. Rom. 6:6; Ephes. 4:22.

compoti sacramento suam ut aquile renouauit iuuentutem.[75] Hec
est mensura etatis plenitudinis Christi,[76] in qua occurrent omnes in
uirum perfectum, receptis denuo spoliis corporum beatorum.
'Beatus et sanctus', inquit Iohannes apostolus, 'qui habet partem in
resurrectione prima'.[77] Resurrectio prima gloriose uirginis
Eadburge ista dicitur, cum de corpore humano quasi de quodam
sepulchro ad perpetue lucis emersit gloriam, et beate immortalitatis a Domino coronam percepit eternam. In secunda uero
resurrectione sanctorum speti/osis induetur uestibus, cum in
modum solis fulgentem resumet in carne decorem, quando felix
anima suo corpori consociata, cum illo deinceps inseparabilem
possidebit unitatem. Cui facta est uox dilecti pulsantis ad ostium
cordis. '"Aperi," inquit, "mihi soror mea, amica mea, columba
mea, immaculata mea".[78] Pande ex intimo affectu cor tuum, quia
dissoluetur in proximo terrestre tabernaculum tuum. Ponam te
electam meam in thronum meum, concupiui enim speciem et
decorem tuum. Quam ea de causa sororem appello, quia regni mei
coheredem facio. Et iccirco es amica, quam archane dulcedinis mee
particeps haberis et conscia. Columbe es etiam designata uocabulo,
quam Sancti Spiritus perfudit unguentum, et suorum illustrauit
copiosa largitate donorum. Immaculata etiam censeris ex nomine,
quia integra es carnis ab operatione. Et cum sis a secularibus remota
negotiis, et superne contemplationis specula sullimata, ecce habes
apparere conspectui meo digna. Veni igitur de Libano sponsa, ueni
de Libano, ueni, coronaberis.[79] Quia candidatum preciosis actibus
gestas indumentum, primo coronata es uiuens in corpore. Ad
percipienda deinde superne beatitudinis premia, secundo
coronaberis soluta a carne. Coronaberis et tercio post
resurrectionem, in eterna immortalitate corporis et anime. Ita ero
premium tuum ego gloria indeficiens, et lux eterna sanctorum, ut
ad fruendum perpetuo hac prefulgeas gratia, et uultus mei
delecteris serenitate gratiosa.'

Ad hec respondeat uigilans uirgo sponso suo, et dicat:
'"Pessulum ostii mei aperui dilecto meo."[80] Templum mei
pectoris habitaculum regis effeci celestis, qui me sue miserationis
preuenit insigniis, et uirginee puritatis decorauit ornamentis.

fol. 97

[75] Cf. Ps. 102:5. [76] Cf. Ephes. 4:13.
[77] Apoc. 20:6. Cf. *Letters*, p. 113, lines 14–16 (no. 31). [78] Cant. 5:2.
[79] Cf. Cant. 4:8. Cf. also *Letters*, p. 90, line 23 (no. 21), to Osbert's niece Margaret, nun of Barking. [80] Cant. 5:6.

Illustrauit me splendoribus suis sol iusticie, et ditauit donorum suorum copia inuisibilis auctor uite. Cui cogitationum mearum nuditatem[z] expono, defecatum innocentis conscientie pandens uestibulum, ut currentem post se in odore celestium trahat unguentorum. At ille dilectus meus qui et candidus ex uirginei splendoris uellere, et rubicundus intinctis uestibus ex purpurea erat passione, declinauerat atque pertransierat.[81] Decli/nauerat a carne ad spiritum, pertransierat a terris ad celum. Declinauerat specietenus communem habitationem hominum, pertransierat ut mihi promissam ueritatem non negaret similitudinis angelorum.'

In his spiritualis uite deliciis dissoluta ut prediximus uirgo insignis, inter filias Ierusalem illius apud superos contemplatur speciem, cuius in fornace Babilonis decocta[82] desiderabilem concupierat beate glorie uisionem. Curat exequias uirginis caterue plebs congrua uirginalis, et dum iste modulis insistunt et psalmis, lacrimis ille et querulis suspirant in lamentis. Sanctimonialis[a] autem celebris illa multitudo feminarum, uirginem sacram oratorium extra sepeliunt, et in paradiso ancillarum Dei arctus exanimes tumulo componunt. Expensas substantie corporalis dispensant egenis, et dum redemptionis[b] nostre mactatur in ara uictima salutaris, Christi fratres in platea temporalibus sustentantur alimentis.

Transiit autem gloriosa et felix Eadburga uirgo tricesimo etatis sue anno, septimo decimo kalendas Iulii de corpore mortis huius migrans ad uitam,[83] de pena temporali ad immarcescibilem gloriam. Que in diademate regis eterni margarita incomparabilis emicat, et inter pretiosos lapides Syon infiniti splendoris radios uibrat.[84] Nec enim in eminentiori loco statuit sibi marmor insigne pretiosa uirgo, nec argento celatum aut ebore preuidit sibi sponsa Christi sepulchrum, quippe quam nichil inanis glorie inclinare preualebat ad lapsum. Sicut enim humilitatis sub disciplina regulari preelegerat uitam, ita in tempore dissolutionis sue foris in atrio humilem elegit sepulturam. In illius speculemur forma quanta sit in

---

[z] *interlined addition MS*

[a] *corr. from* sanctimonalis *MS*   [b] redeptionis *MS*

[81] Cf. Cant. 5:6.

[82] Cf. Dan. 3. Cf. also *Letters*, p. 75, line 6 (no. 10); p. 156, lines 21–2 (no. 42), to Alice, abbess of Barking, concerning the virginity and incorruption of St Æthelthryth.

[83] The feast of Edburga's deposition on 15 June was commonly commemorated in English calendars both before and after 1066: see above, pp. 117–18, 125–9. For the year of her death see above, p. 104 and n. 30.   [84] Cf. Is. 28:16; 1 Pet. 2:6.

moribus deformitas nostra, et per eam edocti sic conteramus carnis lasciuiam, ut sancte pudicitie apprehendamus armaturam. Sicque uirtutes sacras opera nostra redoleant, ut castarum mentium uitrea puritate in uasis fictilibus ipsa patrocinante pernitescant.[c]

Quieuit itaque aliquanto tempore in eodem quo condita est loculo Eadburga incorruptibilis et splendida[d] uirgo, donec choruscantibus / miraculis sepultura ipsius celebris habita est et insignis, et signorum celestium ex undanti plenitudine, per mundum sparsit radios immortalis uite. Ad gloriose preterea laudis Dei cumulum sicut scribendi primo precessit exordium, sic terminandi uitam et transitum glorie uirginalis, meta huius operis ipso auctoris appareat insignis. In Christo et enim regis nostri adiutorio et uirtute confisus quod Sancto Spiritu inspirante de gloriosa eius ciuitate Eadburga summatim decerpere potui, in modicum ut cernitur uolumen extendi. Sit igitur Deo Patri gloria qui eam sapientie sue luce perfudit, sit eius unigenito gratia qui illam sibi sponsam celesti diademate coronauit, sit spiritui ueritatis laus indeficiens, qui eandem templum sue inhabitationis effecit. Trino et uni Deo honor et omnipotentia, uirtus et salus indiuidua, qui nos ad sacre uirginis Eadburge transferat apud superos perhenne tripudium, gloriantes cum illa et de continua sanctorum societate gratulantes, cuius nec incipit nec desinit imperium, per omnes generationes seculi seculorum. Amen.

[13]

Subsequentis[85] series operis effectui suppeditat nostre promissionis, dum triumphalis uirginis exequias plurimum desudata translatio sequitur, quam signis euidentibus actam celitus solennis ecclesia preconatur. Iterum uirgo splendida, iterum illustris Eadburga, preclare sibi laudis erigere titulos imperat, ut ad sanctimonialium gloriam feminarum pulchritudo sue sanctitatis innotescat. Que in area certaminis sui in quo triumphauit principem mundi, nutu celestis sponsi gratiam promeruit sui corporis transferendi, ut ex ignobili sepultura qua primo recondita in Wintoniensi urbe

---

[c] *corr. from* pernitescunt *MS*   [d] et splendida *added in margin MS*

[85] This chapter has the form of a short prologue to a second book (fols. 98–107; cc. 13–19) concerning the development of Edburga's cult at Nunnaminster. For discussion of that cult see above, pp. 103–29.

cognoscitur, crebra miraculorum gloria celebriore loculo
excellentius denuo conderetur.

Gratulentur ergo uirgines tymphanistriarum plausu solennes,
quibus ut luna in translationis sue festiuo modulamine resplenduit
Eadburga signorum celestium admirabili claritate. He sunt / que in
acie celestis milicie uitam eius celibem tanquam uiuentem uirginis
speculantur imaginem; he sunt que cum pretioso gloriosi corporis
sui thesauro dotalem eius custodiunt familiarius edem. He sunt
quibus illa tam copiosa tamque desideratum patrocinantis gratie
Dei impertit beneficia, ut dum illarum queque celestis sponsi
delicias brachiis castitatis amplectitur, hanc ad coronam
immarcescibilis glorie illeso pudore prosequatur. Igitur quoniam
incorruptioni sanctarum uirginum similitudo promittitur
angelorum, ad honorem incorrupte uirginis Eadburge uenerentur
in illa Domini mirabilia sacrate Deo uirgines, que in arce humilitatis
sue uirginee suas imitari professe sunt puritates. Et qui linguas
infantium facit disertas, lingue mee fibras diu clausas[86] aperiat ut
quicunque preclare glorificationis sue preconia legere, eiusque
patrocinia postulare desiderat, in amorem egregie uirginis magis
magisque diuino spiritu uentilatus inardescat.

[14]

Cumᶠ gloriose uirginitatis laurea coronata in celo beata cum sanctis
regnaret Eadburga, et suorum Deus insignia meritorum declarare
dignaretur in terra, locus ille nouus crebrescere cepit circumquaque
miraculis, in quo aliquando reconditus celestis carbunculus radios
occuluerat sue claritatis. Spargendi igitur erant crines fulgoris
insoliti, et infecundis Brittannie prouinciis illuminandus omnis
orbis, ut ex lampade pretiose uirginis prudentie eius faciem
produceret oleum, et extincte per eam repararentur uirginum
lampades fatuarum.[87] Unde et non nulle sanctitatis eius forme
quantum niti preualent spiritualiter impresse, huius exemplo
discunt et populum suum et paternam domum relinquere,[88]
seseque uirtutum uarietate decenter circumdare, ut in uestitu
deaurato celesti sponso mereantur complacere.[89] Quarum uitam

---

ᶜ *MS wrongly foliated; fol. 98v omitted*   ᶠ *addition MS*
[86] Cf. *Vita Edwardi*, p. 106, line 32.   [87] Cf. Matt. 25:1–13.   [88] Cf. Ps. 44:11.
[89] Cf. Ps. 44:10. Cf. also *Letters*, p. 168, lines 18–19 (no. 42), to Alice, abbess of Barking. Cf.
also notes 71 and 107 above and below.

celibem sic Deus a crimine custodit immunem, ut innocentia semper resplendeat ex affectu, et mundicia puritatis uirginee fol. 100^g tam corpore quam spiritu representetur in / actu. Radio itaque tanti iubaris caterua resplenduit illa uirginalis, que sacrate corpus Edburge de ignobili sepultura transtulit, et insignes eius titulos super regale mausoleum et celebre euidenter erexit. Neque uero splendorem uirgineum quilibet existimare debet inglorium, quem Deus e celo signis certioribus approbat, et locus in terra quo sepulta delituit patenter manifestat.

[15]

Secus ecclesie namque maceriam in atrio uirginum, beate uirginis fuerat corpus humatum, cui fenestra desuper contigua aperiebatur in die, et sole ruente claudebatur in nocte. Huius officii sedula quedam uirtutis erat femina flameo Christi insignita, que dum hanc obserare per omne sabbatum studiosius ageret uespere, aliquando passa repulsam sensit uiolentiam a foris imminere. Videbatur sibi quod manus ipsam quelibet inde repelleret, que fenestram claudere exterius uetaret. Hac quassata conqueritur sanctimonialis iniuria, properoque gressu oratorium egreditur, ut tam molestus auctor citius deprehendatur. Ad locum uero ueniens neminem repperit, seseque cucurrisse^h suspirat in uacuum, et sauciato corde regreditur introrsum. Hasque frequenter uices explere cum contenderet, ut aperto foramini clausulam inferret, uirtus huic diuina solet obsistere, eamque retrorsum inuisibili impetu ualidius elongare.

Siluit itaque uernula Christi diuini uoluntatem secreti, et nocte eadem qua sanctam pertulit innocentiam, rem reuoluit animo ceteris ignotam. Femina uero sancta assidue dubio fluctuabat in pectore, quia certum non habebat ueritatis argumentum, utrum opus fantasticum esset an diuinum. Et iccirco expectatione pendula in ambiguo mutantem, exhortatur ratio subtrahere hominum noticie rei predicte difficultatem, donec superuenturis noctibus experimento fidentiori cognosceret, quid hoc sibi negotium futuro tempore parturiret. Custos itaque sacrorum femina religiosa uasorum, intenta mentis acie respexit ad Dominum, orans ut ter sancta illa insurgeret uiolentia, si uoluntas huic concordaret diuina. fol. 100v Excubat in oratorio fidelis uernula Christi Ihesu, / nocturne quietis sompnum luminibus subtrahit propriis, studium sollerter apponit inceptis rei predicte terminandis. Sed uigiliis inseruiens, et absque dispendio laborem consumens, cum non preualeret fenestram recludere, sanctimonialibus studuit ignota reserare. Quod ergo discit una, mox docetur altera, et spargere tante nouitatis indaginem, fama non diffidit per congregationem. A nulla ei inscribitur nota mendacii, dum de eius fide quelibet non diffideret, et de uita sanctitatis nulla dubitaret. Sic igitur fenestra consideratur aperta, ut non desinat uniuersas instruere, gloriose corpus Edburge de loco ad locum celebriorem transferre.

[16]

Cum sponsus itaque celestis post exequias sacri corporis manifestare sic incipit uirginem meriti prerogatiua felicis, epythalamicum de sponso suo concinat sponsa canticum, filiasque Syon mulceat, tonorum fidibus supernorum. 'En,' inquit, 'ipse stat post parietem nostrum, respiciens per fenestras, prospiciens per cancellos.'[90] Quid est gloriosa uirgo? Quid concrepas de dilecto tuo? Quis est ille paries post quem stantem contemplaris amicum tuum? Que sunt ille fenestre, per quas asseueras respicere regem tuum? Qui sunt illi cancelli, per quos astruis prospicere amicum[i] tuum? Sonos exterioris symphonie auribus hausimus, sed interiorem dulcedinem prorsus ignoramus. Doce ergo nos et interioris medulle pinguedinem querere, et gratos ex illa sapores mutuare.

Ad hec Eadburga uirgo sacra respondeat, et desolatos consoletur et dicat: 'Paries iste caro est mediatoris Dei et hominum, qui me dum essem in carne, muniuit assidue a persecutionibus temptationum. Qui de duabus domibus condidit eternaliter unam, dum creaturam in celis angelicam et naturam in terris coniunxit humanam. Bonus paries post quem stat sponsus meus celestis, qui mortalis in carne et immunis a crimine, me effecit participem immortalitatis sue. Pro me duello conflixit cum tyranno, erectusque / uiriliter stetit in acie, et in meo debili corpore hostem dignatus est tryumphare.[91] Respicit de sanctuario suo per fenestram suam dilectus meus sepulturam, nec uult ut sub ignobili cespite caro mea deinceps lateat, quam in minoribus aliquantulum miraculis mundo iam commendat. Per quedam uero signa id est per

fol. 101

---

[i] *interlined addition over erasure* MS
[90] Cant. 2:9. Cf. *Letters*, p. 92, lines 13–14 (no. 22), to Osbert's niece Cecilia, nun of Barking.
[91] Cf. *Letters*, p. 92, lines 14–16 (no. 22), to Osbert's niece Cecilia, nun of Barking; p. 164, lines 24–7 (no. 42), to Alice, abbess of Barking.

fenestras sol celestis ingreditur, totamque domum meam in spiritu illuminat, et corpus in tumulo prodigiis exornat. Per cancellos etiam id est per occulta dispensationis sue me respexit misteria, ut sincere dilectionis uestigia et nouam gloriam ostendat in publico, qua ei depacta sum ineffabiliter admirabili caritatis sacramento.' Sic nos spirituali consideratione plenius instruit uirgo uenerabilis, ut nectarea suauitas diuine dulcedinis anime nostre palato uberius sapiat, et absinthium mundane uoluptatis nostris mentibus amarescat. Veruntamen ad inceptam ex ordine recurrentes materiam, explicemus hystoriam noua incude uirginee maiestati fabricatam.

[17] *Quod sancta Eadburga sanctimonialibus apparuit, nouamque sibi sepulturam fieri precepit*

Crescit itaque diuini magis et magis in congregatione fama miraculi, et matronas ueteres curiosa sollicitat grauitas, ac de transferendo beate uirginis corpore reddit animatas. Deliberant inter se celebrem ei in oratorio debere fieri sepulturam, mysterio uacare nequaquam tantum existimantes prodigium, quod prouenisse fatebantur diuina dispositione celitus adornatum. Sui conqueruntur erroris incuriam, dum tumbam sancte uirginis lamentantur indignam, nec ius nec fas esse quod extra delituerat, que regie dignitatis splendore radiabat. In uirtutum acie et grauitate morum, sic beatam Eadburgam testantur emeritam, ut ubi in agone sudauerat certaminis olimpici, ibi denuo sortiatur debita sepulchri. Et quo deuota loco diuinis diu uacauerat excubiis, eo recenter obtineat insignes titulos renouate mansionis. In hac sententia uirgines uirginalem gloriam declamantes, si pigritauerint animo formidant iudicis gladium, si opus accelerauerint palmam sperant
sideream pro / retributione meritorum. Fit igitur ilico quod diuino nutu statuitur, et de loco ignobili uirgo felix et gloriosa meritis eleuatur. Secunda tumulatione extra chorum reconditur in monasterio, ubi uulgaris turma consueuit assistere, et diuinis ad orationem laudibus solenniter interesse. Censebant profecto ipsam in ipsa decenti transpositam, optinere iam dignas et celebres satis exequias, sed prouidit aliter superne dispensationis excellentissima maiestas.

Quiescentibus namque sororibus beata uirgo Aedburga euidenter apparuit, seque ad supereminentiorem edis sacre transferri portionem imperauit. Secus mensam collocari dominicam appetebat, cui dum carnem circumferret spirituales cibos ipsa parauerat. Et que Spiritus Sancti fuerat effecta sacrarium, in sacrario locum sibi conderet sanctarum deuotio feminarum. Asseuerat etiam celestem promeruisse cum sanctis uirginibus palmam, et in sanctorum numero cum angelis Dei se glorificatam. Maturant hac uisione predicte sorores beate uirginis Aedburge reuerenter imperium, et in eminentiori loco sanctuariiʲ sanctarum transferunt fauillas celebres reliquiarum. Operatur pietas diuina ad sancte uirginis gloriam propalata mundo magnalia, et quid translatio facta recenter innuerit, tumulata uirgine arta prius fenestra clausa denuo patefecit. Que tanta improbitate importuna extitisse dinoscitur, ut ante corpus transpositum clausulum negasse argumento probabili uideretur.

Subsecuntur etiam a Christo innumera sullimius insignita prodigia, et uirtutes cotidie copulantur uirtutibus, et signorum celestium manifestatur effectus. Diuersis afflicti languoribus ad sanctum uirginem ueniunt, et uiribus per eam reparatis ad propria recedunt. Nulla quippe uacare dies miraculo poterat, immo sine multis refusa miraculis nulla prorsus radiabat.

[18]

Ea tempestate sacerdotium ita concordabat et regnum, ut secundum Platonis sententiam et reges philosophyce uiuerent,[92] et philosophi tanquam nudi euangeliste Christi uiciis et concupiscentiis imperarent. Probabile satis sideribusᵏ duobus ostenditur, quorum splendor et claritas mundo spec/tabilis

fol. 102

ʲ *corr. from* sunctuarii MS ᵏ *later addition* MS

[92] The association of Plato with the concept of the *rex philosophicus* was current throughout the Middle Ages and its use here does not imply direct familiarity with the works of Plato. Osbert used the same theme in his *Vita Edwardi* (p. 67, lines 21–4) and it is suggested by Bloch (*ibid.*, n. 2) that his source may have been Boethius, *Consolation*, Bk I, c. 4 or Alcuin, *Epistolæ* (ed. E. Duemmler, in *Monumenta Germaniæ historica, epistolarum tomus IV* (Berlin, 1895), pp. 1–493), no. 229.

For Osbert's views on the concord of *regnum* and *sacerdotium* see also *Letters*, p. 124, lines 11–15 (no. 36), addressed to Theobald, archbishop of Canterbury (1138–61) and written after November 1153: 'tu namque in magna tempestate factus es cum tuis principium passionis vitæ, quando contra te persecutores et tyranni cœperunt vehementer insurgere. Divisum a regno eo tempore erat sacerdotium, sed nunc sacerdotio tua sedulitate copulatum est regnum.'

For the career of Theobald, his quarrels with King Stephen concerning attendance at the papal Council of Rheims (1148) and concerning the succession of Stephen's son, Eustace (from 1150), and his subsequent role in securing the peace of 1153 and the succession of Henry II see especially A. Saltman, *Theobald, archbishop of Canterbury* (London, 1956), ch. 1; see also *CS*, I, ii, especially 778–9, 813–15, 820–6.

uniuerso commendatur. Regnabat tunc Ædgarus Ædmundi principis filius, qui sancte uirginis Eadburge germanus extiterat,[93] quem probitatis titulus dote multiplici perlustrabat. Beatus uero Ætheluuoldus Wintoniensem regebat ecclesiam,[94] cuius tanta sanctitas inter pontifices Anglie fuisse dinoscitur, ut pre nimia claritatis excellentia ineffabilis extitisse memoretur. Cui Deus in clericorum repulsa secularium hoc ad testimonium uere religionis contulit, ut materialis Ihesu Christi forma in figura crucis suspensa uerborum sonos intelligibiles ederet, et auctoritatem sanctorum monachorum et famam celebrem approbaret.[95] Primusque Wintoniensis uir deuotus ecclesie hoc prerogatiue munus distribuit, ut et religiosas personas introduceret, et carnis uoluptatibus deditos exterminaret.[96] Que[l] uero monasterium priuilegia ualebant comprehendere, que ad sanctorum Dei laudem et gloriam studuit diligentius titulis insignire. Quam precipue deuotionis iubilo beate et gloriose uirginis Edeldrede preclaros radios extulit, qui Eliensem insulam integritate morum et murorum reparatione circumcinxit. De Burgensi atque Thornensi plura referre non uacat cenobio, que diuersorum gloria ornamentorum gloria operuit, et adhuc hodie sanctorum intercessione exornare non desistit.[97]

Humana de ipso lingua nescit exprimere, quot et quanta militibus Christi donatiua distribuit, et quot seruorum Dei castra et actu et habitu innormarit. In huius itaque diebus se gloriosus Dei

---

[l] Que . . . insignire *MS corrupt*

[93] Edgar ruled Mercia and Northumbria from 957, Wessex from 959 until his death in 975. He was a son of Edmund, king of Wessex (939–46), himself a son of Edward the Elder and Edgiva and brother of St Edburga. For discussion of Edgar's accession and of his 'deferred' consecration see Nelson, 'Inauguration rituals', pp. 63–71, and A. Jones, 'The significance of the regal consecration of Edgar in 973', *Journal of Ecclesiastical History* 33 (1982), 375–90. On Edgar's relationship to Edburga see also *Vita Edwardi*, p. 69, lines 22–6: 'Beata uero Eadburga, signorum fulgore celestium urbs Wintonie lustrans confinia, sancti huius principis aui, regis uidelicet Eadgari, insignis resplenduit amita, cui frater uirginis Eadmundus in carnali pater extitit genitura.'

[94] Æthelwold was consecrated bishop of Winchester on 29 November 963 and died on 1 August 984. For general references to his role in the tenth-century reform see above, p. 106, n. 35.

[95] This anecdote of the speaking crucifix, which supported the case of the monks against that of the secular clerks, is derived from the legend of St Dunstan. It makes its first appearance in Osbern's Life of that saint, composed towards the end of the eleventh century (*Memorials of St Dunstan*, p. 113) and recurs in later Lives by Eadmer (*ibid.*, pp. 212–13), William of Malmesbury (*ibid.*, pp. 307–8) and Capgrave (*ibid.*, pp. 342–3).

[96] For discussion of the refoundation of the Winchester religious houses see above, pp. 106–7.

[97] For the refoundation of Ely, Peterborough and Thorney see above, pp. 107, 181–96.

confessor Swithunus noua reuelatione glorificauit,[98] quem et recens miraculorum gloria cotidie extollebat ad sidera, et uirtus indefessa magnificabat in uniuersa terra. Tanta uero meritorum prerogatiua gloriosum Dei pontificem donauerat Ætheluuoldum, ut tredecim sanctorum corpora de ignobilibus tumulis deuotus extraheret, et condigna reuerentia sepulturas eorum excellentius honoraret.[99]

De quorum cathologo beatus confessor Dei Suuithunus diuersis in urbe Wintonia fulgurabat usquequaque miraculis, et gloriosa uirgo et felix Eadburga preclaris et innumeris rutilabat signis. Confessor namque insignis tanquam sol celestis uariis radiabat usquequaque prodigiis, et regia proles Ædburga choruschabat uirtutibus, sacris circumdata uirginibus ut luna / sideribus. Claritas sanctitatis amborum aduersas depellebat ualitudines infirmorum, et quicunque ueniebant postulaturi fideliter impetrabant postulata nec tamen difficulter. Lingua mutorum que diebus antea infinitis ferias eterni transegerat silentii, nouas eliminando sillabas humani facta est particeps uerbi. Paralitica solidantur menbra continuo, que torta diutius infesta dissoluerat et manifesta ualitudo. Leprosa facies ex insperato decidit, et nitida cutis recenti innouatione reuirescit. Claudis solida firmantur uestigia, et qui super pedes proprios stare non poterant, reparatis gressibus quasi cerui saliebant.[100] Sic operabatur pietas diuina proflua in sanctis et copiosa magnalia, ut et uirtus eorum in plebe claresceret, et populus Dominum uoce tinnula collaudaret.

Certatim namque confessor et uirgo quasi quibusdam successibus noua determinabant miracula, dum tanquam reciprocis apicibus in prosa et uersu inter se confligerent, et mutuis disputationibus altercarent. Quibus enim sanctus pontifex dominus Suithunus quasi uidebatur negare remedium, beata uirgo Eadburga sue miserationis pretendebat manum. Et quos illa non admittebat ut liberarentur ab egritudine, uir Domini preclarus salutifera dignabatur interuentione. Itatenus ex utroque latere ciuitas munita gaudere non desiit, ut quod clerus et populus in ecclesia ad honorem

fol. 102v

---

[98] The relics of Swithun, bishop of Winchester from *c.* 852 until *c.* 862, were translated at Old Minster by Æthelwold on 15 July 971. For the development of Swithun's cult and its relationship to that of Edburga see above, pp. 108–10, 112–14.

[99] For the importance of the cults of the saints in the tenth-century reform see above, p. 107. I have been unable to verify Osbert's statement that Æthelwold was responsible for the translation of no fewer than thirteen saints.

[100] Cf. Matt. 11:5; 15:30–1; 21:14; Luc. 7:22; 14:13.

Dei celebrare satagerent, per compita^m etiam et theatra saltatores in
citharis et instrumentis musicis personarent. Egregia parilitate
fulgurabat uterque miraculis, precelsa maiestate prodigiis uterque
radiabat et signis. Mirabilis namque humilitas que dum uiuerent
seculo diu delituerat in occulto, reuirescente fidei gratia iam
manifesta creuit in publico, ut utriusque meritum chorusca luce
patesceret operum, et sanctitas inexplicabilis consona diuersitate
resplenderet singulorum. Et licet essent impares ordine, equi
pollebant miraculorum claritate. Dumque gloriosus confessor Dei
Suuithunus dicior fieret in celebri et continua signorum
temporalium serie, insignis et precelsa uirgo Eadburga dignior

fol. 103 appare/bat ex regii sanguinis generosa maiestate. Gratulabundus
applaudit uenerandus athleta domini et pontifex Athelwoldus, et
de geminata luce urbis Wintonie, ineffabili gaudio solenniter
tripudiat, et de beneficiis sanctorum collatis exultat.

[19]

Videns itaque preclarus sacerdos Domini Ætheluuoldus tantis
beatam uirginem Eadburgam choruschare miraculis, quam
inmensis in celo ante uultum Dei non diffidebat radiare meritis,
eam de tumulo transferri ad thecam argenteam disposuit, cuius
benigne uoluntatis uestigia in beneplacito suo gratia diuina direxit.
Crebris enim reuelationibus Domino fuerat inspirante premonitus,
ut tam honestum et utile citius aggrederetur inchoare negotium, et
ad totius Anglorum ecclesie utilitatem perducere et profectum.
Alloquens ergo abbatissam que tunc temporis sacratis Christi
uirginibus preerat, ceterasque sanctorum congregationes et plebem
quas ad Dei opus in urbe Wintonie gubernabat, omnibus pariter
suum manifestauit affectum, cunctorumque concordantem
repperit sue uoluntati consensum. Eadem uero que presidebat
uenerabilis femina uocabatur Alfgheua.[101] Dies ergo certa
solennitatis tante statuitur, ut tam preciosus uirginalis glebe thesau-
rus de profundo telluris eleuetur.[102] Conueniunt ad gloriam et
laudem Dei clerus et populus, et multitudo innumera utriusque

---

^m per compita *an addition MS*
101 For the abbatial succession at Nunnaminster see above, pp. 33–5.
102 The feast of Edburga's translation is commemorated on 18 July in Winchester calendars
of the pre- and post-Conquest periods: see above, pp. 117–18 and n. 83, 125–7. This feast
probably refers to the saint's translation by Æthelwold, though it is not impossible that it
may refer to the earlier translation said by Osbert to have been carried out by the
Winchester nuns.

sexus. Crescit feruor deuotionis et famulatus obsequii, et prorumpit in iubilum, omnis ordo discipline Dei. Agonithete Christi in monachica conuersatione preclari laudem uirginis personabant cum cantico, et clerici eiusdem prosequebantur gloriam tempore oportuno. Virginales etiam symphoniste concinebant uirginem, et populus regis filiam predicabat insignem. Sic in uno quoque gradu ex ore fidelium, concentus et organa resonabant hymnorum.

Cum tante itaque magnificentie pompa, et festiua cum episcopo totius ciuitatis gloria, assumpta est beata uirgo Ædburga solenniter de sepulchro, et in locello / reponitur argenteis floribus aureisque compacto; quibus intexti sunt pretiosi lapides, claritatis sue radios intuentes ministrantes. Cuius celebri glorie illud uterque competit, quod chorus filiarum Syon in cantico canticorum dicit: 'Que est ista que ascendit de deserto, deliciis affluens, innixa super dilectum suum?'[103] Gloriosa Dei sponsa et uirgo felix Eadburga, de telluris profundo tanquam de deserto deliciis afluens innixa, quasi uile et despectum mansionis sue tugurium preciosiore commercio permutauit. Quod enim non curamus desertum dicimus, et quod diligentes amplectimur et inhabitamus, uelud affluentes delicias possidemus. Sic ad nouam uirgo thecam uelud ad regni translata est gloriam, que in huius peregrinationis exilio honore condigno debitam promeruit reuerentiam, ut humilem precelse maiestatis throno mutuaret sepulturam. Et bene innixa super dilectum suum dicitur, quia amoris Christi dulcedine debriata, mente ac spiritu de terris ad celum, et menbris corporeis transfertur ad serenum.

fol. 103v

[20]

Iam uero ut ceptam ex ordine prosequamur historiam, ad materiam reuertamur de qua regressi fuimus, et ad laudem uirginis auxiliante Domino noua incude eius opera retexamus. Cum itaque barbarus ferocis Dacie populus liberiores Anglice gentis proceres inuasisset,[104] et uulgus inerme atque captiuum pati cogeret exterminium, spoliis gaudebat atque direptione miserorum. Hacque in patria debachatur frendens insania, et quoscumque afflictos redimere poterat, argento et auro crudeliter redimebat. Unde sanctimoniales femine uirgines, pro redemptione suorum, ere pretioso spoliauerunt beate uirginis feretrum, et pro suis

---

[103] Cant. 8:5.
[104] Cf. n. 28 above; again the reference must be to the series of Danish invasions which commenced *c.* 980.

293

liberandis dederunt in pretium, sicque facta est redemptio captiuorum. Urna deinde sacra amicta est pallio, sicque permansit tempore diuturno. Verum postmodum uenerabilis abbatissa Aelfleda nomine,[105] oblationibus fidelium uas idem renouauit populorum, totum ex integro per circuitum circumdans argento unius parietis latere subtiliter deaurato. Excreuit postea in deuotis piorum cordibus sancte uirginis memoria, operante religionis femina Alfletha abbatissa, que secundam uirginalis urne particulam, / aureis floribus exornauit, et piarum adminiculo reginarum crucis Christi signum in medio fixum super erexit.

fol. 104

Ecce, o uirgo speciosa et felix Eadburga, integer et unicus uirginitatis tue sponsus pre filiis hominum forma speciosus,[106] quia interiorem in te tuam adamauit pulchritudinem, exteriorem circumdedit tabernaculo tuo decorem. Quoniam eius gratia dum esses in corpore in labiis tuis est diffusa, auri et argenti ipsuis copia in urna tue uirginalis glorie haut tenuiter est extenta. Filie regum in honore tuo iubilant, et filie Iude in tuis laudibus solenniter exultant. In uestitu deaurato quam decorauit doctrina sapientie, a dextris regis astas circumdata uirtutum uarietate.[107] Adducentur post te superno regi uirgines, que tuo cotidie animate exemplo, in eius obsequio de hoste prostrato inueniuntur triumphantes. Gloriosa igitur caro tua pro dotis tue mercede reflorebit ut lilium, et odor tuus ut balsami resperget fragrantiam, in resurrectione sanctorum.

[21]

Ante innumera que operatus est Christus per beate uirginis merita in Wintoniensi urbe miracula, Ieremie lamentationis prophetia uidebatur impleta, que dictur: 'Vie Syon lugent, eo quod non sint qui ueniant ad solennitatem.'[108] Sancte namque uirgines ad supernam Ierusalem suspirantes, quasi uie Syon estimande fuerant, que religioso sue sanctitatis exemplo ad eterna solemnia plurimos ducebant. Que priusquam beata uirgo Eadburga euidentibus sue claritatis radiis esset ostensa, et signis patentibus in populo decorata, lugebant admodum desolationem suam, quia raro populus inter eas contemplationem querere conabantur diuinam. Fama namque sacerdotis Dei Suuithuni omnes ad festiua miraculorum suorum

[105] For this abbess see above, p. 34; very probably she is to be identified with the Alfletha who occurs below.
[106] Cf. Ps. 44:3. Cf. also *Letters*, p. 155, lines 18–19 (no. 42), to Alice, abbess of Barking.
[107] Cf. Ps. 44:10. Cf. also notes 71 and 89 above.
[108] Thren. 1:4.

alliciebat solennia, et iccirco squalide uirgines[109] sua torquebantur depressione et iactura. Sed postquam sol iusticie illuxit illis in gloria signorum magnifice uirginis, creuerunt in eadem ecclesia celestis patrie celebria, et gaudia sanctorum sunt multiplicata. Unde inter pretiosa pretiose mundi uictricis et uirginis insignia, rem uobis refero non minus indignam relatu, quam illis presentibus uisu facta est et auditu.

In predicta namque / ciuitate squalebat quidam languidus fol. 104v mirabili dolore ac morbo contractus, adeo ut neruis exsiccatis et arefactis in poplite, magis repere uideretur genibus quam pedibus ambulare. Hic Aeluricus recte nominatus uocabulo, cognomen ex aduerse ualitudinis contraxit incommodo. In lingua siquidem Anglica cuius hic interserere uitamus barbariem, publico hunc nomine appellabant repentem. Cumque tam contumeliosa grauiter afflictus laboraret molestia, gloriose uirginis Eadburge sibi patrocinium cumulare non desiit, que ueloci clementia adiutricem misero manum porrexit. Tamdiu namque peruigil in precibus sanctis perseuerauit et compunctione cordis, quod ab ea restitui sibi meruit totus incolumis.

Eia, beata uirgo, quam felix es et quam decora, in superni principis thalamo, ex cuius donatiuo balsama egris infundis celestia, ut sospitas in illis conualescat perfecta. Dilectus tuus descendit in hortum suum ad areolam aromatis,[110] quia in ecclesiam tuam per potentiam suam uenit ut decus magnificaret tue glorie uirginalis. Ibi candidus idem uirginis agnus inter lilia pascitur,[111] quia sancte congregationis tue piis exercitiis et uirtutum odoribus delectatur. Et quia tu in dilecto tuo gloriaris, et dilectus tuus tecum uersatur in liliis uirginei pudoris, mirra et aloe et omnibus primis unguentis[112] confecit andidotum, unde pro amore tuo dignatus est clementer sanare contractum. Nisi enim secundum apostolum emulatus esset debilis karismata meliora, prima recepisse non diceretur unguenta. Sed dum in ipso mirre nomine carnis conualuit mortificatio, comitatur aloe penitentie uidelicet amaritudo. Hec interiora purgare uitia consueuit, et peccatricem animam mundatam suo reconciliari creatori. Prima unguenta tria sunt karismata, dilectio Dei, dilectio proximi,[n] dilectio inimici. His uero tribus cum mirra et aloe parata est confectio, unde perfecte salutis integritas innouatur infirmo. Qui diuturno postmodum tempore incolumis

---

[n] *corr. from* proximo MS
[109] Cf. Thren. 1:4. [110] Cf. Cant. 6:1. [111] Cf. Cant. 2:16; 6:1–2.
[112] Cf. Cant. 4:14.

uiguit, artemque didicit sanguinem minuere, et stipem sibi cotidianam tali usu comparare. Durauit autem usque ad tempus Alfgiue uenerabilis abbatisse, que de Colonia ciuitate Germanie ex generoso sanguine natiuitatis traxit / originem, et in nouo sanctimonialium uirginum monasterio quod Capitolium dicitur sancte religionis didicit honestatem.[113] Nomen autem suum quod a repo uerbo diriuatur, usque ad supremum sue senectutis diem retinuit, sicque decollato sibi beneficio testis beate uirginis Eadburge fidelis permansit. Hic prefate quoad uixit abbatisse uenam uel capitalem incidere, familiaritatemque tante femine suis diligenter uotis inclinare.

fol. 105

[22]

Ecce mellifluus flos campi, qui expandit in uirginibus lilia conuallium[114] per latitudinem mundi, in terra salsuginis et inhabitabili austro flante secundo propulsat hyemem, et apparentibus pretiosis beate uirginis Eadburge floribus in terra deserti gratum diffundit odorem. Paupercule namque due ut didicimus femine que eodem hautque dissimili uexabantur languore, diuturni doloris per uirginem sacram euaserunt erumpnam, ipsaque patrocinante sospitatem recipere meruerunt concupitam. Earum una inter sacras sanctimonialium cateruas flammeo Christi insignita gratas° egit in laudibus Dei longo tempore ferias, eiusque uita et honesta conuersatio indicium omnibus prebuit, quod eam gloriosa uirgo Eadburga a corporis incommodo liberauit. Sic traxit ad se dulcedinem incarnati uerbi Dei affectus in illum prospicientis anime, que dum carnis sarcinam gereret, angelica degebat conuersatione. Et quia eiusdem redemptoris nostri uocabulum unguentum est exinanitum, et secundum ethimologiam nominis sui saluum faciet populum suum a peccatis eorum, in odore unguentorum eius[115] cucurrerunt muliercule post eum tracte, ad quas sanandas occurrit uirtus Dei fide prouocata et earum unanimitate. Ergo quia rex precellentem uirginem introduxerat in cubiculum suum,[116] de plenitudine eius

---

° -as *interlined addition* MS

[113] For this abbess see above, p. 34. The phraseology of Osbert's description of her noble birth closely parallels that of *Letters*, p. 53, line 8 (no. 3), to Henry, priest of Westminster and kinsman of Osbert, and p. 135, lines 27–9 (no. 40), to the nun Ida. Cf. also *Vita Edwardi*, p. 69, lines 27–9.   [114] Cf. Cant. 2:1.   [115] Cf. Cant. 1:3; 4:10.

[116] Cf. Cant. 1:3. Cf. *Letters*, p. 91, lines 30–1 (no. 22), to his niece Cecilia, and p. 140, lines 19–20 (no. 40), to the nun Ida.

gratie hausit antidotum, unde sospitatem reparauit debilium feminarum.

[23]

Adhuc lampades gloriose uirginis signorum suorum clarus accendit ignis,[117] et uirtus eius sue claritatis radios inuisibiliter uibrat,[118] quibus uisibiliter mundum et potentialiter / illustrat. De celo namque maiestas adueniens humano intuitu non comprehenditur, et tamen eius potentia in opere sentitur. Res est in propatulo[119] que manifestanda est mundo, cuius splendor ab ortu solis usque ad fines occiduos, illustrabat per secula auditores uniuersos. . .

fol. 105v

De Virmandensi namque castro quod beati Quintini martiris gloriosi subiacet patrocinio,[120] quidam clericus litterarum apicibus probe instructus Brittanniam adiit, et Wintonie hospitalitatis gratiam a sanctimonialibus feminis diligenter impetrauit. Qui uersu et prosa precellebat ceteris, et inter eiusdem temporis grammaticos uidebatur singularis. Hic prefate de qua diximus erat carus abbatisse, eiusque gaudebat tam religiosa honestate, quam honesta uenerabilis femine familiaritate. Cuius titulo precellenti instabilis illa que fortuna dicitur inuidit, eumque per casus uarios inmense aduersitatis attriuit.

Prepeditus namque grauissima uexatione capitis, affligebatur infelix maxime incommodo passionis. Sicque successu temporis laborauit in tormentis, ut dum cotidianam perferret in cerebro uertiginem, morbo conualescente uerteretur in furorem. Unde et cathenis et compedibus[121] tenebatur oneratus, et manicis fortasse ferreis terrebatur astrictus. Adeo namque dira preualuerat insania, ut neminem conuitiorum relinqueret expertem, nullum flagellorum quem attingebat immunem. Antiquus etiam ille humani generis inimicus, qui de eodem misero domicilium suum fecerat, in uerbis blasphemie per os eius triumphabat. Contumeliosa enim eius uerba uerberabant aera, et quiddam execrabile spumabat ad celum, et quod eructabat retorquebat in Deum. Condolet infelici uenerabilis ancilla Christi, et qua pastorali preminebat auctoritate, sacerdotes ecclesie precepit adesse. Religiose quoque illius sancte congregationis femine iubentur

---

[117] Cf. Cant. 8:6.   [118] Cf. notes 4 above and 138 below.
[119] Cf. *Letters*, p. 116, line 12 (no. 33).
[120] Saint-Quentin (*Augusta Veromanduorum*, alleged scene of the martyrdom of St Quentin) in the diocese of Noyon.   [121] Cf. 2 Par. 33:11; Marc. 5:4; Luc. 8:29.

assistere, ut utriusque sexus suffragiis comitantibus, de atrio suo fortis proiciatur armatus. Cum sancta itaque uirago tecti illius subisset tugurium, peruersus et hospes et hostis in aduentu sanctorum infremuit, et per os eius quem captiuum tenebat in huiusmodi uocem erupit: 'Per uirtutis illius potentiam que ubique eternaliter et regnat et imperat, te contestor / et adiuro, ut nomen Patris et Filii et Spiritus Sancti reticeas, nec tuis egressum labiis illud in me refundas.' Latinis autem usus est uerbis dum hec diceret, dum in presentia sancte illius multitudinis auarus predo trepidaret. Hoc intellecto insignis et precelsa uirago, eum deferri ad ecclesiam beate Dei genitricis et Eadburge sacre uirginis imperat,[122] ut sanctorum precibus ab hac egritudine citius conualescat.

Vinctus itaque ferro et circumcinctus cathenis, ante crucem Christi miserabilis sistitur, et in pauimento prostratus ab illis qui aderant beate patrociniis Eadburge cum lacrimis commendatur. Que uero tanquam mater presidebat reliquiis, in psalmis pro misero desudat et lamentis, quodque psaltes David in unum corpus colligens Spiritu Sancto dictante cecinit, uolumen ex integro insignis uirago decantauit. Dolium illic preparatum astitit, quod sacre benedictionis aqua repletum per presentium manus infelicem excepit. Ex arbusto quod sauina dicitur flagellum redigitur, et eo cesus acrius cruciatur. Inuocant sacre uirgines Eadburgam Christi uirginem, ut pro misero supplicet apud Dei maiestatem. Singultus edunt et lacrimas proferunt, et earum libamina usque ad aures uirginales in celum conscendunt. Que sue congregationis uicta meritis, precibus pulsauit superni misericordiam iudicis, ut possessus a demone miseriam euaderet tante calamitatis. Sceptrum enim peruersi superauit exactoris, et iugum oneris eius a ceruice patientis excussit, eumque misericorditer ad integram sospitatem sacra uirgo reduxit. Redit ad se ipsum et secum deinceps habitat, quem extra semet ipsum ducens predo malignus hactenus inhabitabat. Ita in momento leni sopore perfunditur, et teterrimum emittens sudorem, ab omni labe liberatur.

[24]

Fluunt iterum optima gloriose uirginis Eadburge de supernis unguenta, que ex cella caritatis uinaria sponso suo imperante celitus

---

[122] Nunnaminster; for the dedication of the house see above, p. 125.

elicuit,[123] et ad tellurem uirtutibus sterilem ut fecundaretur et fructificaret emisit. Cuius ut dulcedo spiritualis presentie supernorum fragrantiam refunderet aromatum, tabernacula cedar uariis passionibus inhabitantis demonii terribiliter denigrata, sicut pelles Salomonis mutato colore Ethiopis formosa facta sunt rursus / et decora.[124] Referenda est igitur ueritatis hystoria fidelium naribus odoranda, que superiori nequaquam dispar uidetur esse relatu, immundo spiritui uirtute contraria Spiritus Sancti.

Est pagus apud Occidentales Saxones Wiltonia uulgariter appellatus,[125] qui populosis undecumque conuentibus agitur, et nundinarum frequentibus mercimoniis insignitur. In hac infelix quidam homo arreptus est a demonio, quem multa passionum congerie infestus predo cohercuit, et mutato interius mentis habitu per scissuras uarias dissipauit. Patientis itaque cognati precepta opinione solenni pretiose uirginis Eadburge de Wiltonia proficiscuntur, spe bona fulti Wintoniam, ut apud eam impetrent tam aduerse ualitudini sospitatem desideratam.

Memoranda itaque religiose sanctitatis femina de qua prelibauimus abbatissa, eum ante crucifixi Saluatoris flagellari fecit ymaginem, ut sibi propitiaret immensam clementie Dei in hoc incommodo maiestatem. Interpellatur Eadburga uirgo sacra, inuocantur frequentius ipsius presidia. Pulsat celos congregationis sancte deuotio, et unaquaque earum sacrificium offert contriti cordis Deo. Liberat igitur Dominus hominem per Eadburge uirginis pretiose intercessionem, et recedente informis monstri infesta tyrannide, fetor teterrimus locum occupauit intolerabili densitate. Sic in sanctis suis semper Deus laudatur et predicatur mirabilis,[126] et ut redemptor noster apostolis suis predixit in euangelio, hoc genus in nullo eicitur nisi in oratione et ieiunio.[127] Quia uidelicet aperte nobis datur intelligi, quod fortis armatus a congrediente non prosternitur, nisi qui cum eo conflixerit uictoria celebrior et fortior habeatur. Recessit igitur ad propria gratulans et incolumis, Deum collaudans et Eadburgam de immensis beneficiis collate sospitatis.

---

[123] Cf. Cant. 2:4.   [124] Cf. Ier. 13:23; Cant. 1:4.
[125] Wilton, Wiltshire. For some aspects of Wilton's history see above, pp. 37–44, ch. 5.
[126] Cf. Ps. 67:36. Cf. *Vita Edwardi*, p. 81, line 29; p. 113, line 16; p. 119, line 19.
[127] Cf. Matt. 17:20; Marc. 9:28. Cf. also *Letters*, p. 174, lines 27–8 (no. 42), to Alice, abbess of Barking.

[25]

De nectarea mellis dulcedine quam faui miraculorum emanant pretiose uirginis Eadburge, quedam uobis replicanda est ueritatis hystoria, ad Christi laudem et gloriam celebri titulo solenniter declarata. Vinctus quidam ferreis regis edicto in urbe Wintonie fol. 107 atterebatur loris, / qui sanctorum edes locorum per celebres circuire dies consueuerat, et sue captiuitatis erumpnas coram mensa dominica et corporibus sanctorum quibus urbs abundat exponebat.[128] Ingressus itaque aliquando quod corpore sacre uirginis insignitum est beate Dei genitricis oratorium, auxilium postulat Eadburga sacra patrocinante diuinum. Iniuriam replicat quam irremediabiliter tolerat, iudiciique periculum quod sibi futurum imminere formidat. Cum ergo tantis quateretur anxia mens in sua captione miseriis, aliquando suis precibus pium Dominus indulsit auditum, et ex inprouiso ingredienti uniuersa confracta sunt pondera uinculorum. Sonus itaque tam immensus omnium aures reuerberat, quia uelocius diuino confracte sunt imperio compedes, quam artificio conteri possent humano. Mater sancte congregationis solennes eadem hora Deo psalmorum uictimas immolabat, que stupefacta miraculo omnipotentem Deum et sanctam Eadburgam glorificat et adorat. Accitisque sanctimonialibus feminis quibus preerat, in cymbalis benesonantibus[129] Saluatoris potentiam cum eisdem laudat. Detinet secum per aliquot dies uirago insignis cathenis exemptum, sicque auctoritate regali proprie libertati restituit,[130] quem rex regum Dominus pretiose meritis Eadburge ferreis nexibus absoluit.

Plura sunt que seculorum Dominus omnium ad sepulchrum uirginis operatus est insignia miraculorum, quibus illustratur eadem in qua requiescit ciuitas regia,[131] unde superno regi gratias agendo gratulatur et exultat omnis terra. Letemur ergo et nos splendida gloriose uirginis Eadburge uenerando preconia, et celebrem pretiose translationis eius diem egregie laudis prosequamur recordatione preclara. Interpellet ipsa pro nobis

---

[128] For discussion of the several major shrines of the Winchester religious houses see above, pp. 116–17. [129] Cf. Ps. 150:5.

[130] There is perhaps an echo here of the laws of Alfred, c. 2: 'Gif hwa þara mynsterhama hwelcne for hwelcere scylde geseca, þe cyninges feorm to belimpe, oððe oðerne frione hiered þe arwyrðe sie, age he þreora nihte fierst him to gebeorganna, buton he ðingian wille' (Liebermann (ed.), *Gesetze*, I, 148).

[131] For Winchester's status as the principal *ciuitas regia* of late Anglo-Saxon England see above, pp. 114–16.

regem supernum, sacrarum sponsum uirginum, ut per eius nobis
merita gaudia cum sanctis suis tribuat sempiterna, ubi gloriosa
eadem et felix Eadburga cum regum omnium Domino fruitur luce
perpetua, et uirginitatis splendida decoratur corona, in angelorum
societate sanctorum, Ipso largiente, qui uiuit et regnat in secula
seculorum, Amen.

fol. 107vP

[26]

Ihesu Christo[132] in cunctis mundi nationibus principaliter
imperante, cum gloriosa eiusdem redemptoris sponsa et uirgo
illustris Eadburga crebris miraculorum prodigiis in Wintoniensi
choruscharet prouincia, longinqua etiam loca claritate penetrauit
admodum copiosa. Cuius uirtutis potentia non nullos sibi diuitum
conciliauit animos, et ad sue uirginee puritatis obsequium familiari
dulcedine inclinauit obligatos. Inter quos preclarus quidam comes
Alwardus enituit, qui Persorense cenobium in honore beate Dei
genitricis et perpetue uirginis Marie cum summa deuotione
construxit.q[133] Huic agnomen Wada Anglico sermone a
consanguineis ipsius est inditum, quod apud conprouinciales
uetustas usque in diem non deleuit hodiernum. Odor opinionis
tanti uiri mellifluus transcendebat aera, et celos penetrabat puritas
cordis angelorum Domino gratiosa. Trahebatur aureis assidue
bonorum funibus operum, diuinorum redolens fragrantia
preceptorum. Tractus utique currebat in sanctorum desideriorum
odore, promissione delectatus remunerationis eterne. Unde zelo
succensus flagrabat superno, ut pretiose uirginis Eadburge reliquias
adquireret, easque solenniter in monasterio quod restaurauerat
collocaret.

Igitur ab Alfghiua illius temporis abbatissa ausu parentali cum
feruore petiit, quod quia nepos eiusdem erat ei mater
congregationis non negauit. Sinciput itaque uirginis pretiose cum
aliquibus costis et minutioribus sacratis ossibus aliisque suscepit ab
abbatissa reliquiis, centumque latenter libras enumerauit monete
probatioris. Hec siquidem sanctimonialium magistra feminarum
filia Aðeluuoldi comitis extitit, cui Ætheldrida que regi

P *three lines blank both at the end of fol. 107 and at the beginning of fol. 107v, the latter presumably*
   for addition of rubric   q *marginal addition MS; erasure in text*

132 This chapter begins a short third book concerning the translation of some of Edburga's
     relics to Pershore and the inception of her cult at that house. For discussion of Edburga's
     cult at Pershore see above, pp. 19, 30–1, 129–39.

133 For the foundation and early history of Pershore see above, pp. 30–1, 36, 129–39.

postmodum Eadgaro iuncta est conubio carnali genitura mater
fuit.[134] Plures enim sunt qui sicut in preclaro comite sedulitatem
hanc uenerantur religiosam, sic abbatisse detestandam in
predictarum distractione reliquiarum calumpniantur auariciam.
fol. 108 Quia uero summis / annitebatur uir iste illustris gazarum copiis,[135]
quod de sacrata uirgine inspiratum celitus conceperat et
uoluntarium, ab herili magnopere femina tam prece quam precio
coemit extortum.

[27]

Potest heros iste insignis ad honorem beate et gloriose uirginis,
Domino et regi sacre concinere uirginitatis: 'Sub umbra', inquit,
'eius quem desideraueram sedi, et fructus eius dulcis gutturi
meo.'[136] Refrigeratio huius umbraculi amorem, et dulcedo
Spiritus Sancti, cuius rore mellifluo uitiorum extinguntur incendia,
et calore ad superna corda fidelium illuminantur accensa. Quem
noster utique dilectus sanctis immittit animabus, cuius uidelicet
fructus idem dulcedo spiritualis carnis eius et sanguinis, saporem
infundit superne sacietatis. Hac celestis sponsi copiosa prediues
consul inebriatus gratia, sub umbra illius sub protectione scilicet
sanctarum sedit reliquiarum, iocunditatis eterne diu desideratum
percipiens fructum.

[28]

Claruit itaque patentibus indiciis quanta uiri deuotio esset
consularis, ceperuntque uirginis merita in eodem loco crebrescere,
quo imperante Altissimo uirtus de celo eandem dignata est
prouinciam illustrare. Inter mundi huius procellas candidam Deus
in beata Eadburga nutrierat columbam, que ei fructus offerret
pacifice pinguedinis, oleo delibuta integerrime castitatis. Placuit
itaque celorum Domino palam fieri mortalibus se non delectari
auro uel argento, sed pura conscientia et sincere caritatis obsequia.
Hec sunt iocunda que requirit sacrificia gratia diuina, fragrantia
uidelicet sanctarum orationum aromata, et suauiter redolentia
preclare deuotionis incensa. Sicut enim columba quondam a Noe
reseruata est in archa, que ramum uespere uirentis oliue in ore suo

---

[134] For this abbess see above, p. 34. Cf. *Vita Edwardi*, p. 69, line 25, cited at n. 93 above.
[135] Cf. *Letters*, p. 147, line 8 (no. 41).   [136] Cant. 2:3.

302

detulit,[137] sic moderno tempori circa uesperam seculi beatam Deus Eadburgam sua propitiatione reseruauit. Hec est que signum pacis consueuit ingerere dilectoribus suis, hec est que emulatores sue sequipedasque castimonie, introducere non denegat ad portum tranquillitatis eterne.

fol. 108v[r]

[29]

Cum igitur Wintonia quadam ut premisimus sacri corporis portione esset diminuta, rara postmodum uisa sunt urbem illustrare gloriose uirginis Eadburge miracula. Et licet non nullis temporum interuallis prodigiorum suorum signa retraxerit, impreciabilis tamen uirgo diu ocultatos sue claritatis radios noua quasi potentia tandem uibrauit.[138] Vidit et miserta est ut fas est credere contritis corde, et quos in humilitate spiritus et gemituum sciebat anxietate deficere, hos fraterne dilectionis uisceribus affluens celesti non tardauit consolatione recreare. Age ergo solennes et celebres ciuitas regia beate Eadburge gratias et laudes, quoniam que peccatis exigentibus te uisa est aliquanto tempore uoluisse deserere, iterum compatiens copiosis non dedignatur fulgoribus illustrare. Intuetur oculo nequaquam obliquo quanta sit in Persorensibus suborta deuotio, iccirco ut confidimus diuisio ei facta non displicet, cuius uirtutis excellentia in longinquis etiam regionibus[139] plures eius obsequio deditos docet.

[30]

Egregius igitur uir palatinus et uenerabilis consul Alwardus fide susceptis et intimo karitatis ardore reliquiis, ad Persorense quod restaurauerat redit cenobium, thesaurum secum deferens super aurum et topazion pretiosum.[140] Domicilium uero regie uirgini preparat aureum, artificiali opere et ordine preclaro solennibus titulis mirabiliter insignitum. Collocantur uirginis reliquie in urna que fuluo resplendebat ere, ubi fulgurantibus miraculis eius ceperunt merita clarescere, et uenerabilis uiri fides inclitis splendoribus choruschare.

Eia consul preclare, consul uenerande, canta gloriose uirgini

---

[r] *one line blank at foot of fol. 108*
[137] Cf. Gen. 8:8–12. [138] Cf. notes 4 and 118 above.
[139] Cf. Luc. 19:12. Cf. *Letters*, p. 156, line 3 (no. 42). Cf. also n. 142 below.
[140] Cf. Ps. 118:127.

canticum leticie, quod ei sponsus eius precinit perhenni redolens caritate. '"Pulchre sunt"', inquit, '"gene tue sicut turturis, collum tuum sicut monilia, murenulas aureas faciemus tibi, uermiculatas argento."'[141] Quia uero in genis sedes inspicitur Dei, pudoris, recte uirgo inpreciabilis Eadburga a sponso celesti assimilatur turturi, cuius in celibe uita uirtutibus redolens conscientia famulatus obsequium professa est castitati. Amissa namque ad tempus Christo coniugali suo, qui 'in regionem abiit longinquam / accipere sibi regnum'[142] in supernis et honorem et gloriam, ipsa post eum quasi soliuaga et gemitibus plena illesam uirginitatis conseruabat coronam. Que nichil in hoc corpore uiriditatis habuit, quia nichil in temporalibus pretiosum concupiuit. Cuius collum celestibus decoratum splendet monilibus; quia semper in illa uiguit solida castitatis custodia, et sincere mentis claritas inuiolabilis et incorrupta. Et quia in monilibus aureis lapides pretiosi radios solent uibrare splendoris, eius uirginitati inseruntur uirtutes tanquam auro claritatis lapides, castas cordis eius cogitationes in lege mandatorum Dei firmiter obserantes. Sic uirgo insignis et regia suis collaudantibus ostendit exemplo, quod caste mentis conciperent et fouerent in gremio.

Unde etiam fidelis deuotio consularis uiri murenulas ei fabricauit operis aurei, in uarietate uermiculatas nitentis argenti,[143] cum in preclaro uase quod uirgineis preparauerat ultro reliquiis, pretiosa circumdedit diuerse claritatis. Ipsa namque, uirgo conspicua, uirgo preclara, celesti redundauit uelut auro sapientia, et nitenti uelut argento in castis eloquiis resplenduit scientia. Iccirco uir inclitus uir uenerandus, ex metallo ei pretioso condidit habitaculum, quod thesaurum sanctarum contineret reliquiarum.

Cuius fidei deuotio iugi miraculorum roboratur triumpho, que in Persorensi prouincia operari dignatus est Dominus, gloriose uirginis Eadburge suffragio. Surdi recipere merentur auditum, ceci uisum, debiles et claudi reformantur ad gressum. Mutis loquela redditur, et morborum uarietas noua sospitate reparatur.[144] Nec minus celebri uirgo insignis apud Persorenses gloria resplenduit, quam in exactis retro diebus penes Wintoniam signorum potentia radiauit.

Unde tam insignis fame noticiam in multorum auribus sonuit, inde ex diuersitate locorum ad Persorense cenobium innumeros

fol. 109

---

141 Cant. 1:9–10. 142 Luc. 19:12. Cf. n. 139 above.
143 Cf. Cant. 1:10. 144 Cf. n. 100 above.

adduxit. Et qui alia sanctorum loca propter audita miracula deserunt, ad noua beate uirginis Fadburge patrocinia ut illic adorent non mediocriter tendunt. Nec in sua meruit honorem tantummodo patria, sed in regione gloriam et laudem recepit aliena. Sicque factum est, ut cum Persorensibus innumeris choruscet illustris Eadburga prodigiis, et cum Wintoniensibus copiosa redundet / caritate miraculis.

fol. 109v

[31]

Alloquatur itaque sponsus celestis sponsam suam Eadburgam gloriosam uirginem, et supernis magnificet preconiis tam celebris pudicitie splendidam puritatem. 'Ortus', inquit, 'conclusus es soror mea sponsa, ortus conclusus, fons signatus. Emissiones tue paradisus malorum punicorum, cum pomorum fructibus.'[145] Merito beata et inpreciabilis Christi sponsa et uirgo illustris Eadburga conclusus dicitur ortus, diuersarum virtutibus uarietatibus ornatus, et fons salutari caractere sapientia Dei signatus que in baptismate signo crucis Christi insignita resplenduit, et donis Sancti Spiritus consecrata ineffabili uictoria triumphauit, cui illecebre carnalis nullum inhesit uestigium, quia uirginitatis egregie candidum absque macula seruauit indumentum. Et quod de superni fontis dulcedine haurire promeruit, sequentibus suis uirginibus sacris propinante gratia ministrauit. Cuius emissiones non incongrue predicantur esse paradysus, hoc est ortus deliciarum,[146] diuersis arboribus consitus, et iocundis eterne uoluptatis fructibus ad refectionem uite hinc inde constipatus. Que sancte et egregie conuersationis exemplo fideque doctrina precellens, uirgines Christo peperit morum sibi uenustate consimiles, de secreta quiete contemplationis interne ad publicum humane noticie per opera iusticie procedentes. In eius uita celibe mala punica suauiter redolent, dum illam sacra martirum Christi uulnera ad tolerantiam passionum an area gymnasii triumpharis exercent. Quodque rosei sanguinis Christi pretiosam effusionem recolit, hanc ad martirium fortiter perferendum si non desit persecutor accendit. Cetera uero poma que uirent et non redolent[s] sacre confessionis significant propositum, quo triumphat cum gloria uirginum hanc sequentium celibatus sanctarum. He sunt Spiritus Sancti[t] fistule celestibus

---

[s] *later addition MS*   [t] sancte *MS*
[145] Cant. 4:12–13.   [146] Cf. Gen. 2:8.

organis insignite, quarum gloriosa uita beate predicat uirginis Eadburge merita, et preconia resonat uirtutum fidibus in cythara pudicitie temperata.

[32]

In hospita tellure Wigornensis prouincie operante Domino Nostro Ihesu Christo, uirgo celebris et gloriosa Eadburga prodigiis adicit prodigia, Persorensibusque multa confert beneficia largitate copiosa / namque radios suorum adeo celestis gratia multiplicat, ut usque ad in hodiernum diem splendor ueri solis in operatione beate uirginis ab eadem regione non recedat. Infra unius anni spatium tanta refulsit illic claritate miraculorum, ut centum ab aduersa ualitudine liberarentur inualidi, diuturni languoris feruore decocti. Gratulantur Persorenses quia Deus eosdem respexit humiles, triumphant et iubilant quia uisitauit eos oriens superna magnalia personantes. Eadburgam uirginem eximiam solenni fauore magnificant, et speciosum forma pre filiis hominum[147] eiusdem sponsum preconantur et laudant.

Wintonienses lamentantur et deflent, quod antiqua signorum claritate non resplendet.[v] Iccirco satagunt patrocinia uirginis gloriose nudis adusque Persoram pedibus postulature procedere, et ne suum Wintonie domicilium deserat uotis supplicibus exorare. Sed Deus Omnipotens urbem Wintonie misericorditer, et fines Persorensis ecclesie in miraculis patrocinantis Eadburge respexit solenniter. Utrobique predicanda refulgent magnalia, utrobique claritatis potentia rutilat gratiosa. Sit ergo decus Altissimo, qui eam talem ac tantam condidit, quod per eius merita innumera suis fidelibus beneficia prouidit.

[33]

Adiecit itaque Dominus omnium insignem miraculis Eadburge uirginis incrementum, quod Persorensibus maximum in prouincia cumulauit preconium. Mulierem namque quandam paralysis aduersa ualitudo dissoluerat, que interminata prorsus egritudine laborabat. Aurem siquidem et os eiusdem torte[w] pene in unum redegerat, eamque ut uidebatur molestia incurabilis affligebat. Ita

---

u *one line blank at foot of fol. 109v*
v *final* e *?later addition on erasure* MS   w tercio MS
147 Cf. n. 106 above.

funditis a cunctis desperata diutius quatitur, et sub pressura ponderosi doloris uehementer arcetur.

Sed quid est, o mulier, quod non confugis ad eius potentiam, que consueuit inualidis larga salutis conferre remedia? Cur ad Eadburgam non intendis conuolare, celeriter, que iuuare misellos consueuit hylariter? Nunquid non audisti quam celebri refulget inclita uirgo gloria, quot et quanta potentialiter exercet insignia? Nunquid non consideras uirginis sancte potentiam, nunquid non attendis ineffabilem eius predicandamque po/tentiam? Noli differre utramque salutem a sponsa Christi repetere, antidotumque medele celestis a superni regis pretiosa uirgine postulare, et si non potes pedibus ad eius subsidia currere, uel aliorum manibus allata amoris deuotione uelocius curre. Manus namque medici celestis sponse myrram distillant, quam tibi nequaquam diffidas proficere, si te in uitiorum uiderit insignis heros mortificatione persistere. Et digiti eius mirra sunt probatissima pleni,[148] quia claritatis eius radii in miraculorum sunt exhibitione diuisi. Alios namque a febribus sulleuat, alios a cecitate mirabiliter sanat. Ab aliorum corporibus pellit demonia, ab aliis surditas effugatur diuturna. Alios podagra diffluentes liberat, alios a natiuitate contractos reformat. Alios a paralisi misericorditer eruit, alios a languoribus diuersis excludit. Accelera proinde eius suffragia uel desiderando reposcere, quia psalmista testante pauperum solet Dominus desiderium exaudire.[149]

Ad oratorium itaque uirginis sacre torta mulier prefata uenit infirmitate, uitulosque labiorum suorum Deo et sancte studuit Eadburge committere. Que dum uideretur in hac deuotione sedula, pertransiens quilibet eam pedis uexatione fatigauit incautam. Commota itaque die illa sospitati non redditur, ueruntamen in aliud tempus eius curatio prolongatur. Venit itaque non multum longo post tempore ad domicilium uirginis gloriose, ibique tamdiu orationibus sacris incubuit, donec eam splendidis choruschans uirgo miraculis, largiente Domino integra sospitate uestiuit.

Innumeris igitur huiuscemodi radians illustris uirgo miraculis, sicut ab infantia prerogatiua gratie Wintoniensibus iubare sue sanctitatis innotuit, sic Wigornensi prouincie claritate signorum uirtutis sue potentiam efficaciter patefecit. Tota itaque celesti fortitudine apud Persorenses diuersis infirmitatibus potentialiter imperat, que apud Wintonienses in maiore sui corporis portione

fol. 110v

---

[148] Cf. Cant. 5:5.   [149] Cf. Ps. 9,2:17.

triumphaliter choruscat. Colitur itaque dies celebris apud Persorenses pridie idus Octobris, in qua uenerabilis comes eius reliquiis predictum insigniuit monasterium,[150] eiusdemque Deo dicate uirginis cum plausibus et tripudio desideratum excepit aduentum.

fol. 120[x]   Conuertamus itaque ad illa puri/tatis nostre preconia, et solennia beate uirginis Eadburge meritis immolemus uota. Eadburga nobis in ore, nobis Eadburga semper uersetur in pectore, Eadburgam habeamus omni tempore celebrem, ipsaque uirgo custodiat populum sue translationis solennia deuotis excubiis dignis laudibus celebrantem, per regem et sponsum suum Dominum nostrum Ihesum Christum, qui uiuit et regnat cum Patre et Spiritu Sancto Deus in secula seculorum. Amen.

[x] *MS wrongly foliated; fol. 120 follows fol. 110v*
[150] For the Pershore feast of St Edburga see above p. 132. Cf. *Vita Edwardi*, p. 74, lines 25–6.

TWO ITEMS CONCERNING ST EDBURGA OF WINCHESTER FROM OXFORD, BODLEIAN LIBRARY, MS BODLEY 451

(A) FOL. 120: EXTRACT FROM A LIFE OF ST EDBURGA

Probat hoc quedam femina ceca, que in uisu edocta a pedessequis sancte uirginis poscens de lauatis manibus suis beneficia clam ab his accepit, uerentibus domine offensam si rescisceret factum, que omnis latere et Deo soli placere optabat depositum suum. Ubi ergo mulier aqua tactu uirginis medicata oculos tetigit et madefecit, albugo que luci obstabat rupta cecidit quam fluxa cruoris secutus lumina inuoluit; femina eadem sanatrice aqua cruorem abluit, moxque celum ac mundum serenissimo uisu hauriens, in laudes Dei sancteque sue uirginis erupit. Hec signa adhuc uolentia latere, insidiantibus peruersis clarius fulser[e], lampade Dei sub modio tegi non u[a]lente. Consueuerat alma uirgo per singulas noctes orandi gratia a monasterio exire, et beati Petri apostoli basilicam proximam per hortum monasterii interiacentem adire, ibique Deo fam[u]lari affectu precum et lacrimarum contrito corde odoramenta immolare. Hunc eius usum[a] quidam sentientes . . .[b] ex sua impuritate impurum iter e[i] [sus]picantes, uti mos est maligni ing[enii] animis ex sua malignitate omnia metir[i] atque innoxios suis ueneficiis deteriores suspicari, ceperunt quadam nocte sub astante arbore que dicitur alba spina proiecti, ipsius innocentie insidiari.

[a] *corr. from* uisum MS
[b] *several characters illegible* MS

(B) FOL. ii: A NOTE ON KING ALFRED, ST EDBURGA AND ST NEOT[1]

Rex Aluredus et beatus Neotus fratres fuerunt filii Adulfi regis qui terciam partem totius regni sui liberam ab omni tributo fecit, et sic liberam sancte ecclesie dedit. Huius filius ut dixi rex Aluredus qui xxix anno regni sui obiit, sed ante mortem multa passus, ut sibi predixerat beatus Neotus. Huius Aluredi filius fuit rex Edwardus senior, pater sancte Edburge uirginis, que iiii^{or} fratres et iii^{es} sorores habuit, quarum una regina Romanorum, alia Francorum sponsa cuiusdam Karoli, tercia regina Norþamhymbrorum, et ipsa sancta Edburga sponsa Ihesu Christi. A transitu uero Aluredi regis usque m.c.l. annum ab incarnatione Domini computati sunt cc^{ti}.l. anni; obiit enim anno incarnationis Domini d.cccc.i.^{a} A transitu pie uirginis Edburge in eodem m.c.l. anno incarnationis Domini completi sunt cc^{ti}.xix anni. Sunt itaque inter obitum Aluredi regis et transitum sancte Edburge anni xxx et i. Beatus uero Neotus ?plus x. annis ante obitum Aluredi regis transiit.

---

^{a} nongentesimo *superscript MS*

[1] This note is printed, with several errors and omissions, in Braswell, 'St Edburga', p. 304, n. 53. A similar note, breaking off after 'sponsa Ihesu Christi', is found in Oxford, Bodleian Library, MS Laud Misc. 664, fol. i.

BIBLIOGRAPHY

MANUSCRIPTS

Cambridge, Corpus Christi College   MS 393
Cambridge, Fitzwilliam Museum   MS 2–1957
Cambridge, Trinity College   MS O.2.1
Dublin, Trinity College   MS 172
London, British Library
  MS Cotton Caligula A. viii
  MS Cotton Nero A. ii/Galba A. xiv
  MS Cotton Titus A. viii
  MS Harley 64
New York, Pierpont Morgan Library   MS 736
Oxford, Bodleian Library
  MS Bodley 240 (SC 2469)
  MS Bodley 451 (SC 2401)
  MS Laud Misc. 114 (SC 1547)
  MS Rawlinson D. 894 (SC 13660)

PRINTED PRIMARY SOURCES

Major hagiographical works are listed under Vitae etc. Less important works, such as those included in *Nova legenda Angliae*, ed. K. Horstmann, 2 vols. (Oxford, 1901), are not separately referenced.

Abbo of Fleury, *Collectio canonum*, in *PL*, cxxxix, cols. 473–508.
Acta sanctorum Bollandiana (Brussels and elsewhere, 1643–).
Ailred of Rievaulx, *Genealogia regum Anglorum*, ed. R. Twysden, in *Historiae Anglicanae scriptores decem*, 2 vols. (London, 1652), i, cols. 347–70.
Alcuin, *Epistolae*, ed. F. Duemmler, in *Monumenta Germaniae historica epistolarum tomus IV* (Berlin, 1895).
An ancient manuscript of the eighth or ninth century: formerly belonging to St Mary's abbey or Nunnaminster, Winchester, ed. W. de Gray Birch, Hampshire Record Society (London and Winchester, 1889).
The Anglo-Saxon Chronicle, tr. D. Whitelock, D. C. Douglas and S. I. Tucker (London, 1961).
Anglo-Saxon wills, ed. D. Whitelock (Cambridge, 1930).
Annales monasterii de Wintonia, in *Annales monastici*, ii (1865), 3–125.

Bibliography

Annales monastici, ed. H. R. Luard, 5 vols., RS 36 (London, 1864–9).

Annales prioratus de Wigornia, in *Annales monastici*, IV (1869), 353–562.

Archbishop Wulfstan, *Institutes of polity*, tr. M. Swanton, in Swanton (ed.), *Anglo-Saxon prose* (London, 1975), pp. 125–38.

Asser's Life of King Alfred, ed. W. H. Stevenson (Oxford, 1904) (tr. S. Keynes and M. Lapidge, *Alfred the Great* (Harmondsworth, 1983)).

Ælfric's Lives of saints, ed. W. W. Skeat, 4 vols., EETS, Original Series 76, 82, 94, 114 (Oxford, 1881–1900; repr. in 2 vols. 1966).

Bede, *Historia ecclesiastica gentis Anglorum*, ed. B. Colgrave and R. A. B. Mynors, Oxford Medieval Texts (1969).

Boethius, *The consolation of philosophy*, ed. S. J. Tester, 2nd edn (London and Cambridge, Mass., 1973).

The Bosworth Psalter, ed. F. A. Gasquet and E. Bishop (London, 1908).

Canterbury professions, ed. M. Richter, with a palaeographical note by T. J. Brown, Canterbury and York Society 67 (Torquay, 1973).

Cartularium Saxonicum, ed. W. de Gray Birch, 3 vols. and index (London, 1885–99).

The Chronicle of Æthelweard, ed. A. Campbell, Nelson's Medieval Texts (1962).

The Chronicle of Hugh Candidus, ed. W. T. Mellows (London, 1949).

Chronicon abbatiae Rameseiensis, ed W. D. Macray, RS 83 (London, 1886).

Chronicon monasterii de Abingdon, ed. J. Stevenson, 2 vols., RS 2 (London, 1858).

Codex diplomaticus aevi Saxonici, ed. J. M. Kemble, 6 vols. (London, 1839–48).

Councils and ecclesiastical documents relating to Great Britain and Ireland, ed. A. W. Haddan and W. Stubbs, 3 vols. (Oxford, 1869–78).

Councils and synods, with other documents relating to the English church, I, A.D. 871–1204, ed. D. Whitelock, M. Brett and C. N. L. Brooke, 2 vols. (Oxford, 1981).

Dugdale, W., *Monasticon Anglicanum*, revised edn, J. Caley, H. Ellis and B. Bandinel, 6 vols. in 8 (London, 1817–30; repr. 1846).

English Benedictine kalendars after A.D. 1100, ed. F. Wormald, 2 vols., HBS 77 and 81 (London, 1939–46).

English historical documents I, ed. D. Whitelock, 2nd edn (London, 1979).

English kalendars before A.D. 1100, ed. F. Wormald, HBS 72 (London, 1934).

Facsimiles of English royal writs to A.D. 1100: presented to Vivian Hunter Galbraith, ed. T. A. M. Bishop and P. Chaplais (Oxford, 1957).

'Florence of Worcester', *Chronicon ex chronicis*, ed. B. Thorpe, 2 vols., English Historical Society (London, 1848–9).

Die Gesetze der Angelsachsen, ed. F. Liebermann, 3 vols. (Halle, 1903–16).

Die Heiligen Englands, ed. F. Liebermann (Hanover, 1889).

Historia et cartularium monasterii sancti Petri Gloucestriae, ed. W. H. Hart, 3 vols., RS 33 (London, 1863–7).

Historians of the church of York and its archbishops, ed. J. Raine, 3 vols., RS 71 (London, 1879–94).

The homilies of Wulfstan, ed. D. Bethurum (Oxford, 1957).

Inquisitio comitatus Cantabrigiensis, subjicitur Inquisitio Eliensis, ed. N. E. S. A. Hamilton, Royal Society of Literature (London, 1876).

Bibliography

The kalendar of Abbot Samson of Bury St Edmunds and related documents, ed. R. H. C. Davis, Royal Historical Society, Camden Third Series 84 (London, 1954).

Leland, J., De rebus Britannicis collectanea, ed. T. Hearne, 2nd edn, 6 vols. (London, 1770).

Itinerarium, ed. T. Hearne, 2nd edn, 9 vols. (Oxford, 1744).

The Leofric Collectar, ed. W. H. Frere, 2 vols., HBS 45, 56 (London, 1918).

The Leofric Missal, ed. F. E. Warren (Oxford, 1883).

The letters of Osbert of Clare, prior of Westminster, ed. E. W. Williamson (Oxford, 1929).

'The Liber confortatorius of Goscelin of St Bertin', ed. C. H. Talbot, Studia Anselmiana 37 (Rome, 1955), 1–117.

Liber Eliensis, ed. E. O. Blake, Royal Historical Society, Camden Third Series 92 (London, 1962).

Liber memorandorum ecclesie de Bernewelle, ed. J. W. Clark (Cambridge, 1907).

Liber monasterii de Hyda, ed. E. Edwards, RS 45 (London, 1866).

Liber vitae: register and martyrology of New Minster and Hyde abbey, Winchester, ed. W. de Gray Birch, Hampshire Record Society (London and Winchester, 1892).

'The liturgical calendar of Glastonbury abbey', ed. F. Wormald, in J. Autenrieth and F. Brunhölzl (eds.), Festschrift Bernhard Bischoff (Stuttgart, 1971), pp. 325–45.

Materials for the history of Thomas Becket, archbishop of Canterbury, ed. J. C. Robertson and J. B. Sheppard, 7 vols., RS 67 (London, 1875–85).

Matthew Paris, Chronica majora, ed. H. R. Luard, 7 vols, RS 57 (London, 1872–83).

Memorials of Saint Dunstan, ed. W. Stubbs, RS 63 (London, 1874).

Memorials of St Edmund's abbey, ed. T. Arnold, 3 vols., RS 96 (London, 1890–6).

The missal of the New Minster, Winchester, ed. D. H. Turner, HBS 93 (Leighton Buzzard, 1960).

The monastic breviary of Hyde abbey, Winchester, ed. J. B. L. Tolhurst, 6 vols., HBS 69, 70, 71, 76, 78, 80 (London, 1932–42).

Nova legenda Angliae, ed. K. Horstmann, 2 vols. (Oxford, 1901).

An Old English martyrology, ed. G. Herzfeld, EETS, Original Series 116 (London, 1900; repr. 1973).

Orderic Vitalis, Historia ecclesiastica, ed. M. Chibnall, 6 vols., Oxford Medieval Texts (1968–80).

The ordinale and customary of the Benedictine nuns of Barking abbey, ed. J. B. L. Tolhurst, HBS 65 (London, 1927).

Patrologiæ cursus completus, series latina, ed. J. P. Migne, 221 vols. (Paris, 1844–64).

Registrum Wiltunense, ed. R. C. Hoare (London, 1827).

Regularis concordia Anglicae nationis monachorum sanctimonialiumque, ed. T. Symons, Nelson's Medieval Texts (1953).

Sermo lupi ad Anglos, ed. D. Whitelock, 3rd edn (London, 1963).

Symeonis monachi opera omnia, ed. T. Arnold, 2 vols., RS 75 (London, 1882–5).

'Texts of Jocelyn of Canterbury which relate to the history of Barking abbey', ed. M. L. Colker, Studia Monastica 7 (1965), 383–460.

Three Lives of English saints, ed. M. Winterbottom (Toronto, 1972).

Two of the Saxon Chronicles parallel, ed. C. Plummer, 2 vols. (Oxford, 1892–9).

Ungedruckte Anglo-Normannische Geschichtsquellen, ed. F. Liebermann (Strassburg, 1879).

Vitae sanctorum Britanniae, ed. A. W. Wade-Evans (Cardiff, 1944).

Vitae sanctorum Danorum, ed. M. Cl. Gertz (Copenhagen, 1910–12).

William of Malmesbury, *De gestis pontificum Anglorum*, ed. N. E. S. A. Hamilton, RS 52 (London, 1870).

De gestis regum Anglorum, ed. W. Stubbs, 2 vols., RS 90 (London, 1887–9).

William of Poitiers, *Gesta Guillelmi ducis Normannorum et regis Anglorum*, ed. R. Foreville, Les Classiques de l'Histoire de France au Moyen Age 23 (Paris, 1952).

VITAE ETC.

ABBO OF FLEURY *Vita sancti Abbonis auctore Aimoino monacho*, in PL, CXXXIX, cols. 375–414.

ANSELM *The Life of St Anselm archbishop of Canterbury by Eadmer*, ed. R. W. Southern, Nelson's Medieval Texts (1962; repr. Oxford Medieval Texts, 1979).

ÆTHELBERT 'Two Lives of St Ethelbert, King and Martyr', ed. M. R. James, *EHR* 32 (1917), 214–44.

ÆTHELTHRYTH *Vita* (Ælfric), in *Ælfric's Lives of saints*, ed. W. W. Skeat, I, 432–40 (see also *HE*, IV, 19–20; *LE*, Book I).

ÆTHELWOLD *Vita* (Ælfric), in *Three Lives*, ed. M. Winterbottom, pp. 17–29.

Vita (Wulfstan), in *Three Lives*, ed. M. Winterbottom, pp. 33–63.

COLUMBA *Adomnan's Life of Columba*, ed. A. O. and M. O. Anderson (London, 1961).

DUNSTAN *Vita sancti Dunstani auctore Osberno*, in *Memorials of Saint Dunstan*, ed. W. Stubbs, pp. 69–161.

Vita sancti Dunstani archiepiscopi Cantuariensis (Eadmer), in *Memorials of Saint Dunstan*, ed. W. Stubbs, pp. 162–249.

EALHMUND *Vita S. Aelkmundi regis*, ed. P. Grosjean, 'Codicis Gothani appendix', *AB* 58 (1940), 177–204, at 178–83.

EDITH 'La Légende de Ste Edith en prose et vers par le moine Goscelin', ed. A. Wilmart, *AB* 56 (1938), 5–101, 265–307 (*Vita Edithe*).

S. Editha sive Chronicon Vilodunense im Wiltshire Dialekt, ed. K. Horstmann (Heilbronn, 1883).

EDMUND *Passio sancti Eadmundi Regis et Martyris* (Abbo), in *Three Lives*, ed. M. Winterbottom, pp. 67–87 (*Passio Edmundi*).

Passio (Ælfric), in *Ælfric's Lives of saints*, ed. W. W. Skeat, II, 314–35.

Hermanni archidiaconi liber de miraculis sancti Eadmundi, in *Memorials of St Edmund's abbey*, ed. T. Arnold, I, 26–92.

'Geoffrey of Wells, *De infantia sancti Edmundi (BHL* 2393)', ed. R. M. Thomson, *AB* 95 (1977), 25–42 (*De infantia*).

Samsonis abbatis opus de miraculis sancti Ædmundi, in *Memorials of St Edmund's abbey*, ed. T. Arnold, I, 107–208.

'A new *Passio beati Edmundi Regis (et) Martyris*', ed. J. Grant, *Mediaeval Studies* 40 (1978), 81–95.

EDWARD THE CONFESSOR   *The Life of King Edward the Confessor*, ed. F. Barlow, Nelson's Medieval Texts (1962).

'La Vie de S. Edouard le Confesseur par Osbert de Clare', ed. M. Bloch, *AB* 41 (1923), 5–131 (*Vita Edwardi*).

EDWARD THE MARTYR   *Passio et miracula sancti Eadwardi Regis et Martyris*, in C. E. Fell, *Edward*, pp. 1–17 (*Passio Edwardi*).

GREGORY THE GREAT   *The earliest Life of Gregory the Great*, ed. B. Colgrave (Kansas, 1968; repr. Cambridge, 1985).

GUTHLAC   *Felix's Life of St Guthlac*, ed. B. Colgrave (Cambridge, 1956; repr. 1985).

MILDRITH   Goscelin of Canterbury, *Vita Deo dilectae virginis Mildrethae*, in D. W. Rollason, *Mildrith legend*, pp. 108–43.

'A fragmentary Life of St Mildred and other Kentish royal saints', ed. M. J. Swanton, *Archaeologia Cantiana* 91 (1975), 15–27.

OSWALD   *Vita Oswaldi archiepiscopi Eboracensis*, in *Historians of York*, ed. J. Raine, I, 339–475 (*Vita Oswaldi*).

SWITHUN   'Sancti Swithuni Wintoniensis episcopi translatio et miracula, auctore Lantfredo monacho Wintoniensi', ed. E. P. Sauvage, *AB* 4 (1885), 367–410.

Frithegodi monachi breviloquium vitae beati Wilfredi et Wulfstani cantoris narratio metrica de sancto Swithuno, ed. A. Campbell (Zurich, 1950).

Vita (Ælfric), in *Ælfric's Lives of saints*, ed. W. W. Skeat, I, 441–73.

'Vita sancti Swithuni Wintoniensis episcopi auctore Goscelino, monacho Sithiensi', ed. E. P. Sauvage, *AB* 7 (1888), 373–80.

WERBURGA   *Vita sanctae Werburgae virginis*, in *PL*, CLV, cols. 93–110 (*Vita Werburge*).

WIGSTAN   *Vita* (Thomas of Marlborough), in *Chronicon abbatiae de Evesham*, ed. W. D. Macray, RS 29 (London, 1863), pp. 325–37.

WILFRID   *The Life of Bishop Wilfrid by Eddius Stephanus*, ed. B. Colgrave (Cambridge, 1927; repr. 1985).

WULFHILDA   'La Vie de sainte Vulfhilde par Goscelin de Cantorbéry', ed. M. Esposito, *AB* 32 (1913), 10–26.

WULFSIGE   'The Life of St Wulfsin of Sherborne by Goscelin', ed. C. H. Talbot, *Revue Bénédictine* 69 (1959), 68–85.

YVO   *Vita sancti Yvonis*, in *PL*, CLV, cols. 79–90.

PRINTED SECONDARY WORKS

Abbott, T. K., *Catalogue of the manuscripts in the library of Trinity College, Dublin* (Dublin and London, 1900).

Addyman, P. V., 'Saxon Southampton: a town and international port of the 8th to the 10th century', in H. Jankuhn *et al.* (eds.), *Vor- und Frühformen*, pp. 218–28.

Bibliography

Addyman, P. V., and Hill, D. H., 'Saxon Southampton: a review of the evidence', *Proceedings of the Hampshire Field Club* 25 (1968), 61–93, and 26 (1969), 61–96.

Aigrain, R., *L'Hagiographie: ses sources, ses méthodes, son histoire* (Paris, 1953).

Atkins, Sir Ivor, 'An investigation of two Anglo-Saxon kalendars (Missal of Robert of Jumièges and St Wulfstan's Homiliary)', *Archaeologia* 78 (1928), 219–54.

'The church of Worcester from the eighth to the twelfth century', *Antiquaries Journal* 17 (1937), 371–91, and 20 (1940), 1–38.

Banton, N., 'Monastic reform and the unification of tenth-century England', in S. Mews (ed.), *Religion and national identity, Studies in Church History* 18 (Oxford, 1982), 71–85.

Barlow, F., *Edward the Confessor* (London, 1970; repr. 1979).

The English church 1000–1066, 2nd edn (London, 1979).

The English church 1066–1154 (London, 1979).

'Guenta', *Antiquaries Journal* 44 (1964), 217–19.

Barlow, F., Biddle, M., von Feilitzen O., and Keene, D. J., *Winchester in the early Middle Ages: an edition and discussion of the Winton Domesday*, Winchester Studies 1 (Oxford, 1976).

Beaven, M. L. R., 'The beginning of the year in the Alfredian Chronicle, 866–87', *EHR* 33 (1918), 328–42.

Benoît-Castelli, G., 'Un Processional anglais du XIVe siècle', *Ephemerides Liturgicae* 75 (1961), 281–326.

Bentham, J., *The history and antiquities of the conventual and cathedral church of Ely*, 2nd edn (Norwich, 1812).

Bethell, D., 'The Lives of St Osyth of Essex and St Osyth of Aylesbury', *AB* 88 (1970), 75–127.

Bibliotheca hagiographica latina antiquae et mediae aetatis, 2 vols. and supplement (Brussels, 1891–1901; supplement, 1911).

Bibliotheca sanctorum, 12 vols. and index (Rome, 1961–70).

Biddle, M., 'Excavations at Winchester, 1962– ': interim reports 2–10 in *Antiquaries Journal* 44 (1964), 188–219; 45 (1965), 230–64; 46 (1966), 308–32; 47 (1967), 251–79; 48 (1968), 250–84; 49 (1969), 295–329; 50 (1970), 277–326; 52 (1972), 93–131; 55 (1975), 96–126, 295–337.

'Winchester: the development of an early capital', in H. Jankuhn *et al.* (eds.), *Vor- und Frühformen*, pp. 226–61.

'*Felix urbs Winthonia*: Winchester in the age of monastic reform', in D. Parsons (ed.), *Tenth-century studies*, pp. 123–40.

Biddle, M., and Kjølbye-Biddle, B., *The Anglo-Saxon minsters in Winchester*, Winchester Studies 4.i (Oxford, forthcoming).

Biddle, M., and Quirk, R. N., 'Excavations near Winchester cathedral, 1961', *Archaeological Journal* 119 (1962), 150–94.

Blackburn, M., Colyer, C., and Dolley, M., *Early medieval coins from Lincoln and its shire c. 700–1100* (London, 1983).

Blackburn, M., and Pagan, H., 'A revised check-list of coin hoards from the British Isles, *c.* 500–1100', in M. Blackburn (ed.), *Anglo-Saxon monetary history: essays in memory of Michael Dolley* (Leicester, 1986), pp. 291–313.

Blair, P. Hunter, *The world of Bede* (London, 1970).

Bibliography

Bloch, M., *Les Rois thaumaturges* (Strassburg, 1924).

Blunt, C. E., 'The St Edmund memorial coinage', *Proceedings of the Suffolk Institute of Archaeology* 31 (1967–9), 234–55.

Boehmer, H., 'Das Eigenkirchentum in England', in H. Boehmer *et al.* (eds.) *Festgabe für Felix Liebermann*, pp. 301–53.

Boehmer, H., *et al.* (eds.), *Texte und Forschungen zur Englischen Kulturgeschichte: Festgabe für Felix Liebermann* (Halle, 1921).

Bradley, H., 'Clare, Osbert de', in *Dictionary of national biography*, x (London, 1887), 386–7.

Braswell, L., 'St Edburga of Winchester: a study of her cult, a.d. 950–1500, with an edition of the fourteenth-century Middle English and Latin Lives', *Mediaeval Studies* 33 (1971), 292–333.

Brentano, R., review of W. A. Chaney, *The cult of kingship in Anglo-Saxon England* (Manchester, 1970), in *Speculum* 47 (1972), 754–5.

Brooke, C. N. L., *The Saxon and Norman kings*, 2nd edn (London, 1978).

'The Canterbury forgeries and their author', I and II, *Downside Review* 68 (1950), 462–76, and 69 (1951), 210–31.

'Archbishop Lanfranc, the English bishops and the Council of London of 1075', *Studia Gratiana* 12 (Bologna, 1967), 41–59.

'Approaches to medieval forgery', in C. N. L. Brooke, *Medieval church and society: collected essays* (London, 1971), pp. 100–20.

'The archdeacon and the Norman Conquest', in D. Greenway, C. Holdsworth, and J. Sayers (eds.), *Tradition and change: essays in honour of Marjorie Chibnall* (Cambridge, 1985), pp. 1–19.

Brooke, G. C., *English coins from the seventh century to the present day* (London, 1932).

Brown, P., *The cult of the saints: its rise and function in Latin Christianity* (Chicago, 1981).

A catalogue of the Harleian manuscripts in the British Museum, 4 vols. (London, 1808–12).

Catalogue of the manuscripts in the Cottonian library deposited in the British Museum (London, 1802).

Chadwick, N. K. (ed.), *Celt and Saxon: studies in the early British border* (Cambridge, 1963).

Chaney, W. A., *The cult of kingship in Anglo-Saxon England: the transition from paganism to Christianity* (Manchester, 1970).

Chaplais, P., 'The original charters of Herbert and Gervase, abbots of Westminster (1121–1157)', in P. M. Barnes and C. F. Slade (eds.), *A medieval miscellany for Doris Mary Stenton*, Pipe Roll Society, New Series 36 (London, 1962), pp. 89–110.

Chew, H. M., *English ecclesiastical tenants-in-chief and knight service* (Oxford, 1932).

Clemoes, P. A. M., 'The chronology of Ælfric's works', in Clemoes (ed.), *The Anglo-Saxons*, pp. 212–47.

Clemoes, P. A. M. (ed.), *The Anglo-Saxons: studies presented to Bruce Dickins* (London, 1959).

Colgrave, B., 'Bede's miracle stories', in A. Hamilton Thompson (ed.), *Bede, his life, times, and writings*, pp. 201–29.

Cottineau, L. H., *Répertoire topo-bibliographique des abbayes et prieurés*, 3 vols. (Mâcon, 1935–70).

Cousin, P., *Abbon de Fleury-sur-Loire* (Paris, 1954).

Cowdrey, H. E. J., 'Pope Gregory VII and the Anglo-Norman church and kingdom', *Studi Gregoriani* 9 (1972), 79–114.

Coxe, H. O., *Catalogi codicum manuscriptorum Bibliothecáe Bodleianáe*, II (Laudian MSS) (Oxford, 1858; repr. 1973).

Darby, H. C., 'The Fenland frontier in Anglo-Saxon England', *Antiquity* 8 (1934), 185–201.

Davies, W., and Vierck, H., 'The contexts of Tribal Hidage: social aggregates and settlement patterns', *Frühmittelalterliche Studien* 8 (1974), 223–93.

Davis, R. H. C., *King Stephen 1135–1154* (London, 1967).

  'East Anglia and the Danelaw', *Transactions of the Royal Historical Society*, Fifth Series 5 (1955), 23–39.

  'The monks of St Edmund, 1021–1148', *History* 40 (1955), 227–31.

Delehaye, H., *Les Légendes hagiographiques*, revised 3rd edn, Subsidia Hagiographica 18 (Brussels, 1927).

  Les Origines du culte des martyrs, 2nd edn, Subsidia Hagiographica 20 (Brussels, 1933).

  Cinq Leçons sur la méthode hagiographique, Subsidia Hagiographica 21 (Brussels, 1934).

  'La Méthode historique et l'hagiographie', *Bulletin de la Classe des Lettres et des Sciences Morales et Politiques, Académie Royale de Belgique*, Fifth Series 16 (1930), 218–31.

Dickins, B., 'The cult of St Olave in the British Isles', *Saga-Book of the Viking Society* 12 (1937–45), 53–80.

Dickinson, J. C., *The origins of the Austin canons and their introduction into England* (London, 1950).

Doble, G. H., *Lives of the Welsh saints*, ed. D. S. Evans, 2nd edn (Cardiff, 1984).

Dolley, R. H. M., *Viking coins of the Danelaw and of Dublin* (London, 1965).

  'An introduction to the coinage of Ethelred II', in D. Hill (ed.), *Ethelred the Unready*, pp. 115–34.

Donovan, M. A., 'An interim revision of episcopal dates for the province of Canterbury, 850–950: part II', *ASE* 2 (1973), 91–113, at 98.

Douglas, D. C., *William the Conqueror: the Norman impact upon England* (London, 1964; repr. 1977).

Dymond, D. P., 'Coincidence or corroboration?', *Proceedings of the Suffolk Institute of Archaeology and History* 35 (1981–4), 225.

Ekwall, E., 'The proportion of Scandinavian settlers in the Danelaw', *Saga-Book of the Viking Society* 12 (1937–45), 19–34.

Farmer, D. H., *The Oxford dictionary of saints* (Oxford, 1978).

  'The progress of the monastic revival', in D. Parsons (ed.), *Tenth-century studies*, pp. 10–19.

Farrer, W., *Feudal Cambridgeshire* (Cambridge, 1920).

Fedotov, G., *Sviatyje drevnej Rusi* (Paris, 1931).

Fell, C. E., *Edward King and Martyr*, Leeds Texts and Monographs, New Series 3 (Leeds, 1971).

Bibliography

'Edward King and Martyr and the Anglo-Saxon hagiographic tradition', in D. Hill (ed.), *Ethelred the Unready*, pp. 1–13.

Fellows Jensen, G., 'The Vikings in England: a review', *ASE* 4 (1975), 185–206.

Finberg, H. P. R., *Tavistock abbey*, Cambridge Studies in Medieval Life and Thought, New Series 2 (Cambridge, 1951).

·*The early charters of Wessex* (Leicester, 1964).

The house of Ordgar and the foundation of Tavistock abbey', *EHR* 58 (1943), 190–201.

Finucane, R. C., *Miracles and pilgrims: popular beliefs in medieval England* (London, 1977).

'The use and abuse of medieval miracles', *History* 60 (1975), 1–10.

Fisher, D. J. V., 'The anti-monastic reaction in the reign of Edward the Martyr', *Cambridge Historical Journal* 10 (1950–2), 254–70.

'The early biographers of St Æthelwold', *EHR* 67 (1952), 381–91.

Folz, R., *Les saints Rois du Moyen Age en Occident (VIe–XIIIe siècles)*, Subsidia Hagiographica 68 (Brussels, 1984).

'Naissance et manifestations d'un culte royale: Saint Edmond, roi d'Est Anglie', in K. Hauck and H. Mordek (eds.), *Geschichtsschreibung und geistiges Leben im Mittelalter: Festschrift für Heinz Löwe zum 65. Geburtstag* (Cologne and Vienna, 1978), pp. 226–46.

'Saint Oswald roi de Northumbrie: étude d'hagiographie royale', *AB* 98 (1980), 49–74.

Frank, R., 'Viking atrocity and skaldic verse: the rite of the blood-eagle', *EHR* 99 (1984), 332–43.

Gaiffier, B. de, *Recherches d'hagiographie latine*, Subsidia Hagiographica 52 (Brussels, 1971).

'Les Revendications de biens dans quelques documents hagiographiques du XIe siècle', *AB* 50 (1932), 123–38.

Galbraith, V. H., *Studies in the public records* (London, 1948).

Geary, P. J., *'Furta sacra': thefts of relics in the central Middle Ages* (Princeton, 1978).

Gelling, M., *The place-names of Oxfordshire*, 2 parts, English Place-Name Society 23 (Cambridge, 1953–4).

Górski, K., 'La Naissance des états et le "roi-saint": problème de l'idéologie féodale', in T. Manteuffel and A. Gieysztor (eds.), *L'Europe aux IXe–XIe siècles: aux origines des états nationaux* (Warsaw, 1968), pp. 425–32.

Gover, J. E. B., Mawer, Allen, and Stenton, F. M., *The place-names of Wiltshire*, English Place-Name Society 16 (Cambridge, 1939).

Gransden, A., 'Baldwin, abbot of Bury St Edmunds, 1065–1097', in R. Allen Brown (ed.), *Proceedings of the Battle Conference on Anglo-Norman Studies* 4 (1982), 65–76.

'The legends and traditions concerning the origins of the abbey of Bury St Edmunds', *EHR* 100 (1985), 1–24.

Graus, F. X., *Volk, Herrscher und Heiliger im Reich der Merowinger* (Prague, 1965).

Grierson, P., 'Grimbald of St Bertin's', *EHR* 55 (1940), 529–61.

Grierson, P., and Blackburn, M., *Medieval European coinage with a catalogue of the coins in the Fitzwilliam Museum, Cambridge, 1, The early Middle Ages (5th to 10th centuries)* (Cambridge, 1986).

Bibliography

Grosjean, P., 'Catalogus codicum hagiographicorum Latinorum bibliothecarum Dublinensium', *AB* 46 (1928), 81–148.

'De codice hagiographico Gothano', *AB* 58 (1940), 90–103.

Grundy, G. B., 'The Saxon land charters of Hampshire with notes on place and field names', *Archaeological Journal*, Second Series 31 (1924), 31–126.

Hardy, T. D., *Descriptive catalogue of materials relating to the history of Great Britain and Ireland*, 3 vols. in 4, RS 26 (London, 1862–71).

Harmer, F. E., *Anglo-Saxon writs* (Manchester, 1952).

Hart, C., 'Hereward "the Wake"', *Proceedings of the Cambridgeshire Antiquarian Society* 65 (1974), 28–40.

Hawkins, E., 'An account of the coins and treasure found in Cuerdale', *Numismatic Chronicle* 5 (1842–3), 1–48, 53–104.

Hill, D., 'Trends in the development of towns during the reign of Æthelred II', in Hill (ed.), *Ethelred the Unready*, pp. 213–26.

Hill, D. (ed.), *Ethelred the Unready: papers from the millenary conference*, British Archaeological Reports, British Series 59 (Oxford, 1978).

Hohler, C., 'St Osyth and Aylesbury', *Records of Buckinghamshire* 18 (1966–70), 61–72.

James, M. R., *The Western manuscripts in the library of Trinity College, Cambridge: a descriptive catalogue*, 4 vols. (Cambridge, 1900–4).

A descriptive catalogue of the manuscripts in the library of Corpus Christi College, Cambridge, 2 vols. (Cambridge, 1912).

Janini, J., and Serrano, J., *Manuscritos liturgicos de la Biblioteca Nacional* (Madrid, 1969).

Jankuhn, H., Schlesinger, W., and Steuer, H. (eds.), *Vor- und Frühformen der Europäischen Stadt im Mittelalter*, Abhandlungen der Akademie der Wissenschaften in Göttingen, 3 Folge, 83–4 (Göttingen, 1973–4).

John, E., *Land tenure in early England: a discussion of some problems* (Leicester, 1960).

Orbis Britanniae and other studies (Leicester, 1966).

'The beginning of the Benedictine reform in England', in John, *Orbis Britanniae*, pp. 249–64.

'The king and the monks in the tenth-century reformation', in John, *Orbis Britanniae*, pp. 154–80.

'Some Latin charters of the tenth-century reformation', in John, *Orbis Britanniae*, pp. 181–209.

Jones, A., 'The significance of the regal consecration of Edgar in 973', *Journal of Ecclesiastical History* 33 (1982), 375–90.

Kauffmann, C. M., *Romanesque manuscripts 1066–1190* (London, 1975).

'The Bury Bible', *Journal of the Warburg and Courtauld Institutes* 29 (1966), 60–81.

Keary, C. F., *A catalogue of English coins in the British Museum, Anglo-Saxon series*, 2 vols. (London, 1887–93).

Keene, D. J., with a contribution by A. Rumble, *Survey of medieval Winchester*, 2 vols., Winchester Studies 2 (Oxford, 1985).

Kemp, E. W., *Canonisation and authority in the Western church* (London, 1948).

Kennedy, A. G., 'Cnut's law code of 1018', *ASE* 11 (1983), 57–81.

Kennett, White, *Parochial antiquities attempted in the history of Ambrosden, Burcester and other adjacent parts in the counties of Oxford and Buckinghamshire* (Oxford, 1695).

Ker, N. R., *Catalogue of manuscripts containing Anglo-Saxon* (Oxford, 1957).

Medieval libraries of Great Britain: a list of surviving books, Royal Historical Society Guides and Handbooks 3, 2nd edn (London, 1964).

Medieval manuscripts in British libraries, II, *Abbotsford-Keele* (Oxford, 1977).

'Sir John Prise', *The Library*, Fifth Series 10 (1955), 1–24.

Keynes, S., *The diplomas of Æthelred 'the Unready', 978–1016: a study in their use as historical evidence*, Cambridge Studies in Medieval Life and Thought, Third Series 13 (Cambridge, 1978).

'The declining reputation of King Æthelred the Unready', in D. Hill (ed.), *Ethelred the Unready*, pp. 227–53.

Kirby, D. P., 'Bede, Eddius Stephanus and the "Life of Wilfrid"', *EHR* 98 (1983), 101–14.

Klauser, R., *Der Heinrichs- und Kunigundenkult im mittelalterlichen Bistum Bamberg* (Bamberg, 1957).

Knowles, D., *The monastic order in England 940–1216*, 2nd edn (Cambridge, 1963).

Knowles, D., Brooke, C. N. L., and London, V. C. M., *The heads of religious houses: England and Wales, 940–1216* (Cambridge, 1972).

Knowles, D., and Hadcock, R. N., *Medieval religious houses: England and Wales*, 2nd edn (London, 1971).

Kologrivof, I., *Essai sur la sainteté en Russie* (Bruges, 1953).

Korhammer, P., 'The origin of the Bosworth Psalter', *ASE* 2 (1973), 173–87.

Kreusch, F., *Beobachtungen an der Westanlage der Klosterkirche zu Corvey*, Beihefte der Bonner Jahrbucher 9 (Cologne–Graz, 1963).

Lambourn, E. A. G., 'The shrine of St Edburg', *Reports of the Oxfordshire Archaeological Society* 80 (1934), 43–52.

Landon, L., 'The early archdeacons of Norwich diocese', *Proceedings of the Suffolk Institute of Archaeology and Natural History* 20 (1930), 11–35.

Lapidge, M., *The cult of St Swithun*, Winchester Studies 4.ii (Oxford, forthcoming).

'The hermeneutic style in tenth-century Anglo-Latin literature', *ASE* 4 (1975), 67–111.

'Some Latin poems as evidence for the reign of Athelstan', *ASE* 9 (1980), 61–98.

Le Neve, J., *Fasti ecclesiae Anglicanae 1066–1300, II, monastic cathedrals (northern and southern provinces)*, compiled by D. E. Greenway (London, 1971).

Le Patourel, J., *The Norman empire* (Oxford, 1976; repr. 1978).

Levison, W., *England and the continent in the eighth century: the Ford Lectures delivered in the University of Oxford in the Hilary Term, 1943* (Oxford, 1946).

'Bede as historian', in A. Hamilton Thompson (ed.), *Bede, life, times, writings*, pp. 111–51.

Loomis, G., 'The growth of the St Edmund legend', *Harvard Studies and Notes in Philology and Literature* 14 (1932), 83–113.

'St Edmund and the Lodbroc (Lothbroc) legend', *Harvard Studies and Notes in Philology and Literature* 15 (1933), 1–23.

Lynch, J. H., *Simoniacal entry into religious life from 1000 to 1260: a social, economic and legal study* (Ohio State University Press, 1976).

Mayr-Harting, H., *The coming of Christianity to Anglo-Saxon England* (London, 1972).

Meyer, M. A., 'Patronage of the West Saxon royal nunneries in late Anglo-Saxon England', *Revue Bénédictine* 91 (1981), 332–58.

Miller, E., *The abbey and bishopric of Ely: the social history of an ecclesiastical estate from the tenth century to the early fourteenth century*, Cambridge Studies in Medieval Life and Thought, New Series 1 (Cambridge, 1951).

'The Ely land pleas in the reign of William I', *EHR* 62 (1947), 438–56.

Miller, M., *The saints of Gwynedd*, Studies in Celtic History 1 (Woodbridge, 1979).

Morey, A., and Brooke, C. N. L., *Gilbert Foliot and his letters*, Cambridge Studies in Medieval Life and Thought, New Series 11 (Cambridge, 1965).

Morgan, M. (Mrs Chibnall), *The English lands of the abbey of Bec* (Oxford, 1946).

Morgan, N. J., 'Notes on the post-Conquest calendar, litany and martyrology of the cathedral priory of Winchester with a consideration of Winchester diocese calendars of the pre-Sarum period', in A. Borg and A. Martindale (eds.), *The vanishing past: studies of medieval art, liturgy and metrology presented to Christopher Hohler*, British Archaeological Reports, International Series 111 (1981), pp. 133–71.

Nelson, J., 'National synods, kingship as office, and royal anointing: an early medieval syndrome', in G. J. Cuming and L. G. D. Baker (eds.), *Councils and assemblies*, Studies in Church History 7 (Oxford, 1971), 41–59.

'Royal saints and early medieval kingship', in D. Baker (ed.), *Sanctity and secularity*, Studies in Church History 10 (Oxford, 1974), 39–44.

'Ritual and reality in the early medieval *ordines*', in D. Baker (ed.), *The materials, sources and methods of ecclesiastical history*, Studies in Church History 11 (Oxford, 1975), 41–51.

'Symbols in context: rulers' inauguration rituals in Byzantium and the West in the early Middle Ages', in D. Baker (ed.), *The orthodox churches and the West*, Studies in Church History 13 (Oxford, 1977), 97–119.

'Inauguration rituals', in P. H. Sawyer and I. N. Wood (eds.), *Early medieval kingship* (Leeds, 1977), 50–71.

Nightingale, J. E., *Memorials of Wilton and other papers*, ed. E. Kite (Devizes, 1906).

O'Donovan, M. A., 'An interim revision of episcopal dates for the province of Canterbury, 850–950: part II', *ASE* 2 (1973), 91–113.

Oleson, T. J., *The witenagemot in the reign of Edward the Confessor: a study in the constitutional history of eleventh-century England* (Oxford, 1955).

Oman, C. W. C., *The coinage of England* (Oxford, 1931).

Pächt, O., and Alexander, J. J. G., *Illuminated manuscripts in the Bodleian Library Oxford*, 3 vols. (Oxford, 1966–73).

Pächt, O., Dodwell, C. R., and Wormald, F., *The Saint Albans Psalter* (London, 1960).

Parker McLachlan, E., 'The scriptorium of Bury St Edmunds in the third and fourth decades of the twelfth century: books in three related hands and their decoration', *Mediaeval Studies* 40 (1978), 328–48.

Parsons, D. (ed.), *Tenth-century studies: essays in commemoration of the millennium of* the Council of Winchester and 'Regularis concordia' (London and Chichester, 1975).

Plummer, C., The life and times of Alfred the Great (Oxford, 1902).

Pollock, Sir F., and Maitland, F. W., The history of English law before the time of Edward I, 2nd edn, 2 vols. (Cambridge, 1898).

Porée, A. A., Histoire de l'abbaye du Bec, 2 vols. (Evreux, 1901).

Potts, W. T. W., 'The pre-Danish estate of Peterborough abbey', Proceedings of the Cambridgeshire Antiquarian Society 65 (1974), 13–27.

Powicke, F. M., and Fryde, E. B., Handbook of British chronology, Royal Historical Society Guides and Handbooks 2, 3rd edn, ed. E. B. Fryde, D. E. Greenway, S. Porter, I. Roy (London, 1986).

Quirk, R. N., 'Winchester cathedral in the tenth century', Archaeological Journal 114 (1957), 28–68.

'Winchester New Minster and its tenth-century tower', Journal of the British Archaeological Association, Third Series 24 (1961), 16–54.

Reynolds, L. D., The medieval tradition of Seneca's letters (Oxford, 1965).

Ridyard, S. J., 'Condigna veneratio: post-Conquest attitudes to the saints of the Anglo-Saxons', Anglo-Norman Studies 9 (1987), 179–206.

Robinson, J. Armitage, The times of St Dunstan (Oxford, 1923).

Rollason, D. W., The Mildrith legend: a study in early medieval hagiography in England, Studies in the Early History of Britain (Leicester, 1982).

'Lists of saints' resting-places in Anglo-Saxon England', ASE 7 (1978), 61–93.

'The cults of murdered royal saints in Anglo-Saxon England', ASE 11 (1983), 1–22.

'Relic-cults as an instrument of royal policy c. 900–c. 1050', ASE 15 (1986), 91–103.

'The shrines of saints in later Anglo-Saxon England: distribution and significance', in R. Morris (ed.), The Anglo-Saxon church: papers on history, architecture and archaeology in honour of Dr H. M. Taylor, Council for British Archaeology, Research Report 60 (London, 1986), pp. 32–43.

Rosier, J. L., The Vitellius Psalter (Ithaca, 1962).

Royal Commission on Historical Monuments (England), Inventory of historical monuments in Dorset, IV, North Dorset (London, 1972).

Russell, J. C., 'The canonization of opposition to the king in Angevin England', in C. H. Taylor (ed.), Anniversary essays in mediaeval history ... presented to C. H. Haskins (Boston, Mass., and New York, 1929), pp. 279–90.

Ryan, M., et al., 'Six silver finds of the Viking period from the vicinity of Lough Ennell, Co. Westmeath', Peritia 3 (1984), 334–81.

Saltman, A., Theobald, archbishop of Canterbury (London, 1956).

Sawyer, P. H., Anglo-Saxon charters: an annotated list and bibliography, Royal Historical Society Guides and Handbooks 8 (London, 1968).

The age of the Vikings, 2nd edn (London, 1971).

'The density of the Danish settlement in England', University of Birmingham Historical Journal 6 (1957), 1–17.

Sayers, J., 'Monastic archdeacons', in C. N. L. Brooke, D. E. Luscombe, G. H. Martin and Dorothy Owen (eds.), Church and government in the Middle Ages:

essays presented to Christopher Cheney (Cambridge, 1976), pp. 177–203.

Schofield, B., *Muchelney memoranda*, Somerset Record Society 42 (1927).

Schramm, P. E., *A history of the English coronation*, tr. L. G. Wickham-Legg (Oxford, 1937).

Sisam, K., *Studies in the history of Old English literature* (Oxford, 1953).

Smart, V., 'The moneyers of St Edmund', *Hikuin* 11 (1985), 83–90.

Smyth, A. P., *Scandinavian kings in the British Isles 850–880* (Oxford, 1977).

Southern, R. W., *Saint Anselm and his biographer: a study of monastic life and thought 1059–c. 1130* (Cambridge, 1963).

Stafford, P. A., *Queens, concubines and dowagers: the king's wife in the early Middle Ages* (Athens, Ga, 1983).

'The reign of Æthelred II, a study in the limitations on royal policy and action', in D. Hill (ed.), *Ethelred the Unready*, pp. 15–46.

'Sons and mothers: family politics in the early Middle Ages', in D. Baker (ed.), *Medieval women, Studies in Church History* Subsidia 1 (Oxford, 1978), pp. 79–100.

'The king's wife in Wessex 800–1066', *Past and Present* 91 (1981), 3–27.

Stenton, F. M., *Anglo-Saxon England*, 3rd edn (Oxford, 1971).

'St Frideswide and her times' (1935), in D. M. Stenton (ed.), *Preparatory to Anglo-Saxon England: being the collected papers of Frank Merry Stenton* (Oxford, 1970), pp. 224–33.

Stewart, D. J., *On the architectural history of Ely cathedral* (London, 1868).

A summary catalogue of Western manuscripts in the Bodleian Library at Oxford, 7 vols. (Oxford, 1895–1953).

Symons, T., '*Regularis concordia*: history and derivation', in D. Parsons (ed.), *Tenth-century studies*, pp. 37–59.

Tait, J., 'An alleged charter of William the Conqueror', in H. W. C. Davis (ed.), *Essays in history presented to Reginald Lane Poole* (Oxford, 1927), pp. 151–67.

Taylor, C. S., 'Deerhurst, Pershore and Westminster', *Transactions of the Bristol and Gloucestershire Archaeological Society* 25 (1902), 230–50.

Taylor, H. M., 'Tenth-century church building in England and on the continent', in D. Parsons (ed.), *Tenth-century studies*, pp. 141–68.

Thompson, A. Hamilton (ed.), *Bede, his life, times and writings* (Oxford, 1935).

Thomson, R. M., 'Early Romanesque book-illustration in England: the dates of the Pierpont Morgan "Vitae sancti Edmundi" and the Bury Bible', *Viator* 2 (1971), 211–25.

'Two versions of a saint's Life from St Edmund's abbey: changing currents in XIIth century monastic style', *Revue Bénédictine* 84 (1974), 383–408.

Tolhurst, J. B. L., 'An examination of two Anglo-Saxon manuscripts of the Winchester school: the Missal of Robert of Jumièges and the Benedictional of St Æthelwold', *Archaeologia* 83 (1933), 27–44.

Ullmann, W., *The Carolingian Renaissance and the idea of kingship* (London, 1969).

Vaughan, R., *Matthew Paris*, Cambridge Studies in Medieval Life and Thought, New Series 6 (Cambridge, 1958).

Victoria history of the counties of England.

Bibliography

Voss, L., *Heinrich von Blois, Bischof von Winchester (1129–71)*, Historische Studien 210 (Berlin, 1932).

Wallace-Hadrill, J. M., *Early Germanic kingship in England and on the continent: the Ford Lectures delivered in the University of Oxford in the Hilary Term 1970* (Oxford, 1971).

'The *via regia* of the Carolingian age', in B. Smalley (ed.), *Trends in medieval political thought* (Oxford, 1965), pp. 22–41.

Ward, B., 'Miracles and history: a reconsideration of the miracle stories used by Bede', in G. Bonner (ed.), *Famulus Christi: essays in commemoration of the thirteenth centenary of the birth of the Venerable Bede* (London, 1976), pp. 70–6.

West, S. E., 'A new site for the martyrdom of St Edmund?', *Proceedings of the Suffolk Institute of Archaeology and History* 35 (1981–4), 223–4.

Whitbread, L., 'Æthelweard and the *Anglo-Saxon Chronicle*', *EHR* 74 (1959), 577–89.

Whitelock, D., 'The conversion of the Eastern Danelaw', *Saga-Book of the Viking Society* 12 (1937–45), 159–76.

'Archbishop Wulfstan, homilist and statesman', *Transactions of the Royal Historical Society*, Fourth Series 24 (1942), 25–45.

'The dealings of the kings of England with Northumbria in the tenth and eleventh centuries', in P. A. M. Clemoes (ed.), *The Anglo-Saxons*, pp. 70–88.

'Fact and fiction in the legend of St Edmund', *Proceedings of the Suffolk Institute of Archaeology* 31 (1967–9), 217–33.

'The pre-Viking age church in East Anglia', *ASE* 1 (1971), 1–19.

Wildhagen, K., 'Das Kalendarium der Handschrift Vitellius E. XVIII', in H. Boehmer *et al.* (eds.), *Festgabe für Felix Liebermann*, pp. 68–118.

Williams, A., '*Princeps Merciorum gentis*: the family, career and connections of Ælfhere, ealdorman of Mercia, 956–83', *ASE* 10 (1981), 143–72.

Wilmart, A., 'Eve et Goscelin', *Revue Bénédictine* 46 (1934), 414–38.

Wilson, R. M., *The lost literature of medieval England*, 2nd edn (London, 1970).

Wormald, F., 'The English saints in the litany of Arundel MS 60', *AB* 64 (1946), 72–86.

Wormald, P., 'Æthelred the lawmaker', in D. Hill (ed.), *Ethelred the Unready*, pp. 47–80.

Wright, C. E., *The cultivation of saga in Anglo-Saxon England* (Edinburgh and London, 1939).

Wright, T., 'On saints' Lives and miracles', in T. Wright, *Essays on archaeological subjects*, 2 vols. (London, 1861), I, 227–67.

THESES AND PAPERS

Franklin, M. J., 'Minsters and parishes: Northamptonshire studies', unpublished Ph.D. thesis (University of Cambridge, 1982).

Gransden, A., 'The Domesday inquest and the abbey of Bury St Edmunds', paper presented at the Fifth Annual Conference of the Charles Homer Haskins

Society for Viking, Anglo-Saxon, Anglo-Norman and Angevin History, University of Houston, November 1986.

Hahn, C., '*Peregrinatio et natio*: the Life of Edmund King and Martyr', paper presented at the Fifth Annual Conference of the Charles Homer Haskins Society for Viking, Anglo-Saxon, Anglo-Norman and Angevin History, University of Houston, November 1986.

Hamilton, T. J., 'Goscelin of Canterbury: a critical study of his life, works and accomplishments', 2 vols., unpublished Ph.D. thesis (University of Virginia, 1973).

Ridyard, S. J., 'The royal saints of Anglo-Saxon England: a study of some West Saxon and East Anglian cults; unpublished Ph.D. thesis (University of Cambridge, 1983).

Thomas, I. G., 'The cult of saints' relics in medieval England', unpublished Ph.D. thesis (University of London, 1974).

INDEX

Index

Elmham, Theodred; Danes, Vikings in, 61–2, 65–9, 93–5, 211–29 *passim*, 239; ealdormen, *see* Æthelwine; kings, *see* Anna, Æthelbert, Æthelstan, Æthelweard, Edmund, Eorpwald, Offa, Redwald, Sigebert; royal house, 3, 83n, 178n, 195, 196, 217

East Dereham, Norfolk, r.h., 50, 57–8n, 59, 108, 178–9n, 180, 181, 191–2

Eastern Europe, royal saints of, 2–3, 4, 248

East Kirby, Lincs., 215n

Ecgfrith, king of Northumbria, 53, 80, 81, 85–6, 177, 209

Edburga, St, abbess of Minster-in-Thanet, 16–17n, 241

Edburga, St, of Adderbury (and Bicester), 16–17n, 134–8; Life, 135

Edburga, St, of Aylesbury, 137n

Edburga, St, of Castor, 16–17n

Edburga, St, of Lyminge, 16–17n, 241–2n

Edburga, St, of Repton or Southwell, 16–17n, 249n

EDBURGA, ST, OF WINCHESTER, 17–37, 96–139, 144, 235, 237, 253–310

Life: 96–103; genealogy, 16, 18, 27, 83, 96; vocation, 17, 18, 26n, 37, 83–4, 98, 101, 104n, 264–6; humility, 18–19, 27, 86–7, 98–9, 266–9; charity, 88, 89, 102, 274–5; obtains *Canaga* (All Cannings, Wilts.), 26n, 33, 88–9, 98, 99–101, 103, 144, 270–4; *mediatrix ad regem*, 101, 144, 270; status at Nunnaminster, 33–4, 281; death and burial, 19, 98, 102, 103–4, 279–84, 286

Cult: 103–39; at Nunnaminster: 103–27; inception, 103–5, 132, 236; and tenth-century reform, 105–14; and cult of St Swithun, 112–14, 291–2, 294–5; after 1066, 121–7; translations, 26, 136; by nuns, 19, 104–5, 283–9, 293n; by Æthelwold, 19, 29, 30, 34, 106, 110–14, 132–3, 292–3; at Pershore: 129–39; translation to Pershore, 19, 27, 28n, 29, 31, 34, 129–39, 301–2, 303–5; and Mercian St Edburga, 134–8; at Bicester, 137–8; at Great Malvern, 134; miracles: in life, 19, 28, 275–9; at Nunnaminster, 103–5, 112–13, 119–20, 130, 284–306 *passim*; at Pershore, 130, 260–1, 302–8 *passim*; feasts, 25, 118n, 125–9, 132, 283 and n, 293n

Sources: 16–37; Bodley 451, anon. extract, 28–9, 104n, 309; anon. note, 104n, 310; Harley 64, 28n, 30, 36n, 104n, 131, 132; Hyde breviary, 25, 26, 33, 35n, 114, 126, 131, 134; Lansdowne Life (Lansdowne 436), 25, 26, 35n, 132; Middle English Life, 26–7, 30, 35n, 114, 132, 137; Osbert of Clare, *Vita Edburge* (Laud Misc. 114), 16–37 *passim*, 96–139 *passim*, 154, 171, 176, 253–310); William of Malmesbury, 27–8, 31, 110–11, 130, 131; Winchester annals, 134

Eddius, Life of Bishop Wilfrid, 16–17n, 53n

Edgar, king, 25, 31, 34n, 36n, 47, 49, 79, 80, 106, 116, 119, 182, 183, 187, 188, 189, 190n, 191, 192, 194, 290, 301–2; as father of St Edith of Wilton and St Edward, 37, 42–4, 83n, 84, 141–5 *passim*, 153n, 154, 155, 165, 168, 169, 171, 196, 236, 239

Edgiva, daughter of King Edward the Elder, 27n

Edgiva, wife of King Edward the Elder, 16, 27n, 104n, 266n, 290n

Edington, Battle of, 211, 216

Edith, St, of Aylesbury, 135, 137n

Edith, St, of Polesworth, 243

EDITH, ST, OF WILTON, 37–44, 140–75 *passim*, 235, 238

Life: 83–8 *passim*, 140–8; genealogy, 37, 42–3, 83, 154; vocation, 29n, 37, 83–4, 143, 144, 265n; chastity, 84, 140; humility, 86, 87–8; charity, 88; rejects throne, 41, 88, 147; appointed abbess of three r.h.s, 41–2, 87–8; builds *oratorium* of St Denys, 39, 41n, 88, 141n, 146–7, 148; *mediatrix ad regem*, 144, 169; death, 37, 40, 143, 146, 147

Cult: 148–75, 236; monastic patron, 148–71; royal promotion, 152–4, 195, 196; and cult of St Edward, their political significance, 154–71, 239–40; after 1066, 171–5; translation, 40–1, 150, 155, 165; miracles, 39, 40, 44, 149–51, 152; feast, 175 and n

Sources: 37–44; Goscelin of Canterbury, *Vita Edithe*, 29n, 37–44, 49, 79, 80, 83–4, 86, 87–8, 89n, 91n, 140–75 *passim*, 176, 195, 265n; William of Malmesbury, 42–4

331

Milton, Kent, r.h., 57, 90n, 180, 181n
Minster-in-Thanet, Kent, r.h., 241; abbesses, *see* Domne Eafe, Edburga, Mildrith
Modwenna, St, 135–6n
Monenna, St, abbess of Killeavy, 135–6n
Morley St Peter, Norfolk, 215
Muchelney, Somerset, abbey, 164
Much Wenlock, Salop, r.h., abbesses, *see* Milburga
Muluca, 100, 101n, 270–1

Narford, Norfolk, 215n
Neot, St, 28–9n, 310
New Minster, *see under* Winchester, religious houses
Nigel, bishop of Ely, 51n, 52n, 54–5n, 200, 208
Nordvico (or *Nordvic*), 215
Normandy, Normans: Norman Conquest, 6, 65, 121–5, 141, 164, 171–4, 186n, 196–201, 227–9, 244, 251; Norman reception of English saints, 6–7, 121–9, 171–5, 196–210, 226–33, 251–2
Northampton, 215n
Northumbria, Northumbrians, 65–6, 68, 69, 108, 211, 221, 246, 310; kings, *see* Alcred, Eanfrid (of Bernicia), Eardwulf, Ecgfrith, Edwin, Egbert, Osric (of Deira), Oswald, Oswiu
Norðwalde (Northwold, Norfolk), 189n
Norway, royal saints of, 2
Norwich, 215; archdeacons, 70n; bishops, 133n; *see also* Everard, Herbert; cathedral priory, 218n; see of, 228
Nunnaminster, *see under* Winchester, religious houses

Odda, 36n, 134
Odo, bishop of Bayeux, 173n
Offa, king of East Anglia, 73, 80
Offa, king of Essex, 92
Offa, king of Mercia, 21, 217n, 244, 247
Olaf, St, king of Norway, 2
Orderic Vitalis, *Historia ecclesiastica*, 207n
Ordwulf, *princeps*, 152, 161, 164, 165
Osbern, Life of St Dunstan, 43, 44n, 252n
Osbern Giffard, 173n
Osbert of Clare, prior of Westminster, 16–37 *passim*; *Miracula* of St Edmund, *see under* Edmund, St, king of East Anglia and martyr, sources; kinsman, *see* Henry, priest of

Westminster; nieces, *see* Cecilia, nun of Barking; Margaret, nun of Barking; *Vita Edburge, see under* Edburga, St, of Winchester, sources; *Vita Edwardi, see under* Edward the Confessor, St, king; *Vita* or *Passio* of St Æthelbert, *see under* Æthelbert, St, king of East Anglia and martyr
Oscetel, king, 211
Osgod Clapa, 229
Oslac, 187n
Osmund, bishop of Sherborne, 173
Osmund, priest of Wilton, 39–40n
Osric, king of Deira, 81n
Osthryth, St, 243, 246, 247
Oswald, St, bishop of Worcester, archbishop of York, 31, 45, 62, 107, 108, 132–3n, 188n, 225; *Vita* (Byrhtferth of Ramsey), 47–8, 50n, 95n, 155, 158, 162
Oswald, St, king of Northumbria, 92–3, 108, 243–4, 246
Oswen, 64
Oswiu, king of Northumbria, 246
Osyth, St, 134–5, 136n, 243n; 'First Essex Life', 134–5, 135–6n; Life by William de Vere, 135, 135–6n
Oðinn, 69n, 216
Ovington, Hants., 120n
Oxford, 137; r.h., 242; Jesus College, 258; Principals, *see* Thelwall, Eubule; St Frideswide's, abbey, 164

Paschal II, pope, 2n
Passion, relic of, 39, 145–6
Paul, abbot of St Albans, 6
Paul the Hermit, St, Life by Jerome, 10
Peada, king of the Middle Angles, 135
Penda, king of Mercia, 16–17n, 60, 92, 134, 177, 243
Pershore, Worcs., abbey, 19, 21–2, 23, 27, 29, 31, 129–39 *passim*, 227, 255–6, 259, 260–1, 301–10 *passim*; abbots, *see* Foldbriht, Thomas, Wido, William
Peter, St, *monasterium* (or *basilica*) of, *see under* Winchester, religious houses
Peter the Martyr, St, 28n
Peterborough, Northants., abbey, 60, 107, 109–10n, 242, 290
Picot, sheriff of Cambridgeshire, 204–5, 206n
Plato, 261, 289
Plegmund, archbishop of Canterbury, 32, 215

Witchford, Cambs., 187–8n, 189n, 198
WITHBURGA, ST, 50, 59
  Life: 50, 57n, 58, 59, 84, 178–9n, 180
  Cult: at East Dereham, 180; translation,
    57–8n, 59; at Ely, 195n, 201,
    209–10n; translation to Ely, 59, 108,
    180, 185, 186n, 191–2, 194;
    translation in 1106, 57–8, 59, 204;
    miracles, 59, 204; feasts, 185–6n
  Sources: 59; *Anglo-Saxon Chronicle*,
    57–8n; *Liber Eliensis*, 57–8n, 186n;
    Miracula, 57n, 59; *þa halgan*, 59n;
    Vita Withburge, 55n, 56n, 57–8n, 59
Wold, Cambs., 187–8n
Worcester, 132; annals, 104n, 132–3n;
    bishops, *see* Oswald, Simon,
    Wulfstan; cathedral, 107n, 132–3n,
    128, 129; church, 107n; deans or
    priors, *see* Warin; *provincia*, 306, 307
Wulfgeat, 164
Wulfheah, 164
Wulfhere, king of Mercia, 50, 60, 80,
    89–90, 180, 181n
Wulfhilda, St, abbess of Barking, 43
Wulfled, 187–8n
Wulfric, abbot of New Minster,
    Winchester, 124
Wulfric (Spot), 164
Wulfsige, St, bishop of Sherborne, 156,
    161; Life by Goscelin of Canterbury,
    49n, 172n

Wulfstan, St, bishop of Worcester, 128n,
    132–3n
Wulfstan, bishop of Worcester, bishop of
    London, archbishop of York, 166n;
    Sermo lupi ad Anglos, see under
    Edward, St, king and martyr,
    sources
Wulfstan, ealdorman, 141
Wulfstan of Dalham, 190n, 191
Wulfstan, precentor of Winchester, Life
    of St Æthelwold, 34–5n, 106n, 182n,
    195
WULFTHRYTH, ST
  Life: relations with King Edgar, 37,
    42–3, 44–5n; vocation, 37, 43, 84,
    142; virtue, 88, 91n; as abbess of
    Wilton, 43, 141n, 142–8 *passim*;
    collector of relics, 39, 141n, 145–6;
    promotes cult of St Edith, 147–8,
    152, 179, 236; miracles, 145, 146
  Cult: 39, 149, 152
  Sources: Goscelin of Canterbury, *Vita
    Edithe*, 37, 39, 43, 84, 88, 91n, 141n,
    142–8 *passim*, 149, 152; William of
    Malmesbury, 42–3
Wulfwen, nun of Wilton, 142
Wulmar, 232

York, archbishops, 123; *see also* Oswald,
    Wulfstan; calendar, 129; see of, 116;
    Walmgate, 215
Yvo, St, 49n